REBELS AND RENEGADES

REBELS
and
RENEGADES

BY

MAX NOMAD pseud.
„

Essay Index Reprint Series

BOOKS FOR LIBRARIES PRESS, INC.
FREEPORT, NEW YORK

First Published 1932
Reprinted 1968

LIBRARY OF CONGRESS CATALOG CARD NUMBER:

68-20326

PRINTED IN THE UNITED STATES OF AMERICA

FOREWORD

As the title indicates, "Rebels and Renegades" is a series
of portraits of outstanding representatives of contemporary
revolutionary tendencies. No attempt has been made to deal
with the personal lives of these leaders. The biographical
method has been used as a convenient means of bringing
out the cross-currents and internal conflicts which have been
agitating the revolutionary and labor movements during the
last few generations.

It is characteristic of these movements that the laboring
masses were assisted, encouraged and inspired not only by
leaders who had risen from their own ranks but also by
champions coming from the educated middle classes. The
latter have been the exponents of that vast complex of ideas
known under the common designation of "Socialism." These
educated middle class and lower-middle class exponents of
socialism are referred to here as the socialist intellectuals or
the socialist intelligentsia. The term "intellectual" is understood in various senses, the most common in America being
that of "highbrow," or, generally speaking, a person with
cultural pretensions. Here, however, it is used in the more
specifically economic sense of a stratum deriving its livelihood from mental occupations. In Europe great numbers of
this class have played a prominent rôle in the revolutionary
and labor movements of the nineteenth and twentieth centuries.

There is no doubt that these struggles have contributed
toward an improved standard of living for large sections of
the working population and have given them an increased

v

consciousness of human dignity. And yet the achievement is entirely out of proportion to the immense efforts and sacrifices which have been made. Whole strata of the toiling masses, particularly the unskilled and semi-skilled, have benefited very little from the long struggle. And the ever recurring economic depressions, together with the progress of labor-saving machinery, have more often than not rendered illusory all the improvements achieved during the previous periods.

The various tendencies opposed to the present system have tried to make each other responsible for the *impasse* at which the working class has arrived after a hundred years of revolutionary propaganda and activity. Communists, along with Anarchists and Syndicalists, are heaping invective upon the moderate Socialists for having made peace with the powers that be. Socialists and Communists vent their scorn upon the utopian hopelessness of anarchism and syndicalism. The followers of the latter schools, in unison with the moderate Socialists, in turn accuse the Communists of subordinating the interests of the working class the world over to the needs of the Soviet bureaucracy. All of them, in the name of the socialist ideal, are attacking trade unionism pure and simple, with its self-complacent upstart leaders and its labor aristocracy, out of contact with the rest of the working class. Finally, along with the trade unionists, they all curse the Fascist renegades of socialism, like Mussolini and Pilsudski, who have openly allied themselves with the propertied classes.

In these mutual recriminations one issue is nearly always either wholly ignored or skilfully glossed over: the deep conflict of interests which exists between the manual workers and the intellectuals, semi-intellectuals and self-taught ex-workers who are heading the labor movement.

Like Faust, the rebellious intellectual and self-taught ex-worker has two souls dwelling in his breast. Taken as a group, he is originally, like the worker, at the bottom of the social ladder. He shares the worker's hatred and resentment against a system that denies him the good things of life. Side by side with the worker he struggles against privilege and thus develops all the heroic qualities which that struggle calls forth. But his interests are not identical with those of his humbler associates. He has his education, his invisible capital, which, sooner or later, as the struggle progresses, enables him and his social group to rise to a position of comfort within the existing or the "transitional" system—while the worker is told to expect it only under "pure socialism," which only his grandchildren may live to see. Along with the flame of revolt, a fire less sacred burns in the heart of the leader—the lust for power and its material rewards. Gradually his personal, group and class interests prevail with him over those of the laboring masses : and his mind, always ready to rationalize his desires, is forever finding convincing arguments to justify his new course. Having achieved recognition, influence, or power, the apostles of yesterday become apostates, the tribunes turn traitors, and the rebels— renegades.

To be sure, there have always been leaders who, disregarding their personal and group interests, have found a sublimation for their ambition in glory, consistency, and at times in martyrdom. They, too, have found a place in this gallery of portraits.

M. N.

New York, March, 1932.

CONTENTS

ILLUSTRATIONS

REBELS AND RENEGADES

ERRICO MALATESTA

OR

The Romance of Anarchism

ANARCHISM is a dying creed; its faithful communicants are getting scarce. The ghastly glamor once attached to the word itself is fading; other specters—syndicalism and communism—now disturb the slumber of the respectable. One after another, the most prominent figures in the movement have disappeared: the Bavarian bookbinder, Johann Most, of German and American fame, its fiercest master of invective; the Dutch preacher, Rev. Domela Nieuwenhuis, its foremost polemist; the German Jew, Gustav Landauer, its philosopher and esthete, barbarously murdered after the downfall of the Bavarian Soviet Republic; and finally the Russian Prince, Peter Kropotkin, its most scholarly theorist. Those of the old guard who are still alive are gradually passing into oblivion or at best marking time: Vladimir Cherkezov, veteran of veterans, who in 1866 was involved in a plot against the life of the Tsar; Jean Grave, Sebastien Faure and Charles Malato, prominent in France during the latter part of the nineteenth century, and now either discredited or forgotten; Rudolf Rocker in Germany, fighting a losing battle against communist and socialist influence; and finally Alexander Berkman and Emma Goldman, deported from this country during the Bolshevik scare and now most irreconcilable enemies of the Soviet régime. . . .

One name, however, belongs neither among the dead nor among the fading survivals. Its bearer stands out alone, towering mountain high above the rest—the living romance and tragedy of anarchism. That man is Errico Malatesta, upon whose shoulders fell the mantle of the prophet, after the death of Peter Kropotkin.

Errico Malatesta was born nearly eighty years ago (1853) in a small town of Southern Italy. That town, Santa Maria di Capua Vetere, is what has come down to our days of the glorious city of Capua, whose opulence so perniciously affected the fighting qualities of Hannibal's soldiers.

Among the many legends current and recorded about the great rebel, is that of his descent from the famous or infamous dynasty of the Malatesta of Rimini, whose name occupies so conspicuous a place in the history of the Renaissance and the centuries preceding it. Thirty or forty years ago, it was picturesque copy to assert that the dreadful sect of assassins was headed by three princes of the blood— yet the truth was by no means as colorful. While Peter Kropotkin was actually a direct descendant of the Rurik dynasty which preceded the Romanovs, and Vladimir Cherkezov, another famous Anarchist, was a Caucasian "prince" from Georgia—where only descendants of serfs do *not* carry that title!—Errico's ancestors were merely prosperous members of the local gentry, innocent of any halo of blood and romance. The glamor attached to his name is all his own. Hardly one out of a hundred Italians—in whose imagination, as one of his friends said, Malatesta is imbedded as a cross between Garibaldi and Lenin—has ever heard of his medieval namesakes.

He could have been the Lenin or the Mussolini of postwar Italy, if he had so desired. He wanted neither part. It might be said in the words of the Gospel that his Revolution "was not of this world"—but that would not be the whole truth.

He lives in Rome now, with his wife and adopted daughter, until recently earning a living as an electrician, the manual trade he learned after his revolutionary activities forced him to give up his medical studies nearly sixty years ago. Guarded and followed day and night by three agents of the secret police—one for each member of his family— he is virtually a prisoner, though to a certain extent better off than his numerous friends and comrades. For even Mussolini, ruthless and callous as the medieval Malatestas themselves, has not dared to imprison the grand old man whose return from exile he had hailed so enthusiastically two years before his march on Rome. . . .

Malatesta's early youth belonged to the years when the *risorgimento,* the movement for the unification of Italy, was nearing its victorious end. At the age of seventeen, as a young student of medicine at the University of Naples, he hailed the final crowning of the aspirations of all patriotic rebels and martyrs—the occupation of Rome, which hence- forth became the capital of a united Italy.

Mazzini, the apostle, and Garibaldi, the hero of national liberation, had lived to behold the triumph of their vision —and also the reality, which was not quite the same as the ideal they had formed of a redeemed fatherland. Mazzini's motto had been "God and the People." "Liberty," "Equal- ity," "Humanity," and other generous abstractions had been written on his banner. But instead of a theocratic re- public, with himself at the head, as the connecting link be- tween "God" and "the People," what did he behold? "Lib- erated" Italy had simply been conquered by the Kingdom of Piedmont and Sardinia, whose government he had been fighting all his life. Garibaldi, who with his irregulars had dared a hundred deaths against the Hapsburgs and the Bourbons, saw his native Nice bartered away to France and his heroic red-shirts treated with contempt by the military caste of the crowned beneficiary of national unification. A horde of profiteers, job-hunters, and other carpet-baggers were let loose upon the liberated sections of the country.

Modern commercialism and political corruption took the place of the medieval methods of extortion practiced by the former rulers. Not a few of the heroes and idealists of the period of struggle now became reasonable and began to feel perfectly comfortable on the monarchist band-wagon. The nebulous socialist slogans—flaunted to attract the underdog —were now discarded. The revolution of the Italian middle classes was accomplished. But revolutionary discontent still remained.

Every country not over-rich in natural resources or not well-developed industrially, sooner or later finds itself with a surplus of hungry aspirants and a deficit of soft jobs for distribution. With the Italian band-wagon filled to the last seat, there still remained a disappointed residue of young men with college education, but no future—and no present either, for that matter. As usual, this group of malcontents, with a sprinkling of disappointed idealists, formed the nucleus for the development of a new revolutionary movement.

They were to find an unequaled leader in the great Russian revolutionist, Michael Bakunin. After his flight from Siberia Bakunin had settled first in Florence and then in Naples, where he remained until 1867. With his bewitching personality and a halo of heroism comparable only to that of Garibaldi, he soon surrounded himself with a group of young men who later became the nucleus of the Italian section of the International Working Men's Association, founded in London in 1864 (the so-called "First International").

Bakunin's program contained the general socialist postulates. Like most of his writings, it was hazy and nebulous in its wording, but it voiced the dissatisfaction of the masses who had not benefited by the national revolution. It voiced likewise the unspoken desires of the younger set of Italian intellectuals; for, when he spoke of the "Revolution which was to convert Italy into a free republic, consisting of free communes united with each other of their own accord in the free nation," they could easily see themselves as the future organizers of those "free communities," i.e. as the future leaders and rulers of their country. . . . Bakunin, who at that time was working out his anarchist philosophy, might have been surprised at this interpretation of his ideas. But ideas, once uttered, acquire an existence and logic of their own, often quite independent of the intentions of their originator.

In 1870 Malatesta, then a young medical student at the University of Naples, was arrested during one of the student demonstrations frequent at that time. Expelled from the university, he learned a trade as a means of support, but by choice rather than by necessity, for his family was not exactly poor. He stuck to his choice for the rest of his life, however, except during the periods when he was engaged in underground work, in propaganda tours, or in editorial activities which claimed all his time.

Malatesta was at this time a republican, a follower of that faction of Italian republicans which took its inspiration from Garibaldi. In the following year, the struggle of the Paris Commune of March-May 1871—an event as stirring in those days as the Bolshevik Revolution of two genera-tions later—aroused his interest in the ideas of the "Inter-nationalists," as the socialists of the various denominations were called. That historical event, indeed, contributed much to the clarification of the ideas of the younger generation. Mazzini's insults directed against the Commune at a time when it was bleeding to death after an unequal struggle were neither chivalrous nor in good taste and alienated many of his former admirers. On the other hand, the gen-erous but uncouth Garibaldi, now that the wars for national liberation were over, proved himself to be well-nigh illiterate in matters of domestic policy. He accepted Socialism for the distant future, as testified by his famous words, "the International is the sun of the future." He sympathized with the Paris Commune and even considered himself a member of the International—but he was not really interested in the social struggles of the present. Bourbon and Hapsburg rule had aroused his vindictive rage—yet the misery of the tenant farmers who suffered under absentee landlordism he seems never to have noticed.

The younger men did notice it. Some of them were prompted by their own hopeless outlook for the future; some by their revolt against the older generation; and some by their personal tragedy. Strange as it may sound, speaking of an octogenarian who has gone through more adventures than most of his contemporaries, Malatesta was a frail youth, affected, or believed to be affected, with tuberculosis. He did not expect to live long, and facing death, he naturally enough dreamt of immortality. He had been brought up in the heroic atmosphere of the Garibaldian campaigns for a liberated Italy. He had read the pathetic accounts of the revolt of Spartacus, who, two thousand years before, had begun his desperate struggle in Capua, Malatesta's birthplace. In his sensitive and generous heart all these impressions crystallized into a fearless determination to emulate the great heroes of his country's history. As he himself relates in an article of reminiscences of his early youth, it was Spartacus who inspired him most and with whom he identified himself in his dreams. He has held through all the years the inspiration and the resolve.

At the age of nineteen Malatesta had made up his mind as to his immediate allegiance. He joined the Italian section of the International which held a convention and was constituted in 1872.

THE FIRST INTERNATIONAL

The International, founded in London in 1864, was the first attempt at a unification of all existing radical, revolutionary, and even altogether non-political organizations of the workers of all countries, regardless of their differences in theory or program. As the "red scare" of that period, it naturally attracted the rebellious, the adventurous, and the dissatisfied of all countries, all those who bore a grudge against the existing system. British trade unionists who wished to prevent competition on the part of immigrant labor rubbed elbows with French workers interested in co-operatives; Polish patriots who had escaped the Russian hangman's rope after the unsuccessful insurrection of 1863, with Italian republican Irredentists who under Garibaldi and Mazzini still carried on their conspiracies against Hapsburg and papal rule; German followers of Marx, with French disciples of Proudhon: all of them united by a common aspiration for what they called "Socialism"—in reality only a romantic disguise for such very respectable and bourgeois aims as more political democracy and national independence, with State Capitalism as a distant goal.

At the time when Malatesta joined the International, the organization was torn by a violent struggle between two bitterly opposed camps: the followers of Marx and those of Bakunin. This was not a mere duel for mastery between titans, though personal ambition and intolerance played no mean part in it and contributed not a little to its rancor. Nor was it a mere contest for domination between divergent philosophies—Marx's Socialism against Bakunin's Anarchism. The theory of Anarchism, usually connected with the name of Bakunin, had not been fully worked out at that time. Bakunin's followers called themselves Socialists, and Bakunin himself, in a letter to Marx, frankly admitted himself a disciple of the great German scholar. On the other hand, Marx in one of his statements professed that, for the distant future, he likewise was in favor of "anarchy," in the sense of a commonwealth without State compulsion.

What actually divided the two currents of opinion, was

not the "authoritarianism" and "centralism" of Marx, as against the "anti-authoritarianism" and "autonomism" of Bakunin. It was the question of the *tempo* in the revolutionary movement. Marx, in fact, represented the more sedate, reasonable, patient element, as against Bakunin's turbulent, impatient, adventurous following, ready to strike at any moment. This division was, moreover, not merely a question of diverging temperaments—although, no doubt, this element played its part in the case of separate individuals. A glance at the forces marshaled by each opponent shows that Bakunin's hosts hailed chiefly from the economically undeveloped, backward countries, like Italy and Spain, where there was a large body of impecunious, poverty-stricken *déclassé* intellectuals without prospects except in immediate revolution. The situation was similar to that now prevailing in many countries that have suffered through war and revolution; but while the malcontents of the present day turn for inspiration to Communism or Fascism, their grandfathers of two generations ago turned to the Anarchism of Bakunin. Bakunin himself, in a letter to one of his friends, described the situation as follows: "There exists in Italy—and that is what the other countries lack—a class of ardent, energetic youths, without position, without career, without a way out, who, in spite of their bourgeois descent, are not morally and intellectually exhausted like the young bourgeoisie of the other countries. To-day they are throwing themselves head over heels into revolutionary socialism with our entire program". . . .

The economic prospects were not nearly so dark in the countries where the hosts of Marx had the upper hand. In these, particularly in Germany, there were growing industries with an increasing number of industrial workers; the situation offered great possibilities for the organization of a political party of the working class and for the conduct of a "civilized" political struggle with ballots instead of bullets.

Da una fotografia del 1891,
eseguita nell'ufficio antropometrico
delle carceri di Lugano.

ERRICO MALATESTA

Under such circumstances "ardent and energetic" young men from the lower middle classes were not entirely "without career"; they were the prospective leaders, educators and organizers of that potential political struggle. Italy, on the other hand, had hardly any industry to speak of, and its potentialities, as a field for working-class politics, were still in the remote future. In discussing that famous passage from Bakunin's letter, Marx remarked that his opponent's followers in Italy were nothing but a "bunch of *déclassés,* the dregs of the bourgeoisie, . . . lawyers without clients, doctors without patients and knowledge, pool-room students, commercial travelers and other salesmen, and particularly journalists of the small press with a more or less doubtful reputation." This characterization is a fine example of the snobbish contempt in which at that time, the theorist of the aspiring would-be politicians, malcontent but hopeful, held the unlucky desperado who might have to risk his life in order to get anywhere at all. The same contempt, by the way, in the present Marxian camp, marks the attitude of the Socialists towards their Communist competitors, and of the official Communists towards the followers of Trotsky. . . . Ten years later, when the economic situation in Italy began to look more hopeful, large numbers of that very same Bakunist "bunch" began to join the Marxian camp, and then they were *"déclassés"* and "dregs" no longer. . . .

Early in the seventies, however, the Italian section of the International was entirely with Bakunin. Its activities extended over a period of ten years—from 1872 to 1882. It outlasted by several years the official central body dominated by Marx, which died a quiet death in New York. In a packed convention, held in 1872, Marx had all dissenters excluded and the seat of the organization transferred to the American wilderness. This was to prevent the followers of Bakunin and those of the French conspirator Blanqui from getting hold of the organization. If Belfort Bax, the British sociologist, an intimate friend of Marx's *alter ego*, Friedrich Engels, is to be believed, the transfer was effected for the purpose of forestalling the persecutions threatened by the European governments in their alarm after the revolt of the Paris Commune of 1871. Bax's statement only confirms the assumption that the followers of Marx were at the time eager to smother the revolutionary fire, to lay the red specter to rest. They did not succeed, however. For many years to come, the International, as represented by the excluded sections siding with Bakunin, continued to disturb the slumber of the propertied classes of Europe to a degree out of all proportion to their actual strength.

BAKUNISM IN ACTION

Shortly after joining the Italian section of the International, Malatesta visited Switzerland, where he met Bakunin. The impression made by the aging apostle on the mind of the nineteen-year-old "Benjamin," as he was called by the master and the other disciples, remained for life. From that time his story becomes part of the revolutionary history of united Italy. It was then that the two outstanding leaders—Carlo Cafiero, the generous, tragic Don Quixote of the movement, and Andrea Costa, its brilliant but all-too-practical Sancho Panza—became his closest friends.

In 1873-4 the situation in Italy was propitious for a revolutionary movement. The country was in a ferment of unrest caused by the high cost of living. There were strikes and riots in many cities and disturbances in the countryside, for the national liberation had done nothing for the peasantry. The moment for action had apparently arrived.

The Italian section of the International differed from the German, English and Belgian sections in that it was not a federation of workers' societies in which socialist intellectuals were engaged in open propaganda for their ideas. It was rather a blind for the activities of Bakunin's "International Alliance of Socialist Democracy," a secret body within the International, which was to prepare and direct the revolutionary movements in all countries, and as a first step, to eliminate Marx's influence in the International. The situation was grotesque. In spite of Bakunin's denunciation of Marx's "authoritarianism," his own "Alliance" was an authoritarian, hierarchical organization with various degrees of "initiation." In the Italian revolt planned for 1874, Bakunin, Cafiero and Costa were the moving spirits. Malatesta was not in direct touch with the inner circle because he was in jail when the plans were made.

The leaders who had charge of these preparations were not equal to their task. They were unable to weld all the dispersed local uprisings into strong concerted action, and the isolated attempts fizzled out in pathetic failures. Of the three to five hundred men who were supposed to rise in Apulia under Malatesta's leadership, actually only six arrived at the meeting place. These set up their headquarters in the ruins of a medieval castle and tried vainly to induce the peasants of the vicinity to join them. They were soon arrested and were put on trial after a year of preliminary imprisonment.

The jury which tried this group of rebels was composed of the richest land owners of the region and was not disposed to be panicky over their ill-fated attempt to overthrow the existing system. The youthful *opéra-bouffe* insurgents were acquitted amid applause from the audience and with the approval of the whole population of the town. The situation was not substantially different in the other trials held under similar circumstances in other parts of the country. No doubt the lenient attitude of the jurors was influenced by other considerations as well as by the tender age of the culprits. In most parts of united Italy, and particularly in the South, even the middle classes were anything but friendly towards the new government. In the minds of the jurors the violent declarations of the accused in favor of such subversive ideas as anarchism, collectivism, and what not, were translated into nothing worse than a republican protest against the detested Piedmontese dynasty with its parasitic bureaucracy.

As a matter of fact, there was more than a grain of truth in this apparently naïve conception. While the movement of 1874 was in preparation, attempts had been made to induce Garibaldi and many Mazzinians to take part in it. Garibaldi, whose "socialism" was a rather hazy affair, is reported to have promised to join the movement as soon as it would assume larger proportions. These bourgeois alliances would hardly have been sought, if much more than the overthrow of the monarchy had been expected as a result of the revolution.

After his acquittal in 1875, Malatesta enjoyed two years of Quixotic adventure outside of Italy. Venturing into the land of Cervantes, he successfully organized to its final detail the flight of a Corsican revolutionist who was imprisoned in Cadiz; but at the last moment, when it came to boarding the waiting ship, Bonaparte's countryman decided that the regular meals of the prison were too definite a present good to be renounced for the uncertain joys and certain discomforts of liberty.

From Spain Malatesta turned to the Balkans, where the Christian peasants of Bosnia and Herzegovina—now a part of Yugoslavia—had risen against their Turkish rulers. Bakunin tried in vain to dissuade his Benjamin from wasting his efforts in that semi-Asiatic wilderness. His enthusiastic disciple replied that "wherever Carthage is attacked, Rome is being defended." It so happened that in this case the proletarian "Rome" which he wanted to defend was represented by the British Empire, which at that time was following an anti-Turkish policy, and—Tsarist Russia, which soon afterwards joined in the noble cause! Malatesta knew nothing of these implications. He was twenty-three years old, and his heart was craving for sacrifice and glory.

However, it was not given to him to smell the powder of the Turkish guns or to dangle from a Balkan-made gibbet. Twice he tried to cross Austro-Hungarian territory in order to reach the insurgents, and twice he was arrested and sent back to Italy. The Hapsburgs wanted no Italian interference with their own plans for annexing that corner of the Balkans.

When he came back to his own country, the revolutionary unrest, the after-effect of the long struggles for national unity, had begun to subside. Even the most rabid republicans of Mazzini's and Garibaldi's following had become gradually reconciled to the monarchy and its political dispensations. Northern Italy, the most advanced section of the peninsula, was beginning to enter upon the upward path of economic development. The situation was not so hopeless as it had been several years before, and the more "practical"-minded revolutionists were ready to be reconciled, at least to a degree. Andrea Costa, for instance, the brain of the insurrectionary movement of 1874, and who together with Cafiero was next to the heart of Malatesta, was beginning to see things in a new light. The anarchist ideal, he subconsciously began to realize, was after all nothing but an impossible day-dream of sentimental visionaries or desperate romantics bent upon suicide. At best it was an unattainable guiding star to orientate the revolutionary and socialist pilot on his cruise towards a greater measure of political and industrial democracy. It certainly could not be the concrete object of a practical man with a clear vision. When, early in 1877, Malatesta and Cafiero initiated a new insurrectionary movement, purely anarchist in scope, Costa was no longer with them.

The revolt of 1877 was not inaugurated with the hope

of an immediate success, as in 1874, when the participation
of various republican elements had been asked and expected.
In a way, it was the first case of anarchist "propaganda by
the deed"; it was an attempt to stir up the masses and to
spread the revolutionary gospel by the symbolic acts accom-
panying the rising.

The mountains of Benevento, not very far from Naples,
were selected for the performance. It began under an unlucky star. Treason had been at work in the very heart of
the conspiracy. All of the local peasants who had promised
their support—over three hundred of them—were arrested
before the time set for the uprising. As a result, those who
remained, twenty-six in all, including Malatesta and Cafiero,
were compelled to act prematurely, while the region was not
yet fit for band warfare.

Two towns were seized by the insurgents. The king
was declared deposed in the name of the social revolution;
all government records were destroyed; all arms and money
found in the town-halls were distributed among the local
peasants. The revolt, however, did not spread and the
twenty-six were soon surrounded and taken prisoner. After
sixteen months of preliminary incarceration, they were tried
by jury and acquitted. As three years before, Southern
Italians, whether rich or poor, felt no affection for the
Government and were ready to sympathize with all its
opponents—particularly those who had the romantic atmosphere of youth and daring.

A significant detail: most of the members of that little
band, except Malatesta and Cafiero, who were Southerners,
were unable to communicate with the peasants whom they
wanted to arouse! They did not speak the local dialect. Another symbolic detail: the man who betrayed them was an
old Garibaldian, whom they had trusted on account of his
glorious past. The poacher of yesteryear had become the
gamekeeper of today. . . .

Shortly after the trial Malatesta left Italy. Before doing so, he cut the last ties with his bourgeois past. He returned to his home town and donated his property—a few houses left him by his parents—to the tenants occupying them. The Quixotic gesture may appear ridiculous to our present sophistication, but there was nothing sophisticated about the anarchism of those days. It was a new gospel and was taken quite seriously not only by its followers but even by most of its preachers.

Malatesta's bestowal of his patrimony on his poor tenants looked very much like the scriptural gesture suggested to the rich young man by a Jewish radical preacher of two thousand years ago, and unconsciously may have been inspired by it. There is much of primitive Christianity in the generous naïveté of the anarchist gospel. Malatesta's teacher, Michael Bakunin, was dead by that time. He had breathed his last two years before, a broken and disappointed man. The great miracle of the world revolution which he had tried to evoke, had failed to materialize. But the Faith remained. Faith in the ideal of a commonwealth based on altruism, solidarity, voluntary respect for the other fellow's rights—in short, on all the generous qualities with which the highest of the mammals has unfortunately been equipped none too lavishly. To the propagation of that ideal Errico Malatesta was henceforth to devote his life, performing his missionary work in all the corners of the world—wherever people spoke Italian, Spanish, French, or English.

REFORMING THE FAITH

The death of Bakunin coincided with the abandonment of hope for an immediate overthrow of the existing system through the concerted action of determined conspirators who were to arouse the masses. The failure of all the attempts made since the Paris Commune of 1871 suggested to the disciples that the masses were not yet ready for the social revolution and that propaganda was of paramount and immediate importance. Not mere propaganda in the usual meaning of the term, but "propaganda by the deed"; propaganda by the courageous example. It was in this spirit that the revolt of Benevento in 1877 was undertaken by Malatesta and Cafiero. It was only several years later that the expression became identified with individual terrorism.

With the Revolution postponed to a more or less distant future, the disciples had more leisure to discuss the basic principles of their creed and the beauties of the Earthly Paradise they contemplated. Without saying it in so many words, they found that at bottom—paradoxical as it may sound—the Master had been a heretic; or at best, only the Precursor but not the real Teacher. The "collectivist anarchism" of Bakunin—that was the term used at that time—showed a strange likeness to the ideas of "authoritarian" Socialists. While advocating collective ownership of the means of production, it insisted that the producer was entitled to obtain the full product of his labor. This, the disciples asserted, would imply the existence of a constituted authority by which the full product of everyone's labor would be determined. That authority would be in effect a government—a thing anathema to the real anarchist.

A way out of this situation was found by Malatesta and Cafiero in 1876. It was very simple. There would be no accounting authority to evaluate each person's production. Nor would there be merely equal pay for an equal number of working hours, as conceived by certain revolutionary equalitarians. For that again would imply a certain administrative supervision and authority imposing undue restrictions upon personal liberty. With an optimism undaunted by the ugly realities of life, the apostles of the new faith assumed that every human being had the urge to work and to be useful to the community. Quite voluntarily and without compulsion or control of any sort, everybody would produce according to his abilities, and consume according to his needs, by taking freely from the well-stocked store-houses. . . .

This idea, called "communist anarchism", was obviously in the air at that time, for other Anarchists came forth with it simultaneously in other sections of Europe. As a result, the new creed was soon adopted without opposition in practically all anarchist circles. Prince Peter Kropotkin became the "scientific" mouthpiece of the new gospel. Only Spain held out for a while, for the grandsons of Don Quixote remain conservatives and traditionalists, even while they are Anarchists. Or, possibly, they stuck to the less utopian tenets of pure Bakunism because they had not given up their hopes for a revolution, and realized that it would take a few cosmic periods before the beautiful "free lunch" ideal could materialize.

The Anarchists, having removed the last trace of "authoritarianism" from their ideal, now likewise eliminated it from their organization. There is no doubt that for all his dislike—or perhaps jealousy—of Marx's despotic rule in the General Council of the International, Bakunin had wielded no less personal power in his secret "Alliance," which he had organized within the official International. It was actually this "Alliance" which, in case of a successful revolution, would have wielded, to use Bakunin's own words, "the collective dictatorship of the Alliance members—a dictatorship without badge, without title, without official powers, and all the more powerful as it was devoid of all appearances of power." Discarding the shackles of this strictly centralized secret body (not unlike the controlling machinery of the Catholic Church or even the Jesuit order) anarchism, after its reformation, began to wallow in a sort of "new freedom." Independent groups became eventually the favorite form of "organization," with each little group, or rather its leader, jealously guarding its "autonomy." To continue the ecclesiastical parallel, a congregationalist system now prevailed.

THE ODYSSEY OF A CONSPIRATOR

Despairing of the possibility of an immediate revolution in Italy, Malatesta left his country shortly after his acquittal in 1878. His restless spirit and the international police did not permit him to remain anywhere for any length of time. Driven from Egypt to Syria; from Syria to Asia Minor; from there to Switzerland, Rumania, France, and Belgium in turn, he finally landed in London—before the War the asylum of all political refugees to whom the rest of the world denied hospitality.

During this Odyssey he came in touch with well-nigh all the outstanding personages of the movement—and with the prisons of all these countries as well. In Paris he had also the first serious encounter with his Socialist step-brothers. Jules Guesde, once a disciple of Bakunin and later founder of the Marxist *Parti Ouvrier* ("Workers Party"), had inserted in his paper insulting remarks about the Spanish anarchists and refused to publish a rectification. Indignant, Malatesta took up the cudgels for his Iberian friends and actually challenged Guesde to a duel. Medieval tradition was still potent, even among the most advanced elements of the Latin countries.

Two cruel blows marred his exile in London. His two old friends, Cafiero and Costa, passed out of his life forever. These two, with Malatesta, had done more for the organization of the early labor movement in Italy than anybody else. Cafiero, the rich aristocrat who had been slated for diplomatic service, had chosen the revolutionary career instead, sacrificing for it his entire fortune and his very life. Breaking down under the strain of disappointments and persecutions, his mind now gave way, and he died in a lunatic asylum. Andrea Costa, the brains of the movement, had likewise been unable to stand the strain, but his disappointment took another form. Having lost his faith in the immediate revolution, whether for the pure anarchist ideal or its republican substitute, he now began to "face facts." Economic conditions in Italy were beginning to change. Industries were springing up, the wages of skilled workers were increasing. Here was a potential army of dues-paying party and trade-union members, in need of educated leaders. There before him was the example of the German Socialist Party which, though persecuted, was continuously growing and was gradually becoming an important factor within the State. True, the satisfactions it held in store for its followers and protagonists were far from the millenial promises and iconoclastic ambitions of the first "Internationalists." Still, gradual reforms were helpful to the workers, and the political rewards and emoluments that the party organization held out to its leaders in the near future were not to be despised, modest as they were, by the "lawyers without clients" and the other starving white-collar gentry. Revolution was no longer the only way out of a desperate situation. After all, it was wiser to be a living party official, member of parliament, or trade-union leader, than the dead martyr of a hazy ideal. The Marxian doctrine, with its emphasis upon the objective economic forces as against man's subjective desires, was adopted as a justification of law-abiding tactics. To this course Costa, like many others, was now committed. The revolution was definitely relegated to a period when Italy would have reached a much higher step of economic development. It meant a few generations more to wait—a mere trifle in the history of humanity. . . .

Malatesta and his band of irreconcilable rebels were outraged at such apostasy. All the more, as this Sancho Panza gospel was threatening to win over all the most educated and ambitious elements of the movement, and to leave only the unpractical dreamers and violent fanatics faithful to the anarchist creed. Even Cafiero himself, during that twilight period when his mind was beginning to cloud, had begun to give in to the new trend.

In 1883 Malatesta returned to Italy, in an attempt to combat the growing influence of Costa, who a year before had been elected to parliament. He was arrested soon after his arrival, and condemned, with a few of his friends, to three years' imprisonment for belonging to an "association of criminals." This henceforth became established as the specific charge against Anarchists, enabling the courts to dispose of them without jury trial. The prosecuting attorney might admit that the indicted men were *individually* gentlemen of unblemished reputation and pure character; *collectively,* nevertheless, they constituted an "association of criminals," and could be sentenced as such.

The sentence was appealed from, and in the meantime Malatesta took the opportunity to publish a paper in Florence and to conduct a public campaign of propaganda. Shortly before his sentence became valid, he went to Naples, where along with many other prominent Anarchists and Socialists, including Costa, he helped to fight the cholera epidemic then ravaging the city. The Government, which offered him a medal in appreciation of these services, was at the same time anxious to prevent his flight and watched his movements as well as the house in which he lived. Its vigilance was of no avail. He was carried out of the house in a case supposed to contain a sewing machine and carried on board a ship bound for South America.

Malatesta's journey to Argentina was not planned exclusively as a missionary trip for the conversion of the Spanish- and Italian-speaking workers of that country. It was to a large extent an Argonautic expedition, though the golden fleece was not to be used for his own enrichment. He had heard rumors of gold deposits in Patagonia, the southern-most corner of the American continent, and with a few friends he ventured into that desolate wilderness in a des-perate attempt to establish a financial basis for the anarchist movement, in which the "angels" were very scarce. The prospecting trip was successful, but the Argentinian Govern-ment, which had got wind of the expedition, simply con-fiscated the claim of Malatesta and his friends.

Back in Europe in 1889, Malatesta witnessed a beginning revival of the anarchist movement which coincided with the economic turmoil prevailing in those years. This resuscitated his hopes, and from a purely theoretical propaganda of the ideal he turned again to active revolutionary preparations as in the early seventies. Unity in the revolutionary camp was sorely needed, and he launched an appeal for the organiza-tion of a Socialist-Anarchist-Revolutionary Party—an at-tempt to lay down a basis for the collaboration of Anarchists of the various schools. Preparation for an armed revolution and opposition to any government that might attempt to constitute itself after the revolution—these were the two points on which, he thought, there could be no divergence of opinion. The question of the distribution of the products of labor—whether on the "collectivist-anarchist" or "com-munist-anarchist" basis—was to be settled after the revolu-tion, through propaganda, example, and experimentation. In those days his anarchism represented the most radical if rather hazy, protest against the existing system.

His permanent residence after his return from South America was again London, where he remained until 1897. During this period he expressed his ideas in a number of pamphlets (such as "A Talk Between Workmen" and "An-archy") which have become anarchist classics and have been translated into practically all civilized languages. In other respects, too, this period was the most active in his life. He was in his forties—old enough to have become a seasoned

conspirator and propagandist, and still young enough to remain unshaken in enthusiasm and determination.

His artistry in disguising himself enabled him to make a
great number of secret trips to Belgium, France, Switzerland and Italy—all countries which waited for him with open
prison doors, as he had been either sentenced in, or expelled from, their territories. He toured Spain, soon to become a scene of the most atrocious persecutions directed
against the growing revolutionary movement. He went to
Belgium, at the time when the first historical experiment
of a general strike embracing most of the workers of a
whole country was being enacted there as a means of obtaining universal suffrage. Malatesta hoped he could succeed
in directing the movement into more revolutionary channels,
but nothing came of his hopes, for the influence of the Socialist Party, a rigorously law-abiding corporation, was all-
powerful.

Great unrest was meanwhile brewing in Italy. Especially
in Sicily, now in the grip of a wide-spread economic distress, a powerful movement was on foot. Under the leadership of the Socialists, great numbers of starving peasants
and sulphur miners had already organized, and soon they
gave vent to their dissatisfaction in violent clashes with
the armed forces. Malatesta and his friend Malato, a leading
French anarchist of Italian descent, tried to stir up insurrectionary movements in other parts of Italy and to set the
whole country aflame, but the masses failed to respond. The
vagueness of the anarchist slogans and the unwillingness of
the Socialists to coöperate may have had something to do
with their indifference. The riots in Naples and Massa Car-
rara broke out quite independently, and cut telegraph wires
were the only concrete results attributable directly to the anarchist activities of 1893.

At the same time a wave of terrorist acts, sweeping France
and to a certain extent other countries, was raising an-

archism to the sinister grandeur of an omnipresent red specter. Malatesta's secret activities of those years will probably never be fully recorded. Up to the present he has refused to write his memoirs—for he has never considered his revolutionary career at an end. Another reason is also valid. Too much of a gentleman to lie for the sake of propaganda, he is likewise too much of a propagandist to tell all his depressing disappointments. Last, but not least, his complete story could hardly be published before his death, for during this part of his career he had his fingers in every revolutionary pie that disturbed the digestion of the frightened bourgeois world. There was a time during the nineties when he was almost as much of a headliner in all European papers as were Lenin and Trotsky during the first years of the Russian Revolution. He was reported to be everywhere and to have organized and instigated every uprising and every political murder—a modern "Old Man of the Mountains."

The reports were, of course, greatly exaggerated. In spite of Malatesta's efforts, the anarchist movement had never become a really organized affair. Unlike the Russian revolutionists of the seventies and eighties (of the "People's Will"), and their successors, the "Socialists-Revolutionists," the anarchist terrorists nearly always worked without any preconcerted plan. The various terrorist activities carried out by them were either individual acts of protest, committed mostly without preparation, or else simply indirect suicides, prompted by misery, personal disappointment, or Herostratic vanity. Malatesta may have known in advance of some of the more celebrated cases, such as the killing of the Spanish Prime Minister Canovas del Castillo, in 1897, for ordering the mass torturing and execution of Anarchists. But even in these he was hardly anything more than the consultant specialist, and not the initiator. It was against his code of honor to prompt other people to do things he did not do himself. Moreover, he did not attach an excessive importance to individual acts of terrorism—he was a believer in mass action.

On Three Fronts

His activity during these years was really a struggle on three fronts: against the bourgeois world; against the socialist leaders whom he attacked as politicians reconciled to the bourgeois world; and finally against the all-too-numerous nuisances within the anarchist movement itself.

A great deal of his energy was consumed by the latter quite unsavory task. The "reformation" which the faith underwent after the death of the Master had called forth unexpected results. In the minds of most of Bakunin's successors, the social revolution had become as vague and as distant as in the imagination of the most moderate Socialists. Having lost hope in an early revolution that would overthrow the existing system, the believers could afford to indulge in the imaginative joys of an ideal admittedly impossible of realization by the living generation. The beauty of that ideal, connoting a most optimistic belief in the goodness of human nature, was in reality only a compensation for a profound pessimism. While the Socialists postponed their revolution to the moment when the economic conditions would have reached the necessary point of development—in the meantime enjoying what blessings graced the interval and finding arguments for extending the latter indefinitely— the Anarchists saw theirs as still more remote. Their preachers, too, had time to wait—some of them, like Jean Grave, theoretical head of the French Anarchists and favorite disciple of Kropotkin, openly admitting that it might take centuries before they could reach their goal. In the meantime they kept setting up little debating societies of religious dreamers, whose bark was worse than their bite, and who derived as much satisfaction as they could from the occasional acts of protest committed by their more temperamental or desperate brethren. Political democracy had proved a blessing and a sedative not only for the socialist would-be politicians, but also for the priests of the anarchist ideal-worship. A worship which in its pure, unadulterated form knew of no classes, but only of Anarchists and non-Anarchists, believers and non-believers.

That evolution of the once revolutionary gospel showed that at bottom anarchism was not a protest for economic equality voiced in behalf of the manual workers. It was rather the extreme, one might say poetical, expression of the desire for political freedom—an extension of the time-honored demand of the liberal intelligentsia for more political autonomy and less government interference. In many of his writings Peter Kropotkin insists that the society of the future would be the resultant of the various active forces of the revolution—with the "authoritarian Socialists" working towards strict centralization, while the Anarchists worked in the opposite direction. In other words, the Anarchists' extreme demand for "no government" was only meant to be a damper upon the centralist tendencies of modern socialism. What anarchism really aspired to—without most of its adherents realizing it—was a Socialist State with as much local autonomy as possible. And its preachers seemed to be hardly more in a hurry to get there than their socialist step-brethren. . . .

In vain Malatesta tried to break up this ineffective complacency. His attempt to create an organization resembling a revolutionary party met with strong opposition. Men like Jean Grave even accused him of a leaning towards the Socialist Party. To the talkative pygmies for whom the terror-inspiring reputation of anarchism was an escape from their sense of inferiority, subordination to a revolutionary leader seemed to be even more hateful than the existing system. A leader like Malatesta might try to whip them into some risky action; they preferred purely theoretical "negation" of the State, coupled with splendid isolation from the masses.

But there was something worse still. Since the second part of the eighties a new element had penetrated the ranks of the movement. A very distressing heresy, professed and propagated by a few honest cranks, but chiefly sponsored by what might be called "crooks with a philosophy," had taken its inception from a few acts of "expropriation" committed by disinterested comrades who wanted to replenish the war chest of the cause. These acts were emulated by some less devoted individuals who did the same thing for their own benefit. Since the theoretical luminaries of anarchism unanimously frowned upon this confusion of the cause with ordinary crime, a special theory was gradually evolved to suit the requirements of the trade. Poor Stirner with his *Ego and His Own*. Nietzsche with his gospel of amoralism, and last but not least, good old determinism—pragmatism not being invented as yet—became the philosophical bases of a trend which justified any action that benefited the individual: professional stealing, counterfeiting, procuring—even stool-pigeoning! In short, the followers of the new gospel behaved as if Machiavelli's text-book had been written not for princes, prime ministers, and diplomats, but also for malcontent manual workers and white-collar slaves. They called themselves "Individualist Anarchists"—for some people seem to need an ideological cloak for their acquisitive propensities—but they believed neither in revolution nor in any perfect future society. Their only tenet was to "live anarchistically," that is, in disregard of all the shackles imposed by society upon the individual. The respectable anarchists always claimed that this aberration was systematically fostered by the police. It was a natural assumption, for these miniature Borgias did more harm to the revolutionary cause than any amount of government persecutions ever could. Their activities were confined chiefly to France and the other Latin countries. "Anarchist Individualism" in Germany, England, and America, was a perfectly respectable, purely philosophical affair, based upon Max Stirner, Benjamin Tucker, and a few minor prophets. Libero Tancredi—later under the name of Massimo Rocca, one of the chief pillars of Fascism—was the most brilliant exponent and . . . practitioner of this "theory" in Italy. When a few years ago he dared to oppose some of his own heresies to the official Fascist doctrine, it was discovered that he had continued to practice his old "individualist" theories in his capacity as officer of some financial institution of the Duce's realm—and he had to flee the country. . . .

In the middle of the nineties anarchism entered upon a new stage of its development. Police persecutions had greatly reduced the ranks, the terrorist "propaganda by the deed" was declining, the interest that had been aroused by the idea itself, particularly among the intellectuals in France, was abating. The remaining militants now saw themselves faced by the sad prospect of becoming preachers of a dying sect and stewing in the juice of their own sterile phrases and declamations. They decided to descend from their ivory towers and to seek contact with the masses. In France especially, they rushed into the trade unions and gained influence in them. A result of this combination of anarchist theory with trade union practice was the emergence of a new current called "Revolutionary Syndicalism" or simply "Syndicalism." The trade union (in French "syndicat") was proclaimed at once the medium of the revolutionary struggle of the working class and also the basis of the reconstruction after the victorious general strike. "Direct action" and "general strike" became the chief watchwords of the new trend, and soon crowded out the other slogans.

Malatesta was, of course, pleased by this new turn—but he had his misgivings. He was afraid lest his comrades might rush from the ivory tower of pure anarchist philos-

ophy to the prosaic brick-and-stone mansion of trade unionism pure and simple. Time and again he urged his comrades
not to lose their identity in the trade unions; to use these
organizations for the propaganda of anarchist ideas; never
to forget that "the essential and primary consideration is
not 'class unity' but the triumph of anarchism, which af-
fects the whole human race." The later development of
French syndicalism and its once anarchist leaders into trade-
union respectability on the German or British model, showed
that his apprehensions were not unfounded. But it also
showed that no amount of anarchist-humanitarian preaching
could stop that normal evolution. Just as the best intentions
of a romantic Anarchist could not prevent the propaganda
for a vague social revolution in behalf of the "whole human
race" from becoming the harmless pastime of sentimental
phrase-mongers or a pseudo-revolutionary cult exploited by
professional preachers.

In 1896, however, the outlook was still very bright, and
at the International Socialist and Labor Congress held in
London in that year Malatesta represented a number of
Spanish trade unions. The Socialist parties sensed the danger threatening them from their anarchist competitors in
the trade union field and decided to refuse admission to all
those delegates who did not recognize the necessity of using
the ballot. Malatesta and his comrades were excluded on
this ground, the Socialist majority thus emphasizing the fact
that running for political jobs was of greater importance
to them than the collaboration with potential allies in the
struggle for the overthrow of that capitalist system in which
they had begun to feel so comfortable.

Shortly after that congress Malatesta returned to Italy.
The trip was secret, as on previous occasions during that
period, but this time it was not meant as a fleeting visit.
He meant to stay and to work for the cause until stopped
by the police. His best friend, Saverio Merlino, had turned

"pink" and had begun to advocate the ballot. It was as hard a blow as the death of Cafiero and the defection of Costa had been in the early eighties. Merlino was a lawyer of great ability, and had repeatedly and successfully defended Malatesta and other Anarchists during their incessant trials of the previous period. He was likewise an accomplished and learned writer, and his prestige was second only to that of Malatesta. His undoubted sincerity—he had no political ambitions—made his conversion, or apostasy, doubly dangerous.

Malatesta's return was no doubt intended to stave off the effect of this loss to the cause. He began publishing a paper in Ancona, and for nearly a year was able to dodge the police. It was then actually high time for his arrest, for his propaganda among the simple and uncouth workers of the factories and of the harbor was producing alarming results. The police and the courts had previously been kept busy by bloody fights, drunken brawls, and other crimes of violence committed by the longshoremen and other workers; but since his coming they had seen themselves threatened by a dire calamity which was explained during the ensuing trial. The prosecuting attorney, in his simplicity, actually gave vent to his fears in the following argument: Malatesta's influence had destroyed criminality; it had entirely changed the character of the workers of Ancona; owing to him, crimes were no longer committed—and Malatesta certainly ought to be sent to jail, since by destroying crime he was making the courts unnecessary! Malatesta was condemned to six months imprisonment.

A month after his condemnation, while still a prisoner, he was a distant witness of the desperate revolt of May, 1898. That uprising was caused by the high cost of living; starting in the South it spread to the North and assumed particularly violent forms in Milan. It was, no doubt, in accordance with the ensuing policy of bloody repression that after the expiration of his term he was given an additional five years of "forced domicile" in Lampedusa, one of the desolate rocky islands in the Mediterranean now used as a place of deportation for anti-Fascists.

Malatesta's "forced domicile" did not last long. His escape from that island has the true quality of high adventure. While a storm held the guards within doors, he and three comrades, daring what seemed like certain death, seized a small barge and put out to sea. Picked up by a steamer, they arrived safely in Malta and a short time later Malatesta was back in his London refuge.

After a few months rest he went to the United States, where he lectured in Italian and Spanish and edited a paper in his native language in Paterson, N. J. The inevitable discussions as to the merits or demerits of organization now began again, and this time almost cost him his life. During one of these disputes G. Ciancabilla, the leader of the "anti-organizzatori," seeing that the majority was siding with the old champion, emphasized his own argument by emptying his revolver into the body of his opponent. The hero escaped, and Malatesta, unable to leave the place on account of his wound, was arrested. He refused to name his assailant, although the police left him for a time without any treatment in the hope of forcing him to give the desired information. Ciancabilla remained a prophet among the guardians of the Holy Grail of unrestrained individual liberty, and died a few years later in California, where he edited a paper with the fitting title *La Protesta Umana*.

THE "RED WEEK" AND THE WAR

A year later, in 1900, Malatesta was back in London where he stayed until 1913. During these thirteen years, as in his previous London sojourns, he led the obscure life of an electrician, working in his own small shop. In his leisure time he continued the propaganda of his ideas, participated in the publication of several papers, and enriched anarchist literature with a number of popular pamphlets. The movement sponsored by him was meanwhile rather stagnant. All his attempts to create a well-organized Anarchist party were being thwarted continuously, either by persecutions, or by internal dissensions—or by the lack of a definite immediate aim.

However, Malatesta was not disheartened—or, if he was, he did not show it. In 1907 an International Anarchist Congress was held in Amsterdam, at which his point of view prevailed. The Anarchists were now to steer clear of the Scylla of purely abstract propaganda which would condemn them to isolation, and the Charybdis of Syndicalism pure and simple, which would absorb them. Malatesta was elected a member of the International Bureau whose seat was in London. The Anarchist International, thus constituted, showed, however, little activity and vitality. Anarchism as a revolutionary movement seemed at last to be a dead issue, its most energetic elements having been absorbed either by the purely theoretical propaganda of the idea, or by trade union activities.

On two occasions, during this period, public interest again centered about Malatesta. In 1910 he barely escaped being implicated in the then famous "Sidney Street Affair," when nearly the entire London garrison, under the command of Winston Churchill, besieged and exterminated two bandits who had decided not to give themselves up alive. Another member of the band had been mortally wounded a few days before, when jointly with the two other men he had killed several policemen who had surprised him in an attempted burglary. The three desperadoes had behind them a record of daring terrorist activity in Russia, or more correctly, in that Baltic section of the old Tsarist empire which at present constitutes the independent Latvian Republic. During the revolution of 1905-6 they had been engaged in a merciless guerrilla warfare against the Baltic-German feudal lords and their Russian bureaucratic supporters. Later, forced to seek shelter in England, they had first tried to earn a living as workers; but they had lost the habit of work and finally had decided to "live their own lives." For a while one of them had worked on his own account as a mechanic in Malatesta's little shop. Quite unconcerned as to whom he might involve, he had used the address of the shop when ordering an oxygen cylinder, which could be employed for cutting metal rods—and safes. It was not a very sporting thing to do, but desperadoes seldom see the other side of their actions. The number of the cylinder, which had been found by the police at the scene of the burglary, led the chase back to Malatesta's shop, and only the great esteem which he enjoyed as an idealist of the purest type saved him from being arrested and implicated in the affair.

Two years later he made his first and only acquaintance with a British jail. The Italian expedition to Tripoli in 1911-12 had aroused great popular enthusiasm even among radicals and particularly among those sons of the sunny South who expected to be the first colonizers and civilizers of that "ancient Roman possession"; for, peace-time internationalist convictions are not always strong enough to resist the war-time temptations and allurements of conquest. The Italian revolutionary colony in London was now rent by dissension. Malatesta violently attacked the imperialist venture. On the other hand a certain Bellelli, apparently anticipating the methods of political controversy adopted since the outbreak of the World War, accused the old rebel of being an agent of Turkey; Malatesta, who in the meantime had received confidential information about the activities of his opponent, called him publicly an *agent provocateur*. As British court procedure did not permit Malatesta to prove his charge, he was condemned for libel and had to spend three months in prison. Only urgent protests from his many influential friends saved him from deportation, which a vindictive judge had attached to the penalty.

A year before the outbreak of the World War Malatesta, as in 1897, received the invitation to edit a local anarchist paper in Ancona. He returned to Italy and his paper soon became the center of revolutionary propaganda. Early in June, 1914, the moment at last arrived for which he had been waiting all his life. Popular discontent had been aroused to the boiling point by the killing of a few paraders who had protested against some official celebration. A general strike declared in Ancona, where the shooting had occurred, soon spread to many other cities, and during that "red week" nearly all of Italy was in the initial stage of a revolution. Republicans, left-wing Socialists, Syndicalists and Anarchists, forgot their old scores and showed a united front.

Malatesta expected from the movement neither the realization of the anarchist ideal nor the establishment of a socialist republic. But he did hope that "many obstacles would have been removed, and a period of free propaganda, of free experimentation, would have been inaugurated, as well as a period of civil strife, at the end of which we would have seen our ideal shining victoriously." In other words, he expected as the immediate result, the establishment of a democratic republic, with a long period of revolutionary struggles to follow it. It was all very hazy. He had become a manual worker as a supreme protest against the existing system, but he had remained a romantic intellectual thinking in terms of "free propaganda," "free experimentation," and "civil strife" for the sake of an "ideal" which in the opinion of practically all anarchist thinkers is beyond the reach of those now alive. A mass struggle for concrete demands, aiming at the immediate improvement of the situation of the workers and the unemployed, was altogether outside the scope of his revolutionary ideology.

He was disappointed in his hope. At the very moment when the sweep of the movement threatened to assume the proportions of an actual revolution, the bureaucracy of the General Federation of Labor sent out a circular telegram calling off the general strike. The order created confusion in the ranks of the workers; there was no well-knit system of secret communication that could have maintained the contact between the various cities; and the whole affair fizzled out. The leaders of the Italian trade unions did not want a revolution. The existing system, even with the monarchy on top, was good enough for them. Their jobs were soft and steady, and a real revolutionary outbreak, particularly if it failed, would have meant destruction of the unions, imprisonment, firing squads, or even return to manual work. . . .

Malatesta, romantic scion of the middle classes, saw his hopes dashed by the unromantic upstart sons of manual toil, working hand in hand with college-trained socialist politicians who seem to have been more interested in the socialist careers of Millerand and Briand than in the glory of a martyr's death or the romance of an exile's life.

The reaction that immediately set in forced Malatesta to flee. Though hunted all over the country, he succeeded in escaping and was soon back in London.

A greater disappointment than the breakdown of the "red week" revolt awaited him with the outbreak of the War. Not only the Socialist politicians of the belligerent countries had made common cause with their governments; even the leading Anarchists, with a few exceptions, had taken the same stand. Kropotkin, Guillaume, Grave, Cherkezov, Malato —founders, veterans, and classic expounders of modern anarchism—had become bitter-enders pure and simple. Kropotkin saw himself complimented in the *New York Times* as the "great Russian democrat."

Heartbreaking experience as he felt it to be, Malatesta
was now obliged to come out against his old friends and
comrades, particularly when they issued an appeal against
a "premature peace." His article written on that occasion
was entitled "Pro-Government Anarchists," and the stand
he took was very closely akin to that of the Bolsheviks, in
declaring that the slaughter should be stopped by revolutions
in all the countries concerned. Though personally he wished
a German defeat, he declared that it was the business of a
revolutionist not to help one government against another but
to fight his own government. Thus, to a certain extent, he
took his inspiration from the old Marxian slogan—forgotten by the teacher's later disciples—that "the worker has no
country." The "orthodox" Anarchists, as represented by
Kropotkin and his friends, were apparently of the opinion
that the antagonism between monarchist Germany and republican France was of much deeper significance than the
antagonism between the workers and the bourgeoisie, and
that not only the French, but even the Russian and Italian
workers, were duty-bound to shed their blood for the democratic institutions incarnated in Clemenceau and Poincaré.
An attitude which could only be explained by the assumption that they had lost all hope for the overthrow of the
existing system, and therefore were ardently in sympathy
with any government which at least permitted them freely
to profess and to preach their belief in Utopia and in the
goodness of man.

HOME AGAIN

Malatesta's attempts to return to Italy during the war
were not successful. The government of his country simply
refused to let him enter. He was dangerous there, whether
he was in prison or in liberty. Later, in 1919, when the war
was over and an amnesty had removed all the obstacles to
his return, the British and the French governments jointly

tried to prevent his departure; the French by refusing a
transit permit, and the British by issuing an order forbidding any ship clearing from an English port to take him on
board. He finally outwitted the joint efforts of three governments to keep him out of Italy. With the connivance of
Captain Giulietti, brother of the secretary of the Italian
Seamen's Union, he was enabled to board an Italian steamer
and to land in Genoa.

The reception given him by the Italian masses was overwhelming. Wherever he came, he was greeted enthusiastically by the entire working population. Anarchists, Syndicalists, Socialists, Republicans—they all bowed before that
old man of sixty-six, whose whole life had been devoted to
the Revolution. Even the Fascists, at that time still a long
way from their victory, were forced to join in the general
chorus. On December 27, 1919, Mussolini, in his *Popolo
d'Italia,* hailed Malatesta's arrival with these words: "We
are far from his ideas, for we no longer believe in any revealed truth nor in any terrestrial paradise, . . . but all this
does not prevent us from sending our hearty greetings to
Malatesta, for we are always ready to admire a man who
disinterestedly professes a faith." There was probably another reason for Mussolini's enthusiasm. He was afraid of a
Bolshevik dictatorship in Italy, from which in view of his
attitude during the War, he could expect no tenderness.
Malatesta's anarchist influence was in his opinion a convenient counterweight against a successful emulation of the
Russian example.

The Revolution was again in the air in those days, for
in spite of "victory," Italy, owing to her poverty, had suffered perhaps more than any other country. This expectation of an early revolution quieted, to a certain extent, the
mutual struggles among Anarchists of the various schools
and they all joined forces around *Umanità Nova,* the first
Italian anarchist daily, founded in Milan early in 1920.

Malatesta became its editor, but he had to spend a great part of his time on propaganda trips in the provinces.

In the atmospere prevailing at that moment, his personality worked wonders. It was his personality alone, his past, the legend around him, his fifty years of disinterested apostolate—for he is by no means a first class speaker. Some of his experiences read like episodes from early Christian history, when praetorian guards are said to have seen the light and embraced the gospel. Time and again, the State constables ("carabinieri") sent to watch his meetings, were ordered away by their officers, who had noticed that their subordinates had been touched to the quick. There was a case of a sergeant-major of the carabinieri who joined the cheering crowd; his consequent dismissal from service meant to the able-bodied peasant boy the sacrifice of a coveted career.

In spite of the many local outbreaks the revolution itself failed to come. There is no doubt that among the masses many expected Malatesta to give the signal for it, and that they would have followed him if he had done so.

There was a moment—early in 1920—when that revolution was actually within reach. Giuseppe Giulietti, secretary of the Seamen's Union, whose brother had enabled Malatesta to return to Italy, conceived the idea. Giulietti was not an Anarchist, not even a "regular" Socialist. He was in a class by himself, a romantic republican in the Garibaldian tradition; an enthusiastic bitter-ender during the War, but just as enthusiastic for a revolution as soon as the fighting was over. An admirer of Gabriele d'Annunzio, he suggested to his demigod the idea of a "march on Rome"—more than two and a half years before Mussolini carried out this idea to a quite different end. . . . D'Annunzio was to head the "march," winning to the cause the republican and nationalist elements, while Malatesta was to enlist the support of the radical working class contingents.

But nothing came of it. The socialist politicians and trade union leaders were not interested. They were the strongest party in the country, and held several thousand municipal administrations in their hands. A democratic republic, the primary goal of the "march," would have given them no more in the way of jobs than they already had. Moreover, they were certain that the revolution would not stop at a mere democratic republic. That meant civil war—a risk they were not ready to take. Even the leaders of the left wing of the Socialist party—those who later constituted the Communist party—evinced no enthusiasm. Their ardor began to cool as the revolution seemed nearer. They, too, had their safe jobs, and they were interested more in displacing the old Socialist Party chiefs than in overthrowing the capitalist system.

Malatesta himself wavered, not because he was afraid, but because he believed that the revolution should be carried out by all the revolutionary parties and organizations and not by Anarchists alone. He desired the Socialists to unite with the Anarchists in dispossessing the capitalists. A government based upon democracy and civil liberties, to be set up by the Socialists would then permit the Anarchists, through propaganda and experimentation, to win the majority for the anarchist ideal.

There was only one little flaw in his plans. The Socialists had no intention of performing the task so generously assigned them by Malatesta. Courteously and maliciously, they were ready to leave all the revolutionary glory to the Anarchists. Malatesta clearly saw how incongruous was the situation in which he and his followers were placed. They could not help D'Annunzio merely to establish a republic after the French or Swiss model. To do so would have been impossible in view of the expectations of the rank and file, and in face of the example of Russia, where capitalist rule had been overthrown. Should they go further, and carry out the social revolution alone and unaided? Build with their own hands the Socialist State whose evils they never tired of denouncing? Help the Communists to establish their dictatorship? But the Communists demanded absolute submission and were averse to grant any freedom of propaganda or experimentation. Or reach for the anarchist moon outright? But the Anarchists were in a minority; if—to use Malatesta's own reasoning—they wanted to introduce the anarchist millennium by force, they would, by so doing, cease to be Anarchists; for they would have to establish a dictatorship not greatly different from that of their Bolshevik antipodes. Such a course would be a complete moral capitulation. Thus the only course left them was to postpone the revolution to that cosmic date when the majority of the population should be converted to the anarchist ideal. . . . The whole tragedy and hopelessness of anarchism as a revolutionary movement was embodied in that dilemma.

With Malatesta and his following unwilling to start a revolution that would lead to the establishment of a bourgeois or socialist republic, or to the paradox of an anarchist dictatorship,* and with the other radical groups likewise unprepared to take the risk, events hung fire. At the end of August and early in September, 1920, however, the striking metal workers at last took the initiative and occupied the factories. The world was aghast at this new experiment and waited for further developments. Malatesta repeatedly visited the "red trenches" and encouraged the workers to hold out.

* Curiously enough, in 1926 there actually appeared the so-called "Russian Platform" of a group of Anarchists, advocating a sort of anarchist government on the morrow of the social revolution—contradictory as this may sound. A similar position was taken in 1931 by the most prominent French Syndicalist, Pierre Monatte. Immediately after the victory of the revolution in Spain he declared that the Syndicalists of that country ought to work towards the establishment of a dictatorship of the revolutionary trade unions; thus demanding a dictatorship of the trade union officials as distinguished from the dictatorship of the intellectuals heading the Communist Party.

Once again, as seven years before, during the "red week," the revolt of the masses and the courage of the apostle proved powerless against the "machine"—against the collective leadership of the General Confederation of Labor, and the Socialist politicians supporting them. The movement was called off at the price of a few vague promises of "factory control." The upstart ex-workers of the Confederation of Labor, and the lawyers, journalists, professors, and politicians of the Socialist Party who were allied with them, were afraid of the civil war that threatened from a continuation of the struggle. The old saying of Karl Marx, that "the workers have nothing to lose but their chains, and a world to win" did not apply to their leaders. They had their precious lives and their very good jobs to lose. They had, of course, a very plausible excuse for their delay. A revolution in Italy, they said, would not hold out more than a couple of weeks; a blockade on the part of England and France would starve it into submission in less than a month. They would not gamble on the possibility of the revolutionary wave spreading to the other countries of Western Europe. . . .

The old fox Giolitti, who was prime minister at that time, likewise did his share in preventing a revolution, by using the very opposite of the traditional methods. He avoided all violence, all provocation. If the various radical organizations were hesitating in throwing the spark into the explosive barrel of popular discontent—Giolitti, the wise, liberal statesman, was not going to do it for them. After all was over, he was asked why he had not opposed violence to the lawless occupation of the factories. He replied: "I had confidence in the General Confederation of Labor, which proved that it deserved it."

The decision of the trade union leaders had killed not only the revolution but also the *morale* of the workers. Their belief in their leaders and their self-confidence were shattered.

The government, the bourgeoisie, and the new aspirants for power—Mussolini and his crowd of ex-soldiers, intellectuals and semi-intellectuals, including to a great extent transfuges from the various radical groups—saw that the moment had come for a counter-offensive. This notwithstanding the fact that Mussolini himself had hailed and encouraged the occupation of the factories.

REACTION

Not more than four weeks after the surrender of the factories, mass arrests were effected in Milan, including Malatesta and the very active Armando Borghi, secretary of the syndicalist "Unione Sindacale," a revolutionary trade union organization competing with the General Confederation of Labor but not enjoying great influence. One previous attempt to arrest Malatesta had been made early in the year, but the general protest had been so violent that he had been immediately released. This happened in February, when the wave of revolutionary mass sentiment had been rising. That wave was now receding. This time Malatesta stayed in prison for nearly ten months—the intention of the government was obviously to keep him there until the storm had blown over and the work of pacification had been accomplished.

Six months passed after Malatesta's arrest and still no indictment was produced against him. To force the hand of the authorities and to obtain the temporary release to which they were entitled, Malatesta and his comrades went on a hunger strike. It was a risky thing for a man of his age to attempt, but he took the chance, as he had taken that other chance when on a frail barge he braved the stormy sea.

The hunger strike had been endured for seven days, and still the sufferings of the revolutionary veteran failed to call forth a protest from the masses which had celebrated

his return only a few months before. The unrest had not
subsided as yet, but the workers were discouraged, disappointed, cowed. The punitive expeditions started by the
Fascist bands were not meeting with any well-organized resistance. It was in vain that Malatesta's friends tried now
to stir up the activity of the masses for the old leader. The
workers of Milan did not budge. The situation was hopeless,
and Malatesta seemed to be doomed to a slow and painful
death.

The lack of response among the workers called forth a
violent reaction from some of the more desperate elements
among the Anarchists. Stricken in their hopes for a revolution, stricken in their faith in the workers, stricken in the person of their leader, they could at least have their revenge!
The war and the exploits of the Fascists had not done much
to stimulate respect for human life. On the night of March
23, 1921, they went on a mad carouse of mass destruction,
placing bombs in a theater, an electric power plant, and a
hotel. Twenty-one persons were killed, and many others were
maimed by the explosion in the theater.

The massacre did not add to the popularity of the cause
which the fanatics had wanted to advance. The audience of
the theater included workers as well as capitalists and government officials. The Fascists seized the propitious occasion to deal a heavy blow to their Anarchist enemies. They
raided and completely destroyed the offices of Malatesta's
daily paper. It could not appear again in Milan.

In view of the renewed persecutions and arrests, and the
general perplexity, Malatesta and his friends had to give up
their hunger strike. No attention would have been paid to
the struggle of the prisoners, and their death would not have
caused any great commotion.

This failure of the hunger strike was humiliating enough
for the old rebel, who was thus placed in a ridiculous position, but worse still was the further necessity of publicly

dissociating himself from his overzealous disciples. He had never approved of those forms of "revolt" which expressed themselves in the bombing of cafés or theaters. His aim was revolution but not the satisfaction of individual grudges or hatreds against the bourgeoisie. He knew very well that such forms of protest were not really dangerous to the existing system; that they were harmful to the cause and consequently only too often secretly encouraged by the police. He was also fully aware of the fact that some of his comrades or enemies might suspect that his condemnation of the Anarchist Guy Fawkeses was prompted by considerations of personal safety. Nevertheless, he doubted the necessity of ending his days in prison for an act which he condemned, and he declared frankly that the holocaust in the Diana Theater was either the act of a madman or the result of instigation by the worst enemies of the cause. (It actually turned out that of the two main perpetrators of the butchery, one had been exempted from military service owing to adolescent insanity, while the other was a typical example of the saintly and ascetic fanatic.)

The conclusion of the speech which he delivered before the jurors was not in the defiant tone of a fighter to his implacable class enemies. It was rather the farewell message of an old man who felt that he had lost the long game, so many moves of which were already history. "I am sixty-eight years old, now," he said; "mine has been a modest life; but it has been a life during which I have always tried to do what my feeble powers enabled me to do for my cause. The idea of liberty, of justice, and of love, which has stimulated me since my early childhood, I have pursued and I shall pursue to my very death. I have spent ten or twelve years in prison. Not having been able to win the struggle, it might perhaps be an end worthy of myself to die in prison for my ideas. It would not be useless; it might perhaps be of greater use as propaganda than anything I may achieve in the future. If I were concerned with the cause alone, I should hope for a condemnation, a merciless condemnation—for the sake of the propaganda which it would make. But while I am a man of faith, I am not a hero. 'The spirit is willing, but the flesh is weak' as the mystics say. I love life: I love many people, and I am heartily loved by them in turn. Therefore I desire to be freed; I desire to return to the midst of my friends. But if you believe that you ought to send me to prison, well—I shall find sufficient strength of mind to face my sad destiny with serenity. I may die in prison, but I want to die there with my honor intact. I want to die there illuminated with all the sanctity, with all the purity of my ideal; for while my ideal may be only a vain phantom or a mere dream—it is certainly a dream of love. . . ."

Malatesta was acquitted, and so were the comrades arrested with him. The prosecuting attorney, apparently instructed by the government, which feared the effect of a condemnation, did not press for a conviction. His highly liberal and enlightened speech was, in fact, tantamount to a plea for acquittal. After all, Malatesta had been kept in preliminary seclusion for ten months, and he could be rearrested immediately, whenever the situation required. This seemed to the government a better policy than inflicting a heavy sentence, and one just as effective.

PRISONER AT LARGE

Malatesta, however, has not been rearrested. His daily paper, which he had begun to publish again, a few months after his release, this time in Rome, was again destroyed as soon as Mussolini's black-shirts assumed power officially, in October, 1922. Once more, two years later, in October, 1924, he started another publication, a semi-monthly magazine dealing with the purely theoretical aspects of anarchism; no other public activity was possible under the rigid Fascist censorship.

That magazine was a fitting anti-climax to a fifty-year apostolate. With the Fascist dictatorship firmly entrenched and the chances for an early revolution hopeless, the great rebel began to wonder whether the theoretical compass which was to guide his comrades over the rough seas of another revolutionary situation was in perfect working order. For that compass had failed him and left him helpless in the supreme crisis of his life.

With characteristic fearlessness he began to examine some of the most beloved stock arguments of his optimistic creed, and reached the conclusion that "we had no practical program that could be applied after a victorious insurrection"; that "it is time to remedy that insufficiency of ours so that we may find ourselves ready for future occasions"; and that "it is to this task of working out a practical program for immediate fulfilment that we are inviting all our friends."

This after nearly sixty years of anarchist theory and propaganda!

Merciless to himself for bungling a revolution, he was no less merciless to those who, having accomplished a revolution, had, in his opinion, made a terrible mess of it. Referring to some phases of the activities of the Soviet Government, he wrote in his daily shortly before Mussolini's coup in 1922: "What a glorious memory the Russian Revolution would have bequeathed us, had it been quenched at the time when it was still a revolution and not yet corrupted and stifled by the authoritarian spirit of its rulers."

His tone became more and more bitter after the establishment of the Fascist dictatorship, which in his opinion was to a great extent an imitation inspired by the Bolshevist model. The fact that the younger generation of revolutionists, disappointed with the fading romance of anarchism and fascinated by the glamor of the Russian Revolution, had begun to turn Communist, did nothing to mellow his sentiments. He gave free rein to his feelings in attacking the Bolsheviks to an extent which even some of his most ardent admirers considered in bad taste.

Thus on the occasion of Lenin's death, he declared that he could not mourn him because "even with the best intentions Lenin was a tyrant, he was the strangler of the Russian Revolution," and he exclaimed almost with exultation, "Lenin is dead; long live liberty!" Taken to task for this outburst by his most faithful and cultured disciple, Luigi Fabbri, Malatesta explained his attitude as follows:

"Lenin was a tyrant: and when a tyrant dies, it is human that those should rejoice whose friends and dearest comrades have been persecuted, tortured, shot by order of that tyrant, even if at the beginning of his career that tyrant was a sincere revolutionist, and as such acclaimed and beloved.

"I do not question Lenin's honesty and sincerity, but they do not exculpate him before the judgment of History. Loyola and Torquemada were likewise sincere fanatics, ready to suffer and to sacrifice themselves for the sake of the salvation of souls and for the greater glory of God; but they were the most nefarious, as their sincerity was the greater."

The historical rôle of the great Russian revolutionist, Malatesta seems to have been unable to grasp. That Lenin's advent marked an entire epoch—the beginning of the transition from private capitalism to state capitalism: a transition as momentous as that from feudalism to capitalism; that it has done away with the capitalist and landlord, and brought to the fore a new form of class rule, that of a section of the intelligentsia and semi-intelligentsia—all this Malatesta seems to have dismissed as unimportant in face of the tragic acts of intolerance and harshness which seem to be the well-nigh unavoidable accompaniment of every great historical upheaval.

His magazine was suppressed in 1926, and since that time Malatesta has had practically no contact with the outside world. Being under constant guard, he has voluntarily given up paying or receiving visits, or even going out on the street, since those who speak to him or even greet him expose themselves to arrest and deportation to the desert islands.

Malatesta is a very old man. Still he has not made peace with the world. He has seen most of his illusions shattered. But he has not lost his faith in the Future. In his treatises, which he contrives to slip through the tight net of official surveillance, he continues to present his views of the Revolution that is to come. They are simple enough and as far removed from reality as the anarchist creed of his early days. A generous creed and a humanitarian philosophy, but as effective a revolutionary weapon against the existing system as the tomahawk of an Indian brave against a tank.

ARISTIDE BRIAND

Champion of the General Strike

THE generation that knew Aristide Briand at the beginning of his career is slowly dying away or forgetting. To the world at large he is known as the French war premier who preceded Clemenceau; as the man of Locarno; as the initiator of the Pan-European project; in short, as a statesman of the first rank, admired by all that is respectable and conservative on both hemispheres. Eleven times premier and twenty-five times in charge of the Foreign Office and of other government departments, he has a record of service not excelled by any living statesman.

Yet the usual accounts of this extraordinary life are not altogether complete. A veil of discreet and embarrassed silence is thrown over the first forty-five years of his life. For they are not unlike those first thirty-five years of Mussolini's, the mention of which, in Italy at least, is not only bad form but also bad business.

That is to say, Briand began his political career in the same way as did most young men of his social background, since the days of the Great Revolution: as a champion of the underdog and a preacher of socialist ideas.

He was born in 1862—nearly one hundred years after Gracchus Babeuf, organizer of the famous "Conspiracy of the Equals" who at the time of the Directorate was executed as one of the first exponents of revolutionary communism in modern times. But unlike Babeuf, Briand was not destined for the guillotine and revolutionary canonization.

The "Conspiracy of the Equals" might be called the starting point of the socialist movement in France, but it was not the expression of a genuine working-class revolt. While professing communist ideas of the most equalitarian character, it was in reality a protest of the educated section of the lower middle classes against the ascendancy of the moneyed interests which came to the fore after Robespierre's downfall. The aim of the conspirators was a revolutionary dictatorship that was to bring back the democratic achievements of 1793, with Communism as a promise or a dream of the distant future. So little were the "Equals" interested in the actual situation of the working masses, that they took no hand whatever in the many strikes that occurred during the year when they prepared their uprising.

In the first half of the nineteenth century, the tradition of Babeuf served as inspiration for a large section of the revolutionary movement. In counter-distinction to the various brands of parlor socialism of the upper- and middle-class intelligentsia (usually designated as "Utopian" socialism), "Babouvism" represented the revolutionary republican protest of the poorest section of the lower-middle-class intelligentsia, and of the more educated workers. The "Babouvists" found an active leader in Auguste Blanqui, who for a few decades was to impose both his name and his personality upon the conspiratory-insurrectionary movements of the déclassé French intelligentsia. "Blanquism" was practically identical with Babeuf's gospel—a revolutionary dictatorship of victorious conspirators, who were to establish a republican régime which would gradually effect a transition from capitalism to socialism.

During the revolution of 1848, the Blanquists were on the extreme left of revolutionary democracy representing its most adventurous, most radical, elements. They were opposed not only to the liberal bourgeoisie that had assumed power after the overthrow of the monarchy, but also to the moderate Socialists who hoped for a peaceful development once the republic had been established. The attitude of the Blanquists (they were still called "Babouvists" at that time and their leadership was sorely split) to the other Socialists was comparable to that of the Russian Bolsheviks to the Mensheviks in 1917, or of the German Communists to the Socialists in 1918-19. After the closing of the "national workshops," when the Paris workers rose in that desperate June (1848) insurrection, they found support only in what was left of the Babouvists, all of whose leaders had been arrested a month before. All the other socialists were arrayed against them, along with the bourgeoisie. For all that, the Babouvists had never shown any interest in such questions as wages or trade unions. They thought exclusively in terms of power; after they had seized it, they themselves would take care of the needs of the workers. . . .

Under the Second Empire, the Blanquists were the party of the republican students and intellectual *déclassés,* engaged in a heroic underground struggle against Napoleon III. (Georges Clemenceau was at that time one of the "Blanquists of the second rank"—the master conspirator did not trust implicitly his courage and devotion.) At the same time they were bitterly opposed to the "mutualist" followers of Proudhon. These, mostly skilled workers of the luxury trades, in line with the peculiar anarchist theories of their teacher, were law-abiding believers in mutual credit societies and all kinds of coöperative enterprises, and were equally opposed to both revolutionary political action and strikes for higher wages. The Blanquists, with their attention concentrated on seizing power, showed likewise no interest at all in the wage struggles of the industrial workers.

The Bolsheviks of their time, the Blanquists played an important part in the rising of the Paris Commune of 1871.

ARISTIDE BRIAND

Its cruel suppression, its martyred fighters, the solidarity of the First International (1864-76)—a body feared in inverse proportion to its actual importance—all contributed to create the proletarian-communist legend that still surrounds that uprising. It was really no more than a spontaneous democratic protest against a reactionary attempt to disarm Paris and against the election of a monarchist majority to the National Assembly.

At the time of the suppression of the Commune, Aristide Briand was six years old. His father was a small merchant who had formerly been a farmer. Young Aristide had his preliminary schooling and part of his legal training in his native Brittany. He finished his law studies in Paris, where he had the opportunity of meeting the literary and political bohemians of that day. This was in 1883. Socialist ideas, driven under cover since the downfall of the Commune, were now beginning, once again, to stir the minds of educated youth. The recovery after the terrific bloodletting had been slow and painful. The socialist movement was still disunited and sect-ridden.

The alignment, however, was now different from that before the Commune. The followers of Proudhon, those pacific Anarchists who believed in mutual credit societies and coöperative organizations, had gradually disappeared after the fall of the Commune. Part of them had adopted the revolutionary gospel of Bakunin, who tried to combine elements from Proudhon and from Marx to form a higher revolutionary unity; part of them had gone over to Marx. The Blanquists, whose master died in 1881, after having spent half his long life in prison, no longer occupied such a conspicuous place. Like their grand old man, they concentrated all their attention upon Paris, still harboring his hope to seize the power by a sudden coup. But as that hope grew fainter and fainter, many of the malcontent intellectuals began to turn elsewhere. Karl Marx, long ignored in

France, began to come into his own in that land which had itself produced so many original socialist thinkers. In the great orator Jules Guesde, and in his own son-in-law Paul Lafargue, a brilliant theorist, he found two invaluable apostles. The "Guesdists," or *Parti Ouvrier* (Workers Party), professed the orthodox Marxian gospel and combined peaceful electoral and trade-union activities with a revolutionary verbiage concerned only with the distant future. Bitterly opposed to them were the extremely moderate "Possibilists," headed by Paul Brousse, who only a few years before had been the most violent of Bakunin's anarchist followers. It was this former firebrand who, as head of the Municipal Council of Paris thirty years later, congratulated Alphonso XIII on his escape from an anarchist bomb, thrown at his car during his visit to the French capital in 1905. In his early days, as the originator of the famous terrorist gospel of the "propaganda by the deed," he had publicly advocated the assassination of Alphonso XII, the father of Alphonso XIII.

THE FIRST STEPS

Like so many other young men of lower middle class origin, Briand had his grievance against bourgeois society. He understood that the good jobs were reserved for the few who had luck or connections, while the great mass of the bright lads leaving school must needs remain white-collar slaves or fight their way up in the political game. The labor movement, coupled with political propaganda, offered an excellent opportunity for advancement to a man with a speech-making faculty and a ready wit.

Probably Briand was not particularly taken by any of those various socialist schools. He certainly could not have been impressed by the elaborate scientific jargon of the Guesdists, for he was not the man to waste his youth on

the reading of long-winded treatises on Marxian philosophy
and economics. The Blanquists had no attraction for him.
He was temperamentally a pacifist and not particularly interested in risking his life. The Anarchists repelled him by
their utopianism and unworldliness. He was neither a
dreamer nor a desperado. The "Possibilists," with their
frank and unashamed opportunism, were no doubt most to
his liking. But as he grew older he realized that the game was
more complicated, and that in the narrow arena of the labor
movement revolutionary verbiage was as necessary for carrying on a moderate policy as, in the wider arena of world
politics, pacifist assurances are for carrying on preparations
for war.

After finishing his studies in Paris, Briand did not stay
on in the capital, where his youth and lack of experience
were too heavy handicaps in the race for advancement. He
went back to Saint-Nazaire where competition was less
keen. His family had moved to that place from Nantes.
Before long he became known as an able lawyer in criminal
cases, with a tendency to depend more on emotional appeal
than on fine points of law. At the same time he was a contributor to, and later editor of, a local weekly in which he
gradually established his reputation as a defender of the oppressed.

Working up slowly, from the periphery to the center, he
became municipal councillor of his town at the age of twenty-
six. A year later, in 1889, he was already running for parliament as a "Radical" (the French designation for an advanced Liberal), though he got only 3,000 votes. Meanwhile
he was busily helping in the organization of trade unions in
that section of France. In this task he had an invaluable assistant in Fernand Pelloutier, a contributor to the local
paper with which Briand was connected. Pelloutier was a
descendant of many generations of upper-middle-class intellectuals, including in the past well-known Huguenots and

liberals. In many respects he was the very opposite of his older associate. Sickly—he died very young of a particularly cruel form of tuberculosis—he was scholarly, original, and devoted to his ideas. He was the born ideologist in the best meaning of the word, while the husky lawyer was the born politician, who values ideas and theories only so long as they help him in his career and who discards them as easily as an actor washes off his make-up.

It was Pelloutier, no doubt, who inspired Briand with the great importance of the idea of the general strike. That idea was, of course, not original with Pelloutier. It had been in the air since the early seventies, when it was propagated by the Anarchists of Bakunin's school, and even earlier, in England during the thirties. It had first been preached on a large scale in the United States in connection with the eight-hour movement in the middle of the eighties, and it has forever remained connected with the Chicago Haymarket tragedy of 1886 followed by the execution of the four innocent Anarchist agitators in 1887. In France resolutions in favor of the idea had been adopted during the later eighties by various trade-union conferences—more as pious gestures than as serious proposals.

Pelloutier now took the idea and made it the central point of a fundamental revision of all the previous conceptions held by the various socialist and anarchist schools. Originally a Marxian Socialist, he had gradually shifted to anarchism, and finally had arrived at a position, all his own, which placed all the emphasis upon the trade-union movement. The "syndicats" (the French word for trade union) were to break away from the influence of the Socialist politicians with their gospel of the conquest of political power. The general strike was to be the instrument for overthrowing the capitalist system, and the trade union was to be the nucleus for the construction of a new order. Thus Pelloutier became the father of the theory and practice of "Revolutionary Syndicalism" as it is called in France, or simply "Syndicalism," as it is called in other countries. It was left to the legislatures of some of our western States to coin the term "criminal syndicalism," and to apply it indiscriminately to all revolutionary tendencies, however contradictory. The I. W. W., at present almost extinct, is an unorthodox variety of the original French article. Not only a theorist but an organizer as well, Pelloutier was one of the founders of the French General Confederation of Labor; and even now, thirty years after his death, he is held in great esteem by organized labor in France, as one of its most notable pioneers.

In the early nineties the syndicalist theory was still in the making and the conception of the general strike in the idyllic stage of a "peaceful revolt of folded arms." It was in this form that Briand took up the idea as a weapon in his struggle for leadership within the socialist movement.

PRO AND CONTRA THE GENERAL STRIKE

The Marxian *Parti Ouvrier,* led by Jules Guesde, was the strongest of all the socialist organizations then contending for the favor of the working masses. In addition to the usual groups of job-hungry intellectuals and of semi-intellectual *déclassés* which it shared with the other factions, it had connections with workers in many industrial centers in the provinces. It even had under its guardianship an entire organization, the National Federation of Trade Unions, which had been founded under its influence in 1886. True, there were individual trade unions which sided with other socialist organizations; sometimes, indeed, several unions in the same trade, each with its own factional affiliation, a state of affairs which nullified their influence. The Guesdists, however, undoubtedly had the greatest influence. In 1892 they called two conferences at Marseilles; one, of the trade unions affiliated with the party, and another of the party organizations, to be held immediately afterwards. The delegates were practically the same in both conferences, except for a few of the most prominent intellectuals who attended the official party conference only. Briand was a delegate to both conferences: in the trade-union conference he represented the "Bourse du Travail" (local labor center) of Saint-Nazaire, which included eleven trade unions; in the party conference he represented the socialist group of that town, although personally he was not a Guesdist.

Those two conferences at Marseilles definitely connected the name of Briand with the idea of the general strike. At the trade-union conference he reported the findings of the commission on resolutions in favor of the "principle of the universal strike." The resolution was adopted unanimously and Briand's popularity among the trade-union delegates was established.

The reaction was, however, quite different among the Marxian intellectuals who had been watching the proceedings from the audience. Not being delegates to the trade union convention, they were helpless witnesses of the unexpected triumph of a heretic. The oratorical talents and the intelligence of this young man of thirty were incontestable, but what he was saying was against all the well-established traditions of the party and full of danger to the unity of the movement. Alexandre Zévaès, a historian of the French socialist movement and himself a delegate at the party convention of 1892, records in his notes that "Guesde was reserved, while Lafargue circulated among the delegates the rumor that the young lawyer was a stool-pigeon hired by the government." A generation before, similar rumors had been circulated by Lafargue's father-in-law against a better man —Michael Bakunin. Apparently all means are fair not only in love and war, but also in the struggle for revolutionary leadership. . . .

The general strike was not on the agenda of the party conference which followed the trade-union convention. Briand, however, found a pretext for bringing the matter up for discussion. The International Socialist Congress to be held in Zurich in 1893, furnished the opportunity. The "stool-pigeon" took the floor and suggested that the general strike be placed on the agenda of the international congress. The speech which he delivered in support of his motion contained the following passages:

"Until now the Socialists have been envisaging only two methods of bringing about a democratic régime based upon economic equality: Revolution and universal suffrage. Some of them are inclined towards the first; others prefer the second.

"Revolution? But who could dream of it seriously today? It would be childish to dream of beginning once more the bloody and romantic ventures, the heroic armed uprisings, which have filled this century up to the time of the Commune (1871).

"At the present time an insurrection would be doomed to the most tragic failure. Any attempt to build barricades in our large contemporary cities is made impossible by the wide avenues and the long straight streets. The age of street battles is past.

"There remains the ballot. It has certainly given results. But how feeble are these results when compared with what remains to be accomplished!

"While giving up the idea of an insurrection, is it not possible, though continuing to use the ballot, to consider another method, the use of which depends upon the workers themselves, and which would be both peaceful and lawful?

"The law of 1864 permits workers to get together and to go on strike. The working class has amply availed itself of this right. Every year hundreds of strikes occur in various cities or industries. These are the partial strikes. They

are becoming less and less effective. Why should not an attempt be made to render these strikes more general in order
to increase their chances of victory?

"These tactics would have the advantage of being lawful.
The law which makes the strike legal sets no limits to its
extent. Consequently, in undertaking a general strike, the
workers may assure themselves that they are exercising a
legitimate right, and many of them who would shrink from
resorting to violence, to revolutionary action, would not
hesitate to take part in a movement which, while formidable,
would at least not carry them beyond the bounds of legality.
By thus asserting itself, the proletariat will show its power,
its function as the creator of national wealth, and it will
easily obtain those reforms which the government at present
jealously withholds."

The Guesdist leaders were adamant in their hostility to
the idea. They had good reasons for their attitude, for with
all their revolutionary talk, they were at bottom peaceful
politicians, casting hopeful eyes on the success of the German Socialist Party with its tremendous job-dispensing
machine. The general strike might easily throw a monkey-
wrench into the gears of that hoped-for machine. Whether it
was to remain a mere dream of a "revolt with folded arms,"
or whether it was to assume a more actual and turbulent
aspect, the *party* was bound to suffer. The masses might
attempt to get immediately, by the direct action of a general
strike, what they were being taught to expect in the future
as a result of casting the right ballot. Defeated, such a strike
might bring down persecutions on the party and so weaken
its electoral chances. Victorious, it would be an encourage-
ment to further revolutionary activities, with revolution and
civil war. To all of this, in a democratic country enjoying
universal suffrage, Socialists are as a general rule averse.
Capitalism is quite bearable to them as long as it permits
them to organize the workers and to get their votes. To the

German Socialists, for instance, the general strike idea was "general idiocy," until the growing impatience of the workers forced them to incorporate the "political mass strike," as they called it, in their war gear. Even then it was only for electoral use, as a means of defending or extending the suffrage, not for vulgar bread-and-butter objectives. Only one year after that very congress of Marseilles, the Belgian Socialists used this weapon for the purpose of obtaining universal suffrage.

In his reply, Guesde used an argument which did honor to his political astuteness, even if his sincerity was questioned. He actually declared that he was opposed to the general strike because it was not sufficiently revolutionary! It would take half a century, or even a century before the workers would be ready to have recourse to such a weapon—while in less time they could be induced to vote the socialist ticket!

"Is it possible," Guesde said, "to expect such unanimity! Why, at this moment, without any effort, without any risk, the workers, by using the ballot, *by voting for themselves,* for the candidates of their class, could become the masters of the government, could become the government! In spite of that, only a minority has responded to the appeal of socialism. From this alone you may judge the time that would be necessary before, at the risk of their bread and the bread of their families, the majority, nay, *all* the workers, could be induced to desert their shops, their mines and their factories!

"We do not postpone our escape from the social inferno to a period as distant as the time of the general strike. A party of the [working] class, a party of social transformation, we are *ipso facto* a party of revolution, of insurrection —as soon as insurrection has become possible." *That* moment had of course to be determined by Guesde himself, who, by the way, ended his political career as a member of the Viviani-Briand War cabinet—a typical representative of

a large section of the pre-War generation of Marxian politicians in Western Europe, with their pseudo-revolutionary
spread-eagle oratory and make-believe irreconcilability.

The simplicity with which Guesde took it for granted
that by voting for Guesde (or any other aspiring politician)
the worker is voting for *himself,* and that every worker
would be more easily led into voting for the "right man"
suggested by Guesde, than into striking for better conditions, is an interesting example of what one might call
"political Narcissism." But he carried the day, and Briand's
proposal was rejected by a large majority. This majority
consisted mostly of the same men who only a few days
before, at the trade-union conference, had voted in favor
of Briand's general strike resolution. One might wonder
whether Briand's cynicism and contempt for the underdog
did not get its strongest backing from this edifying sight.
The official record of the convention, published by the party,
said nothing about this discussion, though it was the most
outstanding event of the convention and had occupied a
whole day.

Briand's conquest of Paris began in 1893 and was indirectly connected with the wave of anarchist terrorism then
sweeping the French capital. An anarchist had thrown a
bomb into a restaurant to avenge the betrayal of another
anarchist terrorist by one of the waiters. Following his arrest he was advised by his friends to engage Briand for his
defense. Here was a *cause célèbre* which in a day could
have decided the future of the young provincial lawyer. He
came to Paris—practically penniless—but nothing came of
his great hopes. The bomb-thrower had in the meantime
engaged a member of the Paris bar. Briand, however, remained in the capital and found a job on the staff of a
liberal daily, for which he had to cover the labor movement.
His pay was more than modest and he had to work hard
on the side, copying for lawyers and doing other chores.

ENTER SYNDICALISM

Ten years had now elapsed since he had left Paris, as a youth of twenty-one, after completing his law studies. Many changes had in the meantime taken place in the political situation of the country. There was a rising wave of social discontent, and a large number of politicians heretofore active in the various bourgeois parties had begun to show interest in the aspirations of the working masses. Jean Jaurès, a brilliant professor of philosophy and a conservative member of parliament, took up the cause of socialism and brought to its aid the greatest oratorical talent of his time. Alexandre Millerand, a prominent member of the *Parti Radical*—corresponding to the American "Progressives"— and a lawyer of note, followed suit. These converts, as well as great numbers of other intellectuals, budding politicians and *déclassés* who were not interested in the theoretical hair-splittings and personal rivalries of the existing socialist factions, constituted a loose Federation of Independent Socialists, which had neither a strict program nor a rigid party discipline. Belief in "collectivism"—meaning government ownership of industries and public utilities—was their only bond. According to a manifesto published by the Federation, its object was "to rally the socialists who do not want to embody their theoretical conceptions in a formula whose narrowness cannot embrace the multiple aspirations of the modern world, now in the full upswing of economic, political, mental and moral development." Needless to say, Aristide Briand likewise joined the "Independents," who were destined to give to their country a President in the person of Millerand, at least two prime ministers, Viviani and Briand, and one of the greatest orators of all times—Jean Jaurès.

But at that time the young ex-lawyer and hack-writer

was still at the very beginning of his career. At the general
elections held in 1893 he ran for parliament in a Paris district, but another socialist candidate carried the electorate.
It was not until nine years later that Briand entered the
Chamber, yet he was not idle during the intervening period.
Both the socialist cause and the syndicalist movement, then
in its inception, owe much to his activity during these years.
He contributed to the *Petite République,* a socialist daily
which was printing articles by such men as Juarès, Millerand and Viviani. He organized independent socialist feder-
ations and jointly with Pelloutier helped in the general-
strike propaganda among the trade unions.

In 1894 a trade-union conference was held in Nantes, the
city of his birth. This time it was no mere party conference
under trade-union disguise, as had been the case in Marseilles two years before. The convention of Nantes included
not only the National Federation of Trade Unions, which
was a strictly Guesdist creation, but also individual trade
unions and local chambers of labor ("Bourses du Travail"),
regardless of the specific socialist creed they professed or
sympathized with. They had been invited to attend for the
purpose of organizing a "great parliament of labor." This
was the work of the tireless Pelloutier, who was then secretary of the Federation of "Bourses du Travail," and who by
skilful maneuvering had placed the Guesdist body in such
a position that it could not refuse to meet in a conference
with dissenters from the pure Marxian gospel.

All shades of socialist opinion were represented at that
conference: Guesdists, hiding their purely parliamentary aspirations behind a screen of irreconcilable revolutionary verbiage; Blanquists, followers of the great conspirator in name
only, twenty years of political democracy having taught
them that it was not absolutely necessary to overthrow the
government in order to provide jobs for hungry intellectuals
or ambitious ex-workers, but still clinging to the great name

of the martyr as a convenient drawing card; "Independents," working each on his own hook, each with a set of principles of his own, ready to be changed at any moment according to circumstances. Only the "Possibilists" were missing. They had been dismal failures in their hopes of winning over the French workers to a "pink" program that dispensed with all revolutionary talk and would certainly have met with Mr. La Follette's approval. Before dying, however, that group had given life to a new faction, the "Allemanists," so called after their leader Allemanne, who had adopted the general strike as their main plank (besides running for parliament) and who admitted no intellectuals into their ranks, since they wanted to keep all the political jobs for upstart workers exclusively. Their horny-handed gospel had, however, no objection to the admission of employers, as long as they were themselves working in their shops. Allemanne himself was the owner of a printing plant. Last but not least, there were the Anarchists—just emerging disappointed from a heroic period of aimless individual terrorism, during which they had remained without any contact with the masses. Now, under Pelloutier's influence, they were trying hard to free the trade unions from the grip of the socialist politicians and to permeate them with their own ideology.

The conference was one of the most momentous in the history of the French labor movement. The general strike was well in the fore in its deliberations—with the Guesdists, as in former years, opposed to the adoption of a resolution in its favor. Now, however, they were too weak to withstand the concerted attack of all other factions arrayed against them. One common idea, or rather sentiment, had imperceptibly and perhaps unconsciously taken hold of all the other delegates. It was the "Allemanist" spirit of distrust or rather jealousy, of leadership by intellectuals. The Guesdists, with their intolerance and their specifically Marxian air of contemptuous superiority, were the most insupportable of the whole brotherhood of socialist intellectuals. The antagonism between the labor leaders risen from the ranks and the politicians and theorists coming from the intelligentsia, is an old skeleton in the socialist family closet. Apparent differences in principle are often nothing but rationalizations of the struggle for leadership waged between these two groups—which does not preclude the possibility of members of one group occasionally joining forces with the other group.

Aristide Briand spoke as one of the "Independents," and the speech which he delivered in defense of the general strike contributed not a little to the victory of the forces arrayed against the Guesdists.

Beaten in the vote on the general strike resolution, the Guesdists withdrew from the convention. That discomfiture marked the end of their influence in the trade unions. Their own National Federation of Trade Unions soon disappeared altogether. On the other hand, the delegates who constituted the pro-general-strike majority decided to meet again the following year. This they did, and at the convention of Limoges (1895) the General Confederation of Labor was constituted. Following that convention, the various shades of socialist and anarchist thought represented by these delegates—mostly workers or former workers—became submerged in their joint endeavor to build up a strong trade-union movement, independent of all political factions and sects. Syndicalism thus made its appearance as a new factor in French life.

Briand, who had contributed his share to the constitution of this new revolutionary force, did not take part in its further development. Syndicalism did not have much to offer to an ambitious and eloquent lawyer. A life job as a union official—even if interrupted by occasional prison sentences— may have many inducements for an intelligent manual

worker who is compelled to slave his life away at the lathe
or at the bench, with the prospect of being thrown upon the
pavement when he grows old; but its seductions are not to
be compared with those offered by a regular political career.
Moreover, Briand would have been out of place in a *milieu*
that was suspicious of lawyers and other "high-brows."
Even at the Nantes conference, when he was advocating the
general strike, he had been taunted by his Guesdist opponents with the fact that he was a lawyer and did not
belong there. He had defended himself by saying that he
was a lawyer no longer; that he had given up his profession
and was earning a living as a proletarian, being employed as
a salaried man; and he added that he was even unable to
return to his profession, since he had no money to buy the
furniture for an office.

The chief object of this aspect of his activities was, in
fact, now achieved. A crushing blow had been dealt to the
Guesdists and to their ambition of monopolizing the leadership of the socialist and labor movement. The road was now
free for "Independent" talent to work out its own career
unhampered by the dictatorship of Jules Guesde, the *"Torquemada en lorgnon"* as he was called by his enemies in the
socialist camp.

FOR THE GOVERNMENT . . . AND THE GENERAL STRIKE

During the subsequent years until 1899, the political life
of France was occupied to a great extent with the Dreyfus
affair. The struggle for the vindication of a Jewish captain
who had been condemned for no crime of his own, broad-
ened into a life-and-death struggle of all the advanced elements of the country against the supporters of clerical and
monarchist reaction. The Socialists in their majority supported their great orator Jaurès, who had become an enthusiastic champion of the innocent. Aristide Briand was very

active in those days. He became closely associated with
Sebastien Faure, the celebrated though not very scrupulous
anarchist tribune, to whose daily *Journal du Peuple* he contributed. That this peculiar anarchist paper was subsidized
by some Jewish financiers, who during the *Affaire* were
grateful for any help, was a matter of general knowledge.
Briand was broad-minded enough not to raise any objections on the grounds of revolutionary ethics. As time went
by he became more and more broad-minded in this respect. . . .

In 1899 the "Left" won its campaign, and a cabinet was
organized which comprised all the parties that had been
arrayed against the reactionaries. It was headed by the
moderate Liberal Waldeck-Rousseau, and included likewise
Alexandre Millerand, the outstanding leader of the moderate
Socialists. It also included, no doubt to sweeten the pill for
the somewhat perplexed bourgeois world, General Galliffet,
the man who had put down the uprising of the Paris Commune of 1871 and had on his conscience, or to his credit,
the death of thirty thousand revolutionary workers. At that
time, when the mere idea of a socialist cabinet minister
sounded to the whole world like a contradiction in terms,
the appointment of the blood-stained general seemed necessary as a kind of symbolic gesture, showing that the red
peril was well taken care of. Twenty years later that gesture
was no longer necessary. German Socialists of the good old
Marxian school, many of whom had once been workers at
the bench, once for all vindicated the political reliability of
the Socialist Party; for in 1919, 1920 and 1921 the machine
gun exploits of Noske, Scheidemann, Severing and Hör-
sing, ex-workers all, were sufficient to pacify one section
of the working class, with the silent approval of the other
section. . . .

Millerand's entrance into a bourgeois cabinet caused a
rift in the socialist ranks both outside and inside the Parlia-

ment, where since 1893 they had had about fifty representatives, elected by about 900,000 votes. The rift was not healed until several years later. The Guesdists and Blanquists, representing the more radical wing of the Socialist group in the Chamber, had once supported a bourgeois government—the liberal cabinet headed by Leon Bourgeois in 1895—but they balked at having one of their party, by entering the cabinet, assume a responsibility for the actions of the government. It had taken them years to build up their organizations in working-class constituencies, and they were afraid that the first shot fired against striking workers under a government in which they were represented, would wreck their political influence and drive the workers into the arms of the anarchists. They refused to risk their reputation for the sake of a few ephemeral government favors and to jeopardize their future political influence. The "Independents" had no such apprehensions. Not connected with any widely spread organization, elected in constituencies which were to a great extent lower-middle-class rather than industrial, unashamed careerists, impatient to fall in with the government and to become thoroughly respectable at the earliest opportunity— they vigorously defended the step taken by Millerand. For cover they used the untarnished name of Jean Jaurès—a gigantic personality—a disinterested man of genius fallen among grafters and adventurers. Jaurès could have been prime minister for the asking, for any bourgeois party or bloc would have gladly offered him the honors and powers of leadership, but he preferred the more modest and at the same time more glorious part of a tribune of the people, always ready to call the working masses to the defense of their heritage of the Great Revolution. Jaurès was the last of the great liberals in the finest sense of the word. He believed in a gradual transition from the capitalist into the socialist system and he considered the preservation and strengthening of democracy as of paramount importance for this gradual and peaceful process. Socialist participation in the government was in his opinion the best method of consolidating the forces of democracy against the onslaught of nationalist, clerical and militarist reaction.

The whole matter was taken up at a general congress of all socialist organizations, held in Paris in December, 1899. "Antiministériels" and "ministériels," as the representatives of the two sides were called, were arrayed against each other in two hostile groups, with the numerical advantage on the side of the "antiministériels." The congress did not succeed in mending the rift, and until 1905 there were actually two distinct socialist factions in the French parliament—the "revolutionary" composed of Guesdists and Blanquists, which called itself "Parti Socialiste de France"; and the moderate or reformist "Parti Socialiste Français" including the "Independents" and what was left of the "Possibilists." The "Allemanists" remained outside both groups.

During that conflict and particularly during the battle that raged at the general socialist convention of 1899, Briand actively sided with Juarès and the other defenders of socialist participation in the government. In his speech he was merciless to his opponents, and his arraignment of Guesde and his highly disciplined followers was a piece of political sadism. To the delight of "ministériels" and of onlooking Anarchists alike—since extremes meet—he recalled all his foes' sins of omission and commission. How originally they had been so extreme as to oppose any participation in elections and any demands that could be fulfilled within the capitalist system; how later they had given up their hostility to the ballot and to partial reforms; how, to win the peasants' vote, they had even proposed laws aiming at the protection of small peasant property—for which they had been heavily taken to task by Friedrich Engels, the then-still-living incarnation of the Marxian Logos. He recalled that "there is no insuperable chasm between the ballot and

the portfolio," and that "if we have slipped on the slope—
it is only because you soaped it yourselves." He taunted
them with their hostility with regard to the general strike
and recalled that his report in favor of that idea, which had
been adopted in 1892 by the trade-union delegates assembled
in convention in Marseilles, had been rejected two days later
by the same men, when as delegates to the political convention they were under the direct supervision of Guesde. The
Guesdists were furious and retaliated by calling Briand an
Anarchist.* Their anger had good grounds, for his remarks
about the general strike nearly created a rift in the "anti-
ministériel" bloc, the Blanquists, who were in favor of the
idea, applauding some of the passages of his harangue
against their Guesdist allies.

Briand's advocacy of the general strike at the same time
that he was supporting socialist participation in the government may perhaps seem incongruous. The incongruity is
only apparent. In reality this was a clever tactical move,
destined to create confusion in the ranks of his opponents.
Moreover, in order to support the government, one had to
be elected first. In order to be elected, one had to use the
right propaganda. Five years later, at the International
Socialist Congress held in Amsterdam (1904), Meslier, a
Jauressist member of the French Chamber, let the cat out
of the bag as to what the "right propaganda" really was.
"The French workers," he said, "often see in parliamentary
action nothing but a means of assisting the careers of political wirepullers and climbers. In order to combat effectively
this erroneous conception with regard to parliamentary
action, the members of parliament must advocate the general
strike as well." Shades of Machiavelli! Those "petty bourgeois" and "eclectical" Independents had more political

---

* In that speech Briand advocated the strike of the soldiers and threatened that if the authorities persisted in forcing the soldiers to shoot upon
the striking workers, "the rifles might go off but not in the desired
direction."

acumen than the "scientific" Guesdists, so proud of the
Hegelian dialectics of their Marx—whom they never read.
. . . Besides, the French bourgeoisie was no longer afraid
of the revolutionary jargon of the radical politicians. It
knew that free indulgence in oral violence, in normal times,
is an innocent game that harms nobody. It also knew that
the general strike proposed by Briand was exactly as seriously meant as the barricades and rifles flaunted by Guesde
on festive occasions. Particularly it understood that "Rights"
and "Lefts" alike were traders in hope, quite ready to climb
to political influence and reputation on any convenient ladder
of lofty ideals and high-sounding promises.

That speech which Briand delivered in defense of the
general strike has since become a classic. Time and again it
has been republished in pamphlet form by revolutionary
Socialists, Syndicalists, and Anarchists—much to the dismay
of its author, who ten years later, as prime minister, was
to resort to the most dictatorial measures against a general
strike inspired by the ideas he had himself preached! But—
had he not preached the general strike so well, he might
never have achieved the fame which paved his way to power
and influence.

Moving Up

In the meantime Briand was moving up. He had become
editor-in-chief of the *Lanterne,* a daily whose personnel was
composed partly of liberals and partly of socialists. His
journalistic and party activities did not prevent him from
practising law. He did not have the makings of a corporation lawyer—he was too lazy to study his cases and never
had any clients for commercial or other civil suits—but he
was incomparable as a criminal lawyer. His impromptu
speeches—he never prepared them—his entertaining manner, and his comic antics could always carry a jury. Clemenceau, who never liked him—he never liked anybody for that

matter—once declared that if he were to be accused of having stolen the towers of Notre Dame, he would like to be defended by Briand. It was likewise Clemenceau who, referring to Briand's great lack of book-learning—to put it mildly—and comparing it with the great erudition of Poincaré, once remarked: "Poincaré knows everything and understands nothing, while Briand knows nothing and understands everything."

At last, in 1902, a seat was offered him for the parliamentary elections in Saint-Étienne, an industrial city in southeastern France. He won the election, and he has kept that seat ever since. Shortly before the elections he had been appointed secretary general of the moderate "Parti Socialiste Français"—the party of Jaurès and Millerand. He was then forty years old, and the succeeding years became a swift and continuous race from one success to another.

Two years after his election he was appointed to the Commission on the Separation of the Church from the State. The question was at that time agitating the entire public life of France more than any other subject. Under ordinary conditions, the report of that Commission would have taken a year or more to complete. Briand undertook to prepare it, and finished it in less than two months. If one is to believe his critics, the report was full of amusing anachronisms and "bulls." But that did not save the cause of, the Church. The measure was passed, and Briand's speech was ordered posted all over France. There was now no doubt in anybody's mind that he had become "cabinet timber."

The great speech was made in 1905. In the course of that year the socialist ranks, split in 1899, were reunited. Yielding to pressure from the International Socialist Congress held in Amsterdam in 1904, both parties decided to make peace. But as the Marxists had been the victors at that International Convention, the proverbial hatchet was actually buried in the side of the defeated opponents—to use

Whistler's figure of speech. Jean Jaurès and his friends had
to eat humble pie, and to accept the two main conditions
imposed by the victorious "Lefts": refusal to vote for the
government budget, and withdrawal of their representatives
from the parliamentary committee of the "Republican Left"
—that is the liberal bourgeois parties. It was a bitter pill for
Jaurès and his friends, but it had to be swallowed. Their
party was disintegrating; revolt was brewing within the
various sections; and over both factions hovered the threat
of syndicalism, which was making heavy inroads in their
ranks. Both sections realized that a more revolutionary
vocabulary and less dickering with the bourgeois parties
would be needed to stave off that peril. The united party
adopted the name "Socialist Party, French Section of the
Workers' International"—usually called "Unified Socialist
Party."

Nearly a year after the constitution of the unified party,
Briand was offered the post of Minister of Education and
Public Worship, in the cabinet of Sarrien. He accepted it
and was forthwith excluded from the Socialist Party. National elections took place a few weeks after his nomination,
and he was returned to the Chamber from his old constituency. The voters who in 1902 had elected the champion
of the general strike, seemed to be now, only four years
later, even more eager to be represented by a member of a
bourgeois cabinet.

After the elections Sarrien resigned, and Clemenceau, who
had become head of the government, retained Briand in
his cabinet. The task for which the Tiger needed the former
firebrand was of a twofold character. First, he was to continue the application of the Separation Law, directed against
the Catholic Church. By an irony of fate, the religious con-
gregations whose property was to be liquidated by the
government, had engaged Millerand's legal services to protect their interests—the most profitable case any French

lawyer had ever had in his practice. The second task entrusted to Briand's department was an outcrop of the growing syndicalist movement. Encouraged by the successes obtained by various groups of wage earners who had joined the General Confederation of Labor, the school teachers, a very poorly paid category of government employees in France, likewise attempted to form a trade-union organization and to join the Confederation. In this they met with the unflinching resistance of the Minister of Public Instruction.

Jaurès, who in spite of his forced submission to Guesde's antiministerialism never ceased to believe in "collaboration," was greatly dismayed. He had seen his first protegé, Millerand, gradually turning more and more conservative. He now saw the same fate overtaking his younger protegé, whom he himself had advised to accept the cabinet post, and he launched a bitter attack against his former associate.

Briand was of course prepared for such attacks and answered in kind: "When a man joins the government," he replied, "he does not do it for the sake of popularity. It is more courageous to incur invective than to court applause from certain quarters. . . . We were both engaged in a policy of collaboration with the government of Waldeck-Rousseau. I could confront you with certain written statements made by you which might place you in an awkward position. How much ingenuity you displayed at that time! To some people you were then a renegade, and you kept explaining to Viviani and to myself that you were disgusted at the very thought of returning to irreconcilable opposition. Well, I have continued my evolution, and all that I am asking from this Chamber is that it judge me on my actions." He went on to insist that government employees, including teachers, should not be confounded with workers, and that they had no right to organize "against the nation."

It was after he took this stand that Briand, who hereto-

fore had usually been referred to jocularly as "Briand—
la Grève" (Briand, the Strike), began to be called "Briand
la Jaunisse" (Briand the Yellow, literally "the Jaundice").
The originator of that second sobriquet was Gustave Hervé,
father of the revolutionary "antipatriotism" of pre-war
times. A few years later Hervé was himself to turn his
coat and to outdo even Briand in patriotic and anti-revolu-
tionary fervor.*

After a short interlude as Minister of Justice in 1908,
Briand reached the top of his political career in 1909, when
he became Prime Minister for the first time. It was only
seven years since he had first been returned to parliament.
In a statement made on the day he assumed power, he
proudly dwelt upon the fact that he considered himself a
socialist and that he disowned nothing of his past.

The Strong Man

The first year of his premiership passed without conflicts.
On one occasion he might have asserted that his attitude
was much more liberal than that of any previous government. He did not interfere with the turbulent demonstrations staged by Socialists, Syndicalists and Anarchists in
connection with the execution of the educator, freethinker,
and anarchist, Francisco Ferrer—an entirely innocent victim
of Spanish military and clerical reaction. True, no domestic
issues were involved, and attacking the Catholic Church was
at that time a good republican pastime. Still, the Paris police
had heretofore always been very intolerant with all kinds of
street manifestations. . . . The old age pension law for
workers, a social reform expected since time immemorial,
was finally passed during this year. It almost seemed as if

---

* In 1903 Briand, in defending Hervé in one of his famous trials for
anti-militarist propaganda, called army life "an environment of debase-
ment and depravity where they do not reason and where they find nothing
better to do than to plunge a bayonet into the body of a fellow-human."

the Utopia of harmony between capital and labor were finally in sight. . . .

But the idyll was ended sharply by a conflict between the trade union of the railway workers and the companies, during which a strike was called. It was not what might be called a political affair; but, as an expert in these matters, Briand sensed the potentialities of such a strike and lost no time in taking the necessary measures. Army detachments were sent to all the important junctions of the railway system; the leaders of the union were arrested; the workers were mobilized for military service and threatened with court-martial if they refused to return to their jobs.

As in the case of the school-teachers' union, it was Jaurès who, with all the power of his personality and his incomparable oratory, attacked his former comrade. "You were unable to crush the strike," he cried, "except by violating the law. Have you forgotten, now that you are enjoying the prestige of power, the great mass meetings in which you were acclaimed? It is as an inspired propagandist that your memory lives in their hearts. And now, when they read in the papers that it is you, Millerand, Viviani, Briand, who are destroying their right to strike, they will ask themselves whether their life is not an evil dream."

Then he read to the assembly one of the most famous passages of Briand's speech of 1899, delivered at the socialist congress, in which he had taken to task the Guesdist opponents of the general strike: "You can go to battle with the ballot," Briand had said at that time, "I have nothing to object. You can go to battle with spears, pistols and rifles; I shall consider it my duty, when the time comes, to take my place in your ranks. . . . But do not discourage the workers when they attempt to unite for an action which is entirely their own, and in the efficacy of which they firmly believe. The general strike presents this attraction to the militant that it is, after all, but the exercise of an incontestable right. It is a revolution which begins within the law. . . ." *

Briand had to defend and to explain himself: "You are representing me as the man who stirred up the working class, as the man who set in motion the anarchist movement of this country, and you say: 'Where is the difference between your conception of that time and that of the General Confederation of Labor?' You know what that difference is, M. Jaurès. You know that I have always been opposed by the anarchists who are directing the General Confederation of Labor, and that my conception has nothing in common with theirs. You are well aware of the fact that I have always condemned violence. . . . You have isolated my speech from the circumstances under which it was delivered. . . . Our friend Millerand had entered the government. This had caused a certain effervescence within the Socialist Party. . . . At the convention at which the words quoted by you were spoken, I was fighting on your side. On the other side there were Messrs. Guesde and Vaillant, your friends of today. And it was there, not at a public meeting, not before a crowd, but before the congress of delegates of committees, of well-informed people who had already made up their minds, that I expounded my point of view in that speech which I delivered in your interest."

After having thus explained that the revolutionary slogans which had been his peculiar stock in trade for ten years and had made his political reputation, were just a piece of stage play for intra-party squabbles, he dealt with the legal

* That speech of Briand contained likewise another no less interesting passage. "The force of persuasion alone," he said, "even if united with the force of circumstances, is not sufficient to dictate laws to the bourgeois class. Moreover, once these laws have been passed, is there any guarantee that they will be applied if they are not backed by the revolutionary, permanent and continuous force of the organized proletariat?" On another occasion he ridiculed the government which "dreamed of establishing harmony between capital and labor—a dream as chimerical as the search for the philosopher's stone and for perpetual motion."

aspects of the measures he had recently taken against the striking railroad workers: "I am ready to admit," he said, "that theoretically they possess the right [to strike] and that they may use it legally. But there is another right which has not been mentioned in this debate, and which is superior to all other rights. It is society's right to live! There is no liberty, time-honored though it may be, whose exercise can be permitted to endanger the Nation's right to live. . . . The right that is above all other rights—is the right of the Nation to live and to maintain its independence and pride. A country cannot let its frontiers remain open [to attack]. And I am going to tell you a thing that will perhaps make you leap to your feet in indignation: If, in order to defend the existence of the Nation, the government had found no means in the law by which it could remain master of its frontiers—if, for that purpose, it had been unable to make use of its railways, which are an essential instrument of national defense—well, if it had had to resort to illegal measures, it would have done so!"

Upon the indignant cries of the Socialists, who called him a dictator, he stressed again the duty of defending the country against foreign invasion (which nobody was contemplating at that time), and of having recourse to extra-legal measures for that purpose. Finally, he added, "This is the doctrine of the Revolution, the doctrine of Danton! Are you going to disown that doctrine?"

Reference to the Great Revolution for the justification of an unconstitutional procedure in breaking down a peaceful strike was certainly in the grand style. The famous Loi Chapelier of 1791, enjoining the workers from organizing and striking, had likewise been passed in the name of the high principles of the Revolution!

The anger of the Socialists was boundless. Briand's policy was water for the mill of their competitors in the syndicalist and anarchist camps. In his newspaper, Jaurès de-

clared that in view of the violation of the law committed by
the government, it was henceforth useless to legislate at all.
And he warned the privileged classes against the personal
game of Briand—"a miserable, contemptible game, to the
detriment of the public order as well as of the working
class."

The bourgeoisie was elated. Here was a strong man who
was not afraid of the revolutionary Frankenstein he had
helped to create. They urged him to go further yet, to dis-
solve the Confederation of Labor, and to deny the right to
strike and to organize to all the workers employed in
various public utilities. Here he resisted. He believed that
the economic unrest was well taken care of by the suppression of the right of picketing and the arrest of vociferous
agitators; but to outlaw the trade unions altogether—that
was a different matter. It would mean clogging one of the
most reliable safety valves against Revolution and courting
the very danger he was out to avoid.

There had been those who predicted that French syndicalism was bound, sooner or later, to come down from its
revolutionary high horse. With the increase of their membership, aided by the industrial development of the country,
the "syndicats," they argued, would become respectable
trade-union organizations, with well-paid and peace-loving
office-holders, after the British, American or German model.
Did Briand foresee that evolution when he refused to dis-
solve the Confederation? At any rate, by his refusal he permitted that process to take its natural course, thus helping
to tame his country's "enemy from within." Four years
later, when the World War broke out, all the revolutionary
slogans of French syndicalism were discarded by the leaders
of the Confederation, who took their place within the *union
sacrée*. These slogans remained discarded after the war as
well. Their former preachers, headed by the General Secretary of the Confederation, the former Anarchist Leon Jou-

haux, are as respectable now as was Samuel Gompers in his old age.

In 1909-10, however, the Socialists had still another reason to be disconcerted. After having resorted to disciplinary measures against the teachers and countersigned the prosecutions against various labor unions, Briand had begun to carry the war into the socialist camp itself. He made a regular propaganda trip to the industrial sections of the northwest and the north, the latter the practically undisputed domain of Guesde and his upright "revolutionists." The Central Committee of the Socialist Party decided to stage demonstrations against the renegade. But what happened? Thousands of organized workers and a great number of labor leaders, including Socialist members of parliament, a mayor and prominent party officials—most of whom had risen from the ranks—gave the traitor a rousing welcome. They were flattered to have a cabinet minister speak to them as an equal. A mad scramble for government favors followed, in complete disregard of all the proprieties not only of party discipline but of common human dignity as well.

The German Socialists were at that time greatly aroused by the undignified spectacle displayed across the Rhine. Such a thing was not possible in the country of the strongest of all socialist parties. They were right. For Hohenzollern Germany would have never considered giving a socialist firebrand the chance of becoming a cabinet minister and of dispensing favors among his job-hungry comrades. But the German revolution changed all that, and the Briands on the German side of the Rhine outdid even their model.

There were now people who suspected that since the very inception of his career Briand had been an *agent provocateur*. Comparisons were even made between his career and that of Azev, greatest of *agents provocateurs* of modern times, who during the years preceding the War was at the head of the terrorist activities directed against the Tsarist system by the Social-Revolutionists, and at the same time in the service of the police. It would no doubt do credit to the democratic lack of prejudice of the French Republic, to have permitted a stool-pigeon to rise to the highest honor a nation can bestow, but his detractors did Briand an injustice. He was not a traitor in the classical style. He was only courageous enough to do before the War what was done by his socialist fellow politicians in so many other countries after the War: to follow to its logical conclusion a more or less disguised policy of class collaboration and to become the open champion of "national interests" as a whole; in other words—the defender of the existing system.

Since that momentous strike, Briand has been Prime Minister or simply cabinet minister—particularly Minister of Foreign Affairs—more often than any other French politician. Along with Clemenceau, Poincaré, Caillaux, Millerand, he has become one of the leading statesmen of his country. He continued to call himself a Socialist ("Socialiste Republicain") in much the same way as the royalists call themselves "Socialistes Patriotes," and the German Fascists call themselves "National-Sozialisten."

NEMESIS

His further career has been marked by a succession of political intrigues between the leading statesmen for ascendancy among the ruling parties. Continuously evolving toward the Right, he was in 1913 instrumental in having Poincaré elected President of the Republic in the face of Clemenceau's efforts to have one of his own men nominated.

Having become Prime Minister under a President of his making, one of his outstanding actions was the appointment of Delcassé as ambassador to Russia. To those who know the part played by Poincaré and Delcassé in the gentle business of bringing about the World War, the award of the Nobel prize to Briand in recognition of his rôle as Europe's angel of peace assumes a certain ironic significance.

During the War* he was, first, Minister of Justice in the cabinet of the former Socialist Viviani, and again Prime Minister between 1915 and 1917. During those troubled days he shared ministerial honors with a man who had once been his most bitter enemy—Jules Guesde, the patriarch of French Marxism. He, too, had become a "bitter-ender," along with the most prominent socialist politicians in Germany, Austria, and Belgium. The general strike was no longer a bone of contention between the two men who had grown older and wiser. War against the German invader and against the internationalists who wanted to stop the carnage had united them in a cabinet of the "sacred union." Jointly they put their signatures under the decree of expulsion directed against the editor of an internationalist paper published in Paris by a Russian revolutionary exile named Leon Trotsky. . . .

Briand's two important achievements while he was in power as War premier were the winning of Italy to the side of the Allies, and the organization of the Saloniki expedition. In the first task he was greatly assisted by Professor Marcel Cachin, a prominent Socialist, who used every effort to persuade the Italian Socialist Party to come out in favor of Italy's participation in the war. Cachin is now the leader of the French Communist Party. It is a queer world. . . .

In his second task, the Saloniki expedition, Briand was furiously opposed by Clemenceau, who doubted its expediency. Briand turned out to be right—a thing that the Tiger never forgave him. Clemenceau's accession to power in 1917

---

* In 1901 (*La Lanterne*, June 21) Briand had written: "There is no government that would dare to declare war if it were not sure that the people's inertia would countenance its homicidal projects, or if [it knew that] the signal of war were to become the signal of revolt as well."

marks Briand's temporary eclipse. But he came back in 1920, when his activities behind the scenes thwarted the grand old man's presidential ambitions and drove him finally into private life. The Fox proved mightier than the Tiger.

After the defeat of his foremost rival and enemy Briand's importance began to loom paramount in the councils of Europe. Through his person victorious France exercised her hegemony over the rest of the continent. Such trifles as the domestic conflicts between the haves and the have-nots of his own country, no longer held the attention of the former revolutionary propagandist. Attacked by the Communists for his hostility towards the Soviet Union, and by the extreme reactionaries for his slightly conciliatory attitude towards the defeated enemies—he is being warmly supported by the moderate Socialists whose cause, by his defection, he once hurt so painfully. Old scores are now forgotten. Rightly or wrongly, the Socialists are now convinced that his policy is contributing more towards the preservation of European peace than anything that had been proposed by other statesmen of their country. For the French Socialists, patriotic as they may be, do not want war. They feel that another conflagration would strengthen the extreme elements—the monarchist and clerical reactionaries on the one hand and the Communists on the other. To escape the two equally merciless grindstones of Fascism and Bolshevism, they sought the tender embraces of their ancient comrade—in spite of the peccadilloes of his past.

Strange as this may seem, it was this very support, which, by alarming the more conservative elements, frustrated his presidential ambitions and led to his eventual eclipse—one of those tragicomical vengeances wrought by the envious gods in their inscrutable wisdom.

PHILIPP SCHEIDEMANN

OR

From Marx to Hindenburg

BEFORE the War, the German Socialist Party occupied a unique position among the socialist parties of the world. It was, so to speak, the Mother Church, inspired directly by the immortal teachers, Marx and Engels, at whose feet its leaders sat in their youth. To it the younger branches continued to look for spiritual guidance—and material support as well. It was to the socialist parties of the world almost what the ruling party of the Soviet Union later became to the communists. Its two outstanding theorists, Eduard Bernstein and Karl Kautsky, are still alive, venerable octogenarians, who for the last forty years have been supplying the *ex post facto* arguments needed to justify the policies of the frankly reformist and the pseudo-revolutionary wings of their party. But its founders, August Bebel and Wilhelm Liebknecht (father of Karl), are dead. The garrulous and inconsistent "soldier of the revolution," as the older Liebknecht liked to call himself—he had fought in 1848—died in his bed at the age of seventy-four. He was then editor-in-chief of the Berlin *Vorwärts,* the central organ of his party, which nineteen years later, in 1919, was chiefly instrumental in the murder of his glorious son, Karl. August Bebel, the younger and more able of the two, and the real leader, died, likewise a septuagenarian, a year before the War. He was a cautious and practical man even to his death—for had he lived a year longer, he would have shared the disgrace of his successors. . . .

The most prominent of his successors were four men whom he had himself picked for the task—two ex-workers and two intellectuals. Of these four, three are now dead. Hugo Haase, the gifted and successful lawyer from Königsberg, a middle-of-the-roader between the Lefts and the Rights, was murdered by a reactionary assassin. Friedrich Ebert, the "saddler," first President of the German Republic, died during his term of office, mourned by the capitalist press as the savior of his country from the Bolshevist scourge. His humble origin was to large sections of his "nation of poets and thinkers," a greater humiliation than the Treaty of Versailles. Hermann Müller, too, is gone; the man who, from assistant-bookkeeper had risen to the Chancellorship of the Republic, and as holder of that office put democratic dignity to shame by sending to Hindenburg such a servile telegram of congratulation as even a humble bank clerk would not send to the president of his institution.

The sole survivor is Philipp Scheidemann, the first Chancellor of the German Republic, once, like Ebert, a worker. With an eye to his future record in history, he refused to sign the Versailles treaty and thereafter disappeared from the larger political scene, contenting himself with the post of Mayor in his native city of Cassel. The most picturesque of this group of four, he is a living symbol of the rise of what was once the most radical outpost of German democracy, in its struggle against the semi-absolutism of the Hohenzollerns; of its surrender to the imperialist expansionism of German capitalism; and of its final decay, as preserver of the bourgeois *status quo* against the storming forces of revolution.

The son of a small independent artisan who was proficient in his trade as a master upholsterer, young Philipp was not originally slated to become a worker—and a Chancellor. But for the untimely death of his father, who returned from the war of 1870 with wrecked health, the bright scion of an old and respectable burgher family would have continued his studies and would perhaps some day have become a Liberal or a Conservative politician; but he would hardly have reached the heights attained by the orphan-lad who left school at fourteen to learn the "black art" of Gutenberg.

At the time of Scheidemann's birth (1865), that section of the German working class which thought in terms of an independent political activity was still mourning the death of Ferdinand Lassalle—"the man who gave us swords"— the original of the hero of Meredith's *Tragic Comedians*. In a whirlwind campaign begun in 1862, that great orator— the greatest of the nineteenth century—succeeded in founding the General German Workers' Union, the first large workers' organization in Germany to raise the banner of socialism. Lassalle's socialism was a combination of German nationalism—the desire for the unification of all the German lands was in those days a common characteristic of all German socialists—with the usual democratic demand for universal suffrage and a hazy socialist formula of "productive coöperatives with State credits." The immediate needs of the laboring masses gave him little concern; their struggle for higher wages was altogether outside the scope of his activities or even of his thoughts. On the contrary, he believed in the "iron law of wages" and regarded as illusory any attempt of the workers, so long as the present system endured, to raise their wages to any considerable extent above the minimum level required for their subsistence.

Lassalle's career as awakener and organizer of the German workers was cut short after less than two years, but he had started the snowball rolling and growing. Until his appearance in the early sixties, the workers, as yet organized only in educational societies had been politically merely an appendage of the Liberal middle classes. Now they began to organize themselves as an independent party pledged to the democratic postulate of universal suffrage and to vague socialist watchwords. Meanwhile, the leadership of the middle-class and lower-middle-class intellectuals, as well as of the ex-workers who continued the traditions of Lassalle, did not remain unchallenged. Another group of intellectuals and semi-intellectuals, headed by Wilhelm Liebknecht and August Bebel, began to dispute the right of the Lassallians to the leadership of the working class. They took their inspiration directly from Marx and his "International," rather than from his gifted but heretical disciple. . . . The consequent ugly quarrel lasted for several years, until the union of both groups in 1875, in a single Social-Democratic Party, henceforth the official name of the German socialist party. This was not merely a sectarian dispute as to the greater merits of their respective prophets. The Lassallians took rather a contemptuous attitude toward the trade unions, and even while they helped to organize them, treated them as mere duplications of the party organization. The leaders of this section were self-centered intellectuals, politicians above all, with a strong nationalistic bias in favor of Prussia, whose hegemony they supported in the case of Germany's hoped-for unification. Like their teacher, Lassalle, they were ready to support Bismarck and his junkers against the bourgeoisie. Their Marxist opponents, active mostly in the non-Prussian sections of Germany, were against Prussian predominance; they opposed the autocratic organization methods of the Lassallians and advocated intra-party democracy instead; they were in favor of collaboration with the various democratic parties; and they were ready to grant a modicum of independence to the trade unions, which they vigorously helped to organize. The two socialist parties finally merged in 1875 as a result of the changed political situation after the unification of Germany, and of the disgust of the workers at this unsavory quarreling among their leaders.

The united party enjoyed only a short period of open activity. Bismarck became disturbed by its continuously increasing poll of votes—it had reached 500,000 in 1877— and in the following year he found in the terrorist attempts of two paranoiacs, who were neither Socialists nor Anarchists, a pretext for passing anti-socialist laws which forbade any kind of radical activity. The growth of a democratic force that threatened junkerdom and monarchy was to be checked at all costs.

The anti-socialist laws were made effective in 1878. It was during the first years of their operation that young Scheidemann, then an apprentice in a printing shop, became acquainted with socialist ideas. The pamphlets written by Lassalle, then still current as propaganda, though entirely forgotten now, gave him what is called "class consciousness" —and that, to him as to thousands of other workers like him, meant voting the socialist ticket, paying party and union dues, hoping for better conditions in some indefinite future, and mistrusting as "nuts" or "stool-pigeons" all those who advocated somewhat more risky tactics.

Conspirators—with a Difference

By 1883 Philipp had reached the age of eighteen and had become a full-fledged worker; he was sufficiently mature to be admitted as a member of the secret socialist organization and to be entrusted with the collection of money for the exiled, and with the distribution of the party organ in his home town, Cassel in Hesse-Nassau. This was either smuggled in from abroad, first from Switzerland and later from London, or, when smuggling became difficult, occasionally published secretly at home. At about the same time he joined his trade union; for the trade unions, which had been suppressed along with the party in 1878, were once more permitted after 1883, Bismarck having discovered that a legal-

ized trade union was safer for the existing system than the
secret one which inevitably sprang up in its place and eluded
control. He still hoped, however, to suppress the movement
for political democracy conducted by the Socialist Party; he
had overlooked the fact that all the urge for romance, all
the unused revolutionary energy, bottled up in a rising industrial working class, would favor the mildly illegal activities
which propagated the new gospel.

The secret organization of which Scheidemann had become a member was constituted on the classical pattern of
the Blanquist conspiratory groups which had existed in
France during the period between 1830 and 1870. There
was a committee of five men; each of these five was in touch
with another five, and so on. In Cassel alone this secret
body had several hundred members. Here, however, the
resemblance to the pattern ended. Auguste Blanqui and his
associates in France were *déclassé* intellectuals, students,
bohemians, desperadoes. They were ready at any moment
to organize a coup that would secure them power—and fail-
ing that, either a speedy death on the barricades or before
the firing squad, or a lingering one in solitary confinement.
The German socialists of the seventies and eighties were
not of that mold. The steady development of industry and
the increase of the working population, together with the
universal suffrage, had shown them the opportunity to
create a large and powerful political organization which
would offer its leaders all the advantages that one of the
regular parties could afford. The France of Blanqui's time
had presented no such prospect. Much as the German socialists may have liked the prospect of a democratic republic with government ownership when conditions should
become ripe for it, they had been satisfied meanwhile to
hold their jobs as editors, organizers or parliamentarians,
and they were opposed to any kind of unlawful activity.

As a result of this attitude, the anti-socialist laws created

PHILIPP SCHEIDEMANN

great confusion among the party leaders. Bismarck's fears notwithstanding, they had never dreamed of a revolution, and their situation was now quite tragic, for they had lost the jobs in which they had felt so comfortably settled. They were not Brutuses, and they did their best to placate the angry gods by assuming the tamest attitude possible. Friedrich Engels, co-worker of Karl Marx, who, since the revolution of 1848 had lived in England, and who expected a militant policy against the Bismarck régime, expressed in 1882 (in a private letter) his contempt for the "thousands of ruined existences" for whom the party had become "a milch cow which was suddenly slaughtered by Bismarck."

Seeing no other way out, a great number of the old job-holders were driven to illegal activities. These built up that conspiratory machine of which young Scheidemann became a member in 1883—but their aim was not bloody revolution. Only a few of them went in that direction, and those few either were forced to leave their country, like the famous Johann Most—later active as an Anarchist in America—or they repented and swung over to the extreme right of the party. The remaining conspirators were chiefly interested in spreading the party gospel, getting more and more votes, and electing as many members of Parliament as possible. In this they succeeded fairly well, and in the elections of 1890 the Socialists polled nearly one million and a half votes. In the same year, a few months before the general election, the anti-socialist laws were repealed—twelve years after their enactment.

EDITOR

Up to the early nineties, Scheidemann worked at his trade, first in Cassel, where he took part in the publication of a local socialist paper, and later in Marburg, also in the Prussian province of Hesse-Nassau. Gifted and studious, he soon acquired sufficient knowledge of history and political economy to be able to write for papers and to conduct propaganda. At the age of twenty-four, he was chairman of a political society disguised as a social club, district chairman of the Typographical Union, and second-chairman of the local sick-benefit society for general workers. Socialist intellectuals soon became aware of the abilities as well as of the winning personality of the young giant, and in 1894 they induced him to become editor of a weekly paper in Giessen in the Duchy of Hesse-Darmstadt.

Party activity was still in its incipient stage in that section of the country, and Scheidemann had to be party secretary as well as editor, mailing clerk and collector for his paper—all for the royal salary of one hundred and twenty marks a month, on which he had to support a wife and three children. He stuck it out bravely and soon became known all over Hesse for his effective propaganda among the peasantry, designed to combat the propaganda of the Anti-Semitic party, then very active among that section of the population. He remained at Giessen until 1900, when he was called to Nuremberg, Bavaria, to become editor-in-chief of the socialist daily published in that important city.

The two years he spent in Nuremberg were disappointing ones. The party machinery there had become a distressing tangle of cliques, intriguing against each other for jobs, power and political influence. The movement was the property of a few ambitious men, who jealously guarded their vested interests, acquired either by participation in the secret movement during Bismarck's persecution, or as favorites or confidential advisers of local leaders, since deceased. Scheidemann was thoroughly disgusted and seized the first opportunity to go back to Hesse. There he became editor of a party daily in Offenbach and chief propagandist in all the provinces of the Duchy.

In the meantime, "red Philipp" was becoming one of the

marked figures among the party workers of Southern and Southwestern Germany. In 1898—at the Messianic age of thirty-three—he had been put up as a candidate for the national elections in Solingen, an industrial city in the Rhine Province. It was an old stronghold of the party, but internal jealousies almost bordering on civil war between factions, had brought about his defeat. Five years later, however, in 1903, he was finally returned for the same constituency. He had at last achieved the dream of many a class-conscious proletarian." . . .

Scheidemann had been in the party only five years when the anti-socialist laws were repealed, in 1890. The period between 1890 and 1903, between his apprenticeship as party journalist and speaker and his election to parliament, was perhaps the most momentous in the development of German —and to some extent of international—socialism. It was a period of continuous growth, unhampered by any anti-socialist legislation, and, at the same time, of theoretical disputes, which came near to splitting the party into two hostile camps. Yet Ph. Scheidemann's autobiography—over eight hundred pages in the German original—contains no more than two or three lines in reference to this warfare of theories. To the practical politician of today, engrossed in the national and municipal troubles of post-War Germany, it has become, apparently, mere surface froth, of far less consequence than mildly amusing anecdotes about an old party leader's housekeeper or details of party squabbles in his own constituency. Indeed, even at the time, while the dispute was at its hottest, he never showed any real interest in matters of party theology.

The anti-socialist laws had proved a dismal failure. From the twelve-year ordeal the Socialist Party had emerged, strengthened in numbers and in influence among the workers. Even the paternalistic social legislation which Bismarck had fostered in the hope of holding back the red tide, had worked in favor of the party rather than against it. The Iron Chancellor was humiliated by the repeal, but, considering the wavering attitude of the Reichstag, he did not insist strongly upon the renewal of those barbaric laws of repression. Instead, he had a vengeance in mind for the plebeian vermin which the law had failed to crush. As he himself admitted later, he was now on the lookout for a general who, in one way or another, would provoke the laboring masses into some overt act—an excuse for a bloodletting that would keep them in their places for a generation at least. If he had had his own way, no doubt the application of Tsarist methods would have called forth a genuine revolutionary movement in the "Russian" style—and might perhaps have destroyed the semi-autocracy of the Hohenzollerns without the intervention of the War—which, to carry the pipe-dream further, might perhaps not have occurred. But Bismarck was no longer the power that he had been for more than a generation. The young Kaiser wanted to be his own master—and at that time he hoped to stay the red tide by gentleness rather than by force. Moreover, there had grown up a group of savants, who had begun to search more deeply into the true character of the socialist movement. They realized that, given a certain modicum of political liberty, the preachers of the dreaded new gospel would turn out to be respectable leaders of a party of gradual progress, whose ultimate equalitarian aims would be a religious promise rather than a practical program. The Socialist Party was, therefore, permitted to proceed. . . .

BETWEEN LEFT AND RIGHT

Already, in 1890, a strong radical opposition against the old, tried leaders had made its appearance in the party. This was led by the younger elements—and hence dubbed "die Jungen"—who found that the movement had degenerated into a "petty-bourgeois party of reform", entirely too engrossed in parliamentary activities. At the opposite extreme of party policy were a group of outspoken moderates, like Georg von Vollmar, only a few years before a flaming rebel. These—a counterpart of the French "Possibilists"— wanted to abandon the revolutionary phraseology which still pervaded all the party utterances, to give up the socialist aim, and to concentrate the party's effort upon certain democratic postulates; in other words, they wanted frank and undisguised class-collaboration. The rest of the old guard, intellectuals and former workers alike, formed the party Center. To the impatient "Youngsters" of the Left, who wanted not only revolutionary talk but revolutionary action, and to the cynical but honest out-and-out politicians of the extreme Right, who wanted moderate words and moderate action, the more subtle leaders of the Center—Bebel, old Liebknecht, Kautsky—opposed the Machiavellian policy of very revolutionary abstract theory and very moderate action —a combination designed to keep the masses within the party and the leaders out of jail. The Left tactics would soon invite persecution and bring about reaction; the Right tactics, still far from placating the government by their moderation, would, by a ricochet, only strengthen the imprudent Left, or even furnish grist for the anarchist mill. The Center won. The "Youngsters" were expelled from the party, and most of them later joined the Anarchists.

Having disposed of the "Youngsters," Bebel took to task the honest cynics of the Right, and that without any mincing of words, though he did not actually demand their exclusion. Of those moderates who were former workers (such as the famous Karl Grillenberger from Nuremberg), he said flatly that the improvement in their material situation had quenched their revolutionary spirit; to Georg von Vollmar, the once rebellious landed gentleman, he applied as freely the method of economic determinism. Yet he was highly

indignant when the "Youngsters" and the Anarchists judged
by the same method the party leadership as a whole!

Three years later, at the party conference at Frankfurt
(1894), came another revolt, this time from the radical
workers of Berlin. They demanded that the salary of a party
official or editor should not exceed 3,000 marks annually—
more than double the yearly earnings of the average skilled
worker in Germany at that time. The party chiefs were
highly indignant at such an indiscretion, and Bebel, losing
his patience and forgetting his usual caution, blurted out the
untactful truth that, if such a demand were granted, most
of the socialist journalists would throw up their jobs and
go over to the bourgeois press. That comment on the idealism of socialist leadership still stands in the records of the
Frankfurt Party Convention of 1894—but who knows
about it? *

It was in 1896 that Scheidemann took part for the
first time in an annual convention of the party. Since that
time he has taken part in all but one or two; until 1912,
however, when he was elected to the presiding board of the
Party, he spoke very seldom and then only on questions of
secondary importance. During this long time he was still
feeling his way and was apparently mainly interested in
means and ways of getting votes for the party by winning
over the non-working-class sections of the population. Great
was his insistence that the feelings of these sections should
not be offended, and that no publicity should be given to
"foolish statements about religion."

* Bebel had apparently forgotten to have that passage expunged. Convention reports of later years were published with greater caution. In
his autobiography Scheidemann, as if it were the most natural thing in
the world, candidly mentions how, in the minutes of a convention of a
few years later, a sentence that never was uttered was interpolated in
order to smooth over an awkward scene. A whole chapter could be written on the forgeries, substitutions and omissions practiced in the socialist
scriptures and historical records to suit the requirements of the various
warring factions. The analogy with similar proceedings in the history of
the Christian gospels and churches is particularly striking.

The Great Heresy

In the theoretical debates concerning the "Revisionist" heresy of Eduard Bernstein, which kept the party in a state of ideological excitement from 1898 to 1903, he never took part at all—at least, not at the party conventions, at which questions of principle were threshed out before the eyes of the whole socialist world. Was he, the editor of party dailies, the popular agitator, the parliamentary representative, not sufficiently versed in matters of principle to be qualified to speak? Or was he, the practical man, disdainful of this theological hair-splitting? Or, again, was he merely waiting to see which side would win before committing himself one way or another?

The questions raised by Eduard Bernstein in his articles published in 1898 dealt with all the fundamentals of the party's creed. He had been, with Karl Kautsky, the chief luminary of socialist theory, after the great teachers, Marx and Engels. He had lived in exile, first in Switzerland and then in England, through all the years of the anti-socialist law, editing the main organ of the German party. He had been in close touch with Engels throughout this time, and he was considered to be the great master's literary-theoretical executor. And it was his hand that directed a mortal blow against the great principles of socialist orthodoxy. . . .

It was not merely the iconoclastic zeal of a Father-of-the-Church-gone-heretical, that prompted Bernstein to come out with his criticism. He had definite, practical aims in view. He saw that the Party had exceeded the bounds of a propagandist sect; it had become a power in the country—indeed, a power in many countries; and he believed that the traditional assertion of revolutionary beliefs inherited from its two great teachers stood in the way of its progress toward its proper place in the fabric of government. In particular, he found obnoxious in this respect that tenet of the Marxian faith which pictures the continuous concentration of capital as gradually leading to a complete disappearance and proletarianization of the middle layers of society, with the result that a small number of super-capitalists are finally opposed by practically an entire population of pauperized wageslaves. When that moment arrives, according to the Marxian law, the revolution will come—and it will be a comparatively easy matter to dispose of that small group of capitalist leviathans. . . .

Around this point of Marxian theory, the debates principally centered. Bernstein used a great wealth of figures to prove that the number of capitalists was increasing both relatively and absolutely, and that the facts did not bear out Marx's prediction as to the gradual disappearance of the middle layers, but showed, on the contrary, an increase in their numbers. His conclusion was that economic evolution was not leading automatically—or, let us say, inevitably—to a catastrophic breakdown of capitalism; and that it was, therefore, advisable to discard unnecessary talk about revolution and to let the Socialists appear as what they actually were—a democratic party of reform, struggling by continual improvements to achieve a gradual transition into socialism, by which he, of course, understood State Capitalism.

Bernstein's heresies were met with indignation. The more diplomatic Georg von Vollmar had arrived at similar practical conclusions several years before, but he had not ventured to question the infallibility of the theories of the great masters. Bernstein, a scholar and not a practical politician, had carelessly spilled the beans—made a deplorable tactical error. He had not reflected that, by exposing the time-honored fiction of the continuously decreasing and disappearing capitalist and middle classes, he was depriving the party of a proprietary medicine, long used as a specific for widely different ills. Faith in the inevitability of their victory kept the masses from growing disappointed over the slow increase of their wages; it likewise preserved their enthusiasm for voting the socialist ticket and paying their dues. On the other hand, the same faith was very effective in quenching their rebellious impatience; they could always be told that the process of concentration of capital and automatic self-slaying and self-elimination of the bourgeoisie had not yet reached the point at which their overthrow had become scientifically inevitable, and that for a long time to come proletarians would have to content themselves with peaceful, law-abiding, practical parliamentary activity. Revolution as a conscious act of will of the hungry masses, and not as an "inevitable," "objective," mechanical result of economic development, was tabooed by both contending schools.

Though frowned upon officially, Bernstein's policy of open class-collaboration and renunciation of all revolutionary talk was gradually and imperceptibly making headway, among both intellectuals and trade-union officials.

The followers of Bernstein, wherever they had the majority—chiefly in the more democratic southern states—never lost an opportunity of showing that the Socialists were not as bad as their reputation. They voted the budget, they used every chance to take part in the receptions given by the various kings and princes of the smaller states, they exerted themselves to appear, like the Austrian Liberals, as "His Majesty's most obedient opposition." Only the junkers in Prussia kept the potential MacDonalds disdainfully at a distance, by opposing even the mildest democratic concessions.

The resolution adopted at the party convention at Dresden, in 1903, which finally condemned the Revisionist heresy, declared that the Party "could not aim at participation in a government within the bourgeois society."

Events of fifteen years later have supplied the necessary explanation of the real meaning of that decision; for, since 1918, the German Socialist Party has repeatedly not only taken part in, but also headed, various governments "within the bourgeois society," and this with the endorsement of Karl Kautsky and the other official representatives of the old Marxian tradition—except for a few ultra-left dissenters. The opposition against Bernstein was, therefore, plainly intended to forbid not "participation in a government within the bourgeois society," but participation in a government such as existed in the German Reich—that is, a government not responsible to Parliament, and in which a socialist minister, if admitted at all, would have no influence, and would only injure the Party as a whole by preventing it from fighting for more democracy and a parliamentary régime, like that in France or England.

If the German Marxians used their influence at the International Socialist Congresses to forbid cabinet participation to Socialists in a parliamentary country like France, it was only because they were afraid that the disappointing results of that participation might discredit their own propaganda in favor of a parliamentary régime.

Bernstein, by advocating participation in the government, even in such politically backward countries as the Reich, was expressing the point of view of the younger set of ambitious politicians, who wanted to *arrive* as soon as possible—even at the expense of the future interests of the party. He also expressed, to a large extent, the attitude of the trade-union officials, who were afraid that revolutionary talk might have unfavorable repercussions on the safety of their own organizations. These were even more moderate than the politicians of Bernstein's camp. Indeed, some of the latter, in principle at least, accepted the idea of a political strike for obtaining democratic suffrage in Prussia or for defending universal suffrage, should it be threatened. The trade-union leaders refused to take any such chances under any circumstances whatever.

FIGHTING THE KAISER

While all these theoretical and practical questions were debated, Scheidemann, even after his election to Parliament, kept in the background. The study of the Marxian theories, as he himself admits, was to him "seldom a reviving draft, mostly a weariful effort." In this respect he was not a "lowbrow" exception in the Party. The deeper theoretical problems of the Marxian economics and philosophy are subjects involving a study of many years, and their intricacies and frequent contradictions—apparent or real—have left many a student in complete confusion and despair even after the most sincere effort. Marx's writings cover a period of nearly forty years; the political conditions—and the moods of the writer—repeatedly changed during that period and these changes are very often reflected in the text. Moreover, his style is scarcely lucid, giving excuse for endless variations of interpretation for his various sayings—all accepted as gospel truth—which the various socialist sects keep using to discredit each other. This was a favorite game of a dozen or so of super-intellectual scholars, who, with the exception of the many-sided, fiery rebel, Rosa Luxemburg, were not active politicians. But old Wilhelm Liebknecht, the personal friend of Marx, one of the founders of the German Socialist Party, and the chief editor of its central organ, is now generally admitted (among the *cognoscenti*) never to have penetrated the fundamentals of Marxian philosophy—and even his purely political writings abound in most glaring contradictions. Bebel, too, in his debates with Bernstein, openly admitted that he understood but little of the philosophical problems involved in the Marxian theory, while the former worker, Ignaz Auer, the extremely

astute and cynical general secretary of the German Socialist
Party actually boasted of his ignorance. (At the outset of
the discussions Auer had capped the climax of his cynicism
by upbraiding Bernstein in the henceforth historical personal note in which he wrote: "Dear Ed.: You are an ass;
such things are done, but one does not speak about them."
This frankness recalls the "profitable Jesus-fable" remark
attributed to one of the Renaissance popes.)

But the politicians knew what they wanted, however innocent they might be of its philosophical implications. They
wanted more democracy in a highly capitalist, yet nevertheless semi-absolutist, Germany; they wanted more influence
in Parliament; they wanted votes; they wanted prestige with
the working masses. To get these things, they had built up
an enormous political and trade-union machine, with an imposing hierarchy of tens of thousands of leaders and party
employees, almost as impressive as that of the Catholic
Church and, like the latter, prepared to use its spiritual
influence and ascendancy in order to maintain its power and
its material comforts.

In the division of labor necessary in such an enormous
organization, only a select few reserved for themselves the
work of preserving the pure essence of the true doctrine
and of transmitting it to the next generation in a form more
or less diluted and modified according to political necessity.
The rest became journalists, party and trade-union organizers and agitators, and—the particularly astute and clever
ones—parliamentary politicians and leaders.

Scheidemann had been preparing himself for the parliamentary career. Ever since his election in 1903, he had been
a valuable assistant to the aging Bebel, who for generations
had been the parliamentary floor-leader of his party. The
young deputy entered the Reichstag armed with a wealth of
detailed information on a variety of not very interesting
subjects, such as public sanitation or cattle breeding, ac-

cumulated during his years of propaganda among the peasants of Southern Germany. His two maiden speeches, delivered in the same session and almost without preparation, greatly impressed not only his own party, but also the rest of the Parliament with his knowledge, his self-assurance and his humor—the latter no less pleasing to his audience for being neither very pungent nor very subtle.

His parliamentary career, begun in 1903, has lasted to the present time. In 1903 there were eighty-one socialist deputies in a house of 400 members, and a total vote of 3,010,-000 had been polled to return them. Of these eighty-one, forty-nine were intellectuals, lawyers, journalists, party employees; the remaining thirty-two were manufacturers, small employers, publishers, innkeepers, shopkeepers—even one "rentier," i.e., owner of an independent income. A number of these had, like Scheidemann, once been workers, but not a single one of them had been employed as a worker at the time of the election. Four years later, the party's stand against colonial expansion brought about a consolidation of all other parties against the Socialists, and the number of socialist representatives was reduced almost by half (to forty-three), though the number of socialist votes did not decrease. This was a lesson for the party leaders, and one particularly taken to heart by Scheidemann, not to run counter to the chauvinist susceptibilities of the middle classes. In 1912, the party, having made an election arrangement with the Progressives, more than made up for its losses. It now had 110 deputies, elected by a total socialist vote of four and a half millions. Every third voter in Germany was a Socialist.

Scheidemann's career as a parliamentarian was by that time in full swing. In 1908, upon Bebel's suggestion, the party unanimously intrusted him with the expression of its views regarding the general policy of the government. Many parts of his speech were prophetic. He attacked the foreign policy of official Germany, spicing his remarks with veiled but sarcastic allusions to the Kaiser's provocative speeches. He did not conceal his contempt for the clumsiness of German diplomacy, and he predicted a complete isolation in the future. His remarks about the probable alliance of Italy with England and France and his gibing hint that "at war the military leaders were generally not better than the diplomats," were almost those of a clairvoyant.

Attacks against junker rule and particularly against the Hohenzollerns were his specialty, and in that rôle he became a national figure, more hated by the Kaiser than any other man in Germany—save, possibly, Bülow, the Chancellor, who, for the sake of the country, or even for the sake of the dynasty, occasionally had to call his master to task and bid him keep his mouth shut.

In 1909 Scheidemann spoke on the promises made by Wilhelm II, concerning the democratization of the franchise to the Prussian Diet—promises, which had not been kept. He concluded with the impudent remark: "I am well enough acquainted with Prussian history to know that the breaking of one's word belongs, so to speak, to the lofty traditions of the Prussian ruling dynasty."

A year later, in 1910, again speaking in the place of Bebel, who was growing weaker, he attacked German imperialist ambitions in Morocco, in connection with the famous Mannesmann concession, which had brought the war danger still nearer. In the following year he attained perhaps the highest honor in his party's gift, when he became member of the Presiding Board of the Party.

He was at his best in a speech made in 1912, just after the election, when the Socialist success at the polls had fired the self-confidence and courage of their leaders. The Kaiser had been making another of his impossible speeches—in this case, threatening to break to pieces the constitution of Alsace-Lorraine, to withdraw it from the jurisdiction of the Reich, and to make it a part of Prussia. Scheidemann protested against the legal, or rather the illegal aspect of this threat. He hailed it as "a weighty confession on the part of high authority that incorporation into Prussia should be held up as the heaviest punishment which could befall a country for its contumacy; a punishment which, it seems, is comparable to a penitentiary sentence, or degradation to the lowest class of German citizenship—the Prussian class." Such language was a slap in the face, and the Cabinet, as well as the members of the conservative parties, left their benches in protest against the unheard-of insult.

This outburst of Scheidemann's, which at the time made him well-nigh a world figure, was preceded, three months before, by a tragicomic incident. As the largest party in Parliament, the Socialists were allowed to have one of their members selected either as President or at least as First Vice-President of that assembly. An agreement was arrived at, and kept by the parties concerned, by which the two next largest groups—the "Center" (Catholic Clericals) and the "National-Liberals" (big business)—were to have the President and the Second Vice-President, leaving the post of First Vice-President to the Socialists. Scheidemann, after Bebel the most popular man in the party, was thus elected Vice-President of the Reichstag. When the arrangement was put into effect, the true-blue Conservatives and all the other reactionary and dynastic elements made such an outcry about the "desecration" that the Catholic President and the National-Liberal Vice-President immediately resigned. Two Progressives were then elected in their places. Scheidemann refused to accompany them on their formal visit to the Kaiser, and the Kaiser, slighted by Scheidemann's election, refused to receive the new praesidium. A month later, in accordance with the regulations, the first provisional choice of a praesidium had to be ratified by the Reichstag in a regular election; Scheidemann was not reëlected.

Scheidemann thoroughly enjoyed that month as Vice-President, when, in the absence of the Speaker, he could swing the gavel and take his place in the seat formerly held only by aristocrats. With his well-fitting cutaway and his impressive dignified appearance—and all papers had to admit that!—the other parties might well have foreboded in him the new aristocracy. It was the aristocracy of self-made politicians, risen from the working class and from the *déclassé* or adventurous sons of the bourgeoisie, who, one day, no longer "scum" and interlopers, might blossom out not only as Speakers, but as Chancellors and Presidents—yes, even as "saviors of the country" from that "Red Peril" which they themselves had so lately embodied.

Growing More and More Respectable

Meanwhile, the regular annual party conventions were following their course. "Principles" were no longer being discussed. The moderates, theoretically influenced by Eduard Bernstein but actually swayed by their own ambition and impatience to become part of the governmental machine, both in the individual states and in the Reich, were making headway. The party had grown to enormous dimensions. The development of German industrialism had brought about comparative prosperity and steady employment for the German workers. Germany, which previously had been sending large numbers of emigrants yearly to England and America, had now become a field for immigration, absorbing Polish and Italian laborers. The German worker was not satisfied, of course, but in the main he was not revolutionary, either. Ultra-radical talk was no longer so necessary in order to keep the workers in the Socialist Party. Imperceptibly, the Marxist "Center" and the Revisionists became even more alike than are the Democrats and Republicans in America. Only personal grudges over past slights still kept up an antagonism here and there. In his autobiography Scheidemann mentions that in the Socialist group in Parliament there was a Radical and a Revisionist wing, each holding separate and secret caucuses, and that he was in the Radical section. This is the only reference he makes in his two big volumes to his own intra-party alignment. He writes as follows: "Properly speaking, I fitted neither pattern; but the arrogant way in which some of the Revisionist colleagues treated members of the other group disgusted me so much that I got into the Radical camp." In other words, as a former worker, he was indignant at the impudence with which the upper-class and middle-class super-intellectuals, who had come directly from the universities and from comfortable homes, were attempting to run the party and treat as underlings the old militants of working class descent. The latter, perhaps, did not have their polish and their learning; but it was they who, by great effort and sacrifice, had helped to build up the party at a time when Socialism was a dangerous creed, and political rewards for its leaders were not yet within reach.

An attitude of this kind was, however, not the exclusive monopoly of the Moderates. Rosa Luxemburg, who represented the most radical extreme Left of the party, could sin even more in this respect than her enemies of the far Right. In a clash she once had with Scheidemann during a party convention, she so tactlessly asserted her intellectual superiority, as to call forth a deep resentment in most of those delegates who were not Doctors of Philosophy like herself.

In the meantime, Bebel was growing weaker and weaker, and during the last two years of the old man's life—he died in August, 1913—Scheidemann took his place at various solemn international manifestations. In 1913 he was invited to the United States, both to reawaken public interest in the American Socialist Party, and to interpose the authority of his name against the rising tide of the I. W. W. movement.

His visit to the United States was in the year following a propaganda tour, carried out by Karl Legien, Socialist member of parliament and head of the German trade unions. The German Gompers made his visit under the auspices of the A. F. of L. and was solemnly received by the notables of the country, including President Taft and the Senate. Still a year earlier, in 1911, Karl Kautsky, the great theorist of the German party, had written a letter to the American Socialists, refuting the doctrine of violence then preached by Haywood and Frank Bohn, the latter now a thoroughly respectable conservative.

Scheidemann's visit, it was hoped by the American Socialists, would take away the bad taste left in radical mouths by Legien's intimacy with Mr. Gompers and Mr. Taft, and at the same time strengthen Kautsky's propaganda for law-abiding revolutionism. In his lectures here, Scheidemann stressed the point of view that "in our respect for the laws lies our salvation," expressing his belief that "the life of one worker is worth more than an attempted struggle," and his intention "not to secure rights at the high price of the lives and happiness of the toilers."

Ten months later, after the war broke out, he would not even discuss the question of stopping the carnage at the price of returning Alsace to France. . . .

1914

In the meantime, the danger of a world war was drawing nearer and nearer. The Balkan wars of 1912 were rightly felt to be only a prelude to the coming great conflagration. The Socialists of the various European countries were fully aware of what threatened. At that time Scheidemann was one of the most important members of the party's presiding board. He was in charge of drafting most of the party's political proclamations. In 1912 he went to Paris, where he and Jaurès both spoke in favor of a Franco-German rapprochement. An International Socialist Congress, called to Basel during the same year, adopted a resolution pledging the working class to use "all means which seemed to them most effective" in order to prevent war; should the war, nevertheless, break out, they were to use the economic and political crisis brought about thereby for the purpose of stirring up the people and hastening the abolishment of capitalist class rule. Other international socialist manifestations in favor of peace took place in 1913 and 1914 as well—the last shortly before the outbreak of hostilities.

The Socialists, the world over, excepting the followers of Pilsudski in Poland, were actually opposed to war. War meant reaction and possibly revolution. To the mass of Western socialists the latter was as abhorrent as the former. They protested against the impending disaster, and until July 30th, as long as there still was hope that the war might be prevented, the Presiding Board of the German Party and its central organ violently protested against the sacrifice of "a single drop of blood of a German soldier" for the imperialist designs of the Hapsburgs. Scheidemann's personal organ, the paper published in his electoral district, threatened the German Government with the "wrath of the people," should it enter upon the "criminal policy of might engaged in by the Hapsburgs."

The German government knew that there was no serious determination behind all these vociferations, and it paid no attention to them. The party leaders, who still clung to the illusion that the authorities took their revolutionary bark seriously, expected to be arrested as soon as war was declared. They were pleasantly surprised to find themselves mistaken.

The German Socialists showed themselves quite worthy

of this confidence of their Government. On August 4th, they made the famous statement in which, referring to the Tsarist menace, they declared that in the hour of stress they would not leave their country in the lurch.

Scheidemann and his party have generally been charged with committing, by voting the war credits, the great betrayal and denial of socialist principles. In reality they had remained faithful to an old tradition. Time and again, all the luminaries of international socialism, Bebel and old Liebknecht in Germany, Guesde in France, Greulich in Switzerland, had declared that they were ready to defend their country in the case of aggression by a foreign power. This was the generally adopted attitude. At the back of their minds, however, the socialist leaders retained the conviction that, once the hostilities began, it would be easy for any government to prove to its own subjects that their country had been attacked—no matter who had started the fight—and that they themselves would have to do likewise with their own party membership. This was no longer 1847, when Marx and Engels in their *Communist Manifesto* could proclaim that "the worker has no country." To the heretics within or outside the party who harked back to the old "the-worker-has-no-country" war-cry, the official reply was that since the workers had the right to vote and to organize, they had a stake in the country and were therefore bound to defend it. The heretics' counter-blast was the impudent suggestion that the franchise and the labor organizations were chiefly useful to the socialist and labor politicians, and that the workers in each country should react to a declaration of war by general strikes and insurrections.

There was also a middle-of-the-road point of view, which during one of the debates on this point was stated by Karl Kautsky, the great Marxian scholar. He advanced the opinion that under modern conditions it was well-nigh impossible to decide which party was the aggressor, and proposed

that the "proletarian interests, that is, the general interests
of European democracy" should be adopted as the only cri-
terion. He cited as an example the case of Russia in 1905,
where the workers, even though the Japanese were the ag-
gressors, were not interested in defending their country,
since the defeat of Russia would weaken its absolutist government and thus further the cause of democracy. Kautsky
used the example of Russia, but he apparently had in mind
Germany itself. It was a veiled pre-war threat, meant to
calm the bellicose ambitions of the German rulers. The
thought, which he obviously could not speak out, was that
the proletariat might be interested in defending a democratic
Germany, but that it need not show any excessive enthusiasm
for national defense, as long as the semi-absolutist junker
régime prevailed.

Neither Bebel, nor the rest of the influential leaders of
the party saw it that way. They were practical men. Their
party and trade-union organizations were enormous in size;
they had a respectable representation in Parliament; they did
not mean to risk all this by running counter to the nationalist
prejudices of a large section of the workers and of the lower
middle classes, who were joining the party in ever increasing
numbers. Like the Liberal German bourgeoisie, which gave
up its democratic aspirations for the present gains of economic and imperialist expansion under Bismarck's junker
régime, the socialist intellectuals and upstart ex-workers
were content with as much (or as little) democracy as they
had, so long as their business was not interfered with, and
their jobs were safe. To Kautsky's remark that in 1870
Bismarck had succeeded—by means of the notorious Ems
telegram—in deceiving all Germany into the belief that
France was the aggressor, Bebel answered, with obvious
bad faith, that times had changed since 1870, and that such
proceedings could never succeed now. The argument shows
that seven years before the great War the venerable patri-

arch of German Socialism was already determined to play
the part which fell during the War to Scheidemann, his
much-abused successor. . . .

When the war, at last, broke out, the party faced two
alternative dangers. One was immediate—losing its popularity and being crushed by the government for opposing the
War. The other was in the future—losing its soul, becoming
altogether discredited as an appendage to the military
machine, and hence suffering from post-war competition by
more radical elements. The great majority preferred to meet
the second danger. For one thing, it was in the future;
moreover, the prospect of being dubbed "social-patriots" did
not dismay them, for they were sure that the masses would
stick to them even after the war—particularly if the war
was victorious. The possibility of a German defeat they
did not consider.

To support their position, Scheidemann and the majority
of the party used yet another argument—that the country
must be defended in any case, because "a defeat would be
tantamount to collapse, destruction and unspeakable misery
to all of us." This was the good old "My country, right or
wrong." Hitherto it had not formed part of any socialist
vocabulary, for it plainly meant the endorsement of every
imperialist adventure, of every *fait accompli;* its use would
simply have aligned the socialist parties with any of the
old-time nationalist parties, so far as a war issue was concerned.

A small minority within the parliamentary group submitted to the majority decision but were opposed to voting the
credits. They believed in national defense once the war was
on, and they were not for overthrowing the government or
for getting the soldiers out of the trenches. However, they
did believe that even a mild opposition would have certain
repercussions among the people at large, sufficient to disrupt
the complete unity necessary to aggressive war, and so to in-

cline the government not only to a speedier conclusion of
the War, but also to the granting of democratic reforms.
Among the dissenters again, there were a few still more determined elements, headed by Karl Liebknecht, courageous
son of the founder of the Socialist Party, Rosa Luxemburg
and a few others. These, as the war progressed, inspired the
organization of various revolutionary groups, such as "Spartacus" and "Internationale," the precursors of the Communist Party which was formed after the War. They were
of the opinion that "victory or defeat in the War was equally
ruinous to the German people," and that it was necessary
immediately to put forward the most radical demands such
as "popular decision over war and peace" and "control of
the government by Parliament and of Parliament by the people." This was, though in a milder form, the point of view
taken by Lenin and his friends—that war should be opposed
by insurrection and civil war.

After Bebel's death, Scheidemann was generally recognized as the most representative and most eloquent leader
of the party. Treated with great consideration and polite-
ness by the Chancellor, Bethmann-Hollweg, he became more
and more conscious of his own importance. His ambitions
began to exceed the narrow limits of a mere working man's
party. The Socialists were already the largest party-group
in the Reich, and they could easily take advantage of the
present difficult situation to become the most influential body
in Imperial Germany—if only they consented to play up the
nationalist tune. But there was no unity among them. The
Berlin *Vorwärts,* central organ of the Party and mouthpiece
of the radical Berlin workers, kept kicking over the traces
and compromising the good patriotic intentions of the majority leaders. Technicalities made it difficult to drop its
editorial staff, which was to a certain extent influenced by
Rosa Luxemburg, but in this case, as later during the Revolution, the military authorities came to the rescue of the

good cause. The paper was forbidden to print anything about the class struggle, and the matter was settled.

Then there was that impossible Liebknecht, who could not be induced to keep quiet. That "dogmatic fanatic," that uncompromising firebrand, kept on talking of the "immovable principles," no matter what happened. Scheidemann had no patience with principles. They had always seemed to him an encumbrance, perhaps good in their place, in the party school—but what had party principles to do with party politics—and high politics at that?

His naïveté, not to say cynicism, once he began to collaborate with the Hohenzollern régime, knew no bounds. Innocently he reports a trip to Italy, made by the Socialist deputy, Dr. Südekum; that millionaire tribune of the people was known all over Germany as the smartest dandy who ever represented horny-handed proletarians in the aristocratic drawing rooms to which he frantically sought admission.* He returned from his trip greatly dissatisfied with the Italian Socialists. He had obviously tried to win them over to the cause of Germany, and he bitterly complained of their hostility—though, to be quite fair to them, they were just as much opposed to any entanglements with the Allies.

In September, 1914, the Presiding Board of the German Socialist Party was visited by Dr. Victor Adler, founder of the Austrian Socialist Party. The sad fate of Serbia was mentioned. Adler did not refuse the Serbians his sympathy: he merely qualified it with "Quite so, but then, I am not a Serbian." Scheidemann's only reaction to this was the remark made in his autobiography: "He could not have ex-

* It was this Dr. Südekum who, at a reception given by the Kaiser to the members of Parliament, had called forth the envy of all the other parties by being the only one to appear in a lieutenant's uniform and with an Iron Cross at that. It was he again, who as a socialist and republican Cabinet minister of Prussia, after the "revolution" of 1918, ordered the shipping of seventy-two carloads of priceless national art treasures to Doorn because the former Kaiser had claimed them as his property. Even bourgeois politicians were indignant at such servility.

pressed himself more clearly if he had said, 'In such a moment I am first of all a German.' "

In the meantime, the German armies had penetrated deep into the territories of their western and eastern neighbors. The Pan-Germans were asking for enormous territorial acquisitions. The minority of the Socialist Party opposed any further granting of war credits, on the ground that as things were going, Germany was certainly not waging a defensive war. Scheidemann countered with the argument that they "could not refuse the war credits because some short-sighted people (meaning the Pan-German annexationists), put up demands which the government did not approve." He thus actually backed up the fiction that the government had no annexationist intentions.

The government sometimes made it rather hard for Scheidemann to sustain this fiction. In March, 1915, the Chancellor had spoken of "security and greater liberty of movement and opportunity of development for a stronger and greater Germany." Scheidemann, who was not greatly taken with this phrase, tried to convince the comrades of the minority of its harmlessness. "Bethmann-Hollweg, after all his other statements, could not possibly have meant a Germany which had become greater through territorial accretions," he explained. "Such an interpretation seems altogether out of the question. If Germany wins this war, then it will be actually stronger and greater than formerly, even if it does not acquire a square meter of territory." With such arguments he could make little impression on the other side, which was headed by Hugo Haase, one of the best barristers of Germany.

On the other hand, the French Socialists often made Scheidemann's stand easier. Early in 1915, Vaillant, a veteran leader of the French Socialists, and on the party's left wing at that, published an article protesting against a premature peace; so did Renaudel, the main spokesman of the party, in 1916, insisting upon the restitution of Alsace. In the same vein, Scheidemann would not even consider the idea of Germany giving up the contested territory, declaring that Alsace-Lorraine was German land and had to remain so. He ridiculed the French Socialists who denied that a restitution of Alsace-Lorraine would be an annexation, and he pointed to the chauvinism of the French Socialists for justification of his own attitude.

Nevertheless, the opposition within the party grew. In December, 1915, 43 out of 110 socialist members of parliament were opposed to the granting of war credits. Dissatisfaction among the population, and particularly among the workers, was growing. Scheidemann's own constituency turned against him, and though the leader of the largest party in the Reich, he was refused a hearing at meetings in his own district of Solingen. But there was no backing down for him. Early in the war he had coined the patriotic word "durchhalten," to "see it through"; his name had become the synonym and at the same time the insulting nick-name for the socialist patriots. He had to "see it through" even though he must step down to the lowest depths of vulgar patriotism and even imperialism.

To the arguments of the quite imposing minority that the patriotic stand of the majority was endangering the party's good repute among the laboring masses, he replied that "the fatherland is the 'treasure chest,' to be protected, defended, and carefully guarded; it is the ultimate issue of the political struggle, to which the party is only a means."

Unselfish as his devotion to the "treasure chest" may have been, he nevertheless tried to get some jewels out of it for his party. He sounded the government on the question of the Prussian franchise, hoping that the loyalty of the Socialists would finally induce the government to grant this old democratic postulate. The answer was polite but adamant. The Prussian franchise was a controversial subject and would disturb the peace of the realm. In other words, the Prussian junkers were willing to accept socialist assistance and cannon-fodder, but unwilling to make the slightest political concession. Philosophically, Scheidemann wrote in his diary: "After all, we did not vote the credits in order to be rewarded. I had no illusions about it. . . . On the strength of our attitude during the war, it will be easier to obtain, after the war, what was unattainable until now." *Mañana!*

The "treasure chest" demanded the renunciation not only of new political concessions but also of certain established fundamental principles—one of these was opposition to all annexations. In a speech delivered in Parliament on April 5th, 1916, Scheidemann, as Chairman of the Socialist parliamentary group, declared that "only political infants could believe that the frontier posts would not be moved." He denied later that this speech advocated annexations, though it is hard to conceive what else it advocated.

The trend towards imperialism within the German Socialist Party had begun almost with the very inception of the War. Heinrich Cunow, next to Kautsky its greatest living Marxian scholar and a famous anthropologist to boot, along with a number of other brilliant intellectuals in the party, openly advocated imperialist aggrandizement. It was, he said, in line with the Marxian theory, according to which socialism became possible only after capitalism had reached the highest point of its development. As imperialism was the latest development of capitalism, good Socialists, far from combatting it, should actually further it—for the sake of the future triumph of socialism, of course. One is reminded of the arguments used during the Libyan War in 1912 by some of the Italian socialist and syndicalist intellectuals to justify Italy's imperialist enterprise. The language was different, but the intention was the same: to seek in imperialism a provision for the ever-growing number of intellectual workers to whom the homeland did not offer comfortable jobs; to avoid the ever-sharpening class struggle by granting to the workers a part of the profits from colonial possessions or other annexed territories.

It was in this spirit that the organ of the German Transport Workers' Union greeted a German military victory with the words, "The German flag waves over Antwerp, let us hope forever." And Dr. Victor Adler, the uncontested chief of the Austrian Socialists—a brilliant cynic who seldom engaged in any theoretical discussion—simply said: "We Austrians are ready to take Poland and Serbia. That would not be an annexation."—Of course not! It would be only national unification, for was not Austria already holding large Serbian- and Polish-speaking territories? . . . Scheidemann, though he was never as outspoken as this, had only admiration for the Austrian leader, who, in his opinion, had "great understanding of *real-politik*."

THE RUSSIAN REVOLUTION

The year 1917 was crucial both for the rulers of Germany and for the Socialist Party. Unrestricted U-boat warfare was decided on in February; the Socialists opposed the decision, but they declared that once the decision was adopted they would place no difficulties in the way of its execution. A year before that decision, Scheidemann had been one of the signers of a resolution, submitted by all parties, which encouraged U-boat warfare and actually led to the decision of 1917—which, in turn, precipitated America's entrance into the War.

Early in March came the Russian Revolution. This event was greeted with mixed feelings both by the government and by its socialist supporters. It meant relief on the eastern front, where fighting ceased for some time; but it meant also two other things—a weaker grip for the monarchist principle and a stiffer backbone for all domestic opposition

—not only against the government, but also against the majority of the Socialist Party.

The Minority Socialists now saw their opportunity officially to sever all relations with the "Scheidemanns" and to organize themselves as the "Independent Socialist Party." At the same time the starving workers of Berlin and Leipzig gave vent to their long restrained dissatisfaction and went on strike. Scheidemann devised a subtle plan to calm the growing excitement of the workers. In an article which he wrote for *Vorwärts* he referred as follows to the Russian Revolution: "All kinds of reforms were promised for Russia 'after the war,' but the war has lasted too long for the Russians, and the more hunger oppressed them, the less endurable seemed the delay. They said to themselves: 'If it is not possible to get bread and potatoes for everybody, what is there to hinder the granting of equal rights to everybody?' So the 11th of March came, followed by the resignation of the Tsar, and thus democracy was obtained." He concluded with an appeal to the government to postpone no longer the old promises concerning the Prussian franchise. His advice to grant equal franchise to the Prussian Diet as a sop to the starving workers was not heeded by the government. The latter still felt very sure of itself, and the junkers never ceased to advance the argument that any concession of this kind might be interpreted as a symptom of weakness—both abroad and at home. Moreover, not only the junkers but the other privileged classes as well, were angered by the threat of revolution implied in the analogy between Russia and Germany.

Not all bourgeois spheres, however, were indignant at Scheidemann's revolutionary gesture. The long misery of the War and the uncertainty of the future had reawakened in some progressive middle-class elements the rebellious democratic spirit of 1848. The Liberal bourgeoisie had slavishly prostrated itself before the Kaiser and his feudal entourage as long as these had represented victory, preponderance in world politics and prosperity. Now that the halo of invincibility was beginning to fade, some perfectly respectable bourgeois began to put their faith in Socialism, which they were gradually finding out to be no enemy but only a lively younger brother of Liberalism.

Scheidemann relates in his autobiography how he was visited one day by Privy Councillor Dr. Witting, formerly Mayor of Posen, the brother of the famous publicist, Maximilian Harden, and a very influential politician in Western Prussia. "He assured me," the socialist leader goes on, "that I was quite unaware how big my following was, even among the middle classes. He thought that I ought to proceed with a 'courageous action,' drive out the federal government, and take over the leadership myself. The great majority of the middle classes would stand by me, as would the entire working class. The whole nation was eagerly wishing for some action that would bring the war to an end. I answered him that I would not stop at anything if I felt sure that I could thus put an end to the war and to the misery of our people. But I did not feel sure. The 'courageous action' he asked for would mean civil war and a sure defeat of Germany."

To expect that Scheidemann and his fellow-leaders would risk their necks in a serious struggle, was of course a great mistake on the part of Dr. Witting. A bourgeois who has grown up in confortable circumstances may lose his temper and go wild when things begin to go wrong; but upstart ex-workers and lower middle-class intellectuals and *déclassés,* who have risen from poverty and social nothingness to comfort and consequence, do not do such things. They know only too well what it means to be poor and, barring a few romantics, they will take no chances. Moreover, Scheidemann and his party knew quite well that a revolution, once begun in such a highly industrialized country as Germany, would mean much more than a fight against the junkers for a democratic régime. Its later development would bring a death struggle against all the propertied classes, with all the horrible possibilities of a real civil war. To expect the respectable Socialist Party to lend a hand to that, would be tantamount to expecting the Catholic Church to preach and practice the tenets of primitive communism held by the first Christian communities. . . .

THE "SCHEIDEMANN PEACE"

The Russian Revolution and America's entrance into the war toned down the hope of victory and increased the will to peace of all but the most rabid imperialists of the junker caste and the lords of the dominant industries. Foretaste of world dominion made these disregard the ever-nearing specters of Defeat and Revolution. But Scheidemann and the Progressives saw them, and in a speech delivered in Parliament on May 15th, 1917, the socialist leader urged the government to consent to a peace without annexations, if the Russians and the Western powers did the same—otherwise "you will have a revolution in the country."

A month later he was in Stockholm trying to pave the way for peace negotiations by getting in touch with representative Socialists of the Allied countries. Nothing came of it. French and Italian Socialists were refused passports by their respective countries, and Ramsay MacDonald could leave the country only on condition that he would not meet the representatives of the Central Powers. Scheidemann had to be contented with conversations with the Dutch-Scandinavian committee, and worse still, had to see his efforts thwarted to a great extent by the praise bestowed upon him by the Kaiser for his activities.

A month later, in July, Scheidemann's name came into national prominence through a peace resolution adopted by

the Socialists, the Progressives and the Catholic Party in
favor of a peace without annexations. The resolution united
a majority of the members of Parliament; as Scheidemann
had been its chief spokesman, its contents became known as
the "Scheidemann Peace"—and much of the hatred he won
from the annexationists and super-imperialists he owed to
that move.

In the fall of that year, the Socialist Party called a Convention, the first and only one during the war. In his report
on the tasks of the Party, Scheidemann stated that "through
the war, the Socialist Party had become a party with a direct
claim to power in the State"; that "after the war, Germany
will be a parliamentary democratic state"; and that "as it
used to be in England, the party that gets the majority of
the seats will form the government and bear the responsibility." It is plain that his expectations for the outcome of
the war were not very optimistic, for he could hardly have
been so naïve as to expect these enormous domestic concessions from a victorious Germany. There was, too, a certain
energy and determination in the tenor of his speech. Though
Russia—still in the Kerensky stage—was not mentioned at
all, and though nothing was further from Scheidemann's
mind than a revolution, it was evident that he was making
a mild clatter with the sword of revolutionary Russia in
order to further the cause of peaceful democratic changes in
Prussia.

In November the Bolsheviks overthrew Kerensky. They
were quite serious about peace, and they had great hopes
that the German workers would lead the way by starting
strikes and other manifestations that would impress their
rulers. Scheidemann and his crowd—the "Independents"
were not very influential as yet—were as little inclined to
help them in this, as they ever were to mount barricades or
throw bombs. Particularly now, when they were being
courted and flattered by official Germany as they never had

hoped to be in their lives. Only a short time before, there had been a ministerial crisis—and each of the two aspirants for the Chancellorship, Prince Bülow and Prince Hatzfeldt, had invited Scheidemann to a cordial talk, bidding for his support. And Prince Bülow, the greatest pre-war Chancellor after Bismarck, had actually helped the former printer into his overcoat! Was Scheidemann to fight a system whose most aristocratic representatives were now so fair to . . . the working class?

In Lenin's triumph, German official circles, including the Socialists, saw at first nothing but an excellent chance to strengthen their western front and to stiffen their attitude in tentative peace negotiations. Scheidemann packed his suitcase again, to renew his conversations at Stockholm. He met there the old Bolshevik Vorovsky (who later, as Soviet Ambassador to Italy, was assassinated in Switzerland) and told him flatly, not to hope for a revolution in Germany.

BREST-LITOVSK

The Brest-Litovsk negotiations between the Central Powers and the Soviet Government left no doubt as to the intentions of the former. The Bolshevik appeals for solidarity, addressed to the German and Austrian workers, had not been entirely in vain. Mass strikes broke out in Vienna, Berlin and other large cities. Five hundred thousand workers were on strike in Berlin alone. The influence of the Independents and of the "Spartacus" group—later the Communist Party —began to tell. This was not only sympathy for Russia, it was also a protest against ever increasing misery and starvation at home. The situation threatened Germany's military power and the prestige of the Socialist Party alike. Friedrich Ebert, next to Scheidemann the most powerful man in the party, and later president of the Republic, joined the Berlin strike committee. He actually succeeded in breaking up the strike and saved the German militarists from a very difficult situation if not from complete disaster.

Events were now following each other in quick succession. By the end of February the Soviet Government was forced to accept the terms of the Brest-Litovsk peace, the German rehearsal of Versailles. One of the most remarkable figures among the German "negotiators" was General Max von Hoffmann, who showed a brutality and cynicism rare even among the Prussian junkers. This, however, did not make him socially impossible for Scheidemann. The successor of August Bebel sets it down candidly in his autobiography that he repeatedly met the general later on, in private company. . . .

The Majority Socialists, with all their disapproval of Bolshevik methods, were not enthusiastic about the Brest-Litovsk peace. They did not share the optimism of the annexationists, who saw in the "liberated" Russian border provinces an inexhaustible reservoir of man power, food stuffs and raw material for the continuance of the war in the West. The Socialists feared a future war of revenge on the part of Russia, and they were not anxious to see their own militarists too successful, for that might mean failure for their own democratic hopes.

In a speech delivered when the Brest-Litovsk peace was submitted to the vote of the Parliament, Scheidemann said plainly: "The present policy towards Russia is not our policy." He was against bringing Russia's border lands "into a relation to Germany which perhaps they did not want themselves." Perhaps!

Finally, he urged his party to vote against the ratification of the peace. Ebert opposed this point of view, on the ground that a contrary vote "might give the impression that the Socialists were in favor of continuing the war." The Socialists finally decided to abstain altogether from voting on the question. Their consciences were pure . . . and they declared through their central organ that "there was no other immediate solution except the hoped-for complete German victory on the Western front as well."

THE DEBACLE

In August, 1918, Ludendorff knew that he was at the end of his resources—and early in October, six weeks before the armistice, Prince Max, the Liberal heir to the throne of the Grand Duchy of Baden, was appointed to the Chancellorship of the Empire. He was to start a new democratic era that would placate Wilson, control the revolutionary fires already kindled, and do what he could to save their thrones for the Kaiser and the two dozen lesser potentates of Germany.

The Socialist Party was invited to join the Government, but Scheidemann was not particularly eager to enter "a totally bankrupt enterprise at the moment of its absolutely certain breakdown." Ebert, whose only "principle" was power at any price, finally coaxed the party into accepting the proposal. The immortal "saddler" had been privately invited by Prince Max to join the cabinet and would gladly have done so. The party, however, decided to send Scheidemann, who was a more impressive and brilliant personality, though Ebert was generally recognized as the shrewder politician and the "strong man." *Mutatis mutandis* it was a relation similar to that between Trotsky and Stalin—with the same amount of mutual affection.

During the five weeks of his participation in the Cabinet, Scheidemann did his best to earn his hire. The necessity of the Kaiser's abdication—for the sake of better peace terms and in order to preserve the monarchy, as well as to placate popular dissatisfaction—was apparent even to the princely Chancellor. But the Chancellor was too much steeped in the old respect and servility to say it out bluntly to the Kaiser's face. Repeatedly Scheidemann urged Prince Max to speak to the Kaiser, and he as persistently kept on refusing—even though the socialist minister used the "republican" argument that "you must induce the present monarch to abdicate if you want to save the monarchy as an institution." The Socialist Party thought Scheidemann's insistence too radical and too dangerous. Ebert was firmly and violently opposed to it. Having at last become cabinet timber, he had became as cowardly and awe-stricken before Majesty, as any courtier born. . . .

Scheidemann, meanwhile, took his duties as the Kaiser's cabinet minister very seriously. He ingeniously devised a method for "getting the goods" on Adolph Joffe, the Soviet Ambassador, and having him expelled for fomenting revolution. The revolution came nevertheless, on the very day of the expulsion. The sailors of the naval base at Kiel mutinied rather than meet the "hero's death" to which the admiralty wanted to send them at a time when the Government had already asked for an armistice. The new cabinet felt quite sure that the good old methods of quelling a mutiny would be of no avail now. They would only precipitate a general uprising all over the country. It therefore accepted Scheidemann's suggestion to entrust the business of pacification to a Socialist. Gustav Noske, a former worker like Ebert and Scheidemann, was sent to Kiel to promise the mutineers immunity and to induce them to deliver up their arms and to return to their posts. The sailors did not take the paternal advice. They simply left Kiel with their arms and ammunition and dispersed over all the large cities of the Empire, carrying with them the seed of revolt. . . .

The Kaiser saw his days numbered, and, as a last resort, he attempted to save his skin by offering Scheidemann the Chancellorship. The bait did not work. Scheidemann was not interested in a few days of glory under a monarch whose position was no longer tenable; for the revolutionary movement was spreading from city to city, and in Bavaria a republic had been proclaimed, though Berlin still remained quiet.

By November 7th, Ebert, the strong man who held the party in his fist, but who would take no chances, finally realized that the socialist workers, in Berlin at least, might all go over to his "Independent" competitors, and that a revolution was inevitable, if the regular Socialist Party took no action. An ultimatum was sent to the Chancellor, threatening the withdrawal of the party's support, if the Kaiser did not abdicate next day, and if certain democratic postulates were not granted. In a conversation with the Chancellor, Ebert spoke plainly: "If the Kaiser does not abdicate, then the social revolution is unavoidable; but I do not want it, I hate it like sin."

In spite of Ebert's good intentions, the revolution could no longer be stayed. On the day after the delivery of the ultimatum, the socialist shop chairmen of Berlin urged the party leaders to give the signal for an uprising, since otherwise the workers would act without the party. But Scheidemann still hoped for a peaceful outcome, if the Chancellor would only induce the Kaiser to announce his resignation before nine o'clock of the next morning. He made a moving speech. "Believe me," he said, "that my sentiments are all with you, that I would be only too glad to go into action; but do not forget what a great responsibility we all carry; we must not act irresponsibly, like the Spartacists and the Communist babblers, who get on better the more everything turns topsy-turvy. We want to insist on our demands, whatever happens, but we must not endanger the armistice negotiations. . . . Do those who want to go out on the street, whatever happens, know what may be the consequence? We all know how it begins, but nobody knows how it will end. Think of the blood which has been flowing for over four years. Are the streets of Berlin to be reddened with work-

ers' blood? I know that you all agree with me when I say
that we want to get everything that can be had: if possible,
without shedding a drop of blood. We also want to do, and
must do, anything to avoid bloodshed. . . . Think less
about the irresponsible blatherskites in the factories and
more about your families and Germany!"

Thus spoke Scheidemann, one day before the Revolution.
But the Kaiser would not resign. Next day, the historic
ninth of November, Scheidemann tendered his resignation
at nine in the morning. Exactly at the same hour, the general strike started in Berlin and hundreds of thousands of
workers went out on the streets. There was no bloodshed—
the entire garrison went over to the Revolution.

To block further developments towards a Republic or,
perhaps, even towards a Soviet system, Prince Max trans-
mitted his chancellorship to Ebert, who held that dignity
for a day. In exchange, as man to man, Ebert offered to
Prince Max the dignity of Regent of the Empire, without
consulting either the party or Scheidemann, his closest associate as fellow-Chairman of the party. But the regency
of the Empire was not to last even as long as Ebert's chancellorship.

The fate of the Kaiser was settled—but that of the monarchy was still in the balance. With their much-praised do-
cility, the German masses might have accepted the regency
as a preliminary to the selection of another Hohenzollern,
but Karl Liebknecht spoiled the game. While the fiery rebel
was addressing an enormous crowd from the balcony of
the royal palace, Scheidemann was warned of what threatened. Liebknecht's intention was to proclaim a Soviet Republic, with all power vested in the Councils of Workers
and Soldiers. In a second Scheidemann was at a window
of the Parliament building, and in a historic speech, he proclaimed the Republic. The Bolshevik menace was turned
aside. The masses were not likely to ask for another re-

public immediately. . . . In saving Germany from the scourge of "Asiatic socialism," Scheidemann incurred the violent wrath of Ebert, the future first President of the Republic. By proclaiming the Republic, Ebert said, Scheidemann had exceeded his "rights." Only the Constituent Assembly was entitled to decide whether Germany was to be a republic or a monarchy. Compared with that squat Sancho Panza of law-abiding and legitimate revolution, the tall, impulsive Scheidemann almost rose to the proportions of a romantic Don Quixote of irreconcilable rebellion.

The Republic

A government was now formed, including an equal number of representatives of the Majority Socialists and of the Independents, with Scheidemann and Ebert as its most prominent members. One of the first actions of the new government was to proclaim the reëstablishment of all civil liberties suppressed during the war, and the extension of democratic rights in the spirit of the Western democratic countries. Prominent leaders of the Socialist Party were placed in various higher government positions—but the junker rule itself was not affected. The old army commanders and other officers, all the judges and most of the heads of the civilian administration, were left at their old posts. The principle of "continuity" was respected. As the Liberal *Frankfurter Zeitung* pointed out a few months later, the all-important work of giving the junker stable a thorough cleaning could have been done either by calling a Constituent Assembly immediately after November 9th, when the revolutionary fire was still in full blast, or by a short transitional stage of revolutionary dictatorship. The Socialists did nothing of the kind, and so gave the enemies of the Revolution plenty of opportunity secretly and openly to prepare for a comeback.

It was, of course, neither stupidity nor political blindness that kept Scheidemann and Ebert from taking the steps so necessary for the preservation of the Republic. They had not wanted either the Revolution or the Republic, and would have been quite happy to play the peaceful rôle of a Mac-Donald or a Henderson under a nephew of the last Kaiser. They knew that the resisting power of the German privileged classes was formidable, and they were afraid of the uncertainties of a civil war. Moreover, a civil war had been imminent from the very moment the Republic was proclaimed—but so far the war drums were not beating on the Right, which was still cowed and awaiting developments. They sounded from the extreme Left, the communist "Spartacus" group, which had combined with its advocacy of Soviet rule a demand for complete elimination of Scheidemann, Ebert and all of their fellow-leaders. Scheidemann and his friends were not willing to let their hard-won vested interests in German politics be wrung out of their hands by a mob of what they believed to be crazy fanatics and worshippers of the Bolshevik abomination. "If there has to be a dictatorship, then it will be ours," was their idea—as expressed on a later occasion by Otto Wels, one of the most prominent leaders then and now. But they did not need to resort to dictatorship as yet. They still had the support of the majority of the workers—though this support was not certain. The Spartacus movement was growing. Carried on by a minority of the most energetic workers, with a sprinkling of intellectuals, it was determined to obtain more than a democratic republic, French or Swiss style. They had a few arms at their disposal, but no organized armed force. The rank and file of the Independent Socialists sympathized with them, though the leaders were pusillanimous and tried to avoid any dangerous commitments. There were also various armed bodies in Berlin, which, though not Spartacist, were left-wing Socialist in their allegiance. Finally, there was the Workers' and Soldiers' Council of Berlin, which, moderate as it was, loomed as a potential source of trouble for the young democratic republic.

In his great hurry to create a stable government, unhampered by conflicting authorities, Ebert staged a little counter-revolution of his own. A troop of armed men, equipped and financed by members of the old nobility serving in the Foreign Office, arrested the Berlin Executive Committee of the Council of Soldiers' and Workers' Delegates and proclaimed Ebert president of the Republic. But the executive end of the conspiracy had somehow bungled its job. At the last moment, the "saddler" became frightened and double-crossed his "king-makers." The organizers of the coup fled, but they never ceased to insist that Ebert had known all about their preparations. Scheidemann, in reporting the incident says that "the strange undertaking has not been fully cleared up to this very day. It is most desirable that this elucidation should be brought about, for it would certainly silence all talk about Ebert's alleged complicity in the matter." A veiled accusation, it is Scheidemann's belated revenge for all the humiliations he had to bear from this jealous "fellow-proletarian" who always tried to boss him and actually conducted his own policy behind his back. . . .

THE RED WEEK IN BERLIN

Things were now coming to a head. A comparatively trifling conflict broke out between the authorities and the radical (but not communist) People's Marine Division of the revolutionary veterans of the Kiel mutiny, who were stationed in Berlin. The Majority Socialists called in the help of a reactionary general, who had at his disposal troops altogether unaffected by the revolution. The revolutionary sailors with their inferior equipment were subdued after much bloodshed, but the turmoil continued. Scheidemann, not willing to "deliver Germany to Bolshevism," declared that he would stand the "Schweinerei" no longer. The Independents, without whose knowledge the whole bloody action had been undertaken by Scheidemann and Ebert, forthwith resigned from the Cabinet.

Only one Independent official did not resign. This was the president of the Berlin police, Eichhorn, who had succeeded in organizing an auxiliary police force that was "Left" in its sympathies. This force was charged by the "Scheidemanns" with having refused to aid the reactionary troops sent by Ebert against the sailors, and Eichhorn himself was accused of sympathies for the Liebknecht group. In an insulting letter he was declared demoted from his office, the demotion to take place immediately.

This was the last straw. The left wing of the Independents, headed by the septuagenarian firebrand Georg Ledebour, and the Communists of the former "Spartacus-Bund," headed by Karl Liebknecht, called out the masses in an attempt to overthrow the Scheidemann-Ebert government and to establish a Soviet Republic.

The optimism of Ledebour, who expected the entire working population of Berlin as well as the whole garrison of the capital to join the rebels, was not justified. They had a few thousand armed men and the sympathies of a large section of the Berlin workers. But the regiments stationed in Berlin, and even the radical sailors, remained neutral. To the masses the issue was not clear. They saw only a struggle for power between two sets of leaders.

For a few days, however, the most important government buildings of Berlin, as well as the editorial offices of the largest dailies, including *Vorwärts* with the Socialist Party headquarters, were in the hands of the rebels. Armed detachments of picked socialist workers who were loyal to the government were of no avail against the firmly entrenched followers of Liebknecht and Ledebour.

Scheidemann now needed an energetic assistant to help him in organizing his resistance. He found him in the person of Gustav Noske, who two months before had been sent to Kiel to quell the revolt of the sailors; the former printer and the former basket-maker set out to create a force upon which they could rely. Not trusting the ordinary rank and file, which could easily be won over to the "Soviet insanity," they resorted to a step which put a stamp on the whole further development of the Revolution. They got in touch with the old military commanders and empowered them to organize corps of volunteers for the defense of the government. Thus a mercenary troop was created, composed of nationalist students, adventurers, ruffians, yokels—in short, a body as inaccessible to any Red propaganda as the hosts of Mr. Pinkerton. With these, they entered Berlin on January 11th, and broke the resistance of the rebels. One by one the buildings were stormed. No quarter was given. A few days later, after the fight was over, Karl Liebknecht and Rosa Luxemburg were arrested and murdered by the escorting soldiery.

The unsuccessful revolt and the death of the two leaders was a tragedy in more than one respect. The two had actually been against the uprising, for they knew that the moment for the establishment of a Soviet dictatorship had not as yet arrived. Even if the revolt had succeeded in Berlin, it could not have maintained itself against the opposition of the rest of the country. The All-German-Congress of the Soldiers' and Workers' Councils, held in the middle of December, had shown an overwhelming majority of Scheidemann's followers. Karl Liebknecht and Rosa Luxemburg had not even succeeded in being elected as delegates to this Congress, which had decided in favor of elections to the Constituent Assembly and declined a proposal that it should itself assume all power. Two weeks later, at the first convention of the Communist Party, Liebknecht and Luxemburg had advocated participation in the elections to the Constituent Assembly. They both considered as preposterous an attempt to prevent the elections and to seize the government at a time when the masses were still entirely under the sway of the democratic illusions nourished by the two socialist parties. Rosa Luxemburg suggested that a campaign of strikes for higher wages be initiated, in the hope that the inevitable opposition of the Government would drive the workers to the Left and thus prepare the ground for the seizure of power by the Communists.

This was a very subtle strategical move on her part. At that time the Socialists in power had come out openly against the fast multiplying strikes. Now that *they* were provided for, they considered it mean profiteering on the part of the masses that—in the words of Noske—instead of showing "real social and socialist sentiment, they were trying to get as much as possible for themselves."

The impatient younger element which constituted the majority at the Communist Convention would not listen to reason. Three to one the delegates decided to boycott the elections, with an eye towards an immediate revolution— Bolshevik style. The dismissal of the revolutionary Chief of Police was the provocation that led to the tragic climax.

The death of Karl and Rosa, whose sterling character and absolute disinterestedness had placed them high above the great mass of politicians and careerists composing the bulk of socialist leadership, aroused a wave of sympathy even among those workers who had heretofore been hostile or indifferent. Philipp Scheidemann, who never tired of declaring how deeply moved he was by the death of the two revolutionary leaders, disclaimed all the responsibility for the party. But the facts speak a different language. The murderers of the two leaders were delivered for judgment to the military court of their own regiment—the same regiment that had ordered the murder. The instigating officers were acquitted; the actual assassins got away with trifling sentences and were allowed to escape. The trial was a farce, and the delegates of the Berlin Soldiers' and Workers' Council—not Communists—who had been entrusted with watching the investigation, left in disgust and denounced the attempts made to hush up important circumstances. But this was not all. Immediately after their assumption of power in 1918, the Majority Socialists had organized their own terrorist group, which carried the unassuming name of "Help Service of the Social Democratic Party, Section 14." This "Service" was designed to track down revolutionary militants and put them out of harm's way. Only a few years ago records of its activities during those January days were unearthed, and these established beyond any doubt that it was this "Service" which discovered the hiding place of Karl Liebknecht and Rosa Luxemburg and passed on the information to the monarchist mercenaries who did the actual job. Quite recently, something else has come out: The socialist Chief Justice of the Supreme Court of Prussia (who has now passed over to Hitler) was First Lieutenant of the Guard-Cavalry-Sharpshooters Division, which supplied the murderers of the two great rebels. It was his orderly who clubbed to death Rosa Luxemburg, while the later socialist appointee for Chief Justice was officer of the day at the Eden Hotel, headquarters of the monarchist officers. . . .

AMONG FRIENDS

The elections to the Constituent Assembly gave 163 seats to the "Scheidemanns" and 22 to the "Independents." The total number of deputies to the Assembly being 421, the other parties formed a majority, though they never combined to form an anti-socialist bloc. As representatives of the strongest party, the Majority Socialists got the two highest posts which the new republic had at its disposal.

Fritz Ebert became President and Philipp Scheidemann his Chancellor.

He was not to enjoy his chancellorship for long—and while it lasted it was hardly a pleasure. Ebert had no intention of being a mere figure-head, such as a president is supposed to be under a parliamentary régime. In contradiction to the spirit of the Constitution, he wanted to be a President, American style, determining the policy of the Government, with the Chancellor merely his representative mouthpiece. Always anxious to be subservient to the old monarchists, Ebert, quite unconstitutionally, reintroduced the imperial flag in the army; in the same spirit, he later broke with his foreign minister, Rathenau, a Progressive, for concluding the treaty of Rapallo with Soviet Russia.

Scheidemann's opposition to Ebert's reactionary inclinations had no opportunity to ripen into a more determined conflict. He resigned after only a few months in office, deeming it impossible for him to sign the Versailles Treaty, a document which would stamp the Government as "dispossessor and hangman of its own people" in the interests of the Entente. Having pronounced those henceforth famous words: "What hand would not dry up which signed that peace?"—there was no backing out from the decision he had taken. His "friends," Ebert and the others, who had always talked in a similar vein, but not from his exposed position, were mightily pleased that he had taken this stand. They were now rid for good of a dangerous rival, whose personality stood mountain high above their own. *They* signed the treaty, and Scheidemann's career as a leading statesman was ended, though he remained a member of Parliament and was still important in the councils of the party.

Scheidemann's heroic gesture in sacrificing his political career rather than have the shame of Germany's enslavement forever attached to his name, was after all of no great avail, at least so far as his contemporaries are concerned. To the monarchists, Fascists, and other reactionaries, he is still the old firebrand of twenty years ago, who insulted the Hohenzollerns; he is also the mythical traitor of the "Scheidemann Peace," who "stabbed the army in the back," and who "signed the Versailles Treaty." And the one great achievement of his life, the salvation of his country from the horrors of "Asiatic socialism," is never credited to him in these circles.

"THE ENEMY IS AT THE RIGHT"

This propaganda of hate skilfully concentrated against him has had certain concrete reasons. Immediately after the defeat of the Spartacus revolt of January, 1919, the monarchist officers who had thus saved the democratic republic had begun to lift up their heads. Two months later, Berlin was again in the throes of a "bloody week," far bloodier than the Spartacus revolt had been; but this time neither the Communists nor the left-wing Independents had anything to do with it. The mercenaries, organized by the reactionary officers upon the invitation of Scheidemann and Noske, were again victorious; their opponents now were chiefly the men of the non-communist People's Marine Division and of the Republican Guard, which had been organized in the first days of the Revolution by the Majority Socialists themselves. No one in either of these two bodies had wanted or provoked the fight, but the old military men used some altogether non-political incidents as a pretext for destroying the last remainder of armed force that was not imbued with the monarchist spirit. In this they had the full support of the Socialist, Noske, already Minister of War of the Republic. Firmly convinced that the Republic was best protected by monarchist officers, Noske expressed the conviction that he preferred a frankly monarchist officer to one who pretended to be a republican. The fact was that these re-

publican "pretenders" were being systematically forced out
by their monarchist colleagues. Noske did nothing to stop
this process. Scheidemann was watching it all, and so far,
had made no objection.

Then, all of a sudden, something happened that waked
him up. In a speech delivered to the Berlin troops, Colonel
Reinhardt, Commander of the Berlin garrison, the man who
had quenched the Spartacus revolt in January, 1919, referred to the Government as "riff-raff." The papers reported
the incident, and Scheidemann, then on a visit in Cassel,
delivered an indignant speech in which he "regretted that the
dismissal of Reinhardt was postponed so long." President
Ebert and War Minister Noske were very angry at Scheidemann's interference. They had no intention whatever of
discharging for this reason "an officer who otherwise is so
efficient." And, Ebert added on the following day, "You
must consider that Reinhardt did not take into account the
fact that the statements he made before the troops would be
published." Scheidemann's insistence that "an immediate dismissal of Reinhardt would be a salutary lesson to all officers hostile to the Republic" met with a rude rebuttal on the
part of Ebert.

Scheidemann was amazed. It began to dawn upon him that,
if this was the attitude of the President toward an insolent
and mutinous colonel, then the colonel was the master, while
the President and the Cabinet members were simply flun-
keys, tolerated until they were dismissed—like the proverbial
Oxford- or Harvard-trained Chinese students whom the
various bandit generals of the Celestial Empire usually put
forward as their civilian government. Ebert and Noske
seemed to take such a situation as a matter of course, but
Scheidemann balked. Clearly he saw before him the tendency towards monarchist restoration—and with it all the
impudence and arrogance of Prussian junkerdom which he
had fought all his life. He thought himself as fit as they

were to rule the German masses, or even to chastise them with machine guns, if necessary; but his personal dignity required that it be in the name of democracy and socialism, with a new aristocracy of gab; not in the name of outlived idols with an aristocracy of birth and possession alone.

In a Reichstag speech delivered in October 1919, less than a month after the Reinhardt incident, he raised the cry, "The enemy is at the Right!" It has since become a winged word in the German language.

The Kapp Interlude and After

Scheidemann's warnings were not heeded at the time. He no longer lived in Berlin, but retired to his home town, Cassel, where he was elected Mayor. From there he urged Ebert to "pay much greater attention to the propaganda of the Nationalists (the monarchists) if we are not to endure a very sad experience." But Ebert and Noske were unshaken in their confidence. They obviously considered the symbiosis of a "proletarian" government with a monarchist and reactionary officer caste as a permanent and safe arrangement that should not be distrubed by meddlers with no sense of realities. Moreover, they were actually greatly flattered by this symbiosis. This is evidenced by a remark of Noske, at a party conference held in September, 1919, at which he was attacked for his leniency towards Colonel Reinhardt. Speaking of the struggles against Spartacus, he said: "It was the bearer of one of the best-known names, who, risking his life a thousand times, stole the ammunition for my volunteers out of the various barracks. If you want to know it, it was a Count Bismarck. If they had caught him, they would have killed him. Am I now to forget what these officers have done for the salvation of the country?"

In their gratitude to the monarchist officers for saving their political jobs, Ebert and Noske apparently thought that

these officers were just as grateful to the Republic for taking
them back to service, and would not make any effort to get
back their old power. Three weeks after the above mentioned letter from Scheidemann, the monarchist conspirators, headed by the Prussian junker, Kapp, and the chief
generals, with the entire army of mercenaries behind them,
took Berlin and forced President Ebert, his War Minister
Noske and the rest of the Government to flee to southern
Germany. A general strike was called, and Kapp's government had to give up after four days. Scheidemann, whose
warnings had been contemptuously scorned, expected to have
his revenge now. With all his vigor he pleaded with Ebert
for the resignation of Noske, who had so pitifully shown
his inadequacy in dealing with the Right danger. Ebert would
not hear of it, and the Socialist parliamentary group likewise upheld its War Minister. Scheidemann had become too
"red" for his friends.

The "victory" of the general strike turned out to be a
tragic farce. Kapp had fled—but Kappism remained in full
force. In the Ruhr region, where the workers had organized
a kind of Red Army for the defense of the Republic, these
defenders of the Republic were massacred by Kappist generals and their mutinous mercenaries—with the approval of
the Socialist cabinet ministers, who had resumed their seats.
As many as 705 crimes were charged to the various officials
of the short-lived Kapp régime, including 74 murders committed by soldiers and students: Yet the total punishment
was the condemnation of one man to five years in a fortress,
the mildest form of seclusion. Of the 775 officers who had
joined Kapp, forty-eight were dismissed. The rest stayed,
and not one was punished. The property of the leaders of
the Kapp rebellion was not confiscated as promised, and the
payment of their pensions as retired government officials and
army officers was continued. When, a year before, a Communist revolt had occurred in Bavaria—with a much smaller

number of casualties—every member of the short-lived
Soviet Government and seventy-two military commanders of
the Red Army were punished severely, involving a total of
615 years of prison and three executions. In Berlin, as in
Munich, the government which dispensed that equal justice
was headed by a socialist prime minister. . . .

The monarchist conspirators, though granted impunity by
the Socialists, never forgave Scheidemann for his attempt
at a more energetic attitude. Tirelessly they prepared for a
new uprising, meanwhile continuing the terrorist activities
against radical leaders and militants which they had begun
even before the Kapp adventure. During the first two years
of the Revolution they committed 354 murders, for 93 per
cent of which no penalty was exacted. Of the twenty-two
political murders committed by the "Lefts" only four remained unpunished. Not a single monarchist was executed,
while ten radicals had to suffer the extreme penalty. Statistical material collected by a German pacifist, Dr. Gumbel,
was presented to the socialist Minister of Justice, Dr. Rad-
bruch, showing that two months of imprisonment were the
average penalty for a monarchist murder, while fifteen years
was the average for those radicals who were not executed.
The socialist Minister pointed politely to a slight error which
had crept into the report of a speech mentioned in Dr. Gumbel's letter. And that was all.

Such an attitude on the part of the socialist authorities
was an opportunity not to be wasted. Emboldened by their
impunity, the reactionary terrorists aimed for bigger game—
the "traitors" in high positions. These were the men who,
though stanch supporters of the Hohenzollerns during the
war, had been ready after the breakdown to go along without them. Erzberger, the leader of the Catholic People's
Party, was the first to pay. An ultra-imperialist and annexationist at the beginning of the War, he became a supporter
of the "Scheidemann Peace" in 1917, when the hopes for

world conquest were gone. His "radicalism," it has recently come out, was such that he procured the visas for the false passports which were to facilitate the flight of Liebknecht's murderers. Still, he was a "traitor"—to the monarchists—and fell a victim of their bullets in 1921. Next came Scheidemann in 1922, miraculously escaping from a particularly ingenious attempt upon his life. And shortly afterwards it was the Progressive, Walter Rathenau; in this case the terrorists succeeded in robbing post-war Germany of the most gifted industrial leader, economist and statesman brought forth by the liberal bourgeoisie.

These murderous attempts against the life of the most prominent leaders of republican Germany made the Parliament wake up. A "law for the protection of the Republic" was adopted—but it was applied against the "Lefts," and not against the monarchists, as Scheidemann sadly admits in his autobiography. . . .

Three Hundred Thousand Marks and Three Hundred Thousand Jobs

Since that time, Scheidemann has been retiring more and more from active participation in national politics. He was a deeply injured man. To be branded a "traitor" by the reactionaries after having lost his reputation as an internationalist by his unfailing support of Hindenburg; to be considered an unreasonable extremist by his comrades after having earned the undying hatred of all radical workers and intellectuals: thus to be misunderstood was surely enough to dishearten a man who was nearing sixty. For six years he devoted himself chiefly to local politics as Mayor of his native city. He left the post after the elections had returned a bourgeois majority to the municipal council; but as his election for Mayor had been for life—the German democratic republic has its peculiarities—he exacted, and obtained, the payment of 300,000 real gold marks as balm for his resignation. The Republic is truly good to the workers. Impoverished as the country has become as a result of the defeat, the Republic provides 248,000 more political jobs than graced the government payroll under the Kaiser. The War and the Revolution have not been in vain after all. . . .

Scheidemann retired from the Berlin scene just in time. From his retirement he could observe the further vicissitudes of the party, one of whose great leaders he had been for a few decades. From a small group of impecunious, *déclassé* intellectuals and self-educated ex-workers with a small following among the industrial workers, it had developed into the largest party in the country, controlling an enormous electorate, holding the trade unions under its sway, numbering among its adherents a large section of the lower middle-classes, including hundreds of thousands of intellectuals and semi-intellectuals. It had at its disposal hundreds of thousands of easy jobs in party, trade-union and government institutions. The "Independents," who in the latter part of the War and during the Revolution had stayed away from the main body, now rejoined the old party, or more correctly, the leaders went back, while the following turned communist.

With this growth of influence came a growth of appetite. This was not merely the ambitious politicians' lust for power and social prestige with its concomitant comforts—but common greed for whatever crumbs might fall from the generous tables of all kinds of speculators and shady business men. The famous Barmat scandal of 1925 presented to the whole world a malodorous sore of graft, corruption and favoritism, not unlike the Ohio Gang scandal. The most prominent leaders of the Socialist Party were involved. Among these was Gustav Bauer, Scheidemann's successor as socialist Chancellor of the Republic—who took all the

blame and was shelved by the Party (he has been readmitted since). Scheidemann, however, was not in it, and his
hands remained clean. Bebel's successor was now out of
national politics.

The Barmat scandal drove many workers into the communist camp. Two years before, the attitude of the Socialist
Party during the inflation period, when the value of the
mark dwindled to insignificance, had the same effect. In
order to remain within the Government bloc, the Socialist
Party permitted a form of taxation which practically relieved the employers of all payments, while the workers,
through the immediate deduction of the taxes from their
wages, had to supply 95 per cent of the entire income tax
receipts. For the same reason the party voted for the construction of new cruisers, while the doles of the unemployed
were being reduced.

Staying in the Government, or remaining on good terms
with it, has become the only principle of the party. A mere
allusion to the possibility of including the Fascists in the
government majority, which would forbode the quick destruction of all socialist organizations, makes the Socialists
amenable to all, even the most reactionary, demands of the
government. As W. Sollmann, one of the strong men at the
head of the Party, declared at the Convention of 1931 : "The
most important thing is *to keep what we have,* and to remember that the words of Marx to the effect that the proletariat has nothing to lose but its chains are no longer correct." Marx wrote these words eighty-four years before, at
a time when his entire following was no more than a small
band of *déclassé* intellectuals. Since that day the little sect
of desperadoes has grown to a quarter of a million of office
holders in party, trade-union and government institutions.
Even though some of these jobs are still unpaid and only
honorary until further advancement, the job holders are
doing their best to "keep what they have." But they can no

longer hold the rank and file of their party; the electorate, which has nothing to "keep," flocks in masses to the Communists or occasionally to the Fascists. For whatever the principles or lack of principles of these latter parties may be —they do not tell the starving workers and the malcontent white-collar slaves and other lower-middle-class elements to "keep what they have."

How much longer Scheidemann and his friends will be able to enjoy the benefits of being the largest party in their country is hard to predict. The "National-Socialist" avalanche of German Fascism, with its millions of hungry wolves from the impoverished middle classes and lower middle classes, is rolling on. Hitler's hosts expect to install themselves comfortably in all the hundreds of thousands of soft jobs hitherto held by the socialist politicians, office-holders, trade-union leaders, journalists, ward-captains and other henchmen. The steel and coal interests, whose money has helped to create that enormous organization of Mussolini's emulators, expect to get their share in the Fascist victory in the form of a still greater reduction of the workers' standard of living. Cornered, the Socialists are looking for help to the right and to the left. In order to placate Hindenburg and Brüning, the socialist Police President of Berlin, a former metal worker, suppresses the weekly *Syndicalist* for advocating a general strike in case of a Fascist coup! At the same time the Socialist Party is stretching out feelers in the direction of the Communists with a view to an alliance in case of that very same contingency. The Communists, who a dozen years ago were massacred by the Scheidemannites with the help of the reactionary crowd now arrayed around Hitler, are spurning the advances of their step-brothers. They seem to take the attitude that a Fascist victory is inevitable anyhow, and that the destruction of the Socialist Party will in any case be a great advantage, since it will leave the Communists as the logical leaders of the

German working class, and in line to succeed the Fascists, as soon as the latter have had their day and completely discredited themselves. . . .

Late in 1931 the radical left wing which opposed the silent partnership in the semi-absolutist Hindenburg-Brüning régime, was expelled from Scheidemann's party. The dissenters have since constituted a new organization—the Socialist Labor Party. The new body is attracting those combative working-class elements of the old organization who for one reason or another are unwilling to join the Communists, though not opposed to collaboration with them in the struggle against Fascism. This split seems to be another symptom in the great party of office holders, of that disintegration which has gone on ever since its accession to power and influence. Shortly after the outbreak of the War, Rosa Luxemburg called her party "a stinking corpse." Will Scheidemann live long enough to see her prophecy come literally true?

J. RAMSAY MacDONALD

Last Rampart of Empire

I n one of his earlier novels, H. G. Wells envisioned a time when what was once humanity would have differentiated into two entirely separate animal species, one descending from the masters, the other from the slaves, of capitalist civilization. This ghastly vision was not without a certain sociologic-anthropological basis, in England at least. There, a fast developing and merciless industrialism well-nigh led to a physical degeneration of the industrial wage-working population, largely because the farmer class, whose migration to the cities might have instilled fresh blood into the exhausted organism of the manual workers, had largely become extinct. This process of physical degeneration has now been arrested to a certain extent—though it still manifests itself in the fact that of a hundred applicants for the navy ninety are rejected as unfit.

Meanwhile another process has been going on; a differentiation between the opinions of the sophisticated few and the beliefs and prejudices of the great mass of the people, who are too ignorant to penetrate that dense screen of fictions, delusions and falsehoods which shuts them out from a realistic conception of actual facts and conditions—particularly in the field of public affairs.

The career of Ramsay MacDonald is a case in point. To the sophisticated, he has been for years the leader of a new Liberal Party which is faithfully carrying out the task of preserving the continuity of the best traditions of the British Empire. The idea that with his ascent "the lower class" has obtained "place and power," expressed from time to time in cold type by one adult infant or another, strikes them as funny. They concur with the greatest American daily in the opinion that the "MacDonald régime merely represents British Liberalism in a new form, and that, despite a Labor Government, the English aristocracy is more firmly in the saddle than ever." The fact that, for many years, MacDonald was Secretary of the Socialist ("Second") International does not stamp him a rebel in their eyes. The word "Socialist" has lost its disreputable edge now. It is gradually rising to the same dignity as the word "Patriot"— which, as late as the great French Revolution was still a synonym for rebel and regicide.

However, for the majority of the working people in the United Kingdom, as well as for millions of the downtrodden in other countries, he was until 1931 something quite different. For them, he was the messenger of a new day; a new Moses, who, less violently than Lenin, perhaps, but all the more surely, would lead them out of capitalist thralldom to the land of justice and equality. They were stunned and dumbfounded when, after forty years of preaching and protesting, the only justice and equality he offered them in their hour of greatest need was "equality of sacrifice," the cutting down of their meager unemployment benefits. . . . Yet it would not be surprising if in a few years they were again acclaiming him as their Savior. . . .

His life reads almost like a Horatio Alger story of the poor boy who after many vicissitudes reaches success as the reward of his efforts and hardships. Born in Scotland, in 1866, in the family of a farm laborer, he went through all the heartbreaking struggles of the gifted son of a manual worker, who craves for the higher education his father cannot afford to give him. His misery in London, where he went at the age of eighteen; his chores as an addresser of

envelopes and as an invoice clerk; his superhuman efforts
to acquire more knowledge until he was able to make his
living as a journalist—these will supply a moving chapter
in the schoolbooks of the next generation of English children; provided no violent cataclysm distorts that peaceful
and gradual transition process to State Capitalism, which has
been envisioned by this last savior of the existing system.

The reflex influence of experiences like those through
which Ramsay MacDonald passed during his first years in
London, is usually seen in a bitter class hatred permeating
the early socialist career of every struggling lower-middle-
class intellectual. Yet one looks in vain for any expression
of such a sentiment in his writings and public utterances.
True, he soon had an opportunity to overcome it, for at
twenty-two he had already obtained a good position as secretary to a Liberal would-be statesman, who was exerting
himself to get a seat in the Commons. It was in the service
of this generous employer that he learned the intricacies of
the political game, and the lofty generalities of that liberal
and humanitarian small talk at which he was to become the
supreme master throughout the United Kingdom and its
overseas possessions.

But at the age of eighteen, that spirit of revolt and bitterness did find its expression, if not in words that were to go
down in history, at least in a symbolic gesture. Strange as
it may seem now, young Ramsay joined the Social Democratic Federation, a most radical organization that had the
ambition to represent the pure and undiluted spirit of Karl
Marx on British soil, though its leader, Henry Mayers
Hyndman, was not exactly a personal favorite with the
Teacher. Ramsay has since done more than his share to wash
off that shame.

MacDonald had become familiar with the ideas of social
protest while still in his native village. At that time their
most popular expression was Henry George's celebrated

Progress and Poverty, which had established its author's
reputation as a social critic but had failed to convince any
considerable group of people that the private ownership of
land was the only cause of all social ills, and the single
tax their only remedy. A theory which disregarded the gulf
existing between capital and labor and presented both as
victims of the predatory landowner could not very long hold
the attention of a young man with open eyes.

Looking Backward

The British socialist movement of those years was a
hopelessly small affair. Groups of intellectuals were engaged in lively discussions on the merits of various economic
and philosophical theories—but they seemed to be performing in a vacuum. The British workers were as little interested in their theories as are present-day American workers
in the theoretical squabbles of the various radical groups in
the United States. This was the more disconcerting, as
England was far from being virgin soil for working-class
movements and socialist ideas. Half a century before, and
even earlier, Great Britain had been the scene of violent
industrial and political struggles, which anticipated most of
the ideologies that were to agitate the continent during the
latter part of the nineteenth and the early part of the
twentieth century.

The first decades of the nineteenth century, with their
economic depression following in the wake of the Napoleonic wars, saw a wave of discontent sweeping the country.
The middle classes, the intellectuals, the workers, all in
various ways, expressed their dissatisfaction with the Tory
régime. Demands for the repeal of the Corn Laws, for
democratic franchise, and for nationalization of the land,
agitated the country, creating an atmosphere of turmoil, conspiracy, terrorism and brutal repression, such as can be

compared only with that of Russia in the beginning of this century. Side by side with the articulate campaign for political reform, there was a blind, desperate revolt on the part of the industrial workers, a revolt which throws a ghastly light upon the conditions created by the appearance of modern industrialism. Many of the greatest spirits of England uttered violent condemnations of what was literally mass degeneration—the extermination by slow starvation and overwork of whole generations of British workers and their children. The workers themselves, at bay, organized secretly and offered a desperate resistance by destroying machines, setting fire to factories, and even killing some of their masters. The "Luddites"—the name given to these early rebels after a mythical Ned Ludd—were finally put down by bullets and gibbets; but the terror they inspired, and the acts of violence that were committed, even after their disappearance, helped not a little in removing the restrictions against labor organizations.

With the removal of these restrictions (1825) the road was clear for the development of the trade unions. As a result, England's laboring masses gradually broke up into a minority of well-organized, better paid skilled workers, and a large majority of unskilled and unorganized laborers. With the further development of industrialism the split was to become even more sharply defined. (Recent technical improvements in turn, tend to reduce hosts of skilled workers to the ranks of the unskilled or semi-skilled.)

For a hundred years, now, the British working masses have constantly been vacillating between the purely industrial fight for higher wages and the political struggle for more democracy and representation in parliament. The middle classes, by assisting the workers in their fight against the "Combination Acts," won the support of the workers in the political struggle; but the Reform Bill of 1832, which was the first result of that campaign, entirely excluded the lower middle classes and the workers from the vote. All the benefits of the reform went to the well-to-do merchant and manufacturing classes.

As a result of this disappointment, the trade unions became a promising field for the socialist propaganda conducted by Robert Owen, a successful manufacturer and philanthropist, who advocated the transition of industries into the hands of workers' coöperatives. At the same time, two of Owen's former followers, James Morrison, a self-taught building worker, and James E. Smith, an intellectual, elaborated theories which anticipated by nearly seventy years the ideas of the French Syndicalists. Parliamentary action was deprecated and direct action and the general strike were put forward as the most effective weapon of the working masses. Robert Owen, who in his Tolstoyan naïveté hoped to establish the millennium by converting the privileged classes to his gospel, used all his authority and ascendancy among the newly organized workers to counteract the revolutionary influence of his heretical disciples, and the general strike, which they had urged, was never attempted. Needless to say, Owen with his doctrine of class harmony rather than Marx with his class struggle has been the determining force in shaping MacDonald's political philosophy. Although it was hardly naïveté that directed MacDonald's choice . . .

In their disappointment at the failure of the strike movements of the early thirties, many of the workers turned to the political program of Chartism. The Chartist movement with its emphasis upon universal suffrage, was to a great extent headed and controlled by the lower middle classes, particularly the lower-middle-class intellectuals, who were incensed because the Reform Bill of 1832 had left them out in the cold. The Chartist movement played a most important rôle in English history for nearly two decades—but it did not achieve its object, and with the economic upswing that began in the middle of the century it gradually died out.

J. RAMSAY MacDONALD

FROM MARX TO . . . FABIUS

During the ensuing period, roughly from the middle of the century up to the early eighties, British industry dominated the rest of the world and a share of its enormous profits, enhanced by the exploitation of colonies, went to the workers. This relative prosperity, such as they had never before enjoyed, sounded the knell of all revolutionary activities for over a generation. The workers lost all interest in radical political struggles or ideological schemes. The trade unions which helped them to maintain a high standard of living, entirely satisfied their aspirations. Even the unskilled were much better off than ever before. And in 1867, when the urban workers were granted the franchise, no doubt as a repercussion of many continental struggles and of the American Civil War, during which the British workers had sided with the North—it was the Liberal Party which controlled the workers' vote. With the free-trade issue as a stock argument, the trade unions and their leaders were brought completely under the sway of the employers and their Liberal Party.

In the beginning of the sixties, it is true, a section of the British trade unionists had shown interest in international labor unity, but it had been frightened away by the reaction that set in after the downfall of the Paris Commune in 1871. Their interest in the International Working Men's Association, founded in 1864 with the active participation of Karl Marx, had not been aroused by any revolutionary or anti-capitalist spirit. It was due to a prosaic desire to find ways and means for restricting the immigration of foreign labor, which some employers had just begun to play off against the London building workers. Naturally Marx had no tenderness for the British trade-union leaders, and he even went so far as to say, "it is an honor, rather

than the opposite, not to be an English labor leader, for the
majority of these leaders are all sold to the Liberals."

This was the period of the so-called "Old Unionism,"
when the trade unions became to a large extent mutual-
benefit societies, when conflicts such as strikes were avoided,
and when all efforts were centered upon removing what
restrictions still existed against the full development of
trade-union organizations. The unskilled workers were left
to their fate.

But that period was not to last forever. The glorious days
of British industry began to decline toward the end of the
seventies. By that time British industry, which heretofore
had occupied a monopolistic situation in the world market,
saw itself confronted by growing competition from Germany and America. A period of depression set in, wages fell,
and employers were no longer so ready to grant concessions.

As a result, the eighties saw a revival of the revolutionary
and critical spirit of forty years before—particularly as this
depression had its repercussion upon the educated classes as
well. Increased facilities for public education had begun to
produce an excess of young people of middle-class or lower-
middle-class origin who saw an uncertain future staring
them in the face. Various schemes of social reform involving
a degree of public control of industries as against private
monopoly, were taken up with ardor not only by impecunious malcontents but also by a few upper-middle-class
intellectuals. Some of the latter saw in Socialism either a
philanthropic protest against the growing misery of large
sections of the laboring masses, or a peaceful means of
averting the cataclysm that seemed to them inevitable, unless
certain reforms were effected. Others came in a spirit of
dilettantism or ambition, ready to play with, or to direct,
the potential forces of a history-making upheaval. Hyndman himself, the founder of the Marxist Social Democratic
Federation, belonged to the latter group. Workers and for-

mer workers, leaders among the trade unions, were still scarce in the various radical groups—but they too began to show more and more interest, though only individually at first. From this element, which had been affected by socialist ideas, the "New Unionism" of the later eighties and nineties originated.

At the time (1884) when young Ramsay joined the Social Democratic Federation, that organization had been in existence for three years. Its founders had set themselves a very ambitious aim—nothing less than the revival of the Chartist movement, modified in accordance with the theoretical and practical experience of the intervening decades. The franchise which the workers had obtained in 1867 was inadequate, and in spite of the occasional election of labor representatives to the House of Commons, the workers had no party of their own that could be depended on to stand up for their interests as against the two other parties. The labor representatives, in spite of occasional sulking and insubordination, always remained part of the Liberal Party.

Henry M. Hyndman, the head of the organization, was a man of superior achievements; an outstanding speaker and writer, with vast historical and economic learning. He was also, however, a domineering personality, with a strong chauvinist bias and excessive conceit, bound to conflict with other socialist intellectuals who did not intend to submit meekly to his authority—particularly as he had no jobs to distribute. Hyndman's attempts at the creation of an independent labor movement, inspired with the socialist ideas current on the continent and particularly in Germany, never went beyond the incipient stage, and his organization never exceeded 12,000 members. The workers had their trade unions already, and with the help of these had substantially improved their standard of living. Their unions had been a natural growth, and they were not indebted to the socialist intellectuals for their achievements—whereas, in many continental countries, the socialists had greatly helped the workers in their early trade-union struggles. Hyndman and the other socialist intellectuals, who had done nothing for the workers, were now offering them the socialist ideal and urging them to form a political party pledged to realize it. Like many leading socialists in other countries, Hyndman in a kind of egotistic self-infatuation, expected the working masses immediately to prefer his political doctrine and his candidates to those of his opponents of the bourgeois camp.

Hyndman's brilliant effort was wasted. He succeeded in attracting to his organization a great number of first-class intellects, such as Belfort Bax, a famous barrister and sociologist; William Morris, the poet and artist, Walter Crane, a painter of the Pre-Raphaelite school, very well known in those years; Eleanor Marx-Aveling, the brilliant daughter of her famous father; and, last and worst, her husband, Dr. Edward Aveling—the original of Bernard Shaw's Dubedat in *The Doctor's Dilemma*—most charming and scintillating of all unscrupulous scoundrels that ever infested any political movement. For awhile Shaw himself considered entering the organization.

Young Ramsay MacDonald found himself from the very beginning involved in a confusion of the most heterogeneous ideas, ranging from regular Marxism to anti-parliamentarian socialism and communist-anarchism. The exponents of these were united only by bitter opposition to the existing system; and they were soon to be as bitterly arrayed against each other in a struggle of personal ambitions and diverging conceptions. In the split that ensued, many of the most outstanding personalities, such as William Morris, Bax, Crane, and the Avelings, parted with Hyndman and founded their own organization. This, however, soon disappeared.

The violent language indulged in at that time by Hyndman—who over thirty years later, was to outdo all the "bitter-enders" in their hatred of the "German agents," Lenin and Trotsky—was most remarkable. He advocated "dynamite against capitalists," and during the unemployment agitation of 1886 he cried out that "the unemployed would attract the attention of the public only if a rich man were sacrificed on the grave of every poor man." One of his chief lieutenants, a former army officer and the son of a Major-General, even resorted, in his zeal for similes, to the hackneyed ferocity of Caligula, expressing the wish "that the propertied classes had but one neck, so that misery might be terminated by one blow."

Was MacDonald impressed by this language? If he was, he never recorded it, but in his writings he never conceals his great aversion for the Social Democratic Federation. True, he took part in the violent unemployment demonstrations of 1887, organized by the radical elements; but when later he recalled those struggles of the hungry unemployed—when there was no "dole" to keep them from starvation—his remarks concerned neither his personal sentiments, nor the immediate effect of the riots, which shamed or rather frightened the wealthy public into considerable contributions. His interest centered upon the impression a few of the undeserving poor who had resorted to plundering might have made upon the respectable. "Trade was bad," he wrote, "and men out of employment were being told for the first time in their lives that 'they ought not to starve in private.' They were told to come out in their rags, and they came, the just with the unjust, and, as usual, those who looked on saw only the unjust."

What must have affected him much more was Hyndman's attitude in 1885 with regard to the Tories. Eager to get its candidates returned to Parliament, and short of funds, his organization actually applied to the Tories and got from them financial assistance in its electoral campaign against the Liberals. Considering Toryism as a dead issue, Hyndman and his following saw in the Liberals the true party of capitalism, the main enemy that had to be destroyed at any price, regardless of what allies might be used.

The taking of "Tory gold" greatly scandalized many socialist elements and no doubt greatly contributed to MacDonald's joining the Fabian Society, then, as now, the gathering point of the flower of England's advanced intelligentsia. George Bernard Shaw and Sidney and Beatrice Webb were the main exponents of a "pink" gospel that was attempting to make socialism palatable for the privileged classes. It was not their intention to form a new party. Their only ambition was to "permeate" the other parties with socialist ideas. They were against the class struggle, and they substituted a set of their own economic theories for those of Marx. In the light of present developments—with government control of industries advocated by many upholders of the existing system as the only way out of the impasse and the chaos of planless private capitalism—the policy of the early Fabians assumes a certain prophetic significance. The Fabians represented the most advanced and enlightened wing of the Liberal middle classes, and they understood—without saying so in plain words—that government ownership, the time-honored socialist remedy for all ills, was perfectly compatible with the preservation of economic inequality. High salaries in the administration and management of the nationalized industries, or compensations in the form of life annuities, would be substituted for the profits formerly derived by owners or stockholders from the privately owned industries; and these, as well as increased security and safety, would be sufficient compensation for the loss of private ownership rights. As MacDonald later put it, the capitalists under that scheme would certainly lose less than they are now losing through stock speculation. Strange as it may sound, this mild program of State Capitalism was in its essentials not greatly different from the scheme proposed in the seventies by Marx for democratic countries, such as England and the United States, where, in his opinion, violent revolution and expropriation were not necessary, and Socialism could be established by "buying off" the capitalists.*

The only difference was that Marx and his followers represented the lower-middle-class intelligentsia, which was somewhat more impatient than the self-complacent middle-class and upper-middle-class intelligentsia of the Fabian group, and, for this reason, they considered revolutionary class-struggle verbiage, and pressure by a separate labor party, as necessary for hastening the process.

(Bernard Shaw's latter-day personal postulate for equality of incomes, though bearing all the earmarks of undiluted communism, does not really imply any falling-off from the state capitalist character of his early Fabian doctrines. To postulate economic equality and to reject class struggle and revolution, which alone could accomplish it, is the substance of one of those periodical tomfooleries with which the author of the *Revolutionist's Handbook* dutifully exhilarates a world anxious for entertainment. Thus the working class finds itself in a pleasant dilemma as between preachers of equality who reject the revolution and revolutionists who postpone economic equality to a distant future, altogether removed from the living generation.)

The Fabians, whom MacDonald joined while he was serving his political apprenticeship as secretary of a Liberal would-be politician, could not hold his allegiance for more than a few years. In his *Socialism,* published in 1907, he expressed his attitude towards the first two socialist organizations to which he had belonged at the beginning of his career: "The foreign outlook, phrases and criticisms of the Social Democratic Federation never quite fitted themselves into British conditions; whilst the Fabian Society, much more successful in adapting socialism to British evolution,

* Quoted in Lenin's *The Tax in Kind* and *State and Revolution.*

never succeeded in applying it to the movements of contemporary politics, and never faced the problem of how to organize the masses so that they might be available for the advancement of socialist legislation." This probably means that he preferred the good manners of the Fabians to the harshness of Marxist class-struggle vocabulary; but that, at the same time, he saw no hope for the satisfaction of his political ambitions without a strong pressure by the organized power of the working masses.

The New Unionism

The new departure within the trade-union movement was to pave the way in this direction. The economic stagnation caused by growing German and American competition on the world market dealt a hard blow to the self-complacency of the old trade unions—and made the British workers more inclined to listen to the preachings of some of the revolutionary agitators, who, like John Burns and Tom Mann, workers themselves, had gone through the school of the Social Democratic Federation.

Realizing the difficulties which they themselves had had in digesting the economic, philosophical and political vocabulary of the Marxist creed, they used very little of it in speaking to their fellow workers, whether organized or unorganized. They attacked the old policy which had made of the trade unions mutual benefit and old-age pension societies, and had thus relieved the government of the obligation to take care of this side of public-welfare activities. They called for more militancy and for strikes in order to obtain higher wages and shorter hours. Once the workers got into a fighting mood, they thought, they would soon become interested in independent political activity, and then the time for a great socialist party, German model, would finally arrive.

John Burns was one of the main leaders of the demonstrations of the unemployed of 1886 and 1887—he was then "the man with the Red Flag"—and it was he again, with Tom Mann, who led the victorious strike of the London dockers in 1889. This victory marked the beginning of the decline of the old conservative trade unionism. The leadership of the unions now began to come under the influence of the "new unionists" and a number of unions of unskilled workers were organized, though these were unable to achieve anything like a permanent existence.

The Social Democratic Federation was not to enjoy the credit of this great success, to a large extent obtained by workers or ex-workers who had gone through Hyndman's school. One after another, as their reputations as labor leaders became established, John Burns, Tom Mann, and Ben Tillett turned their back upon the old leader in the frock coat who had taught them the revolutionary thunder that had made their career. They did not need him any more; they were tired of their subjection to the leadership of middle-class or *déclassé* intellectuals. Moreover, many of the ideas officially propounded by the organization were obviously jeopardizing all chances of its success among the working masses. For instance, in an appeal addressed to the trade unions in 1884, the Social Democratic Federation actually stated that the struggle was to be directed not towards the attainment of higher wages, but towards the removal of the wage system and the establishment of socialism. This sounded revolutionary all right; but it was the revolutionism of the outsider—out of contact with the masses—who expects the worker to forget his present-day needs for the sake of a socialist millennium, of which the worker knows hardly more than that the well-dressed, white-collared gentleman promises to establish it for him. It was not even good Marxism, for Marxists in other countries were usually much more cautious, and, though at heart opposed to the industrial struggle for higher wages, were wise enough not to express themselves openly against what, in their eyes, was a necessary evil.

THE INDEPENDENT LABOR PARTY

The activity of these "new unionists" in the later eighties and early nineties prepared the ground for a new socialist party; this in turn became instrumental in creating the British Labor Party. The Social Democratic Federation had become a hopeless group of sectarians, speaking a Marxist esperanto which the British workers refused to learn or to understand. These workers, though growing increasingly restless under the changing economic conditions, were politically still largely in tow of the Liberal Party, whose parliamentary group always included a few labor representatives. That party, however, was now doing nothing to meet the growing demand for social reform. Disappointment on the part of the workers was bound to come sooner or later and to vent itself in violent action, plunging the country into turmoil, calling forth violent counter-measures, and thus disturbing regular and progressive development along democratic lines. Even the most advanced element interested in the labor movement was far from wishing such a really revolutionary turn of affairs. For, in a country enjoying democratic institutions, "revolution" in radical terminology is, as a rule, meant only in a Pickwickian sense, to express a peaceful transition from one historical period to another, such as took place at the time of the industrial revolution. A number of social reforms, including municipal or government ownership of certain public utilities, if forced upon the legislative bodies by the political pressure on the part of organized labor, voting for a party of its own, would improve the condition of labor and obviate the danger of a social cataclysm. Last but not least, these reforms would

open the road to an advantageous political career for new
talent rising from among the self-educated ex-workers and
those intellectuals who were willing to work with them and
to forego the overbearing dictatorial attitude of the high-
brows of the Social Democratic Federation.

Out of this situation was born the Independent Labor
Party, which had found an effective and colorful leader in
Keir Hardie, a former Scottish miner, labor union organizer
and journalist. He was supported in his efforts by the best
of the leaders of the "new unionism" with the exception of
John Burns, for whom the uphill road of an independent
labor party was apparently too slow a process and who
wanted immediate results, for himself at least. Tom Mann
had supported Keir Hardie's efforts from the very inception of the idea, late in the eighties. Friedrich Engels, life-
long friend and collaborator of Marx, also encouraged the
plan—much to the discomfiture of the orthodox Marxist
sectarians.

The new party did not call itself "socialist," lest it frighten
away the many working-class elements which had been
prejudiced against that name by capitalist newspaper propaganda. Neither did its speakers and its publications use
the time-honored revolutionary vocabulary of Marxian socialism, which had become generally current on the continent. The British trade unionism of past generations had
developed under the tutelage of upstart ex-workers, and
these had taken their political and intellectual inspiration
from their Liberal masters, with whom a certain harmony
had been established during the halcyon days of British industrial predominance. As a result, British labor spoke the
political language of Liberalism, with its denial of the existence of classes, its insistence upon such generous generalities as "justice" and "fair play" and its characteristically
English admixture of ethical, religious, and democratic
verbiage.

MacDonald, who in 1891 had left his secretarial job, had in the meantime become a competent newspaperman. For a time he had been associated with the "Fellowship of the New Life" founded by a very high-minded Scotsman, Thomas Davidson, whose aim was "to reconstruct human society according to the principles of the highest morality." Mac-Donald's connection with these Tolstoyan anarchists did not last long, but it stood him in good stead. It greatly increased his supply of high-sounding phrases, so indispensable for a respectable politician.

When the Independent Labor Party was constituted in 1893, the young newspaperman did not join it immediately, but cautiously waited to see whether it had any vitality at all. The probation period was obviously successful, for the future leader of British Labor joined it in 1894.

When two years after the foundation of the party, general elections to the House of Commons took place in 1895, MacDonald was one of twenty-eight candidates running on the Independent Labor Party platform. In his address before the electorate of Southampton he advocated a program of partial and general reforms, identical with the minimum and maximum program of any other socialist party, and culminating in "nationalization of land and public control of the means of production, distribution and exchange." Of course he never used such expressions as "working class" or "class interests," but in sound English fashion he greatly emphasized the question of "principle."

He was not elected, nor were any of the other candidates of the party. The opposition on the part of the old labor leaders, who feared the competition of these rebels, was still very strong; the campaign speeches centered chiefly about "principles," or general promises, with which the Liberals could be as lavish as the next, and not about the crucial question of higher wages, which were not in the control of Parliament; it was therefore natural that the greater number of the workers preferred to follow their old leaders. For, while the worker is always alert to enter a direct struggle for economic betterment, he is a traditionalist when it comes to matters of a "higher order." Like most of his fellow-citizens, he has only a very hazy understanding of public affairs at large, and he is likely to persist in his traditional opinions, or lack of opinions, impressed upon him by his masters, or to rely upon the judgment of his trusted old leaders. Only an entirely changed general situation can work the miracle of shaking people out of their firm habits of thought and behavior. That change was soon to come in England.

So far the progress made by the new party did not come up to its great expectations. True, it won a membership of 6,000 soon after its organization, while its Marxist rival, even after forty years of existence, never had more than 12,000. On the other hand, its electoral successes (44,320 votes polled in 1895) were as nothing compared with the success of the German Socialist Party, which in 1893 had polled nearly 1,500,000 votes. Attempts were made to join forces with the Social Democratic Federation, but nothing came of it. Hyndman's followers insisted upon a complete merger, while the Independent Labor Party hesitated to effect anything more than a loose federation. It was another instance of the old suspicion which leaders risen from the ranks of manual labor feel against the intellectuals whose domination they fear.

Then came a number of blows which finally shook the mass of organized workers out of their complacency. A few large strikes of machinists and miners took place in 1896 and 1897 and were lost after several months. Slowly but surely encroachments were made upon the hitherto established rights of the labor unions. Picketing was forbidden in 1896, and courts declared that the trade unions were responsible for the illegal actions of individual strikers. These attempts were crowned in 1900 by the historic decision of the House of Lords with regard to the strike directed against the Taff-Vale Railway in Wales. The railway company sued the trade union for damages, and the House of Lords, acting as the highest Court, decided against the union.

THE BIRTH OF THE LABOR PARTY

These developments were gradually creating an entirely new atmosphere. The trade unions saw the increasing danger that threatened their very existence, and they were no longer contemptuous of the assistance of those whom they had hitherto looked on as visionaries and dreamers. At the Trade Union Congress held in 1899, a resolution drafted by MacDonald and other members of the Independent Labor Party was submitted, advocating the calling of a special congress of coöperative and socialist organizations as well as of trade unions. This congress was to discuss methods of securing a large labor representation in Parliament, in order to defend the menaced rights of organized labor. The proposal was carried.

A committee was appointed to make arrangements. It included four representatives of the Parliamentary Committee (lobby committee) of the trade unions; two representatives of the Independent Labor Party (Keir Hardie and Ramsay MacDonald); two representatives of the Social Democratic Federation; and two representatives of the Fabian Society, one of whom was G. B. Shaw. At a special congress held in 1900, attended by representatives of trade unions and the various socialist organizations, the Labor Representation Committee—for the next six years the official name of the Labor Party—was established. It was not a party in the usual meaning of the word, since it did not admit individuals. Only organized bodies as a whole could be affiliated with it. Individual membership was rendered possible only eighteen years later.

MacDonald, then only thirty-four years old, became the first secretary of the new organization. The choice of an intellectual may appear strange, when a great number of self-taught labor leaders who had risen from the ranks were available, but the qualifications of this appointee were really extraordinary. A striking personality with a wide culture, he was not only a fluent speaker and an able journalist with a facile pen, but also an excellent organizer with long experience in the labor movement. For several years he had been a member of the National Council of the Independent Labor Party, and he had at the same time been working for various trade-union organizations, including the London Trades Council, the central labor body representing most trade unions of the capital.

During the year 1900, forty-one trade unions and three socialist organizations joined the new party. They brought in a total membership of 380,000 trade unionists and socialists, including about 13,000 members of the Independent Labor Party, 9,000 members of the Social Democratic Federation and 861 Fabians. The same year saw a general election in England, carried on in the atmosphere of the Boer War. It was an atmosphere of jingoism, to which the workingman is just as susceptible as are all the other classes of society. MacDonald opposed this exploit of British imperialism, for, like many other Radicals and Liberals, including David Lloyd George and Winston Churchill, he feared a strengthening of the Conservatives as a result of the war-fever.

In his memorable speech to the voters of Leicester, before whom he came as one of the fifteen candidates representing Labor, he was very bitter against his Liberal opponents. There was not a single item in the Liberal platform, he told them, "which some candidates were not willing to sacri-

fice if a vote were to be gained by doing so." A generation
later, there was not a single point or principle that Labor
had stood for originally, which MacDonald and his crowd
were not ready to sacrifice for the sake of staying in
power. . . .

He was defeated in 1900, as he had been five years before. Only two candidates of the party were elected, Keir
Hardie being one of them. Over one-third of all the votes
cast in the fifteen districts which the new party had contested had gone to Labor. This was hopeful enough, and the
number of trade unions giving their adherence to the Labor
Representation Committee was growing. MacDonald, at any
rate, was full of optimism, for he stuck to the new organization throughout its lean years, though his salary as secretary was no more than twenty-five pounds a year.

It was during the Boer War that he severed his relations
with the Fabian Society. MacDonald's opposition to war was
part of the idealist armory of his ethical socialism—and also
a consequence of his unwillingness to countenance and to aid
an adventure that would enhance the power and the ascendancy of the Conservatives. A cautious body of practical
idealists, the Fabians, in their majority vote, refused to take
sides in the struggle between the British lion and the two
other carriers of the white man's burden, who, tiny as they
were, could occasionally outdo even England in their heroic
treatment of the colored natives. Anxious as the Fabians
were to permeate all classes of British society with their
notions of socialism, they refused to commit themselves to
an anti-imperialist point of view which was very unpopular
with the crowd. Their mouthpiece was Sidney Webb, until
1931, as Lord Passfield, Secretary of State for the Colonies in the Labor Cabinet. Bernard Shaw also refused to
array himself with the pro-Boer partisans, for he considered Paul Kruger's régime in the Transvaal as a despicable
piece of Puritan medievalism which could not command the

sympathy of any civilized person. MacDonald and his
friends, however, refused to see the matter in this light.
They bolted, and since that time MacDonald has been carrying on the policy of the Fabians outside of that organization.

THE LABOR PARTY MARCHING ON

In the meantime the Conservatives, against whom he directed his thunder, were working for him. The Taff-Vale
decision, already mentioned, declaring the trade unions liable
for strike damages, as well as similar judgments following
that precedent, had greatly depleted the funds of the unions
concerned. In protest the unions began to come over to the
Labor Representation Committee, which, in 1906, officially
took the name "Labor Party." It had then 900,000 members,
and the elections held in that year brought it an unprece-
dented victory. Twenty-nine out of its fifty candidates were
returned. In addition, fourteen labor members from the
mining districts, who had been returned as Liberals, joined
the Labor party a few years later. A number of by-elections
brought similar successes. True to his idealist thesis, that
the struggle was one of principles and not of interests, Mac-
Donald, against all appearances, maintained that the Taff-
Vale decision had only a very small part in the sweeping
victory of his party. There was, of course, more than doctrinaire blindness in this stubborn exaltation of the spiritual
as against the material factor. Emboldened by success, the
laboring masses were likely to demand concrete bread-and-
butter results, attainable only at the price of conflicts more
serious than those of the ballot. Insistence upon "principle"
rather than "interests" might prove an effectual barrier
against such untoward "greediness" of the underdog.

The election of 1906 had been a complete rout of the
Conservatives, whose cabinet had resigned even before the
dissolution of the House. The new Liberal cabinet of Camp-

bell-Bannerman, who appointed John Burns as President
of the Local Government Board, proceeded to undo the revolutionary effects of Conservative anti-trade-union policy and
to check the rising tide of Labor Party competition. All the
restrictions and pitfalls designed to hamper trade-union
activity for which a precedent had been made in that famous
Taff-Vale decision of the House of Lords were removed.
Moreover, a number of reforms were adopted—such as the
eight-hour day for miners, an improvement in the laws concerning old-age pensions and sickness insurance, as well as
unemployment insurance for a section of the working class.
Progress in political democracy was likewise marked. A
campaign was begun to abolish the veto of the Lords, and
regular salaries out of government funds were allowed to
members of Parliament who had hitherto been unpaid. This
was a great relief for the Labor Party, which out of its own
resources had been paying each Labor member two hundred
pounds annually. The government appropriation per member
was twice that sum, bringing about a decided social revolution in the personal circumstances of those labor leaders
and sympathizers who were lucky enough to be elected.

All these reforms were important for a large section of
the workers, though not of course for the great majority
of them, the unskilled and unorganized. There seems to be
a law of nature—or is it a divine law?—that "to him that
hath shall be given—" as for the others, they must be patient
and wait for further peaceful developments. For, as Mac-
Donald said at that time, "the socialist change must be
gradual and must proceed in stages, just as the evolution of
an organism does"; the sentence to a certain extent epit-
omizes his "biological socialism," a theory which he has
consistently developed in all his numerous writings. The
same "inevitability of gradualness" has since been proclaimed in a famous phrase of Sidney Webb. It may be
called the classical formula for the gradual transition from

individualist private capitalism, with the owners of land, money and the industries in the saddle, to monopolistic State Capitalism with an all-powerful bureaucracy (composed of all persons with higher education) in charge of the management of the country's economic and political life. This would be the concrete aspect of the anti-capitalist "ideal" haunting the imagination of the socialist intelligentsia: no capitalists, but instead all degrees of inequality of income: from the *prima donna* salaries of the experts down to the bare subsistence of the unskilled laborer.

Simultaneously with the progress of the Labor Party the star of its most gifted speaker and parliamentarian was rising. In 1906, Ramsay MacDonald was elected Chairman of the Independent Labor Party. Five years later, in 1911, Keir Hardie, the patriarch of both the Independent Labor Party and the Labor Party, gave way to MacDonald as leader of the Labor Party in the House.

The Syndicalist Wave

The progress of the working masses was far from keeping pace with the progress of their leading politicians. In spite of various reforms adopted by the House since 1906, the general standard of living of the working masses showed in these years a downward tendency. Caught between the merciless vise of decreasing wages and rising prices, the workers turned to direct action.

A violent strike wave swept the whole country. Miners and railway and transport workers, as well as those in other sections of industry, departed from their traditional patience; the course of their struggle was marked by many stubborn encounters between strikers and the armed forces. This movement marked an entirely new departure in British labor history. Two decades before, a man had been a "radical" if, within the trade unions, he advocated the formation of a political Labor Party to pursue a policy altogether independent from the Liberals. Only after a number of serious judicial encroachments upon the rights of the trade unions did these decide to assert their political independence, thus creating the Labor Party. Now, ten years after the formation of that party, a continuous rise in the cost of living entailed a lowering of the real wages; moreover, a certain disappointment was felt with the achievements of the Parliamentary Labor Party. The workers were being driven beyond mere politics. Syndicalism with its gospel of direct action and the general strike had crossed the Channel and had found in Tom Mann an enthusiastic and influential advocate.

During that stormy period which began in 1911, the railway men were the most important single group who engaged in the struggle against a declining standard of living. In the negotiations undertaken during the strike, proud directors were for the first time compelled to meet the representatives of their employees on an equal footing. Ramsay MacDonald was one of these representatives, Arthur Henderson the other.

The strike greatly strengthened the organization of the railway workers, whose various unions now merged. An incidental and ironical result was the rise to power of James Thomas, later member of the first and second Labor cabinets, and of MacDonald's "National Cabinet." For the last ten years the more radical elements have been charging him with having betrayed every strike movement undertaken on a large scale since the conclusion of the War. . . .

These strikes and their potential results greatly disturbed the ruling classes of the British Isles, and not the ruling classes only. It looked as if the country were about to face a new period of civil strife, like that of the thirties and forties of last century. The leaders of the Labor Party were alarmed. Their beloved policy of "gradualness," with its unexciting but quite secure rewards for the well-paid parliamentary and trade union leaders, was in danger of being swept away by the impatient masses. The Chairman of the Labor Party and his friends did all they could to smother the revolutionary fire, or, as the author of one of his biographies puts it, "to turn the unrest into political channels"; that is, to inspire the masses with the hope that a bigger and better Labor representation, obtained at the next election, would put a stop to the decline in their living standards. He wrote vehement philippics against syndicalism and the idea that "society can be divided into two classes," but without avail. The unrest smoldered on, kept alive by economic causes, and the number of strikes continuously increased. A revolutionary situation was at hand, when the whole course of history was suddenly changed by the great conflagration of 1914.

TRAITOR

During those years of industrial strife, war clouds had been gathering on the European horizon. MacDonald, who was opposed to violent disturbances of the normal development, both in domestic and foreign policy, had worked hard to impress the popular mind with ideas of pacifism. In 1910, during the International Socialist Congress in Copenhagen, he, usually so moderate, had supported a motion advocating the general strike for the purpose of preventing war. It was, no doubt, a mere gesture, intended to impress the British ruling spheres, for he never even for a moment suggested a resort to this weapon when the War was actually imminent.

When the War was finally at hand, during the first days of August, 1914, he made his last stand, on August 3rd, in a speech delivered during the debate concerning the British ultimatum to Germany. For that speech he has been branded as a defeatist, as an enemy of his country, as a traitor. He was confounded at the time with those extreme revolutionists who, with the Marx of 1847, believed that "the worker has no country," and his stand was likened to that taken by the German and Russian extremists, such as Liebknecht, Lenin or Trotsky. Those accusations did him a grave injustice—or too much honor, depending on one's point of view. "If the Right Hon. gentleman [Sir Edward Grey]," he said in that speech, "had come here today and told us that our country is in danger, . . . we would be with him and behind him. If the nation's honor were in danger, we would be with him. . . ."

"Country," it seems, and even "honor"—he was willing to defend; he doubted that these two were involved. He was only against British intervention in a Continental war, an intervention prepared by an "Anti-German Foreign Office" and an "Admiralty anxious to seize any opportunity of using the Navy in battle practice." He believed that either a winning or a losing war would hurt the cause of his party: a victory by strengthening reaction, and a defeat by strengthening revolution. He wanted neither.

These ultimate considerations appeared to him more important than the immediate advantage he and the Labor party might derive from an alignment with the government; he hoped that if he and Labor took a firm stand at the beginning, they would, at least, even if they could not prevent war, be vindicated later—when the national hysteria was calmed, as was the case after the South-African War. He did not reckon with a very important fact: that while individuals may be consistent to the point of grave personal risk and danger, groups and organizations of men who have certain interests at stake, are governed by the immediate consideration of these interests and not by uncertain future developments. The ruling group of the Labor Party consisted of comparatively well-to-do labor bureaucrats and politicians, recruited from among intellectuals and self-taught ex-workers. They were not a group of revolutionary militants, whose whole life, even while they are out of prison, is anything but a bed of roses, and who are ready to take chances. MacDonald's friends had for the most part attained the ambitions of their lives; the labor movement was their vested interest. It was in the power of the Government to wreck their fortunes, and they were not willing to sacrifice their comforts even temporarily.

Therefore, although they endorsed his speech at the time, they disowned him only a few days afterwards, as if it were the most natural thing in the world. When it came to the question whether MacDonald, as the Chairman of the Parliamentary Labor Party, was to voice the opinion of this body *after the declaration of war,* the great majority of the party decided that pacifism was not a proper policy for wartime, and that he should not be permitted to speak in their name. MacDonald resigned from the Chairmanship of the Party, and was replaced by the former worker, Arthur Henderson. He could not then go back on his own words without disgracing himself altogether. He had, however, the consolation that among the few leaders of the Party who sided with him, were Keir Hardie, founder of the Independent Labor Party, and foremost in organizing the Labor Party, and Philip Snowden, second only to MacDonald himself in brilliance and intellectual acumen. He has since more than made up for his step aside. . . .

By knifing MacDonald from behind, the leaders of the Labor Party were actually expressing the sentiments of the rank and file. No sooner was war declared, than the workers in their mass, like the rest of the population, went mad with enthusiasm for a cause, the deeper motivations of which were hidden from them. Not only did they believe in all the official arguments given for their country's participation, no matter how ridiculous these may now appear to everybody, but also, subconsciously and even consciously, large masses went into war with the same spirit in which their masters had for years prepared for it. Actually it was not very hard for the war-mongers to impress the British worker with the belief that a large part of his poverty was due to German competition, which had deprived England of its predominance in the world market. British workers had all along been beneficiaries, to a large extent, of British imperial expansion, and they fully expected to get more benefits from the war now in hand: against such a spirit of economic and political imperialism no pacifist propaganda for "righteousness" could hope to prevail.

Moreover, the skilled workers, who were the backbone of the trade unions and of the Labor Party, were being kept busy producing war materials. They generously left all the glory and all the risk of the actual fight to the less fortunate unskilled workers, who could be easily replaced by women or children.

Under these circumstances, MacDonald's opposition to war was a hopeless venture. "Traitor" he was, to all the enemies of Labor, and to the great mass of workers alike. The Labor Party leaders, however, must have felt that when the war madness was over, his attitude would be vindicated, and that when the time came his upright stand would benefit the Party; for in spite of diversity of opinions, he was never excluded from the Party and even remained its Treasurer throughout the war.

To be sure, he was very guarded in all his expressions. Only once, in an article printed at the outset of the War in the *Labor Leader,* organ of the Independent Labor Party, did he rise to a tone of fierce accusation, tearing to shreds the argument based on the violation of Belgium's neutrality. He recalled to his readers that "Mr. Gladstone made it clear in 1870, that in a general conflict formal neutrality might be violated"; and added that "if France had decided to attack Germany through Belgium, Sir Edward Grey would not have objected, but would have justified himself by Mr. Gladstone's opinions."

But after that, he always insisted that, once the country was at war, it was necessary to see it through to a victorious conclusion. "We are fighting," he said in one of his speeches, "because . . . we have prejudices against a very strong commercial rival. . . . We are in it and we must see it through. . . . How one almost hates the diplomacy that has brought us to this!" Almost!

In a letter which he wrote to the Mayor of Leicester, the city he represented in the House, his "we-are-in-it-we-must-win-it" point of view was expressed in that peculiar style which, florid as it may be, is all his own:

"Victory, therefore, must be ours. England is not played out. Her mission is to be accomplished. She can, if she would, take the place of esteemed honor among the democracies of the world, and if peace is to come with healing on her wings the democracies of Europe must be her guardians. There should be no doubt about this. Well, we cannot go back now, nor can we turn to the right or the left. We must go straight through." And so on.

This was certainly not the language of a "traitor," but he did even better. In a speech delivered in Parliament about two years after the beginning of hostilities, he declared that "this country, if it retains any shred of honor at all, cannot accept a peace . . . which means the sacrifice of Belgium's sovereignty to any extent."

Nevertheless he was considered a traitor, his name was vilified, his meetings were broken up, though, as time went by, considerable sections of organized labor began to realize that his "treason" consisted chiefly in the fact that he was trying to defend the rights of the workers, which under the pretext of war-time stress, the Government was trying to invade. He fiercely opposed conscription of labor, sponsored as he said, by "men who have been the bitterest enemies of trade-unionism," and in general he warned the workers against all the actual and impending encroachments upon the rights and achievements which had been the prize of long and bitter struggle. For already, in 1916, some of the leading men of Great Britain, in speaking of possible post-war developments, had expressed the expectation that "the British workmen would have to consent to work for lower wages than hitherto"; and mine owners, who were themselves making excessive profits, accused the workers of lack of patriotism because, having been spurred on to greater effort, they were asking for an increase in their wages.

While the Labor Party leaders were prudently shunning the "traitor," and the masses at large were only slowly recovering from war hysteria skilfully fostered by an all-powerful press, MacDonald found some comfort in the support given him by the Independent Labor Party. Like MacDonald, the leaders of that comparatively small organization were liberal pacifists rather than radical revolutionists, opposing the war on the same grounds as he did, and continuously losing influence during 1914 and 1915. When the death of their leader, Keir Hardie, brought about a by-election, the pacifist Independent Labor Party man was left far behind, and a patriotic bitter-ender of Hyndman's Marxist organization obtained the seat. (The Marxian Socialists of the old Social Democratic Federation had undergone various splits, reorganizations and renamings since their constitution as a separate organization in 1884. During the War, Hyndman and the rest of the "Old Guard" of sedate upper-middle-class intellectuals, took an openly patriotic stand. Finding themselves opposed by an internationalist majority of the younger set of intellectuals, then somewhat influenced by syndicalist ideas, Hyndman and his friends withdrew and founded a separate organization which obtained a few seats in the House, but remained unimportant. After the War the larger section of the split organization, with another Marxian group, formed the Communist Party.)

Meanwhile, as the War dragged on, and the Russian Revolution entered its second, or Bolshevist, stage, the temper and behavior of the English working masses began to change. A growing labor unrest began to manifest itself in an increasing number of strikes. The cry for peace was growing louder, and MacDonald's voice was no longer shouted down. The Labor Party, which hitherto had not been officially committed to Socialism, adopted public ownership of industries as part of its platform. Thousands of intellectuals began to understand that at bottom socialism meant the substitution of their rule for that of the capitalists. They accordingly began to stream into the Labor Party, which now changed its constitution and opened its doors to individual membership.

Post-War Dangers

The elections which were held immediately after the conclusion of the War were entirely under the spell of the great hopes evoked by the victory. The time for MacDonald's return to political leadership had not yet come. He was not re-elected by his old constituency, and he was forced to spend the subsequent four years in helping his country to avoid the difficulties of the uncertain period of reconstruction.

Dangers were many. The workers, who had been promised so much as a result of victory, saw that in 1919 their standard of living was actually lower than in 1913. They gave vent to their dissatisfaction in many strikes and in increasing sympathy for the Communists, who had formed a party out of the merging of two Marxian groups. The Independent Labor Party, sneered at by Hyndman as a refuge of "weak brethren" and actually a rallying point of many middle-class intellectuals who had become disappointed with the Liberal Party, left the Socialist International and opened negotiations with the Communist International.* MacDonald himself paid lip-service to the great popularity achieved by Lenin: "when the tale of his errors, his evil necessities and his tyrannies has been told to the full, the balance will remain in his favor."

One of the effects of that militant mood of the workers, and particularly of those of them who had just returned from the trenches, was the granting of unemployment insurance, the much-deprecated "dole." It was the greatest single reform directly affecting the bread-and-butter status of all workers in England which had yet been achieved; and, as Lord Derby and Lloyd George declared, it was granted as an alternative to a revolution, which, after the conclusion of the War, was nearer than at any other time. Events in Russia had likewise pointed to that necessity. MacDonald needed and used all his ability to fight against this spirit of direct action, more and more pervading the masses. The books and treatises which he wrote at this time are a depository of all the stock arguments which from time immemorial have been used against revolutions in general, and particularly against revolutionary methods in a democratic country. Whatever the theoretical value of his commonplaces, they were good propaganda. Certainly they convinced the other politicians of the Labor Party, as well as all the other intelligent elements of the middle classes, that MacDonald's assistance was needed to avert a revolution in England.

For awhile, indeed, the world situation forced him into almost active defense of Soviet Russia. This was after the collapse of the White Armies, when Pilsudski invaded the Ukraine and was promptly driven back almost to the very

* Five years later, when the revolutionary wave had abated, this same Independent Labor Party concurred in excluding the Communist Party from the Labor Party.

gates of Warsaw. That turn of events had been quite unexpected, and England and France were again contemplating
intervention. Large sections of British labor took this contemplated action not as a move for the defense of Polish
"independence," but as a thrust, aimed not only at Red
Russia but also at all progress achieved by the workers in
the West. Successful intervention would have meant also a
victory of the Tory elements in general, a blow to all the
democratic hopes nourished by the advanced progressives
of the MacDonald type. From these considerations a "Committee of Action" was organized to protect Soviet Russia
against the threatened intervention, and MacDonald concurred in its activities.

Pouring Oil on Stormy Waters

At the same time serious trouble was brewing in the coal-
mining situation. The gradual decline of the British coal-
mining industry, as a result of the changes in Europe and
the general situation of the coal market, had rendered the
mine owners increasingly unyielding and aggressive in their
treatment of the workers. Between 1913 and 1915 the
miners had succeeded in arranging a fighting agreement
with the railway and transport workers. This was the so-
called "Triple Alliance."

The smoldering conflict between miners and mine owners
came to a head early in 1921. Under the Triple Alliance
agreement, the railway and transport workers were to join
the miners in their strike, and a strike of these three categories would have involved the stoppage of many other industries. The country was thus faced by a general strike, with
further developments not to be predicted. Long-drawn-out
negotiations had given the government ample opportunity
to prepare for the emergency, and when the date set for the
strike finally arrived, on April 15, 1921, the leaders of the

railway and transport workers came to the conclusion that it was safer to break their word than to risk breaking their necks. They canceled the strike. That was the famous "Black Friday" of British Labor, which became henceforth associated with the name of J. H. Thomas, leader of the railway workers, and later member of the three Cabinets formed by MacDonald.

The fighting spirit of the trade unions was not particularly enhanced by the defeat of the workers in 1921. Notwithstanding a trade-union membership of 6,505,000, four and a half millions of whom were at the same time members of the Labor Party, the leaders of the best organized working class of the world "faced facts," by accepting without a struggle almost incredible wage reductions, totaling about 500 million pounds ($2,500,000,000) a year. However, even this sad situation offered some sweet compensations. Speaking of the defeat which the miners suffered as a result of the "Black Friday" of 1921, MacDonald, in a lecture delivered to an American audience in England, remarked candidly that "the defeat of the miners in the coal lockout turned the tide toward political action. The effect has been to emphasize the political aspect, the importance of public opinion and parliamentary control. The British labor movement is at heart more political than industrial in its emphasis and it is conscious of this." Thus the efforts of the laboring masses were henceforth to be openly directed not towards better wages but towards better representatives in Parliament, with a view to establishing a "labor" government in the national administration, and "workers' control" in industry. This was certainly a nobler goal, appealing not to the base instinct of material greed but to the spiritual side of the worker, as a man and a citizen who does not live by bread alone. . . .

Disappointed in their efforts to improve their condition—or even to hold it at the former level—by the old process of industrial warfare, the workers began to listen to the siren songs of industrial pacifism and the more civilized and less costly method of war by the ballot. Over twenty years ago labor representatives in Parliament had repulsed the attacks directed by the judiciary against the unions, and they would no doubt repel the new attacks directed by employers against the workers' standard of living. There were no heretics in their midst to disillusion them. The Syndicalists had disappeared since the War. As in most other countries, the War and the Russian revolution had driven a wedge into the syndicalist ranks. One part became frightened by the responsibilities involved in a consistent abiding by their radical slogans and reverted to moderate socialism and trade unionism; another part, fascinated by the Bolshevik revolution and its international possibilities, became more or less communist in their sympathies. The Communists, on the whole, represented the younger and more impatient set of the impecunious semi-intellectuals and ex-workers. With all their militancy and revolutionary ardor, they were more interested in the political aspects of the labor movement, than in the bread-and-butter question of higher wages. The working masses, faced by two sets of competitors for their favor, both clamoring for a labor government and for workers' control, while using different terms and proposing different methods, gave their preference to those whom they had known longer, and whose method, the ballot, presented the lesser risk.

Thus the revolutionary wave, which had surged so high after the conclusion of the War, ebbed ineffectually away. During all this time MacDonald was doing his bit to pour oil on the troubled waters of social discontent and class hatred. "We are not out merely to get votes," he said, late in 1920, in a famous address, "we are out for having a very fine type of mind and character. I should like to see it that in every workshop the manager may say 'he is a perfectly honest fellow; we can trust him, he belongs to the Labor Party.' " A manager who could trust his workers because they were members of the Labor Party, would be a potential voter for, and member of, that party himself. The great dream of the Fabians of "permeating all classes with socialism" was at hand. . . .

HEAD OF THE GOVERNMENT

MacDonald was reëlected in 1922, and reinstated as head of the Parliamentary Labor Party. After another contest at the polls in 1923, he was called on by the King to form a Cabinet. There were those in his party who had some compunctions about forming a Cabinet when they had no majority in the House, believing that any measure, even remotely attacking the privilege of private property, would be defeated by their Liberal allies. But MacDonald's voice prevailed. He ridiculed the gesture, suggested by some, of proposing a socialist program in the House and going down to defeat against a combination of Conservatives and Liberals, only to appeal once more to the electorate. He did not want to call new elections on a clear-cut class or bread-and-butter issue. That was dangerous. He explained that the voters expected from them more than an empty gesture, and that there was plenty of work to do without provoking the Liberals to turn against them. He succeeded in placating the scruples of the doubters, for they wanted to be placated. They were quite confident that they could overcome the sullenness of the workers, even supposing it ever dawned upon the latter that all they had achieved with the ballot was to procure very enviable positions for a great number of organizers, journalists, lecturers, lawyers, and other representatives of the speaking and writing brotherhood. For the worker, though he may occasionally rebel, is likewise receptive to all those sentiments and arguments that make for slave psychology; and the elevation to power and opulence of his leaders arouses his admiration, rather than his envy and hatred.

The nine months during which the first Labor Cabinet was in power were marked chiefly by the recognition of the Soviet Republic. The cabinet fell on a minor issue—the actual reason being the conclusion of the treaties with Soviet Russia. In the ensuing electoral campaign, the Conservatives made skilful use of the notorious "Zinoviev letter," an obvious forgery, prepared in a sort of international factory of "documents," which eventually discredited itself by trying to involve Senator Borah as a hired tool of the Soviet Government. That "letter" contained minute instructions as to ways and means for organizing mutinies in the British army and navy.

Duped by a Conservative Foreign Office bureaucrat, who double-crossed his chief according to all the rules of old-time intrigue, MacDonald was involved in a very unpleasant exchange of notes with the Soviet Government, in which the honors were not on his side. Once more it became only too apparent that, whatever party sat in the Government benches, the real control was in the hands of a permanent Tory bureaucracy. The Labor Premier did not have the courage to fight that bureaucracy. On the contrary, though beyond any doubt stabbed in the back by his own subordinate, he felt it his duty as a "good sportsman" to cover the Tory gentleman.

The election campaign was fought on the issue raised by the "Red Letter"—the safety of the Empire, threatened by the wicked Bolsheviks. Labor was beaten, though the number of Labor votes had increased. After the striking experiment of a Labor Government in a country with a majority of industrial workers in its population, the Conservatives were still able to command enormous numbers of workmen's votes, as soon as they succeeded in putting the question of the Empire to the front.

THE GREAT STRIKE

The Labor Party was now excused for five years from Government duties. The industrial unrest, which had subsided somewhat during MacDonald's régime, broke forth again, particularly in the coal-mining industry. In the summer of 1925, in view of the exceedingly bad situation in the industry, the mine owners decided to impose a reduction of wages. As the standard of living of the miners had by that time reached the lowest level compatible with existence, the miners were ready to resist, and they had the assured support of other categories of workers. To avoid a general strike conflagration, the Baldwin government decided to offer a subsidy to the mine owners, so as to enable them to maintain the old wage scale. That subsidy was due to expire on April 30, 1926.

This victory following the mere threat of a general strike, greatly enhanced the prestige of direct action, and the whole affair greatly dismayed MacDonald. In a speech delivered before his constituency during that year he thus explained his stand with regard to the impending struggle:

"There is talk about the miners, railwaymen and engineers coming to an arrangement. No greater calamity could come over the country than that there should be raised a great block of unions on the one side and Capital on the other engaged in a great suicidal fight in industry. What I want to see is a real combination of workmen demanding their rights and doing their duty to society while they are making that demand, and so appealing to the moral and intelligent sense of society that public opinion would stand by them and see them through their difficulties. The biggest union that can support the miners is the union of public opinion and reason. I want to see every right-thinking man and woman, whether railwayman, engineer, or in any other

trade, stand by the miners in their claim for a living wage
and decent human conditions; I want to see all organs of
public opinion, the Churches and Chapels, the House of
Commons itself, stand by and see that the miner gets his due
and is not sacrificed to profit-making capitalism."

In other words, the leader of the British working class,
a former secretary of that Socialist International which
is officially arrayed against capitalism, saw the salvation of
the miners from "profit-making capitalism" only in the
Christian assistance extended to them by all the institutions
and organs of that very same "profit-making capitalism." . . .

When the term of the subsidy expired, the government
had still done nothing to put the mining industry on a more
efficient basis, so as to enable it to pay the workers a living
wage and to remain a paying proposition. Any effective
measure would have involved great expense and would have
meant pressure upon private capital and an experiment in
the direction of "Socialism," that is, State Capitalism. Instead, the government had made every preparation in case
the workers should reject the threatened wage reduction
and counter the lockout by a strike supported by other workers. Efforts on the part of the extremely moderate labor
leaders and politicians, such as MacDonald and Thomas, to
induce the government to find a middle way that would
avert the conflict, were of no avail. The general strike,
originally meant only as a threat to spur the government to
some action, as during the previous year, now became unavoidable. The Conservatives were ready for a show-down.
They were playing with fire, perhaps, but they were fairly
sure that, even if the general strike were to materialize, it
would be promptly strangled by the leaders themselves. Their
expectations were not deceived. MacDonald was a member
of the General Council in charge of the strike, as representative of the Labor Party. With Thomas, of "Black

Friday" memory, who was the actual strike leader, he was
firmly opposed to the whole enterprise. Thomas, indeed, was
so alarmed at the possibilities which the General Strike
opened up, that, during the Parliamentary debates of May
3rd, he declared: "I have never disguised that in a challenge to the Constitution, God help us, unless the Government won." Having been unable to call off the strike, as in
1921, he therefore assumed its leadership in order to break
its edge. In a similar way, Scheidemann and Ebert, by heading the "Revolution" of 1918 had saved their country from
a serious social upheaval. Thomas succeeded even better
than Scheidemann. The general strike was called off ten
days after it started, leaving the miners still in their predica-
ment.

That the leaders succeeded in calling it off without difficulties was inherent in the very nature of the strike as a
"sympathetic" strike. The "sympathetic" strikers were more
or less aware of the fact that a lowering of the miners'
standard of living meant indirectly a weakening of their own
position; but that was the concern of a more-or-less-distant
future, while the loss in wages they were suffering belonged
to the actual present. If the general strike had been accompanied by a demand for wage increases in all the trades—
that would have been a different matter. Then the workers
would have held out even against the decree of the General
Council, and a really revolutionary situation would have
followed. Such a situation could not, of course, be welcome
to the thousands of leading labor-union officials and politicians, whose standard of living differed in nothing from
that of the middle and even upper middle classes. The strike
was therefore called off before any such heretical thought
could enter the minds of the workers.

As in 1921, MacDonald did not conceal his satisfaction
over the failure of the strike. "The political Labor Party,"
he wrote after all was over, "never regarded the strike as

a political instrument. It was industrial in its conception, in its conduct, and in its close. I believe that the result will be a very strong swing on to the side of political action, and a far closer coöperation between the industrial organizations and the political one."

The benighted miners probably did not understand at first how their defeat could be conceived of as an advantage to labor and socialism. In due time, however, they saw that their only way to salvation was to return as a parliamentary majority the very men who had opposed their desperate struggle against lower wages. Such seems to be the tortuous road on which the emancipation of the working class proceeds. Continental labor leaders with a Marxian vocabulary, engaged in similar hocus-pocus, justify similar procedures as the "inevitable dialectical contradictions of the proletarian struggle for emancipation from wage slavery."

MacDonald's expectations, expressed after the General Strike of 1926, were realized. The masses actually turned once more to political action, and once more the old leader became Premier, with 287 members of Parliament and 8,300,000 votes at his back. He had still no majority, and he was probably mighty glad of it. This may sound like a paradox, but it is far from being so. Lord Birkenhead, Secretary of State for India in the Baldwin Cabinet, speaking in 1925 of the possibility of a Labor Government which should command a majority, uttered the significant words: "I venture to say quite unprovocatively and sympathetically that if and when the time comes that, with real power, our place is taken by them [Labor Party], they will retain that power only if they make themselves the mouthpiece, not of one section of English life, but of the nation as a whole, and make themselves the responsible trustees and guardians of the ordered continuity of English life."

If words mean anything, what Birkenhead intended to say was that no abrupt changes in property status would be permitted by his party, even if the Labor Party had every constitutional opportunity to decree and to effect those changes. In other words, that the Conservatives would defend their property by establishing a military dictatorship, if, under the pressure of the electorate, a Labor Cabinet attempted any nationalization schemes on a larger scale, without full compensation to the former owners, that is, in any way that would actually benefit the laboring millions.

That such was the firm determination of the Conservatives, MacDonald was fully aware even before that frank and cynical threat. About ten months before, at a time when the Labor Party was still at the helm, he declared, as if in anticipation of Birkenhead's speech, that no government is a wizard, and that even if the Labor Government carried five hundred seats at the next election, it could attempt to proceed only along the road of evolution—because it was a problem of growth and not of revolution. This, in plain English, meant that the "growth" would be a very slow process, so as not to interfere with the gentlemanly pleasures of Lord Birkenhead and his noble offspring. It explains, too, MacDonald's impatience with the left-wing war cry of "Socialism in our time," which could only give rise to unreasonable hopes and inconvenient demands on the part of the impatient multitude. . . .

When MacDonald took office as Prime Minister, the *New York Times* described his "official program" as "so moderate and cautious as hardly to be distinguished from that of the Conservatives." When the House opened, the *New York Times* thought that the King's speech sounded "almost as if it might have been written by a Tory Prime Minister." And in further reassurance: "Except for vague allusions to possible nationalization of coal-mines, there is hardly a passage which might not have done as well for the Conservative or Liberal party as for Labor."

No wonder, then, that Winston Churchill, the die-hard

firebrand, offered his "cordial coöperation in the Government's self-imposed task of carrying out the Conservatives' policy and making the world easier if not safer for capitalism." Fear of a socialist menace was thus changed into simple jealousy of a political competitor for office, particularly as this competition was gradually attracting the best Liberal talent, including some of the most prominent captains of industry.

MacDonald and the Empire

This fear has been particularly allayed by MacDonald's attitude toward the Empire. Notwithstanding theoretical protests against imperialism and the subjection of colonial peoples, the socialist parties of the world have in reality been in favor of the very policy which they denounce. They openly showed their colors at the Internationalist Socialist Congress, held at Stuttgart in 1907. On that occasion the Socialists of England, Germany, Austria, Holland and Belgium, as well as half of the French delegation—in short, those of every country which benefited by colonial exploitation—voted against a radical resolution condemning colonial exploitation. The generous gesture of renunciation was indulged in only by the socialists of those nations which had no colonies to renounce.

At the beginning of his political career, MacDonald had some qualms about the cynical endorsement of imperialism by some of the Fabians, as witnessed by Bernard Shaw's manifesto written in 1900. This was at the time when he opposed the South-African venture. Aside from other reasons already mentioned elsewhere, his disapproval might have owed something to the fact that this particular enterprise was directed against white-skinned people of the Protestant faith.

Ten years later, however, he came out openly for re-

taining the colonies—in the interest of the colonial peoples,
of course. In his book, *The Awakening of India,* written in
1910, at a time when he had already begun to see the governmental possibilities of his party, he used the century-old
arguments of all defenders of the British and other colonial
empires. "Thus," he explains, "for many a long year British
sovereignty will be necessary for India, for the warring elements in Indian life need a unifying, controlling power.
Britain is the nurse of India. Deserted by her guardian,
India would be the prey of disruptive elements within herself as well as the victim of her own too enthusiastic worshippers, to say nothing of what would happen to her from
incursions from the outside." On the eve of his accession to
power in 1924 he warned the Hindu Nationalists that "no
party in Britain will be cowed by threats of force or by
policies designed to bring government to a standstill. If any
Indian sections are under the delusion that that is not so,
events will sadly disappoint them." And six years later, in
1930, the head of the British Labor Government broad-
casted into the universe the following defense of British
past and present policies of conquest and oppression: "We
have not only planted colonies and founded nations, but
we have undertaken the care of people who could not take
care of themselves. They were doomed to civil war or
to systems of government which cut them off from the benefits of civilization. We have duties regarding them. We must
see, so far as we are able, that weakness on our part or a
too ready withdrawal of the guardianship we have assumed
does not abandon them, so they relapse into the conditions
from which our intervention rescued them."

The fact that India has a more than sufficient number of
native English-bred intellectuals, who could "take care of
themselves" and of their country just as well as MacDonald's
Labor Party intellectuals have been taking care of the
United Kingdom, does not impress the British defenders

of the underdog, probably because those swarthy sons of
India . . . are not Socialists. No wonder that shortly after
the Labor victory of 1923, Lord Birkenhead, in congratulat-
ing his opponents, called them "the trustees of the majestic
fabric of the British Empire" to whom the Conservative
lord and the rest of England owed a "debt of gratitude." . . .

In speaking of this "debt of gratitude" the noble lord
apparently anticipated MacDonald's attitude towards Egypt,
Mexico and China, the air-bombing of Mesopotamian villages for a refusal to pay taxes, the imprisonment of over
25,000 persons in India, and similar measures of most ruthless repression, dictated by the lofty principles of "Socialism" and "Labor."

In this connection one recalls the resolution protesting
against the oppression of colonial peoples submitted at a
conference of the Labor Party held in 1923. MacDonald
then pointed out that, as the Labor Party was fighting for
the oppressed peoples anyhow, there was no sense in wasting the time of the Conference on that subject. That was
exactly one year before the Mesopotamian villages were
visited by MacDonald's tax-collecting bombing planes. Yet
the Labor Party, and particularly Ramsay MacDonald, have
all the time actually been champions of the oppressed peoples.
To this day, MacDonald never loses an opportunity to protest against Bolshevik occupation of the Caucasian republic
of Georgia, which, after the establishment of the Soviet
régime, seceded from Russia and formed a Menshevik
Republic, under British tutelage. The occupation of that
territory by the Red Army, effected in 1921, was a painful
blow to British hopes. Here was a very important territory
with the greatest manganese deposits in the world, a natural
outlet for Soviet oil, which was due to become, if not the
most precious jewel in the British crown, then at least a
very effective British gun in the ribs of Soviet Russia. And

as matters turned out, England had to be satisfied with nothing more than the addition of a very remarkable stamp to the famous collection of her King: a stamp with the imprint, "Batum British Occupation." Batum is the chief port of Georgia. . . .

In a moment of impatience, Snowden, then second only to MacDonald in the councils of the Labor Party, once declared that no such thing as independence of colonies was possible, since if one country released them from its grip, another country would take them. That was the reason, as some Soviet journalists maliciously suspected, why the British Laborites insisted upon the independence of Georgia from Russia. . . .

The British Worker's Burden

While MacDonald was engrossed in international relations and in affairs of Empire, the situation of the manual workers kept growing steadily worse, with wages shrinking and the number of unemployed increasing. To inquiries concerning the unemployment situation, the Labor Government continued to use the familiar answer, found so unsatisfactory by Labor representatives when given by their Conservative predecessors in office. This stock answer never so much as hinted at any thorough-going reform, such as a scheme of industrial or agricultural nationalization, which would provide work for the unemployed and mark a radical departure in the country's progress toward government ownership. Any suggestion of this kind would, of course, have brought about an immediate downfall of the government, and that was not exactly what MacDonald and his friends wanted. Instead one hears Miss Bondfield, of MacDonald's Cabinet, suggesting that the unemployed cotton mill girls become servants, with the alternative of losing the "dole." In a country where the workers are the "ruling class," the

socialist government had become an employment agency to
find domestics for the idle rich! The jest goes even beyond
that whimsy of Aristophanes which pictures the socialist intelligentsia of his time demanding nationalization of the
slaves—a very important property item of the Greek city.
At the same time, another Cabinet member, the former en-
gine-driver, James Thomas (with an annual salary of $25,-
000 and a handsome private fortune), sat in a meeting of
manufacturers and scolded the workers for taking the "dole"
that "destroys and saps the independent spirit." And it was
Philip Snowden, Labor Chancellor of the Exchequer, who,
on another occasion, actually suggested that for the salvation of British industries, "wage reductions may possibly
be necessary."

Impatient elements in MacDonald's party occasionally
kicked over the traces. The prominent members of the
younger set were anxious about the future of their party,
whose reputation among the workers began to suffer. Mac-
Donald countered their criticism in 1930, by severing his
relations with the Independent Labor Party, that nursery
for the future leaders of the Labor Party, to which he had
belonged for thirty-six years. He had grown impatient and
contemptuous with dissenters. He knew that theirs was the
spurious radicalism of the young who coveted the positions
of the elder statesmen, but who were afraid to take any
determined step. Was it not James Maxton himself, Chairman of the Independent Labor Party, and firebrand leader
of "red" Clydeside, who at the Labor Party convention,
held late in 1930, had helped to defeat a motion of censure
against MacDonald?

Thus no real principle was involved in all this internal
opposition. Indeed, MacDonald and his party had only one
guiding "principle"—to attain and to hold power against
the other parties and against competitors within their own
ranks. Although a champion of "democracy" and "political

justice" MacDonald has consistently opposed proportional representation with an elaborate set of rationalizing arguments—simply ·because the present, highly undemocratic, electoral system, has seemed likely to give him a bigger following in the House than any other system. A humanitarian with the loftiest ideas, he has maintained such venerable institutions of old England as the whipping post and the jail for debtors, both abolished in practically all civilized countries of the world. A secularist, he makes concessions to the Roman Church in the matter of school control, in order to keep the support of the forty Catholic members of the Labor Party, who take their instructions from the Vatican. A socialist and a pacifist, he yields to powerful capitalist interests and rejects the project of a Channel Tunnel on the ground that the steamship companies engaged in Channel traffic would suffer heavy losses, and that there would be no compensating military advantage. With Sidney Webb, an advocate of the removal of "passport barriers," he rejects Trotsky's plea for a political asylum in order not to expose himself to any anti-Bolshevist mudslinging on the part of his opponents; though before the "war for democracy" both Conservative and Liberal governments granted hospitality to political murderers like the Russian terrorist, Stepniak, and to anarchist conspirators like Malatesta. Leader of a party that has been built up by the trade unions, he openly comes out against the only effective weapon of the laboring masses, saying, for instance, in the preface to *Socialism: Critical and Constructive,* that "strikes for higher wages and shorter hours not only do not lead to socialism but are liable to bring the socialist movement on the wrong path." An enemy of dictatorship and of the personal régime, he keeps important matters of state to himself, withholding them from his Labor Cabinet members as if they were untrustworthy, talkative underlings. Son of a farm laborer and spokesman of the underdog, in his personal contacts he puts on the forbidding aristocratic airs of a Lord Curzon.

In the course of 1931, the financial situation of Great Britain became desperate and humiliating in the extreme. As if the general depression were not bad enough, the British banks light-heartedly engaged the country's finances by reckless speculation with money borrowed from abroad. England's honor and the gold standard were at stake. The situation called for such heroic remedies as are applied at great historic moments, and the two financially soundest countries of the world are reported to have suggested these remedies: a reduction of the insurance benefits of the unemployed and a general lowering of the workers' standard of living. MacDonald took the advice, or obeyed the command —and took it for granted that a very substantial section of his party would follow his lead. But of the hundred labor members he expected to join him, all but a few shrunk back. To use a mixed metaphor, it was a case of Judas betrayed by his brethren. Not that they had the interests of the workers more at heart than he did, but such an obvious and sudden lowering of the workers' living standard might have jeopardized their chances of reëlection and their whole standing as politicians and labor leaders.

The last-minute refusal of the Labor Party to follow MacDonald, and even the sonorous radical phrases of its election appeals, did not save it from disaster. That disaster, though not to such a catastrophic extent, would have come even if its former chief had not become an open agent for the Conservatives. The Labor electorate had hoped for better things from its own government after more than two years of office-holding, than a continuous reduction of its standard of living. That electorate, in its simplicity, believed that the men it had entrusted with defending its interests might have done something more than merely hold their jobs. Maybe it expected at least a defiant gesture against the combined representatives of Liberal and Conservative capital; a gesture which would have defeated them in the House but which might have led to a real struggle outside the House. When that unavoidable defeat in the House finally came, three of Labor's foremost leaders were in the camp of the enemy, and all the issues were confused. In a controversy over technical questions of higher finance, which they could not possibly understand, large sections of labor preferred to listen to the man who so persuasively displayed the bogey of inflation; his former comrades-in-arms offered only empty promises which had lost all lustre.

No doubt MacDonald feels himself fully justified in choosing the course he has taken. Any other, in his opinion, was bound to lead to grave domestic conflicts, endangering the normal "biological" process of the country's development:

That "biological" process implying, though with a new vocabulary, the firm maintenance of the good old principle set forth in Menenius Agrippa's immortal fable about the indispensable harmony between the working limbs and the digesting belly.

LEON TROTSKY

OR

Grandeur and Misery of Power

S ENSITIVE souls in both hemispheres have found in Trotsky's fall from power a subject for melancholy meditation. They have expatiated upon the ingratitude of revolutions which devour their own children, the mercilessness of human hatreds and jealousies, and the fleeting character of popular favor. Generous as these sentiments may be, the famous exile has certainly nothing but contempt for them. A realist, he sees human history not as material for moral tales in which virtue triumphs and wickedness is punished at the end, but as a perfectly amoral succession of struggles for material comforts and power, between classes, cliques and leaders. In such a combat no quarter is given, and its inexorable rules hold good for revolutions as well as for other mass tragedies of the human race. Having lost the game, he probably consoles himself with the thought that historical figures like Danton and Napoleon, to whom he has often been compared, have likewise succumbed to men of lesser merit—for not even defeat has shaken his self-confidence.

Trotsky's life is a striking episode in the century-long fight of Russia's educated classes for the westernizing of their country. This struggle began early in the nineteenth century, when the hosts of Napoleon carried in their wake the gospel of more efficient, more intelligent methods of ruling a world, then entering upon the stage of industrialism. In the Russia of a century ago a group of young officers, and a few high-minded intellectuals, all recruited from the landed nobility, appeared as carriers of the ideal of a national renaissance. This was then practically the only group with a modern education, a civilized outlook, and a deep resentment at the contempt in which their country was being held, regarded as it was as a sort of extension of Asiatic barbarism. These aristocratic rebels—after their ill-fated revolt attempted in December, 1825, they were called Decembrists—were not unanimous as to their aim. Some of them wanted a constitutional monarchy, while others believed in a military dictatorship, revolutionary in scope, preliminary to the establishment of a republic. They paid dearly for their patriotic daring, and it took nearly a hundred years before Russia rid herself of the nightmare of Tsarism.

The revolutionary torch wrung from the hands of the liberal officers was taken up by the intellectuals. These were still, for the most part, descendants of the nobility who were being trained to become the bureaucrats of a medieval State, or molders of the minds of the next generation of bureaucrats and officers. Time and again, the most brilliant members of that group, after visiting Western Europe or getting indirectly acquainted with western political and philosophical ideas, came out in favor of political and social reform. Circles discussing western socialist ideas were formed secretly, and their participants were brutally punished upon discovery. With the progress of economic development, the circle of the intelligentsia widened. It began to include a growing number of commoners from the middle and lower middle classes. Too weak for an open revolt, out of touch with the masses—whom only the reactionary clergy were able to approach—the great majority of the intellectuals found escape from, and a compensation for, their political humiliation, in philosophical speculation, with an iconoclastic rejection of all accepted values. Groups of conspirators flared up sporadically and disappeared again.

In the meantime, economic factors were causing deep general dissatisfaction. The insufficiency of the peasants' land allotments after their "liberation" from serfdom in 1861, coupled with their excessive tax-burdens, as well as crop failures and famines in several sections of the country, drove home the necessity of thorough changes. Other motive forces were the extremely reactionary, obscurantist educational policy of the government, on the one hand, and the great revolutionary ferment called forth all over the civilized world by the revolt of the Paris Commune of 1871, on the other.

The university students now became the banner bearers of discontent for all those sections of the educated classes which were not directly interested in maintaining special privileges enjoyed under the Tsarist system. In the early seventies, thousands of young students who had become acquainted with western ideas at the universities of Switzerland and France, formed an impressive army of apostles who "went among the people" to raise the cultural level of the peasantry and to spur them on to revolt. Their ideology called "narodnichestvo" ("populism") was a more or less genuine Russian product. It was a hazy anarchoid socialism, to a large extent inspired by the ideas of Michael Bakunin, with his postulate of an immediate abolition of the State and the establishment of free communes. It likewise included the ideas of the revolutionary philosopher Peter Lavrov, who spoke of the "debt" which the educated classes owed to the masses whose toil had enabled them to partake in all the benefits of intellectual progress. At the bottom of it all was a mystic faith that the quasi-collective character of Russian rural land-holding—it was in reality a bureaucratic device to simplify the payment of taxes—would enable Russia to pass over to socialism without the intermediary stage of capitalism. Generous and naïve as these theoretical formulations were, they concealed the uncon-

scious desire for a democratic peasants' republic, in which
the intellectuals would be the advisers and organizers or,
to put it more bluntly, the new ruling class. . . .

The students' crusade "among the people" turned out to
be a tragic failure. The Russian peasants, who had risen in
formidable insurrections during the seventeenth and eighteenth centuries under leaders of their own, did not take
kindly to the generous and unsophisticated youths who came
to them from the outside. The moujiks distrusted their attacks against the Tsar, suspecting some devilish machina-
tion on the part of the landed nobility to restore serfdom
which had been abolished in the early sixties. More often
than not the peasants themselves arrested the students and
delivered them to the authorities of their Tsar.

Having learned their lesson, Russia's educated youth
turned from cultural, propagandist and insurrectional activity among the peasants to a more heroic, if less ambitious,
struggle. They became "Liberals with a bomb" and engaged
in a direct terrorist combat against the Tsar aiming at the
very prosaic goal of political democracy.

The main plank of the "Will of the People"—as they
called their terrorist organization—demanded a Constituent
Assembly. This was to convene after the overthrow of the
Tsarist régime, and would, they hoped, carry out the popular socialist ideals propagated by them during the earlier
period. Made bolder by that mortal combat, the terrorists
for awhile contemplated the conquest of power by their
party alone, that is, a sort of revolutionary dictatorship that
would carry out the necessary economic changes before calling a popular assembly. Unlike the Bolsheviks of a generation later—who based their hopes upon an armed uprising of
the working masses led by an organization of professional
revolutionists—the "Will of the People" relied exclusively
upon the terrorist efforts of a few hundred determined conspirators, supported by the sympathy of the intelligentsia

LEON TROTSKY

and the Liberal bourgeoisie. Later, however, when Tsarism showed a greater power of resistance than they had anticipated, they were ready to be content even with a constitutional monarchy—upon the introduction of which they would have become perfectly respectable Liberals-without-a-bomb. . . .

THE NEW IDEOLOGY

Leon Trotsky was born in 1879, and his childhood fell in the period when that heroic band of terrorists, mistakenly called "Nihilists," was bleeding to death under the counter-blows of the Tsarist authorities. He was eight years old, when Lenin's older brother, Alexander Ulianov, was tried and executed for an attempt on the life of the Tsar—the last effort of the terrorist struggle which had begun nearly a decade before. From the ashes of "populism"—both in its vaguely anarchist aspect of the early seventies and in its terrorist and purely political aspect of the late seventies and early eighties—a new revolutionary ideology began to take shape in the minds of the Russian intelligentsia. This was Marxism, and it emphasized the inevitability of capitalist development and of class struggle of the industrial workers, as preliminary conditions for the overthrow of the Tsarist system. George Plekhanov, a former "populist," became the theoretical founder of the Marxist school in Russia and the teacher and spiritual father of generations of Russian intellectuals. It was he who launched the henceforth famous war-cry—"the revolution in Russia will succeed as a working-class revolution, or it will not succeed," calling on the Russian workers to accomplish in Russia the counterpart of the French bourgeois revolution, since their own bourgeoisie was too weak for the task. When speaking about it to the workers, however, the Russian intellectuals preferred to use the expression "political revolution" or "democratic revolution." This was less explicit, but sounded better than "bourgeois revolution" for which the workers might not feel the same degree of enthusiasm. . . .

As the son of a prosperous Jewish farmer, the future organizer of the Red Army did not have to taste the misery of the Jewish lower-middle classes, from which so many revolutionary intellectuals were recruited. Nor did he have in his own family the ever-present memory of a brother who had been hanged for the cause of progress, as was the case with young Ulianov-Lenin. But he was a member of that fortunate race which, as a convenient scapegoat for the various ills racking the country, had incurred every refinement of religious, racial, economic and political sadism which a government steeped in oriental medievalism could devise. Was it not Pobiedonostzev, the Procurator of the Holy Synod and foremost ideological spokesman of the Tsarist system, who cynically suggested as a radical solution of the Jewish problem, that one-third of them be forced to leave the country, another third constrained to accept the blessings of the Gospel of Love, and the remainder left to starve? The educated Jew, unless he happened to be born in the family of a very rich business man, had no peaceful avenue of escape except through conversion, emigration, or Zionist dreams of future Palestinian grandeur—various forms of resignation to fate. But if he had a mind to fight, there was still another way to preserve his self-respect as a man and to defend his interests as an intellectual. He could join the forces of opposition. These were of various shades —from the moderate Liberalism of the successful lawyer and physician, to the "Populist" or Marxian socialism of the students and lower-middle-class intellectuals. The result was that the Jewish intellectuals—along with those of the other oppressed nationalities, such as the Poles, Ukrainians, Letts, Georgians, and Armenians—made up a considerable part of the revolutionary forces.

In his autobiography Leon Trotsky says frankly, "racial

discrimination has probably given a subconscious stimulus to
my dissatisfaction with the existing régime," though he
denies that this was a determining factor. There is hardly
a doubt that the racial humiliations of his school years have
contributed more than he realizes, in stimulating his spirit
of revolt, his ambition and his will to power.

While Trotsky was still in his teens, the radical spirit of
general dissatisfaction with the Tsarist régime that pervaded all educated classes, merged with his Jewish woe into
what he believed to be "sympathy for the down-trodden and
indignation against injustice." That it was in the main sympathy with, and indignation over, his own hopeless situation, as a budding middle-class intellectual with scant prospects in a world of medievalism and privilege, he has never
realized.

At the time when the seventeen-year-old youth graduated
from high school, Russia's political life was beginning to
recover from the stupor and passivity into which it had been
plunged after the bloody suppression of the revolutionary
movement in the early eighties. The labor movement, incipient in the seventies, had shown its latent force and
possibilities throughout the eighties and the nineties, when
spontaneous mass strikes for higher wages broke out in
Petersburg and Moscow. The radical intelligentsia, who for
more than a decade had been lying low, began to feel the
coming of a new day. That new day was to belong to those
who turned their eyes towards the industrial worker, yesterday a peasant, but now alert, combative and eager to throw
off the age-old prejudices and superstitions by which his older
brother in the village seemed still hopelessly befogged.

The Russian following of Marx was a variegated company. There were respectable scholars like Peter Struve,
Bulgakov, and Tugan-Baranovsky, who quite intelligently
acclaimed Marxism as the theoretical justification for Russia's entrance upon the road of capitalist development. These

were the representatives of the so-called "legal Marxism," the Marxism of the university professors. There were the theorists Plekhanov and Axelrod, living in Switzerland, who nearly fifteen years before had set forth the gospel of Marx with more ardor than success. There was too, a galaxy of younger intellectuals—already considered as "old men" because they were nearly thirty—still active "underground," but soon to be arrested. The most outstanding of these were Julius Zederbaum, who, later, under the name of Martov, became the most brilliant leader of the Mensheviks, and Vladimir Ulianov—a man of many aliases, the most enduring of which was Lenin—whose future greatness the Marxian elders had even then·begun to sense and to fear.

Last, but not least, there were a number of influential heretics known under the name of "Economists," who for the present and the near future advocated exclusive emphasis upon the industrial, or as the Russians say, the "economic" struggle for higher wages and shorter hours. They believed that in order to win the confidence of the workers it was necessary, for the time being, to disregard all other issues— such as propaganda for socialist principles or the political struggle against absolutism—leaving politics to the Liberal bourgeoisie. They argued that until the workers had found out that it was impossible to obtain any improvements under the Tsarist system, the time was not ripe for open politico-revolutionary activity. It was a subtle plan, but the other Marxists sensed danger in it. Without speaking it out in so many words, they realized that the workers, fighting for higher wages only, and ignorant of any political issues, might eventually get out of hand; the movement might lead to wild, chaotic wage revolts, in the course of which the workers would be more anxious to force as much as possible from their employers, than to obtain for the latter a more civilized form of government. Or if, in the course of the fight, the Tsarist government should find it expedient to

grant political liberties, the workers, having obtained the
right to organize, might become steeped in non-political
trade-unionism, pure and simple. In any case the socialist
intelligentsia which sought political influence and power,
would come out empty-handed.

Such was the situation of the revolutionary forces when in
1898, at a conference composed of nine delegates who assembled at Minsk, the "Social-Democratic Labor Party"
was constituted. It included the various revolutionary groups
that took their inspiration from Marx.

His First Revolutionary Steps

At the time when preparations were being made for organizing the Social-Democratic Labor Party, young Bron-
stein, who a few years later was to assume the name of
Trotsky, was weighing the old ideology of "Populism"
against the new, of Marxism. The swing was towards the
new faith, and at the age of eighteen, during his last year
in school, spent in Nikolayev on the Black Sea, he was
actively engaged in underground propaganda with its excit-
ing accompaniments—secret meetings, hectographed leaflets
and assumed names.

It is interesting to note that, as Trotsky himself recounts,
the workers who were interested in his propaganda were
mostly highly skilled mechanics, earning good wages, who
were not so much interested in striking as in the "truth in
social relations." One senses here that element—the highest
stratum of the manual-working class—part of which, after
the revolution, was to combine with the *déclassé* intelligentsia in taking charge of the country and forming a large
percentage of the new bureaucracy.

Young "Lvov" (his first alias) was the leader of his local
group and the author of its "literature." He had practically
broken with his well-to-do father and was making a living

by tutoring; with a number of other congenial boys he "lived a Spartan life, without linen, nourished on soups cooked by ourselves."

A few months of activity, and then came the fate of every "underground" militant—he was arrested along with a great number of his friends and comrades. After two and a half years of imprisonment, during which he read voraciously, he was finally sentenced to four years banishment to Eastern Siberia.

His newly acquired faith in Marxism did not remain unchallenged during his exile. Criticism from socialist "Revisionists" and from downright bourgeois adversaries could easily be dismissed. A young rebel suffering for his cause is not likely to succumb to counsels of moderation. But in Siberia he stumbled upon a truly disconcerting critic from the Left. This was Waclaw Machajski, an exile like himself, but banished to a still more distant region in the Northeast.

As a conscientious journalist and historian, Trotsky refers to that critic—whom incidentally he never met personally—both in his autobiography and in his book on Lenin. But the short reference to an obscure Polish "Anarchist"—for Trotsky considered it necessary to classify him under one of the old political categories—does not do justice to a man who created a marked sensation among Russia's revolutionary intelligentsia of the early years of this century.

Waclaw Machajski (his pen-name was A. Wolski) had paid with ten years of prison and exile in Siberia for his early activities as a revolutionary Marxist in Poland. During the last years of his banishment in the frozen wastes he developed a theory of his own, which went as far beyond that of his original revolutionary creed as Marx's Socialism went beyond his democratic Liberalism of the early forties. In Machajski's conception, the socialist theories of the nineteenth century expressed the interests of the intellectual

workers—not those of the working class, in which he placed
the manual workers only. The mental workers, he argued,
were a rising privileged class, fighting for a place in the sun
against the old privileged classes, the landed owners and
capitalists. Higher education was their specific "capital"—
the source of their actual or potential higher incomes. Political democracy (or a revolutionary dictatorship, according to circumstances) was the first, and State Capitalism the
next, step to their domination. To achieve these objects
they needed the support of the manual workers. The confidence of the latter they won by helping them in their early
struggles for better wages and by dangling before them
the socialist ideal of equality. That socialist Beyond was
meant only as propaganda, as a sort of proletarian religion
—not as an object of struggle for the living generation.
The socialism which the radical intelligentsia really aspired
to was nothing but State Capitalism: a system of government ownership, under which private capitalists would have
yielded place to office-holders, managers, engineers; the coming form of exploitation, in which the intellectual workers
receiving higher salaries than those paid for manual labor,
would constitute the new and only ruling class, absorbing
into their ranks the former capitalists and the self-taught
ex-workers.

As a champion of the manual workers, particularly the
unskilled and the unemployed, he advocated revolutionary
mass struggle for higher wages and government provision
for the unemployed, as the only issues of actual interest to
the working class. The leadership of that struggle he visual-
ized in the hands of an international secret organization of
revolutionists. Engaged exclusively in unifying, and in extending the scope of, the spontaneous uprisings of the
manual workers and of the unemployed, this organization
"would dictate the law to the governments," using the
weapon of "world-wide strikes." In other words, it would

force the privileged classes and their governments to provide either work or support for the unemployed and to grant
sweeping increases in the wages of the manual workers.
Elimination of private capitalist profits, automatic transition
to State Capitalism, and finally equalization of the incomes
of the manual workers with those of the new rulers would
be the progressive steps of the revolutionary mass struggle.
Equality of income would secure to all an equal opportunity
for higher education and thus would do away with all class
divisions. The function of government having ceased to
be the privilege of an educated minority, the State as an
instrument of oppression and exploitation would disappear.
Marx considered that exploitation ceased with the disappearance of the private capitalists. In Machajski's opinion
the Marxian scheme of eliminating capitalists but maintaining higher rewards for mental than for manual labor
would "substitute for the capitalists a class of hereditary
soft-handed intellectuals, who would perpetuate the slavery
of the manual workers and of their offspring."

Machajski's ideas gained some converts * among his fellow exiles. The majority of the latter, however, including
young Bronstein-Trotsky, though impressed at first by these
theories, were mainly shocked. Machajski ignored the struggle for power as a mere family quarrel within the educated
classes and reduced the rôle of the revolutionary intellectual,
if he wanted to join in, to that of a disinterested champion
of the workers' bread-and-butter demands, leaving no place
for his political ambitions. . . .

* The revolutionary years of 1905-06 saw the formation, in Russia and
Poland of a few groups inspired by Machajski's ideas. But, as if in
tragic-ironic confirmation of his own theory, he never succeeded in
winning an important number of active revolutionists. Their interests as
intellectuals (or semi-educated workers with the prospects of becoming
intellectuals) were better served by the old-time revolutionary ideologies.
Machajski and his followers were, however, full of hope. They believed
that the working class would inevitably become disillusioned with the
various socialist schools and would eventually force many of their old
leaders to change their course.

Among the Elders

In 1902 Leon Trotsky escaped from Siberia, made a round of various cities to acquaint himself with the situation of the revolutionary movement, and finally crossed the Austrian frontier. This was not an easy task, for the high-school boy who was in charge of the underground railway for revolutionary fugitives nearly balked when he found out that his charge was a political opponent. This political purist belonged to the Socialist-Revolutionist * Party and was accordingly a mortal enemy of all Social-Democrats, such as Trotsky. The Socialist-Revolutionists were the successors of the terrorist "Will of the People" of twenty years before. They placed their hope for the success of the Revolution in the terrorist activities of their fighting organization, and in the pressure of the intelligentsia and the peasantry. Like their predecessors of the early eighties, they were at bottom "Liberals with a bomb," and as the party of the peasantry, they were rivals for power of the Social-Democratic Labor Party, representing that section of the revolutionary intelligentsia whose strength lay chiefly in the support of the industrial workers.

When the young fugitive reached London, he found himself immediately in the intellectual center of the Social-Democratic Labor Party, including the finest spirits of the Marxist intelligentsia. There was, first of all, Lenin, little over thirty, but already a seasoned revolutionary thinker and leader; a man of one idea and one passion, thoroughly convinced that his was the only way to carry the revolution to a victorious conclusion and taking his own supreme leadership as a matter of course. A man of no doubts, to whom other men were hardly more than robots for the revolution,

---

* Their official name was "Socialists-Revolutionists." They are usually referred to as "Social Revolutionists," or, in abbreviation as "Esers."

working in unison under the instructions of the all-powerful engineer. He fascinated the younger generation, but he was quite naturally disliked by the elders—the Marxian veterans, particularly George Plekhanov and Paul Axelrod, who heretofore had been the traditional revolutionary mentors. To them, at best, Lenin was the future Robespierre of the Russian Revolution; at worst, an unscrupulous fanatic with Bonapartist propensities. At the opposite extreme from Lenin, was Julius Martov, the future leader of the Mensheviks, brilliant and learned, but lacking Lenin's sacred fire of fanaticism and unshaken self-confidence. The older generation was represented by Vera Zasulich, not less brilliant than heroic, who in 1878 had fired the first shot in the terrorist struggle against the Tsarist government and a few years later had become a convert and apostle of Marxism. A little later, after the party headquarters had been transferred to Switzerland, Trotsky came into closer contact with Plekhanov and Axelrod.

THE SPLIT

Young Trotsky's literary and oratorical abilities were soon appreciated by his elders. He was permitted to write for their organ, the *Iskra* ("Spark"), as famous in the history of Russian revolutionary thought since 1900, as was the *Liberator* at the time of Abolitionism. He was sent as a lecturer to various capitals of the Continent, wherever Russian students were expected to be won over by his oratory. The following year was fateful in the history of Russian Marxian Socialism. The contradictions smoldering within the organization blazed out at the party conference in 1903, which was followed by a split. Henceforth there was no longer a united Social Democratic Labor Party but two separate camps; the majority faction of the Bolsheviks and the minority faction of the Mensheviks. That split, which grew

deeper and deeper as time went on, was caused by questions
of organization rather than of principles or tactics. Both factions believed in Marxian principles; they agreed in advocating a revolutionary political struggle to establish a democratic form of government, with socialism as an ideal of
the distant future only. They disagreed on the question of
party membership and authority. In his book, *What is to be
done?* published in 1902, Lenin had laid down his specific
conception of the methods of revolutionary activity. The
crucial point in his argument was his insistence upon the
great importance of a body of professional revolutionists,
to conduct the whole movement in an efficient manner. With
this insistence was connected his belief in the necessity of
recognizing as party members only those who were also
actual members of the secret organizations in Russia. This
would leave out all those middle-of-the-road sympathizers
from among the bourgeois intellectuals—professional men,
students, and high-school boys alike—who had not the
courage to burn their bridges and risk everything. In Lenin's opinion this course would avoid the danger of swamp-
ing the party with weak-kneed adherents who would dampen
its combative spirit.

From this point of view, Lenin insisted also upon the
greatest possible extension of the powers given to the Central Committee of the party, which was to direct all revolutionary activities. These powers were to include that of
confirming the personnel of local committees, and even of
nominating their members. Except for Plekhanov, who for
awhile sided with Lenin, all the members of the editorial
board of *Iskra* came out against these proposals, which
they condemned as "Blanquist." Instead of a movement
based on mass support, they asserted, Lenin wanted an organization of conspirators—his attitude implying a belief
that revolutions could be planned in advance—as opposed
to the Marxist point of view that revolutions occurred but

were not made. Some of Lenin's opponents, indeed, went so far as to call his postulates Bonapartist, because, if carried out, his scheme would have concentrated all the power in his own hands.

When the split occurred, Leon Trotsky joined the Mensheviks. He was bound to Martov by strong ties of personal admiration and friendship. He was particularly attached to the two veterans, Vera Zasulich and Paul Axelrod, and he was highly indignant at Lenin's demand that they be removed from the editorial board of the *Iskra*. He admitted no necessity for a centralization of power behind which he was inclined to suspect Lenin's ambition for personal dictatorship, and he bitterly denounced that ambition. Thus, in 1904, he wrote that for the dictatorship of the proletariat, Lenin wished to substitute the dictatorship of the party over the proletariat; for the dictatorship of the party, the dictatorship of the Central Committee over the party; and for the dictatorship of the Central Committee, the dictatorship of Lenin over the Central Committee.

The Revolution of 1905

In the meantime the signs of an approaching revolution were multiplying. In 1903 a general strike hurricane swept Southern Russia, from the oil fields of Baku to the industrial centers of the Ukraine. The strikes were spontaneous in character, with higher wages as their objective. The various groups of the socialist intelligentsia were amazed and thoroughly displeased. The Socialists-Revolutionists, who had been all along dealing one terrorist blow after another to the various Tsarist ministers and governors, forgot their irreconcilable hostility to the system and expressed satisfaction whenever they saw the movement proceeding as mildly as possible. The Social-Democrats took a similar attitude. They found the "news from the South not particu-

larly cheerful." * because the movement "did not assume a
sufficiently conscious-political tinge." A revolt in which the
workers were asking for higher wages only could be of no
particular interest to the revolutionary intelligentsia—
whether it took its inspiration from the "native" socialism
of the "Populists" or from the western socialism of Marx.
In their eyes, it could only retard the real, the political, revolution. Being directed against the capitalists, it was likely to
frighten the liberal bourgeoisie and drive them into the arms
of Tsarist political reaction. Lacking leadership, that great
mass movement soon ebbed away. Had the Socialists of
various denominations made themselves the spokesmen of
the wage demands of the masses already in revolt, the movement, as it developed, would have swept away the Tsarist
system. But a revolution, started under such auspices would
have exceeded the limits of a strictly bourgeois revolution. It
might have developed into a real working-class revolution
engulfing in its continuously growing wage demands the
incomes of all those who were better off than the manual
workers. That was not the aim of the revolutionary intelligentsia, who simply wanted to be one of the several dominant groups in a westernized capitalist Russia. . . .

In the year following the great Southern strike, came
the war with Japan. A wave of discontent began to shake
the whole country—and this time the liberal bourgeoisie
and the students led in protest against the Tsarist system.
Political revolution now seemed at hand. The Socialist-Revolutionists increased their terrorist activities. The Mensheviks began to dream of a Revolution which would bring the
Liberals into power, with the Socialists as a law-abiding
parliamentary opposition party. A government by the Liberal Party was in their opinion the only solution under
the prevailing economic conditions. Lenin's solution was dif-

* Quoted from A. Wolski's (W. Machajski), *The Mental Worker*,
Part III. Geneva, 1905.

ferent: history had taught him that the liberal bourgeoisie was too pusillanimous, too cowardly, to take the energetic measures needed to hold what had been won. The forces of reaction, in his opinion, were bound to come back—as they had done in Western Europe in 1848—if the Liberals were left to defend the political achievements of the Revolution. His way out was a "democratic dictatorship of the proletariat and the peasantry." These two classes must assume power and by ruthless measures destroy all vestiges of Tsarism and render its return impossible. This, however, was not to be a social revolution. The "proletariat and the peasantry" were to exert their dictatorship only for the purpose of establishing an honest-to-goodness bourgeois-democratic system on the Western-European model. The only social difference would be that the big land-holders, the mainstay of absolutism, would be abolished and their land distributed among the peasantry. The capitalists, too, would be forced to make some concessions to the workers. Stripped of its specific terminology, the Bolshevik program of that period called for the destruction of Tsarist power and the establishment of a coalition government composed of representatives of the Bolshevik intelligentsia, controlling the industrial workers, and the Socialist-Revolutionist intelligentsia, speaking for the peasantry.

At last the Revolution broke out early in 1905; but it offered no opportunity for applying either the Menshevik formula of helping the establishment of a bourgeois-liberal régime or the Bolshevik "democratic dictatorship" of the radical intelligentsia.

Of all the active and well-known revolutionists then living abroad, Trotsky was one of the first to return to Russia. The young orator went to Kiev, in the Ukraine, at first, moving under assumed names from one hiding-place to another, writing revolutionary appeals, and having them printed in a secret printing plant. From Kiev he went to Petersburg, where he was likewise forced to live "illegally"—that is, under an assumed name. He belonged neither to the Mensheviks nor to the Bolsheviks, but entertained friendly relations with both. He had left the Mensheviks shortly after he had joined them, for he objected both to their conciliatory attitude towards the Liberals, and to their coolness toward the idea of a reunion with the Bolsheviks. Arrests among his Menshevik friends caused him to go for awhile to Finland which, though connected with the Russian Empire, enjoyed a certain freedom from police surveillance. During that interval of quiet he worked out his famous theory of the "Permanent Revolution."

This theory held that the Russian revolution could not remain purely democratic in scope. The revolutionary government, Trotsky believed, would be obliged to make substantial concessions to the workers, such as providing for the unemployed and taking over those industries whose owners refused the demands of the striking workers. He assumed that the peasant party, which would control the government jointly with the Social-Democrats, would not agree to these reforms and thus would come into conflict with the workers. In case the workers should prevail in that conflict, the economic backwardness of the country would make it impossible to carry out all the necessary socialist measures. The only way out of the situation was thus a revolution in Western Europe, which would join hands with the Russian proletariat in establishing socialism.

Thus, in 1905, twelve years before the revolution of 1917, Leon Trotsky envisaged the idea of a sort of social revolution arising in Russia in the wake of the democratic anti-Tsarist revolution, and thence spreading over all Western Europe as well. This was something new in the European socialism of that time, when it had become almost an axiom that the ambition of the socialist intelligentsia hardly went beyond a career as comfortable politicians and office-holders in a democratic world ruled by the industrial and financial oligarchy, with State Capitalism as a distant dream.

As a result, Trotsky's opinions were not taken seriously either in Russia or abroad. Even by the orthodox Marxists, particularly in Austria, "Trotskyism" (the term was already heard in 1905) was treated as a joke. That it was meant in red-blooded earnest was proved by the development of the revolution of 1917, which to a great extent bore out his predictions.

Lenin's conception of the possibilities of the expected revolution—as recorded in his writings since 1905—underwent many changes and finally came very close to that of Trotsky. A literature that would fill dozens of shelves has since been turned out, in Russia and abroad, on the various "interpretations" of Lenin's and Trotsky's respective formulas. In his *Permanent Revolution,* written during his Turkish exile, Trotsky boils down the difference between his opinion and Lenin's to the question whether "the participation of the representatives of the proletariat as a minority in the democratic government" (established by the revolution) was "theoretically permissible." This question was answered in the affirmative by Lenin, who was ready for a peasant (i.e. Social-Revolutionist) predominance in the government, while Trotsky insisted upon a "proletarian" majority—that is, a majority composed of Marxian intellectuals. The historical test of the second revolution actually settled the controversy. "In November 1917," Trotsky writes in his *Permanent Revolution,* "a struggle raged in the summits of the party around the question of the coalition government with the Social-Revolutionists and the Mensheviks. Lenin was not opposed in principle to a coalition on the basis of the Soviets, but he categorically demanded a firm safe-guarding of the Bolshevik majority. I went along with him hand in hand." It was, therefore, Trotsky's point of view which in fact prevailed in 1917.

In 1905, however, the revolution was still far from becoming a "permanent" affair—though for a moment it actually looked very hopeful. In October a political strike
forced the Tsar to issue the famous October Manifesto,
granting some modicum of constitutional liberty. Leon
Trotsky returned to Petersburg while the strike was on, and
simultaneously with the Mensheviks he conceived the idea
of forming a non-partisan "Council of Workers' Delegates"
to represent the interests of the masses and to keep up the
revolutionary spirit. Lenin was still abroad, and the Bolshevik militants kept aloof, until the arrival of their great
leader made them change their position.

Trotsky, at twenty-six, became the soul of the first Russian Soviet. He wrote all its appeals and resolutions and
was the best of its revolutionary speakers. Soon he was
elected Chairman of the body. At the same time he joined
the Mensheviks in publishing a big political daily which
enjoyed great success. The Bolsheviks had a paper of their
own, but there was no mutual bitterness or acerbity between the two step-brothers. Their eyes directed towards
the success of the political revolution, both papers were in
favor of a reconciliation of the two factions.

But the victorious progress of the Revolution which had
begun so hopefully in October, 1905, came soon to a stop.
The Tsarist government became aware of a very fundamental weakness of its enemies. Chiefly concerned with the
political aspects of the revolution, that is, with changing the
country's régime to the pattern of a western democracy, the
revolutionists showed no particular enthusiasm for the wage-
demands of the hungry masses. They had won over the
skilled workers who were interested in trade unions. But
the hungry crowds of the cities, as well as the village poor,
cared little for all the talk of political democracy, and even
the promise of land meant nothing to them. They wanted
bread, work, higher wages. To get these they would

have risen in irresistible revolt, like that which quite spontaneously swept Southern Russia two years before. But even the most radical sections of the socialist intelligentsia were not interested in such a departure. . . .

Thus, the Tsarist government was given the opportunity to let loose against the revolutionists those same hungry masses whose interests had been disregarded by the revolutionary intellectuals. A wave of massacres was skilfully arranged by the Machiavellian statesmen of the Romanov Empire—the Russian city-and-village poor arrayed against the Jews, the Turko-Tartars against the Armenians, the laborers and other slum dwellers against the students and the intelligentsia in general.

After less than two months existence the Petersburg Soviet was arrested and Trotsky was once more in prison. But this time he was no longer the obscure schoolboy of seven years before—he was one of the most popular figures of the Revolution—may be, at the moment, the most popular.

Again in Exile

After fifteen months in various prisons he was banished to Siberia. He succeeded in escaping before he reached his place of destination and was once more abroad—staying mostly in Vienna, where he published a semi-monthly propaganda paper to be smuggled to Russia.

A new development began to come markedly to the fore during the years of Trotsky's second exile. The rift between the Mensheviks and Bolsheviks, after their short reconciliation in 1906, was now becoming wider and wider. More and more it became obvious that the Mensheviks, after their brief flare-up during the Revolution of 1905, were gathering around their banner the more conciliatory, less determined, elements, who were tired of the romance of the revolutionary underworld. Having lost hope in the Revolution, they

were ready to forsake "illegal" methods of struggle altogether, and to make use of the few rudiments of constitutional rights that had still remained from the wreckage of
the Revolution. For this they were contemptuously called
"Liquidators" by their adversaries—because they wanted to
wind up the revolutionary struggle. The Bolsheviks, who so
mercilessly applied that term, included the more desperate
and energetic elements—and a statistical survey would have
no doubt established that on the whole those of the intelligentsia who followed Lenin were even more *déclassé* economically than their conciliatory Menshevik rivals. They did
not believe that the revolutionary flame had been extinguished for good, and they hoped for a new revolution.

Leon Trotsky remained in the air between the two factions and tried to bring them together, in the hope of winning the Mensheviks over to the renewed revolutionary
activities which he saw to be at hand. A number of Bolsheviks sympathized with his efforts, and a general Social-
Democratic conference was called at Vienna in 1912. But
Lenin was adamant—he was fully convinced that it was
useless to form a bloc with elements that he no longer considered revolutionary, alliance with whom was sure to be
a liability; as a result the Bolsheviks stayed away. Trotsky
found himself in uncomfortable association with Mensheviks, with whom he disagreed on most points, and a few
disobedient Bolsheviks. This venture of his put a further
strain on his relations with Lenin.

Already, two years before, Trotsky had had an unpleasant conflict with the great revolutionist, a conflict in which
the honors were not exactly on his side. During his years
of exile, Trotsky was a free-lance littérateur, supporting
himself and his family with contributions to progressive
papers in Russia and socialist papers in Germany and Austria. In 1910 an International Socialist Congress was to be
held in Copenhagen, and on this occasion he wrote an article

to the Berlin *Vorwärts,* central organ of the German Socialist Party, in which he dealt with the revolutionary situation in Russia. He took to task the Mensheviks, with whose
moderation he did not agree, but he also attacked the Bolsheviks, chiefly on the score of the "expropriations"—the
armed hold-ups of government funds which some of their
fighting groups carried out—in order to replenish the party
treasury chest. With all his contempt for the philistinism
and respectability of the Western socialists, Trotsky had
apparently become contaminated by the same disease. The
Bolsheviks, not having many rich "angels" at their disposal, needed money badly—and took it. Stalin, then a
humble revolutionary worker in the vineyard of which in
time he was to become the undisputed Lord, was one of
those heroic dare-devils who, like Pilsudski at the same time,
were braving bullets and the gallows to get the Tsarist
"dough." Some of the many revolutionary "expropriators"
—whether Bolsheviks, Socialist-Revolutionists, Anarchists
or Polish Social-Patriots, at times went wrong and turned
common bandits, much to the discredit of the revolutionary
cause. It is to this sad feature that Trotsky referred, attacking the Bolsheviks for not abandoning this method altogether. That the tactics of parliamentarism, as practiced
by the Western socialists, were incomparably more demor-
alizing, having gradually converted each Socialist Party into
a little Tammany Hall with its climbers and job-hunters,
Trotsky entirely overlooked. He likewise overlooked the fact
that it was in very bad taste, to say the least, to denounce,
on such a ticklish score, the most militant section of the
Russian revolutionists to a gloating public of pink politicians—and indirectly to the bourgeois authorities as well.
Lenin, who was known not to be opposed to the expropriations, was extremely bitter on that score, and what Stalin
must have thought and felt at that time can be easily sur-
mised.

WAR AND REVOLUTION

The great War found Trotsky in Vienna. Being an "enemy alien," he was forced to leave and went to Switzerland. He did not stay there long, but soon left for France, where he could earn his living as the war correspondent of a Liberal daily published in Russia.

A year after the beginning of the War, the first attempt was made to bring together from their various countries all the internationalist anti-war elements of the socialist parties, and to begin a campaign against the world slaughter. At the historic conference at Zimmerwald, a small mountain village in Switzerland, the revolutionary internationalists found themselves opposed by moderate internationalists who were merely pacifists. Lenin, who headed the former, believed in the necessity of converting the World War into a world-wide civil war. Trotsky took a similar stand—though he refused to join the so-called "Zimmerwald Left"—the body dominated by Lenin. The old personal grudge and his unwillingness to recognize a boss had more to do with his aloofness than any difference in principle.

Another year, and Trotsky was forced to leave France. A mutiny in the ranks of the detachments sent by Tsarist Russia to France, and the death of a Russian colonel killed by his soldiers, were charged to the propaganda conducted by a small Russian daily edited by Trotsky. This was preposterous, for the paper was censored and could not have possibly had anything to do with that affair. But the Russian authorities, supported by the reactionaries in France, carried the day; Trotsky was expelled and was smuggled over to Spanish territory, where the Spanish authorities did not want him either. Accordingly, about three months before the outbreak of the Russian Revolution, he had to leave his last European refuge and to sail for the United States.

The American episode lasted hardly longer than ten weeks. Trotsky was in the process of helping to organize a left wing within the Socialist Party, when news of the downfall of the Tsarist régime and the establishment of a provisional government made the American socialist scene appear to him about as important as the internal squabbles of a sick-benefit society on the lower East Side. In his reminiscences of this country, he is not very tender to the socialist leadership, with its "prosperous and semi-prosperous physicians, lawyers, dentists, civil engineers, and so on," to whom socialism was not so much a political career as part of their social entertainments and business connections. He has a few good words for old Gene Debs—who wouldn't?—but spoils it all by referring to the great orator's bibulous inclinations. It appears that Debs was in the habit of affectionately embracing and kissing the visitor whenever he met him. Trotsky was amused at this effusion, while Debs did not realize that the man whom he admired as a hero and a symbol of Revolution and Socialism, was at heart as cold as steel, and as contemptuous of men and their affections, as the great Corsican himself.

Trotsky's return to Russia was delayed by the cautious British authorities, who scented the danger that threatened the Provisional Government and its determination to go on with the War on the side of the Allies. Arrested on the boat which was to take him to Russia, he spent a month in a Canadian concentration camp, until pressure from the Petrograd Soviet—then still in the hands of the Mensheviks and Socialist-Revolutionists—forced Professor Miliukov, the Liberal Minister of Foreign Affairs, to demand his release. The British Embassy in the Russian capital tried to impress Trotsky's countrymen with stories of German subsidies granted for the overthrow of the Provisional Government and for the betrayal of the country. But the public refused to be alarmed.

Immediately after his arrival in Petrograd, Trotsky proved that English official apprehensions were but too well justified. His propaganda against the continuation of the War and against the Provisional Government became more and more embarrassing to the Liberals, Socialist-Revolutionists, near-Socialist-Revolutionists of the Kerensky brand, and Right-Wing-Mensheviks, who constituted or supported the Government.

In the beginning he stood almost alone in his demand for the conquest of power by the Socialists alone. The only other man in the socialist camp to advocate the same course was Lenin, who had arrived in Russia a month before Trotsky. Independently of each other, Lenin in Europe, Trotsky in America, they had come to the same conclusion. In his own party, Lenin was altogether isolated on that issue. Lenin's old demand of 1905 for a "Democratic Dictatorship of the Proletariat and the Peasantry," was now forgotten by his disciples. The peasants were with the Socialist-Revolutionists—and the Socialist-Revolutionists were in coalition with the Liberals. To call for the overthrow of the government meant to demand a purely socialist government, something very much in line with the "Trotskyism" of 1905—the generally scorned "utopian" formula of a romantic free-lance, which neither the Mensheviks nor the Bolsheviks had taken seriously.

With much glee and vindictiveness, Trotsky tells how, in the early days of the Revolution of 1917, Stalin and the rest of the Old Guard, without a single exception, stood for supporting the Provisional Government and for merging with the Mensheviks. It took Lenin three months of struggle within the party before he succeeded in winning it over to his side. Trotsky's insistence on this point is easily explained. For what were all his old-time casual flirtations with the Mensheviks—he seems to imply—as compared with his perfectly correct stand at the crucial historical

moment; a stand which placed him beside Lenin, as against
the rest of the Bolshevik leaders?

Meanwhile the Provisional Government was preparing
its defense. It could not possibly arrest Trotsky and Lenin.
As old veterans of the revolutionary struggles, these two
had a certain grip on the imagination of the masses, who
would have rushed to defend them, even while disagreeing
with their extreme proposals. So the old weapon of Don
Basile was resorted to : a barrage fire of calumny was started
in the Liberal press. Professor Miliukov personally directed
the fire, and the good work was later continued by Kerensky.
Both Lenin and Trotsky were accused of being German
agents, hired and paid by the Kaiser's general staff. . . .

November 7, 1917

Slander, diligently repeated, like a permanent advertise-
ment, rarely misses its effect. Otherwise it would not be
the favorite instrument of that astute statesmanship which
knows that man rules not by the sword alone. Large sections
of the middle classes soon became aroused against the
"traitors," and that mood rose to a frenzy after the unsuccessful uprising which the workers of Petrograd, with
part of the garrison, had attempted early in July. Lenin had
to go into hiding, or he would have been lynched or "shot
in flight," if he had been arrested. Party headquarters were
destroyed, and many of the members were attacked. Trotsky,
meanwhile, though collaborating with the Bolsheviks, was
still outside their party, his official adherence being scheduled
for the party convention, together with other near-Bolshe-
viks who later became prominent in the councils of the
Soviet régime, such as Lunacharsky, Joffe, Karakhan, he
belonged to a separate organization. A few days after the

July revolt, he was arrested for publicly declaring his solidarity with Lenin.

This imprisonment did not last long. In August the counter-revolutionary General Kornilov—probably in secret agreement with Kerensky—began his march on Petrograd. It is generally assumed that Kerensky, who had hoped to use the general in consolidating his power against the rising tide of Bolshevism, had at the last moment some misgivings about the purely constitutional intentions of his subordinate. Rather than be the dupe of a Tsarist general—who might have dispatched him in the same batch with the Bolsheviks— he appealed for the help of those "German agents" and freed them to get their aid in repulsing the "patriotic" soldier. Yet ten years later, in a book on the Russian revolution, he again accused the Bolsheviks of complicity with the German general staff.

The counter-revolutionary attempt of General Kornilov, and the sad part played by Kerensky during the whole af- fray, greatly increased the prestige of the Bolsheviks in the Petrograd Soviet, which hitherto had had a Menshevik- Socialist-Revolutionist majority. At the vote taken in Octo- ber for the election of the presiding board, the Bolsheviks had a majority, and Trotsky was elected Chairman. That election decided the outcome of the struggle for power. The great majority of the Petrograd workers and soldiers were with the Bolsheviks. They were tired of the War, and the Bolsheviks offered them peace. This argument was more convincing than any political program could be.

Lenin was still in hiding in Finland. Trotsky, constantly in communication with him, from the headquarters of the Petrograd Soviet, almost openly directed the preparations for the revolt. Not all the prominent Bolsheviks favored the undertaking: Zinoviev and Kamenev were against it. For years they had been the closest associates of Lenin, and later, after Lenin's death in 1924, they formed with Stalin the "triumvirate" which ruled the Soviet Republic until 1926. Likewise opposed to the uprising was Rykov, who for nearly eight years was Soviet Premier; so was Kalinin, who since 1919 has occupied a post corresponding to that of a President of the Republic. None of these thought that the party would be able to hold power. Stalin supported Lenin and Trotsky, but he was at that time still quite inconspicuous and unknown to the public at large. The coup was timed for November 7, the day when the Second All-Russia Soviet Congress was to convene. The Bolsheviks were sure that their action, aiming at transferring all power to the Soviets, would be endorsed by the Congress. Trotsky's leading rôle in these historical events was generally recognized at the time. The issue of the *Pravda,* published in 1918, on the first anniversary of the revolution, contains a statement by Joseph Stalin to the effect that "all the work of practical organization of the insurrection was conducted under the immediate leadership of the President of the Petrograd Soviet, Comrade Trotsky. It is possible to declare with certainty that the swift passing of the garrison to the side of the Soviet, and the bold execution of the work of the Military Revolutionary Committee, the Party owes principally and above all to Comrade Trotsky."

But the official appreciation of Trotsky's merits has changed. All things are fleeting, as Heraclitus said. . . .

THE NEW RÉGIME

In the new cabinet, headed by Lenin, Trotsky assumed the post of Commissar of Foreign Affairs. It had not been the intention of the Bolsheviks to form a government alone, to the exclusion of all other parties. The Mensheviks and Socialist-Revolutionists, however, though they were offered participation, refused to join in a venture which they believed doomed to speedy failure. The only other party that

finally rallied to the Bolsheviks was that of the "Left Socialist-Revolutionists," the romantic younger set of the great
party of intellectuals and peasants. Though shunned by the
two large socialist parties, the Bolsheviks had the support
of the war-weary workers and soldiers. They had likewise
the sympathies of the peasants, whose land-seizing activities
were officially endorsed by the new régime.

That the Revolution, in order to survive, would have to
make big steps towards satisfying the demands of the
workers—even though capitalist property rights were violated in the process—had as early as 1905 been one of the
chief contentions of Trotsky's theory of the permanent
revolution. Lenin's conception, in 1905, had not gone beyond that of a "democratic" (that is, bourgeois) revolution,
with socialist measures rather far in the future. But in
1917, at the approach of the November revolution, his statements of the postulates of the party went somewhat beyond
any purely political demand for complete democratization.
Nationalization of the banks, and government control—not
ownership—of industries, became a party cry: a step
towards State Capitalism, but not yet a real challenge to the
system of private capitalism. It was the general opinion in
the Bolshevik party that the time for nationalizing the industries had not yet come—at least not in a country as backward economically as Russia. The land was "nationalized"—
that is, it could not now be sold by those who held it—but
in reality the land decree took no forward step toward collective land tenure. It was rather an extension of private
ownership, permitting all degrees of inequality—from prosperous "kulaks" down to landless farm-hands, with only the
great landlords eliminated. There was thus very little "Socialism" after the victory of the November revolution, except that the men at the helm, intellectuals and a few former
workers, held socialist beliefs and were firmly determined to
use their power in carrying out a gradual transition from

private capitalism to government ownership, or State Capitalism. Under normal conditions that process would have taken decades, and in the meantime the revolutionary firebrands might have settled down to something like the respectable socialists of Western Europe.

Conditions in 1917 were, however, not "normal" and it took only ten months for that nationalization of industries which Trotsky had predicted in 1905. A multiplicity of causes led to this development. In many cases the workers were infuriated by the refusal of the manufacturers to comply with their demands, and simply chased out the owners and occupied the factories. The Soviet Government, based as it was upon the support of the laboring masses, could not restore these plants to the former owners, and the factories were taken over by the government. In other cases, enterprises were taken over, to protect them against sabotage by the owners, while the country was in the throes of civil war. There were also numerous cases where the plants were seized by the government in order to prevent their being sold to German capital after the Brest-Litovsk treaty.

BREST-LITOVSK AND THE CIVIL WAR

Trotsky's Homeric struggle with the German statesmen and generals constitutes one of the most dramatic pages of contemporary history. Undaunted by the brutal threats of the German militarists and unhurried by the impatience of Lenin, who was rightly afraid lest the postponement of the signing might lead to stiffer peace terms, he persisted in his attempts to gain time, hoping against hope that the workers of Germany and Austria would rise and restrain the iron fist that was trying to crush the Russian revolution. Indeed, the workers of Central Europe made some attempts in this direction, only to be discouraged and thwarted by their socialist leaders.

The peace had to be signed at last, for it was obvious that all thought of resistance was futile. The Russian front had ceased to exist long before the Bolshevik rise to power. After signing the Brest-Litovsk Treaty, Trotsky gave up his post of Commissar for Foreign Affairs and was entrusted with the organization of the Red Army. Writing of those years Maxim Gorki quotes Lenin as saying: "Well, show me another man who would be able, within a year, to organize an almost exemplary army and moreover to win the respect of the military specialists. We have such a man. We have everything. And miracles are still going to happen" . . .

The organization of a Red Army had become an urgent necessity with counter-revolutionary armed forces threatening the young republic from all corners of its vast territory. There were times when attacks were being made on seventeen different fronts. During these three years of war against counter-revolutionary armies and foreign invaders, Trotsky had opportunity to display all his exceptional gifts. His sweeping energy, his fascinating oratory, the gripping force of his appeals, his dauntless physical courage, his cold mercilessness—all combined to form a personality as exceptional and as indispensable for the survival of the new régime, as were Lenin's genius and statesmanship; and Lenin was the first to recognize the fact. It almost seems that the Revolution needed these two altogether different types: the impersonal idealist who, like Lenin, submerges his superhuman stature in the cause; and the ambitious egotist, who, like Trotsky, identifies the cause with his own super-human personality. During these three years he rose, with Lenin, to the stature of a demi-god; his pictures were featured everywhere and on every occasion, and his achievements were celebrated in flattering accounts by some of the most outstanding leaders and writers. But all this is forgotten now, and the rising generation knows little of his past glory.

It has been drowned in a sea of recriminations, called forth by the intra-party struggle.

Yet those years likewise nurtured the forces which were finally to drive him from power and to strike his name from Russia's text-books. Trotsky knew his own importance and made those about him feel it. Whether he was conscious of it or not, he assumed the bearing and began to nourish the ambition of Cromwell, the Lord Protector, and Bonaparte, the First Consul. He would, of course, never have stretched out his hand to the symbolic insignia of the old world; but he might have outdone both Cromwell and Napoleon in absolute intolerance of wills or opinions other than his own. There was in him no spark of that human kindness which made great rebels, like Bakunin or Malatesta, Lenin or Liebknecht, not only admired but also beloved by their contemporaries. To Trotsky these human traits were childish, unworthy of a great man, obliged to assert his greatness by keeping all lesser mortals at a rigid distance. To be sure, he made an exception of Lenin—to whom he gave such grudging reverence as Napoleon, for reasons of State, gave occasionally to the Supreme Being.

Unlike Lenin's, his ascendance was not accepted ungrudgingly. True, to the younger intellectuals, who, one day, as the new bureaucracy, were to rule the new State, he was the symbol of what every one of their group would have liked to be—the military hero, the fascinating, virile personality, the great orator, the brilliant writer, the versatile erudite. They did not aspire to be treated as equals—as one does not aspire to be God. It was different with the old militants of the Bolshevik Party, the Zinovievs, Kamenevs, Rykovs, Stalins, Frunzes, Voroshilovs, Bubnovs, Unshlikhts, who had witnessed all the acrimonious literary skirmishes between Lenin and Trotsky. They had always considered the brilliant free-lance as an arrogant mountebank, and they did not relish the idea of being his subordinates. After all, he was only a newcomer; he had been in the Bolshevik Party only since 1917, while they had been with it ever since the split in 1903. Seniority means a great deal in Russia's new upper crust. The years of one's party membership prior to 1917 count no less than a similar number of ancestors in the true-blue aristocratic families of England and Germany. Trotsky had, so to speak, no ancestors. Moreover, Napoleon-like, he plainly intended to be the first great ancestor himself, to set up a nobility of his own, a nobility of merit and daring, composed of young men devoted to him alone and unconcerned with the seniority rights of the old guard.

The danger of Bonapartism, as against, let us say, revolutionary legitimism, was staring the old guard right in the face, a Bonapartism all the more detestable as Trotsky's self-confidence was boundless and as human life meant nothing to him—even the life of good old communist commissars and commanders. (Since 1918 Communist Party became the official name.) It was known that army commanders and commissars who disobeyed orders or showed cowardice were shot by his orders, and that on one occasion Bela Kun's life was saved only through Lenin's intervention: not to speak of decimations of rank and file communists, whenever this seemed necessary in order to bolster up the courage of the waverers. Perhaps the civil war could not have been won otherwise; and Lenin himself, in reply to complaints against the War Commissar's harshness, issued to him a special authorization giving him virtually power over life and death all along the fronts.

Yet Lenin, too, seems to have been worried by the meteor-like success of his invaluable assistant. It was not jealousy. He was as truly above jealousy as his own teacher, Marx, was subject to it with regard to Ferdinand Lassalle—the Leon Trotsky of his time. But the suspicion of Bonapartism, of a possible ambition to establish a Cromwellian dictatorship, based upon the Army alone, with all its inevitable consequences, was not easily to be dismissed. Trotsky's own record of Stalin's and Voroshilov's activities at the front, and of Lenin's reaction to Trotsky's complaints, unwittingly points to Lenin's apprehensions on that score. Stalin and Voroshilov—the latter since 1925 at the head of the War Department—while in charge of certain sectors of the civil war front, had more than once openly defied Trotsky's orders in the most insulting manner. Lenin's only reaction to such breaches of discipline was never more than a suggestion for peace and better understanding between the War Commissar and his mutinous subordinates. All of which quite plainly points to the assumption that Stalin and Voroshilov must have had the backing of the grand old man himself—in order to make his grand young man feel that his possible ambitions would not remain unopposed. . . .

The history of the train which carried Trotsky from front to front, in which he covered a distance about six times the circumference of the globe, is one of the few heroic epics of history. But it is an epic not of victory alone. The Red "War Lord" was not always infallible in his judgment, and in at least one very important case his opinion was superseded by the Council of People's Commissars.

This was the question whether the Kolchak front at the East or the Denikin front at the South was to be given more attention at a given moment. The reversal of his order was a rude shock to his great self-confidence, but the resignation which he offered was not accepted. Later he more than made up for his strategical misjudgment, for his personal urgency defeated Lenin's determination to give up Petrograd, then threatened by another White Army coming from the Northwest. He himself led a regiment to battle, as did young Bonaparte at the famous Bridge of Lodi, turned by his example a panicky retreat into a successful attack, and was wounded during the fight. He had indeed risked his life on many previous occasions, when he insisted on being very close to the actual fighting—a heroic pastime in which the general-staff man of a civilized country never indulges.

His great achievement in saving Petrograd is gradually falling into oblivion. So is likewise the fact that on another occasion his judgment, if it had not been superseded by Lenin and the other powerful men in the Kremlin, would have saved the young Soviet régime one of the greatest setbacks in its history. This was his opposition to the forced march on Warsaw, which he knew was strategically inadmissible. The Polish war had been practically won by the Red Army, and Russia would have received satisfaction for Pilsudski's invasion and all the necessary guarantees, if the hope for a Polish revolution and a communication of the conflagration to Germany and perhaps to the rest of Europe had not tempted the civilian rulers of Moscow to send the army on a military venture which turned out disastrously.

TROTSKY'S BANQUO

Trotsky's last military achievement was an anti-climax. This was the suppression of the Kronstadt revolt of March, 1921, at a time when the civil and foreign wars had just come to a close. The sailors of the great Soviet naval base were not exactly "Whites," and Lenin, after it all was over, said of them that "they did not want the counter-revolutionists, but they did not want us either." They had once been "the pride and the glory of the Revolution," to use a compliment bestowed upon them by Trotsky.

The period of military, or war-time, communism, which set in after the nationalization of the industries in the middle of 1918, and which lasted all through the civil war, had called forth strong dissatisfaction in practically all classes of the population.

It was "communism" of a sort, with the whole country

converted into a kind of a besieged camp, and every function
of society under the control of the army command and of an
immensely inflated bureaucratic apparatus. Food was requi-
sitioned from the peasants, as it had been during the French
Revolution—for the cities had nothing to give them in exchange and must produce for army requirements alone. The
peasants who had taken the land were loath to give away
the fruit of their toil without any equivalent. They could
not see the other side of the story: namely, that requisitions
were only a simplified, barbaric form of taxation, and that
the revolution must preserve itself, though at the price of
those hated foraging expeditions.

Bureaucratization of the entire national life had reached
incredible proportions. At one time there were more government officials in Moscow than there were industrial workers,
though Moscow was an industrial city and not merely a
bureaucratic capital, like Washington. The population at
large suffered from a lack of commodities that might have
been available had it not been for the fact that small-scale
production by independent artisans had been practically
stamped out, since it fostered a class of small capitalists
who might become dangerous during the civil war.

The man in the street had nothing to say about all this.
True, there were Soviets, but the elections being open and
not secret, many people, and these not only reactionaries or
moderate Socialists, began to suggest that these were actually no elections but only confirmations of official lists. The
Bolsheviks felt that, given secret elections, the dissatisfaction engendered by the miseries of the long civil war would
lead to the victory of the Mensheviks, or Socialist-Revolutionists—a victory which would have brought to naught all
the sacrifices that had been made; for their adversaries
openly advocated a full restoration of private capitalism. It
was one of those undeniably ticklish situations, when the
cause of general progress clashes with certain specific demo-

cratic demands. The Belgian Socialists once found themselves in such a situation, when they opposed woman suffrage advocated by the Catholic Party; for such an extension of the franchise at that time would have delivered the country into the hands of reaction.

The Bolsheviks might have found it simpler to dispense with elections altogether and to proclaim the dictatorship of their party; but this would have been an open admission that their opponents in the socialist camp were right in charging them with "Blanquism"—that un-Marxian heresy which approved revolution and dictatorship by a socialist party without bothering about the support of the working masses. The imputation of exerting a Blanquist dictatorship *over* the proletariat rather than a Marxian dictatorship *of* the proletariat, the Bolsheviks indignantly resented. The Bolsheviks took pride in being the most faithful and consistent followers of Marxism—the religion of the most advanced section of the Russian intelligentsia. True, a frankly Blanquist stand had been taken by Lenin in 1917, during the reign of Kerensky, when there seemed to be little hope of the Soviets (still under the sway of the Mensheviks and other Moderates) going over to the Bolsheviks. At that moment (it was shortly after the unsuccessful revolt of July 1917), Lenin published a pamphlet in which he virtually demanded all power for his party, and no longer "All Power to the Soviets," as the original slogan had run. But that episode was buried, and it had become rank heresy to speak of party dictatorship. Open Soviet elections, with their returns determined in advance, were thus a workable, face-saving hybrid between party dictatorship and proletarian democracy.

Early in 1921, the workers of Petrograd gave expression, in one strike after another, to their dissatisfaction with their difficult living conditions. The sailors of Kronstadt thought this was the proper moment to present their own demands, in the hope of winning over the support of the rest of Russia. They practically declared their independence and rejected Trotsky's command to surrender immediately and unconditionally. The suppression of the revolt was merciless and won Trotsky the undying hatred of the Anarchists, who sympathized with the uprising.

The revolt of Kronstadt, though suppressed, was victorious to a certain extent. Its political demands for a "secret vote and free Soviets" amounting indirectly to a renunciation of its dictatorship by the Communist Party, were rejected, of course; but the economic postulates of the rebels, expressing the dissatisfaction of the peasants and their demand to be permitted freely to dispose of their grain, were actually heeded. The New Economic Policy, which reëstablished a certain modicum of private enterprise—mainly in domestic retail trading and small home-crafts—was inaugurated as a direct consequence of the Kronstadt rebellion, and of a local peasant revolt which occurred at the same time in Central Russia.

This New Economic Policy had been advocated by Trotsky as early as 1920—a year before the Kronstadt revolt. His proposal had been turned down then—and it was he who had been obliged to crush the rebels who, so to speak, stood up for his demand. It was a cruel irony of fate. Eight years later, having seen his own faction within the party hopelessly crushed, as a result, he thought, of the open vote, Trotsky was to declare himself in favor of the secret ballot within the party, in the trade unions and even in the Soviets under certain circumstances; that same secret ballot whose advocates he had mowed down in 1921, when his power was still well established. When he came out with that demand, Karl Radek, his former oppositionist comrade in arms, having repented by 1928, harked back to the old argument by declaring that a demand for a secret ballot within the party was "counter-revolutionary." Which was rather peculiar reasoning, for it implied that the majority of the party membership was composed of counter-revolutionists. . . .

TROTSKY VERSUS LENIN

The year before the inauguration of the New Economic Policy found Trotsky involved in numerous disagreements and conflicts with Lenin and the majority of the party. One of these concerned the experiment of the "labor armies," which he had inaugurated against Lenin's advice. When the civil war ended in 1920, and the Soviet Government had on its hands an army of over five million soldiers, it had occurred to Trotsky that part of the men, instead of being sent home, should keep their uniforms and take up the task of reconstruction under military command.

The idea did not work. Trotsky's labor armies simply melted away. In their naïveté the Russian doughboys did not believe that this was the freedom they had been fighting for. Lenin had his chuckle at the expense of his enterprising associate, to whom it never had occurred that projects of a similar kind had been proposed by a certain Louis Bonaparte, later Napoleon III, while he was still a political prisoner.

In the same year Trotsky experienced a serious setback—this time in frank and open opposition to Lenin—on the question of trade unions. He did not think they fitted into the new scheme of things. Once the capitalists had been eliminated, he argued, the proletariat, through the State, had become the owner and manager of all industries. Being owner and manager of the country, the working class could obviously no longer be exploited by anybody; for nobody exploits himself. Hence, Trotsky concluded, the trade unions, with their elected officials, and with the degree of independence which they enjoyed, were no longer needed for their old function of defending the workers' interests. Against whom were they to defend them? Against the

State? But the State—that meant the workers themselves! Therefore he suggested that the character of the trade unions be changed entirely. Let them be managed by appointed efficiency engineers, rather than by elected labor leaders, and concern themselves chiefly with stimulating the workers to greater effort and output.

Lenin saw the dangers of Trotsky's attitude. He, and with him the majority of the party leaders, understood that the workers, deprived of their trade union organizations through which they could voice their grievances against the directors, managers, engineers and other persons in authority—who for all practical purposes had become their new bosses—would soon join illegal trade unions. These the Mensheviks and Socialist-Revolutionists from the Right, and the Anarchists and Syndicalists from the Left, would be only too glad to encourage as a weapon for fighting the Bolsheviks. He explained to Trotsky that this was not yet a workers' republic, but rather "a workers' republic with bureaucratic distortions" and that for this reason the workers still needed special bodies to protect them against the evils of "bureaucratic distortions."

Lenin understood quite well that his country was passing through a military form of State Capitalism, with the bureaucracy as the ruling class; he considered this necessary for the historical period through which Russia was passing, as he considered necessary the use of such expressions as "workers' republic." These were good in their place as propaganda, but were fraught with danger when less sophisticated men, like Trotsky, threatened to mess up affairs by taking or pretending to take these figures of speech literally. For, with all his brilliancy and occasional lack of candor, the great Tribune, from time to time, betrays a quite disconcerting naïveté and lack of understanding of the more subtle moves of revolutionary strategy.

Seven years later, in his *Opposition Platform,* Trotsky

somehow modified his original all-too-simple conception of the Soviet State. "We have a workers' state with bureaucratic distortions," he said, adding, "the swollen and privileged administrative apparatus devours a very considerable part of our surplus value." This was another way of stating that a considerable part of what prior to the Revolution constituted the profits of the capitalists was now being paid out in salaries to a privileged bureaucracy—which in turn was unconsciously harking back to some of the long forgotten predictions of the Polish exile in Siberia with whose criticism he had become acquainted nearly a generation before. (In 1917, Waclaw Machajski had hailed the November Revolution of 1917 as the beginning of a world-wide working-class revolt which would sweep away all privilege. The expropriation of the capitalists in Russia was, in his opinion, a powerful revolutionary stimulus for the western workers. That stimulus, he thought, would have been accentuated, if the Russian Revolution had shown a tendency towards an equalization of incomes.* He believed that by arresting this tendency the Russian Revolution had become a purely national affair of the extreme left wing of the Russian intelligentsia, and he held this fact responsible for the abatement of the revolutionary wave in the West.)

THE BEGINNING OF THE END

The Party Convention of 1921 was marked by two decisions which later were to prove fateful to Trotsky's career.

* Machajski did not believe in the possibility of a "workers' government," maintaining that governing was a function of educated persons only—whether intellectuals or self-taught ex-workers—and that these would consciously or unconsciously defend the interests of the educated minority. In his opinion, the workers' demands, culminating in full equality of incomes with resulting equality of educational opportunities, could be satisfied only as a consequence of constant pressure from below. It could not be an outcome of governmental benevolence, however radical that government might be.

On their face they were harmless enough. One of them stipulated that a question, once thrashed out at a convention, should not be taken up again in party discussions. By this proposal Lenin hoped to avoid the creation of factions and the repetition of futile discussions at the party conventions. In that period of transition from civil war to reconstruction, and from military communism to the New Economic Policy, the party was torn by the criticism of various dissenting groups. There was the "Workers' Opposition," which was very close to the conception of French syndicalism, and demanded that the management of the industries should be transferred to the trade unions. There were also a number of other heretical communist groups. Some of these thought that once the civil war was over the restrictions directed against the various shades of unofficial opinion should be abolished and civil liberties restored. Others argued that by leveling the standard of living of all groups of the population and eliminating the inequalities in the rewards of mental workers, skilled mechanics and unskilled laborers, the Soviet Government would rally the enthusiastic support of the great mass of the poorest strata of the population. They thought that it was in the various inequalities still existing that hostile propaganda from the Right as well as from the Left found its most fertile soil. Many dissenters who, after being repudiated by the party conventions continued to conduct propaganda for what they considered a correct policy, were arrested or sent to distant parts of the country.

Trotsky and his personal following found nothing improper in this procedure. This was the period of reconstruction, and the party could have no patience with its obstreperous and quarrelsome members.

The other decision of the Convention was much more momentous. It created the post of General Secretary of the Party, and nominated Stalin to that post. Suggested by Zinoviev, it was obviously meant as a move against Trotsky;

yet in the final reckoning, Zinoviev suffered from it as much as Trotsky, if not more. The position of General Secretary, in the hands of a strong personality, carried with it great possibilities. The Communist Party was not a democratically organized body. Since its very beginning it had been an army rather than a regular party, with extremely high power attached to the general staff. For the organization of a revolution and the conduct of a civil war, such military features appealed to many as indispensable. The Red Army, as soon as it was faced with a really serious situation, had to give up the principle of election of officers and other idyllic liberties at first enjoyed by its soldiers. Similarly, the Communist Party, to be more effective, had established the principle that the provincial, district or local secretaries did not necessarily have to be elected by their corresponding membership. More often than not, they were simply appointed from the party center of the State, province or district; at least they had to be so confirmed. This was intended to secure efficient local leadership. The result was a condition which some people sometimes likened to the administrative system established in France by the Empire and still existing in the Third Republic—where all the prefects are appointed from the center. The local party secretaries, being directly or indirectly appointed by the General Secretary, were consequently sure to support his policy and to see to it that the elections of delegates to the conventions were satisfactory. With the open vote and the absence of the principle of proportional representation, this was easy. The Central Committee elected by the Party Convention was thus sure to support the policy of the General Secretary. This was not exactly an innovation introduced by Stalin, but his opponents charged that he utilized his position for the consolidation of his power.

As long as Lenin was in good health, Trotsky's position as first in the councils of the republic and of the party after the unquestioned Father of the Revolution, was not challenged. This, notwithstanding occasional disagreements between the two great leaders, and the scant popularity the great Tribune enjoyed among most of the members of the Old Guard. But things changed as soon as Lenin's illness gave rise to the worst forebodings.

The two years between Lenin's first stroke, early in 1922, and his death early in 1924, were years of underground warfare in anticipation of the struggle for succession to Lenin's power. Trotsky had on his side the flower of the younger intellectuals, the students and the "red professors." He was not exactly popular with the workers. His attitude with regard to the trade unions was known. He was an efficiency fanatic—to whom the human element counted for nothing. In 1922 he had proposed the concentration of all industries—a measure which, as Stalin asserts in his book *About the Opposition* would have thrown one-third of all the workers out of employment. The opposition to Trotsky was headed by Stalin, the General Secretary of the Party; Zinoviev, the President of the Communist International and head of the Leningrad party organization; and Kamenev, Chairman of the Moscow Soviet: a "triumvirate" of unequal merit, Stalin as the shrewd, fearless and energetic man of action, towering mountain-high in character over his associates who at bottom were only eloquent pamphleteers. That triumvirate had on its side what is called the "apparatus," the party machine of which all members were directly or indirectly nominated by the General Secretary. Against this actual accumulation of power, Trotsky could oppose only his past achievements, the sympathy of the younger generation, and Lenin's so-called "Testament." That document unmistakably pointed to Trotsky as the most competent man to take over the helm. His possible Bonapartist ambitions, now that the civil war was over, were no longer a cause for apprehension.

The struggle for power was of course conducted under

the guise of a struggle for divergent policies. Trotsky's "permanent revolution" and his reputed hostility towards the peasantry, or at least his disregard and underestimation of them, were dug out of the pre-revolutionary past and presented to the public as timely issues.

Trotsky himself was not silent either. He too dug out old skeletons, reminding the Soviet public in a book which apparently was not meant to be one of purely historical reflections, that Zinoviev and Kamenev had not been altogether heroic during the November Revolution of 1917; and that they were certainly not called upon to be the leaders of a revolutionary nation.

He also set up an interesting theory which was intended to hit the Old Guard a knock-out blow. He spoke of the "degeneration" that had overtaken the old leadership of all the European socialist parties. He pointed to the indisputable fact that practically all the Marxian veteran leaders had turned either pink or yellow during the War, and even before it—and concluded that a similar danger was threatening the "Old Guard" of the party in the Soviet Union. The conclusion was that the party needed fresh blood—an obvious and unmistakable bid for the favor of the younger generation of intellectuals, the "outs" or "not-yet-quite-ins," who were only too anxious to step into the shoes of the older men. As a theory this was rather poor; for the pinkness and yellowness of the old socialist leaders was a result not of their age but of the natural development of every political party which achieves power and influence; and barring some honorable exceptions, the younger leaders of those socialist parties were not better than their elders. If they occasionally rebelled, it was only to crowd out the old leaders and then to continue their policies. But the argument was effective—the younger set hailed Trotsky as their leader.

In the party discussions Trotsky and his followers now kept insisting upon "democracy in the party." Stalin was so heartless as to remind them that as managers of the various sections of Soviet economic life, all of Trotsky's cronies had used the most undemocratic methods; and he concluded with his usual bluntness that the party was faced now by the "democratism" of dissatisfied party-aristocrats, who saw the essence of democratism in substituting one set of men for another.

Still, that statement did not dispose of the fact that the "democracy" practiced by the existing party régime was, to say the least, somewhat curious. Trotsky, in a pamphlet that aroused very much bitterness in the ruling Stalin-Zinoviev-Kamenev group, had said: "The Party lives on two floors. Upstairs decisions are made; those who live downstairs merely hear about the decisions." His gibe had been borne out by a stanch supporter of his opponents— the party's outstanding theorist, Bukharin. In a since famous speech Bukharin had inadvertently admitted that the party elections were elections in name only; that the party meetings were simply asked, "Who is opposed?" to the candidates suggested by the higher authorities, and that "since the members are more or less afraid to declare themselves opposed, it is understood that the suitable person has been elected secretary of the group." * In fact, not a single member of Trotsky's following—and it was very large at that time—could get a nomination as a delegate to the Party Convention; Trotsky himself appeared there not as a delegate but as member of the Central Committee.

At that time the number of workers actually working at their benches were a minority in the party, and the influence of the younger generation of intellectuals could in time have become dangerous to the Old Guard. The Old Guard countered the danger by organizing a mass campaign to admit 200,000 manual workers into the party "for the pur-

---

* Quoted from Louis Fischer's Moscow correspondence, dated June 1, 1924, in the New York *Nation.*

pose" as Molotov, premier since 1930, declared "of training them for government work." These 200,000 potential office-holders were to be an effectual counter-weight against the college-trained intellectuals. Some people saw in this enroll-ment an assertion of the working-class character of the party, as against the bourgeois-intellectual onslaught of the Trotsky crowd. Others saw in it simply the pitting of up-starts from the working class against ambitious younger intellectuals in a struggle for power between two groups of leaders, in which the theoretical issues were only a blind for personal and group ambitions. Certainly these former-workers-raised-to-office have ever since been the chief main-stay of Stalin's power. The grumbling "man in the street" of middle-class origin, sympathized with the Opposition, as he would have sided with any other group opposed to the official régime, and as four or five years later he sided with the Right-Wing opposition headed by Bukharin and Rykov. The workers as a mass seemed to be rather indif-ferent to the outcome of this struggle in higher spheres. Moreover, it was understood that the quarrel should remain *en famille* and that the non-party mass should not be dragged into that contest. (It was only during the intraparty struggle of 1926-27 that the Opposition began to appeal to the outsiders as well.)

Before long Trotsky and his friends began to be treated as if they were enemies of the Revolution. His adherents were removed from positions of importance; a thorough "cleansing" was effected in the universities, and students were expelled in large numbers as "undesirable elements." The procedure was fraught with many personal tragedies.

At last Trotsky had to resign his post as Commissar for War—that vantage point from which his adversaries were afraid he might be able to strike back more effectively than by outworn recriminations and the platonic sympathies of the "red" students and younger professors.

STRANGE BEDFELLOWS

The game was now practically up—at least for the time being. Moments of bitter humiliation came to Trotsky. The obliteration of his name had already begun while he was still a member of the Political Bureau of the Party—the highest council of the country. During the celebrations of the seventh anniversary of the organization of the armed forces of the Republic, only a few weeks after his resignation as War-Commissar, the Red Army daily did not print a single word about the man who more than anybody else had contributed to the victorious conclusion of the civil war.

In 1925 an American admirer of his, Max Eastman, published a book, *Since Lenin Died,* in which he attacked the Old Guard, on account of the methods used by them in their struggle against the great Tribune after Lenin fell ill. Trotsky wrote two statements in which he damned the book as "counter-revolutionary." He had no choice; a refusal would have meant expulsion from the party and political death. He still had hopes for a better day, and in the meantime he worked at his modest post of Chairman of the Concessions Committee and a few other assignments in the organization of national economy.

The campaign designed to undermine his authority in the party and in the masses at large went on unabated. Zinoviev, whom Lenin had called a "deserter" and a "strikebreaker" in 1917, went so far as to ask for Trotsky's expulsion from the Central Committee and even from the party itself. But Stalin was satisfied with his removal from actual power. It was supposed by many that he expected to use the fallen demigod as a potential ally in his forthcoming struggle against the other two triumvirs. When the Central Committee, backing Stalin, opposed the demand for Trotsky's expulsion, Zinoviev was indignant at the spirit of "semi-Trotskyism" prevailing in that body, and protested against too much intra-party democracy. A year later he was one of the loudest champions of democracy in the party!

This struggle had become inevitable. Stalin was not the man to share power with anybody, and Zinoviev and Kamenev as well as their personal following among the party dignitaries, began gradually to realize that their hate and jealousy had duped them into setting up the rule of one as firm and unbending as the fallen giant. Finally, what must have seemed almost incredible to those who had read their studied attacks and learned insults against Trotsky, actually happened. Zinoviev and Kamenev made a complete volte-face and offered their alliance to their erstwhile enemy against the inexorable master of the party machine.

Trotsky accepted. He was not very proud of his bargain. His opposition, which so far had been carried on in the name of a principle, such as "democracy in the party" and a more planned economy, was unmistakably becoming a struggle for power, a contest of personal grudges and ambitions. It seemed, however, his only chance of ever getting back. Zinoviev, moreover, the chief culprit in all the attacks of the past year or two, showed a spirit of contrition which was almost convincing. He declared humbly that he had committed two great mistakes in his life— the first in opposing the November insurrection of 1917, and the other in fighting Trotsky in 1923-24. On the other hand, Trotsky had to make a statement "that in all those questions of principle upon which he disputed with Lenin, Lenin was right—and particularly upon the question of the permanent revolution and the peasantry." Stalin called the affair "an undisguised business transaction"—and he was not altogether wrong. For, later on, particularly after the capitulation of Zinoviev and Kamenev, and his own arrest and deportation, Trotsky again began to parade his "permanent revolution," which he had repudiated for the sake of the alliance of 1926.

One of the chief arguments advanced during the struggle by the new opposition was that under Stalin's régime the bourgeois elements were taking the upper hand. The party was accused of falling under the influence of hostile class elements—the "Nepmen," or new capitalists of the cities, the "Kulaks," or more prosperous farmers, and the bureaucrats. In this growing influence the opposition saw a threat to the proletarian character of the revolution. They used, in this connection, the phrase "impending Thermidor," harking back to that momentous day in the Great French Revolution, when, on July 27th, 1794, the ninth Thermidor of the revolutionary calendar, Robespierre was overthrown by another faction within his party—an event which inaugurated the rule of the big bourgeoisie. The Opposition demanded a decisive struggle against this development. They demanded greater democracy in the party, in order to counteract bureaucratism, and a quicker tempo in the development of the country's industries, in order to strengthen the working-class elements and to make possible the collectivization of agriculture. To get the necessary means, they insisted upon taxing the peasantry—they usually spoke only of the "Kulaks"—to the limit of their resources. One of the chief protagonists of the Opposition, Preobrazhensky, a celebrated Soviet economist, was rather candid in one of his statements concerning the peasantry. Other countries, he said, used their colonies to get the necessary means for building up their industries. We have no colonies, but we have the peasantry. So simple!

At the same time, the Opposition insisted that Stalin's idea of building socialism in one country, while the rest of the world remained capitalist, was un-Marxian, notwithstanding the fact that Stalin tried hard to use some quota-

tions from Lenin to such purpose. The oppositionists had at
their disposal a large crop of quotations to the contrary.

In reply to demands for a more militant policy of the
Communist International (the body directing the activities
of all communist parties) with the world revolution as
its goal, Stalin spoke of the stabilization of capitalism in
the West, as precluding an early revolution in other countries. Many revolutionary non-conformists, however, were
heard to imply that this "stabilization-of-capitalism" argument was only another way of saying that the ruling group,
having consolidated its power, had abandoned the idea of
world revolution in order to avoid military complications
with other countries.

When Stalin pointed to the development of socialist elements in Russia's national economy, Trotsky and his associates incautiously asserted that what was being built in
Russia was not Socialism but State Capitalism. To which
Stalin again replied that if what was being built in Russia
was State Capitalism, then the government was not a
workers' government but a capitalist government—and
dared them to draw that conclusion. . . .

The Opposition, with an eye to the dissatisfied elements
among the workers as well as the minor intellectuals, pointed
to the inequalities of income existing among the various
categories of government officials and workers. (There was
no economic equality in the Soviet Republic, even during the
period of "military communism." The more important one
was in the hierarchical scale, the more one got; not in
money, it is true, for money had almost lost its meaning,
but in actual comforts.) Joseph Stalin, in his book *About
the Opposition* (p. 220) retorted that "there can be no
equality as long as there are classes and as long as there is
skilled and unskilled labor * (see Lenin's *The State and the*

* It should be borne in mind that in "skilled labor" the Marxists usually
include mental work as well.

Revolution) ; we must talk not of an indefinite equality but of the elimination of classes—of socialism"; and, further, on the same page : "one must not play with phrases about equality, for this is playing with fire." The Opposition could have replied that "socialism" without equality was State Capitalism; that no "elimination of classes" was thinkable while there was inequality; and that the lower reward paid to manual labor perpetuated its lower social status. Yet the spokesmen of the Opposition were not insistent on that point,* for at bottom they agreed with their adversaries.

The last few weeks before Trotsky's expulsion from the party were crowded with highly dramatic incidents. His speech at the Central Committee on October 23, 1927, when his expulsion from that body was proposed, if read, as spoken, along with the interruptions and insults hurled at him from well-nigh the entire assembly, sounds like the record of one of those stormy sessions of the French Convention of 1794 which ended by abruptly concluding the career of Danton, or Hebert, or Robespierre. Trotsky was cornered and knew it. He spoke out all his bitterness at the persecution on the part of the secret police, which after all had been set up to fight the enemies of the Soviet system and not dissenters within the party; at the harsh methods used against the Opposition, including the expulsion of some of the most glorious figures of the Revolution and the civil war. He recalled that Lenin had demanded Stalin's removal from the General Secretaryship of the Party; he attacked

---

* In his criticism of the program submitted to the Gotha Congress of the German Socialists of 1875, Marx said that in the "first phase of communism," after the elimination of the private capitalists there would be "no class differences because each [would be] but a worker like the other"—even though there were quite substantial differences in the rewards. Modern socialism, as the ideology of the intellectual worker, protests against the privilege and inequality involved in private capitalist profits; the privileged rewards for "unequal individual endowment" (Marx) it accepts as a matter of course.

what he called "falsification of party history" consisting in "fabrications, distortions, hiding of facts and documents, and perversions of Lenin" committed by the Bureau of Party History; he taunted the majority with the famous "enrich yourself" slogan with which Bukharin had encouraged the well-to-do farmers, and which he had dropped later under the onslaught of the Opposition. He attacked, as insincere and demagogical, the sudden announcement of the seven-hour working day, which was to win over the sympathies of the workers on the eve of the tenth anniversary of the Revolution. He pointed to the "well-established bureaucrats, including the trade union officials, the administrators, the industrial managers, the new private capitalists, the privileged intellectuals in city and country, all those elements which are beginning to show their fist to the working man, telling him 'this is no longer 1918!' "—implying that the time when the worker was paramount in the councils of the Republic, has passed for good. . . .

The struggle had been full of unworthy moments. Hand in hand with serious quotations from Lenin, which were supposed to discomfit Trotsky on the intellectual plane, special reprints were made of all the out-dated morsels of abuse which, prior to the revolution, Lenin had written against Trotsky and the latter against Lenin—both to be taken as proof of Trotsky's moral depravity. Special squads of whistlers and noise-makers were organized and put in action whenever a speaker of the Opposition tried to present his point of view—at least so the Opposition charged. The Opposition resorted to secret meetings and to a secret printing of their platform, its publication having been forbidden as an anti-party—that is, counter-revolutionary—document. The Party retaliated with the help of the secret police, and the Opposition complained that "frame-up" methods were used to compromise them as allies of the monarchists. It was all in the good old style of the French

Revolution, when the various revolutionary factions were striving for power and accusing each other of connivance with the foreign invaders.

Worst of all, a very ugly turn was given to the conflict with the introduction into it of the racial element. In an item, published in the *Pravda,* the central organ of the party, the Communists were enjoined *not* to use as an argument against the Opposition the fact that some of its most prominent leaders, such as Trotsky, Zinoviev, Kamenev, Radek and others, were Jews. This was interpreted by some as a subtle way of putting things in order to play up racial jealousies and prejudices, both within and without the communist ranks. It was done, no doubt, in the heat of the struggle, for the ruling faction was entirely exempt from any anti-Jewish sentiments and tendencies.

The high point of the struggle came on November 7, 1927, the tenth anniversary of the Bolshevik seizure of power. On that day the Opposition participated in the official parades in Leningrad and Moscow, but carried banners and placards of its own, with its slogans directed against the Kulaks, Nepmen and Bureaucrats. Trotsky's automobile was attacked and a policeman fired a shot at it. "Somebody guided his hand," Trotsky insinuates in his autobiography . . .

Shortly after November 7 Trotsky and the other leaders of the Opposition were expelled from the Party and banished to various far-away places within the Republic.

STALIN'S GREAT CAMPAIGN

The suppression of the Kronstadt rebellion had marked the beginning of the New Economic Policy, which at bottom had been the economic platform of the mutineers. In a similar way, the elimination of Trotsky and the other leaders of the Opposition was followed by the adoption of most of the economic measures which they had proposed during their struggle for power.

At the time of his expulsion from the party, Trotsky's following extended far beyond the university students and the young "red professors." In one of his speeches, Bukharin, then the main theorist of the ruling group, inadvertently threw some light upon the real situation. He pointed to the fact that the success of Trotsky's propaganda had its roots in the great distress then prevailing (1926-28) among a large section of the intellectual workers of the country. In fact, two or three hundred thousands of them were unemployed.

Thus it was once more, the old, old story of the "outs" turning on the "ins." Trotsky's victory would have meant to them not merely the vindication of a more deserving leader over the unworthy "epigones," nor even the triumph of a more practical and correct economic program—for Stalin was only too ready to learn from the Opposition. The victory of the Opposition meant to them chiefly the creation of two or three hundred thousand new office jobs, or, at least, their own accession to already existing jobs, as supporters of the Stalin régime were eliminated . . .

Stalin understood that the arrest and banishment of the Opposition leaders would not solve the question. The unemployed and starving intelligentsia had led and organized the revolutions of the past, including those against the Tsar and against Kerensky. Those two or three hundred thousand unemployed intellectuals were a potential menace. In fact, danger signals were already appearing. The Opposition had delved deep into the masses; they had begun to stir up the workers; strikes, which had become a rarity since the establishment of the Soviet régime, began to pop up again. The unemployed manual workers, not all of whom were receiving insurance benefits, were beginning to show an ugly temper. A net of secret connections, more dangerous than those of the Whites and the Mensheviks, was beginning to spread in the cities with the "old man"— as Trotsky was called by his followers—directing and encouraging these activities from his exile on the Chinese border. If, on top of this dissatisfaction in the cities, should come a foreign invasion, the situation might become really desperate for the Stalin régime . . .

Stalin met the situation in a heroic way. The questions of national defense and unemployment must be solved in the shortest possible time. He not only borrowed Trotsky's thunder, he let it roar ten times as loud. Stalin, who had formerly sneered at the billion rubles which the Opposition demanded for accelerating the industrialization of the country, and who had defended the poor peasant lamb which Trotsky was ready to shear so close, was now going to spend many times that amount. The agricultural population, not only prosperous "Kulaks," but middle peasants as well, were now taxed to desperation. A tremendous, unheard-of campaign of industrialization and rural collectivization was begun. With a courage in which he has no equal, Stalin actually ran counter to the will of the great majority of the rural population. At the same time it was declared officially, in a speech delivered by Molotov (Soviet premier since 1930), in July, 1929, that "Trotsky's super-industrialization policy was and remains pernicious and antiproletarian, because this policy did not hesitate at rending apart the bond with the middle peasant." . . .

The collective farms were to provide the Treasury with the exportable grain needed to purchase machinery. To carry out these two campaigns of industrialization and collectivization, millions of additional workers and hundreds of thousands of new clerks, organizers, bookkeepers, agronomists, in short, intellectuals and semi-intellectuals, were necessary. Soon not a single white-collar man was out of employment. Trotsky's army of malcontents was absorbed in the State machinery and forgot about its exiled leader. A large section of his general staff deserted even before that time. Kamenev and Zinoviev were of course the first to capitulate and to be readmitted to the party. Others followed suit, some by claiming that there was no longer any real reason to hold out, since the party had now come round to their point of view; but most of them by humbly bowing their heads and admitting they had been wrong. An undignified scramble set in, each anxious to be first to deny his leader and get the best available higher job.

However, not all the oppositionists deserted the old leader. Christian Rakovsky, former Soviet Ambassador to France, and a few unbending men bound to Trotsky by ties of personal friendship or by romantic devotion, remained in exile. The Trotskyist publications are full of reports of persecutions, suicides, and even occasional executions of the followers of the great Tribune. In his autobiography, Trotsky speaks of "violence, beatings, physical and mental torture applied against the best Bolshevik workers for remaining faithful to the November Revolution." The official press ignores these accusations and it is hard to establish the facts. . . .

RUSSIA WITHOUT TROTSKY

It was not given to Trotsky personally to behold all these developments. Late in 1928 he was requested by the authorities to discontinue his propaganda activities once and for all. When he indignantly refused to give any assurances to this effect, he was expelled from his country for "counter-revolutionary activities, consisting in the organizing of an illegal anti-Soviet party, whose activity was lately directed towards the provoking of anti-Soviet uprisings and the preparation of an armed struggle against the Soviet power."

It was a foregone conclusion that no other country, except Turkey, would admit him. One after one, all his applications for asylum in the various countries were turned down. He has remained on the shores of the Bosporus ever since.

Trotsky is a lonely man now. He derives little joy from the fact that Stalin has adopted many of his suggestions. For, as he wrote to one of his friends "what is decisive in politics is not only the *what* but also the how and the *who*." But the defeated giant has likewise his consolations. His former enemies in the Stalin camp, have fallen, one by one, into disgrace—Bukharin, the chief theorist of the party; Rykov the Soviet Premier; Tomsky, the head of the trade unions. Of a less audacious temperament than Stalin, they became frightened by, and opposed, the excessive tempo of industrialization, extreme rural taxation and collectivization which the new master had initiated.

They had really plenty of reasons to be frightened. Bukharin, as an economist, and Rykov as a practical politician, each of them with a finger on the pulse of village life, foresaw a catastrophe. Bukharin coined the famous expression, "military-feudal exploitation of the peasantry," which Stalin never forgave him. It was even worse than the "Thermidor" and "Bonaparte" accusation coming from the Left. Rykov and Bukharin, of the so-called Right Wing of the Communist Party, speaking in behalf of the middle and prosperous farmers, dreaded a peasant uprising that might spread all over the country, overthrow Soviet rule and bring about some sort of Fascist or Bonapartist reaction. Many commanders of the Red Army, which after all is composed mostly of peasants, were alarmed, and protested. The leaders of the trade unions, headed by Tomsky, likewise balked. True, unemployment had been done away with, but the standard of living of the average worker had been reduced considerably. Fats, eggs, wool, everything, was sent abroad to obtain new machinery. The workers were grumbling, and the authority of the trade union leaders who could not remedy the situation, was declining. In the end the resistance of the peasantry forced Stalin to relent and to heed the warnings of the "Rights."

Stalin had actually so outdone all the proposals ever made by the Left Opposition in the matter of industrialization and collectivization that even Trotsky was moved to protest against what one might almost call "Super-Trotskyism." In Trotsky's opinion the attempt to execute the Five-Year-Plan in four years was a false step. It was too great a strain upon the endurance as well as upon the loyalty of the workers whose standards of living were considerably lowered. With an eye to the progress of revolutionary communist sentiment abroad, he wrote that "what would immediately impress the broad circles of foreign workers is not the abstract figures of statistics, but the actual and substantial improvement in the condition of the workers in the Soviet Union." He had been less interested in the human element when he himself was in power.

In his opposition to Stalin's rapid tempo, though on different grounds, he found himself in unexpected harmony with his opposites on the Right Wing. In fact there were efforts towards a *rapprochement* between Bukharin's Right-Wingers and Trotsky sympathizers—"semi-Trotskyists" in high position and repentant Trotskyists who at heart had remained opposed to Stalin. (Moreover, during the polemics raging in the American communist camp in 1929, it was revealed that the real cause of Trotsky's deportation to Turkey was "the danger that Bukharin might conclude an alliance with him.") Stalin, however, succeeded in foiling every attempt to bring about a joint attack directed against his administration.

Trotsky, seeing that what he dreamed of is now being carried out by his rival, denies the alleged socialist character of the country's achievements. "We were told," he wrote in 1931, taking exception to a much heralded speech by

Joseph Stalin, "that at the third year of the Five-Year-Plan the Soviet Union has entered into socialism. If that were true, we should have witnessed a tendency toward the gradual equalization of wages." In pointing to various other features concerning the workers' situation in the Soviet Republic, he seems to imply that under Stalin's régime Russia is moving towards State Capitalism rather than towards equalitarian socialism, or communism, as conceived or aspired to by the workers.

Stalin's momentous speech before mentioned, dealt not only with methods of stimulating the workers' zeal but also with the Government's new attitude with regard to members of a heretofore openly hostile group—the technical intelligentsia. The long struggle of the high-class "specialists" and engineers against the political intelligentsia and semi-intelligentsia which runs the government machine, has ended with concessions on both sides. The inequality, inherent in State Capitalism is still more to be emphasized by granting to the technicians incomes considerably exceeding those of the ordinary bureaucracy—not to mention the manual workers, of course. In return, the technicians will give up their sabotaging activities, with which they had hoped to bring about the economic breakdown of the system, and the restoration of private capitalism, with its generous rewards to high-class technical talent. They will do it the more readily, as by now the idea of government control or ownership of industries, i.e. State Capitalism,* is opening

* The Russian Communists dislike to have the designation of State Capitalism applied to the present economic system of their country. That term, however, has now been adopted not only by the various "right" and "left" critics of the system. It is likewise being used by the growing number of warmly sympathetic radical and liberal intellectuals the world over who, by pointing to the Soviet Union, have familiarized the public mind with the great advantages of government ownership and planning. The term expresses the combination of the socialist principle of State ownership with the capitalist feature of inequality. The Communists prefer to call that system "Socialism," reserving the term "Communism" for the reign of equality that is to come in a distant future. . . .

out more and more, the world over, as capitalism's only escape from the dilemma of slow disintegration or violent revolution. . . .

IN KEMAL'S CAGE

In the meantime Trotsky in his Turkish exile is engaging in the entertaining pastime of issuing encyclical after encyclical and thesis after thesis to his scant number of faithful followers in Russia and in the rest of the world. The situation in Russia, the crisis in Germany, the revolution in Spain, the civil war in China, and the mistakes committed in all these questions by the Russian Communist Party and the Communist International—all these come in for a merciless analysis under his trenchant pen. As in former years, his articles, pamphlets and books are translated into, and read in all languages, but it is no longer the Communist International or the parties affiliated with it, that cover the expenses. He has become a kind of International all his own, a highly centralized one-man-affair, with himself as the chief inspiration, the only theorist, the principal "angel," and the sole Inquisitor. It is not his intention, so he avers, to create a new Communist International and new communist parties in competition with the official bodies, as it is not his intention to overthrow the existing Soviet régime by force. By boring from within and from without he expects, sooner or later, to see the triumph of his cause in Russia and in the Communist International.

But he has a rather hard time of it, and this hope of his seems much like a willful self-deception, enabling him to keep up his spirits under the weight of his own personal crushing defeat.

Far from making headway in Russia, against his openly hostile rivals, he is not even able to assert his authority among his followers either at home or abroad. De-

fections and desertions of his Russian followers are com-
plemented by distressing heresies of his admirers elsewhere. In their bitterness against the official communist
parties, many of the communist dissenters in Germany,
France and other countries, went much further than their
champion was ever prepared to go. They not only doubted
the revolutionary judgment of the Stalin group, but even
began to question the proletarian character of the Soviet
régime, as it is at present. They adopted the criticism
of some earlier dissenters who declared that "Thermidor,"
that is, a reactionary overturn, had already taken place, and
that the Stalin régime expressed the rule of "classes hostile to the workers." Once Russia was no longer regarded
as a workers' republic, the energetic steps taken in 1929
on account of the Chinese-Eastern Railway, became in their
eyes an ordinary imperialist enterprise. As a result of this
stand of theirs, Trotsky broke with some of his most faithful supporters abroad. With the capitalists removed, he
argues, workers' rule has been definitely established, and
Stalin's régime is not "Thermidor"—but is only, by its
mistaken policy, unconsciously preparing the way for it. If
the Russian Revolution had reached its Thermidor, he said,
a new revolution would be necessary; all that is actually
needed, in Trotsky's opinion, is a readjustment in the party
apparatus; to be accomplished, one may suppose, either by
substituting Trotsky for Stalin, or by readmitting Trotsky
to the party under not-too-humiliating conditions.

Trotsky's hope for readmission to the party has so far
been vain and will probably remain so. His last attempt—
late in 1929 he endorsed an appeal of his friend Rakovsky
—was useless. The appeal was not humble enough and
Stalin was adamant. Nothing less than full repentance and
submission would do.

Will Trotsky ever take that last step? He predicted to
Zinoviev and Kamenev that their abject capitulation meant

their political death, and he was not mistaken. Stalin for-
gives his repentant foes, but he never readmits them to any
position of real power. Trotsky will not kowtow for a
mere living. He prefers to stay in his lion's cage, the unbending head of a little, insignificant sect, but fully conscious of his rôle in history and expectant of his inevitable
vindication in his own country as well.

Whether or not Trotsky lives to witness that vindication himself, his name, as the inspired advocate of State
Capitalism with its super-industrialization and collectivization, will hold a place in history along with that of Stalin,
the fearless executor of his ideas, and that of Lenin—
the leader of a Revolution that, by destroying all vestiges
of Russian feudalism, paved the way for that momentous
development.

BENITO MUSSOLINI

An Adventure in Caesarism

THE wave of enthusiasm that has greeted the rise of the Italian dictator has been receding for some time past. The trains-running-on-time argument has lost its luster. The last great convert on that score, Bernard Shaw, has likewise fallen away—to worship at other altars. The successor of the Caesars still has his admirers abroad, but their number has been shrinking as the "red peril" which he went forth to stamp out has become less menacing and as he himself has begun to dicker with and to abet the "Red Trade Menace." His merciless destruction of all vestiges of Freemasonry, his ever changing attitude with regard to the Catholic Church, his alignment with the former enemies of the Allies, have somewhat cooled the ardor of sundry groups of his worshippers. Others have been alienated by the ever recurring outbursts of primeval savagery on the part of his adherents, ever ready to beat, maim and kill, not only Communists and ordinary trade unionists of the American Federation of Labor type but also highly respectable dissenters of the Count Sforza, Amendola, Nitti, Salvemini type, who were never suspected of being red, pink, or in any other way connected with even the most moderate forms of labor activities. Last but not least, his various encroachments upon the sacred right of property—as when he forces private manufacturers to abstain from cutting down their labor force—as well as other desecrations of time-honored taboos, have

drawn upon him the fire of many of the most conservative publications—in other countries, of course. And instead of being respected as a champion of the existing
capitalist order, he is disparaged as an erratic later-day im-
itator of the classical tyrants of old, whose histrionic antics and high-sounding pronouncements need not be taken
too seriously.

Still, this evaluation of Benito Mussolini fails to consider
adequately the actual historical forces that have brought
him to the fore. His methods of dealing with his opponents may be archaic—borrowed as they are either from
the Marius-and-Sulla or from the Abdul-Hamid periods
—and his various ex-post-facto philosophies may be reactionary, but historically speaking, the movement he per-
sonifies is something new. It is part of a new historical
process—the rise to power of a new class, whose Pro-
tean character has expressed itself during the last hundred years in the most contradictory currents and activities, from the loftiest idealism of a Malatesta or Liebknecht, to its exact opposite as exemplified by the Italian
dictator and his would-be imitators in other lands.

In the early eighties, at the time when Mussolini was
born, Socialism had just begun to get a foothold in the
working masses. Benito's father was one of the early converts from among the manual workers to the revolutionary
gospel of Bakunin, and no doubt this fact had a great share
in shaping the revolutionary career of his son. The sons of
radicals may be indifferent to their fathers' gospel in countries like America, where until recently socialist or related
ideas were never taken seriously and the individualist gospel
of "equal opportunity" had for many something of a convincing ring; but in Italy there has never been the semblance
of such "opportunity"—not only for a gifted and studious
son of a worker but even for an educated scion of the middle
classes. Mussolini was quite lucky; for, owing to particularly

favorable circumstances—his father had become an inn-keeper—he was enabled to acquire a secondary-school education, including training for a public school teacher. But he was not to remain a rural teacher at fifty-two lire ($10.20) monthly.

At the time of his graduation in 1902, Italian socialism was a rather peculiar affair. It professed the same theories as the socialist parties of other countries; it pursued the same tactics—propagating the gospel and getting votes at the polls—but the composition of its upper crust was different. In the other Western European countries, the advent of democracy and the rapid industrial development had succeeded in taking care of a large section of the malcontent intellectuals who had constituted the chief ferment in all the revolutionary movements of the preceding period. Moreover, the public-school system had been organized to a tolerable degree and had rendered elementary education accessible to large sections of the working class. As a result the manual workers had produced from their own ranks large numbers of self-taught leaders. These formed a counter-weight to the middle-class or lower-middle-class intellectuals who had joined the socialist and labor movement either for the sake of a political career or, occasionally, for romantic reasons. In Italy, public-school education was still in its infancy, and consequently the manual workers had exceedingly few leaders who had sprung up from their midst. On the other hand, the number of intellectual *déclassés* was larger than in any other country except Russia—and for the same reasons as in Russia. The middle and lower middle classes had provided their offspring with a higher education for which, however, the country because of its economic backwardness could find no application.

As a result, enormous numbers of *déclassé* intellectuals avidly embraced revolutionary ideas, particularly those of

BENITO MUSSOLINI

the most extreme coloring. With the development of modern industrialism, they first nursed and finally flooded the labor movement, for it offered them what a saturated bureaucratic apparatus of the state, as well as a limited market for their abilities had denied them : jobs and prospects for a political career. Large numbers of higher intellectuals, who in other countries would have joined the "regular" parties, but who in Italy were comparatively underpaid and were discouraged by the great competition in the bourgeois parties, likewise discovered their tenderness for the horny-handed underdog, and for a whole period the Socialist Party was called the "party of the professors." Many of these professors, lawyers and journalists, who learned the political game as representatives of the working class used their experience five, ten or fifteen years later to become regular bourgeois politicians.

At the time when young Mussolini was imbibing socialist ideas, the Socialist Party was in the throes of an internal struggle for leadership. The party was gradually becoming a power in the country. It had succeeded in organizing large masses in the political, trade-union, and coöperative fields ; it had a large electorate and a considerable number of representatives in parliament—all of them intellectuals of the first rank—and the moment seemed near when they would finally reap the fruits of their strenuous labor. The appointment of the first socialist cabinet minister in France (1899) had just startled the world, and the Italian Socialists might soon be called to follow in the footsteps of the French comrades. Socialist opinion, in Italy and elesewhere, was divided on the admissibility of such a step. The future successor of the Caesars, though following all these controversies, had no say in such matters as yet. No sooner had he finished school than he became a homeless vagabond and expatriate. Nineteen years old, he had given up a pedagogical career which meant only unmitigated misery for the rest of his life. For

if Italy or any other of the poor and backward countries of
Southern Europe, had an ideographic system of writing like
the Chinese, it might express hopelessness or resignation by
the symbol of a village school teacher. His enemies, and they
are many, in countless publications printed in all countries
of Europe and America, have claimed that his departure for
Switzerland was due to more intimate reasons, as well as to
his desire to escape military service—but these may just as
well be disregarded.

REVOLUTIONARY APPRENTICESHIP

The few years he spent in Switzerland were filled with
fiery revolutionary propaganda which brought about his expulsion from various Swiss cantons. This was the time of
his revolutionary apprenticeship, and, considering his extreme youth, he did his job extremely well. For a while he
worked as a bricklayer; he worked for various socialist papers published for the Italian workers living in Switzerland;
he headed bricklayers' strikes; he violently attacked the moderate leaders of socialism, who were anxious to prevent any
demonstrations or other turbulent scenes. At the same time
he read copiously, not only the socialist classics but also
modern philosophers and historians, and his lectures against
religion, which he always combined with the gospel of working-class revolt, would have done honor to Robert Ingersoll
and Clarence Darrow.

He seems to have . . . forgotten that period altogether.
In his "Autobiography" he says: "In that period (1904) I
experienced the greatest sorrow of my life: the death of my
mother. . . . All the independent forces of my soul, all my
intellectual or philosophical resources—even my profound
religious convictions were powerless to relieve my boundless torment." It was in the very same year that he lectured
on the proposition—"God does not exist. Religion is an ab-

surdity in science, an immorality in practice, and a disease in man." In summing up his arguments on the subject he declared that "the religious man is abnormal," and that "religion is surely the cause of some 'epidemic diseases of the mind' for which a cure by psychiatrists is necessary." Published and republished by his former comrades, that lecture is still one of the bibles of atheist propaganda among the Italian workers in the United States.

When he returned to Italy in 1905, the country was being rocked by a violent strike movement, an aftermath of the great general strike of 1904. That strike had been called as a protest against the shooting of striking workers in Sardinia and Sicily. It was a gesture of protest, and the Socialists were doing their best to keep the movement within the bounds of legality, though they did not always succeed. The movement could have easily developed into a violent revolution, but the Socialists—already established as one of the political machines of democratic Italy—were not anxious to face the horrors of a civil war. The most they were ready to do was to present the rather naïve demand that the government should once for all desist from using armed forces against the striking workers.

The turmoil continued during the subsequent years, with railway strikes, agricultural strikes and general strikes of protest following each other in quick succession. A new force had made its appearance in the Italian labor movement, which threatened both the social peace of the country and the rule of the old moderate or "reformist" majority in the Socialist Party. It was syndicalism, that new school of revolutionary thought and action which ten years before, in the middle of the nineties, had begun to shape itself in France. However, on crossing the Italian border it had taken on a somewhat different aspect.

In France, syndicalism had, to a very great extent, been the expression of the revolt and jealousy of the self-taught trade-union leaders who had risen from the ranks of the manual workers, as against the socialist intelligentsia. Its ideas were greatly influenced by the anarchist protest against the parliamentary dickerings of the socialist politicians. Only after the syndicalist movement had taken shape, did it find a philosopher in the person of Georges Sorel, who himself had been inspired by the modest originator of French syndicalism, Fernand Pelloutier. But Sorel never was more than a name to the French syndicalist militants, and his works were read even less by them than is *Capital* by most of the socialist politicians who swear by the name of Karl Marx. In Italy, however, syndicalism was readily adopted by large sections of the radical intelligentsia; these constituted themselves an opposition within the Socialist Party—a course entirely at variance with the original conception of syndicalism, which altogether rejected any party allegiance.

The Italian converts of the new gospel, led by two professors of political economy, Arturo Labriola and Enrico Leone, accepted most of its basic tenets—the general strike, direct action and the revolutionary rôle of the trade unions as instruments both of struggle and of reconstruction after the victorious general strike. But they did not accept its hostile, or rather indifferent, attitude with regard to parliamentary action, insisting instead that the workers should elect their own representatives to the Chamber of Deputies. The candidates, it is true, were to be nominated not by the party but by the trade-union organizations; but considering the scarcity of self-taught workers competent for such a task, preference more often than not would have been given to the syndicalist intellectuals. In other words, they adopted the revolutionary vocabulary of anti-parliamentary syndicalism for the purpose of putting fresh blood into the depleted veins of parliamentary socialism. They were out to conquer the party by an assault with new arguments that sounded better in the ears of the impatient worker. And they were also out to get hold of the trade unions, which were, just as much as the party, in the hands of the most moderate elements. Once in possession of these two machines, they would have gradually drifted back to law-abiding normality. Their militant activity in connection with the various conflicts between the workers and their employers was designed to hasten that process of conquest. But the party politicians did not wait. They expelled the syndicalists before it was too late.

Benito Mussolini, then twenty-three years old, had at first, immediately after his return from Switzerland, joined his father, helping him run his little country inn. In his leisure time, of which he had a good deal, he read the philosophers of pessimism and individualism—Schopenhauer, Nietzsche, Stirner—and last but not least, Machiavelli. Thus, while a wave of strikes and violent struggles was rocking all sections of the country, he was assembling the building stones for a philosophy that was to justify his activities of fifteen years later. After two years, he returned to his activities as a public-school teacher. His prospects in this career were better now, than they had been three years before. He had acquired a good knowledge of French and some kind of a certificate permitting him to teach this language. From the teaching proletariat his road was now open, so to speak, to the teaching lower-middle-class. The revolutionary and atheist peccadilloes of his later 'teens and early twenties would not have stood in his way. Born as a result of violent revolutionary struggles, and still on non-speaking terms with the Vatican, modern Italy did not look very closely into a man's political or religious past, or even present.

However, Mussolini's turbulent spirit and his growing self-confidence needed another outlet for his energy than teaching children. Or perhaps, if one is to believe some of his opponents who tried to analyze him in the Adlerian fashion, he needed this outlet to combat a strong sense of inferiority and to compensate for a lack of physical courage—the latter a characteristic as to which there is a practical unanimity among all of his former friends who shared his early struggles.

Be that as it may, after a year he again went abroad, this time to Austria, where he became editor of a Socialist daily published by Cesare Battisti, socialist deputy to the Vienna parliament from the Trentino, the Italian-speaking section of the Hapsburg monarchy. Six or seven years later, Battisti was hanged by the Austrian authorities as a "traitor." He had joined the Italian army during the great War, and when taken prisoner was accorded the fate meted out by England to another "traitor"—Sir Roger Casement.

Riding the Revolutionary Phrase

Expelled from Austria for a remark that was interpreted as an expression of Irredentist sentiments, Mussolini returned to his native region of Romagna and became secretary of the Socialist Federation of Forli. Soon afterwards he was placed in charge of a local weekly published by the organization.

The files of that weekly, which he edited from 1910 to 1912, can no longer be found in the town library of Forli; and anyone who asked for them in the large public library of Milan or Rome, would show more courage than judgment. Founded at the time when the syndicalists had already been excluded from the Socialist Party, the *Lotta di Classe* ("Class Struggle") was not following in the track of that new heresy. In his revolutionary heyday, Mussolini never assumed an actually syndicalist attitude and never laid emphasis upon the industrial struggle. The ideas which he propounded, in violent opposition to the ruling ultra-moderate majority of the Socialist Party, were a mixture of most of the extreme doctrines of political radicalism. They represented an intensely effective juggling of elements from Marxism, with its class struggle and economic interpretation of history; from Blanquism, with its readiness to resort at any moment to a political "coup" or "putsch"; from Hervéism (of that period) with its "anti-patriotism" and hatred for imperialist adventures; from Anarchism, with its "negation" of the state and its "propaganda by the deed." Georges Sorel, the philosopher of syndicalism, with his glorification of violence, contributed nothing to this mental hodge-podge. Sorel was still the monopolistic property of the Italian syndicalist intellectuals, and only after most of them had become ardent followers of the Mussolini of ten years later, was the French philosopher acclaimed as one of the great teachers who had helped to form the mind of the Duce. Sorel himself, as a matter of fact, died as an admirer of Lenin.

There are terrorist exploits of which not all revolutionary Anarchists would approve—for instance, the bombing of cafés or theatrical performances attended by the bourgeoisie. In those days Mussolini's sympathy for the turning worm and his hatred for the well-to-do went to the extreme. When in July, 1910, a bomb was thrown into a theatre in Buenos Aires, Mussolini in two successive issues of his *Lotta di Classe* voiced his satisfaction with what had occurred. "I admit without discussion," he wrote in the issue of July 9, 1910, "that in normal times bombs do not form part of socialist methods. But, when a government—be it Republican, Imperial or Bourbon—gags you and puts you beyond the pale of humanity, then no one condemns violence in reply to violence, even if it finds some innocent victims." In the subsequent issue he continued: "In the Colon Theatre, on that famous gala evening, all those present represented government reaction. Why call the bomb-thrower a coward, simply for disappearing in the crowd? Did not even Felice

Orsini attempt to hide? And did not the Russian terrorists, when their coup had been carried out, try to avoid arrest? Are they heroic madmen who carry out individual (terrorist) acts? They are heroes nearly always, but scarcely ever insane. Was Angiolillo* a madman? Was Bresci a madman? Or Sophia Perovskaya? No! Their behavior drew words of admiration even from bourgeois journalists of high intelligence. In judging these men and their acts, we must not place ourselves on the mental plane of the bourgeoisie and the police. It is not we Socialists who must cast a stone. Let us acknowledge instead, that individual acts have also their value and sometimes are the first signals of profound social transformations."

At about the same time the world was resounding with the famous Sidney Street affair of London. After Winston Churchill, with nearly the entire London garrison, had succeeded in exterminating two Lettish desperadoes, Mussolini gave vent to his sentiments in the following passages printed in *Pagine Libere* of January 1, 1911, a magazine published in Lugano, Switzerland: "So they were Anarchists?" he wrote. "Yes, Anarchists! But not in the classical sense of the word. Haters of work, because physical work—and let us have the courage to proclaim it once for all—embrutes not ennobles man; haters of property, which fixes the differences between man and man; haters of life, and above all, haters, deniers, and destroyers of society. . . . Anarchism, adapted to the masses, loses all its heroic grandeur, because the mass, whether it be a crowd or an army, is vile. It is good that the upper layers of society should be warned from time to time that below the surface there are being prepared volcanic explosions with a voice of dynamite."

* Angiolillo was an Italian anarchist, who, in 1897, killed the Spanish Premier Canovas del Castillo. Bresci, another Italian anarchist, killed the Italian King Umberto in 1900. Sophia Perovskaya was a Russian terrorist, who, in 1881, participated in the successful attempt on the life of Tsar Alexander II.

Two elements of Mussolini's mental make-up of those days show forth from the last paragraph: his personal, individualist hatred for the rich, and his contempt for the "vile" mass. This contempt is admitted even by his official biographer, Margherita Sarfatti. Whether he realized it or not, the revolt he was advocating against those in power, was not a revolt in behalf of the "vile" mass—but rather the revolt of a hungry aspirant for power against those who were well established in it.

But between the power of the bourgeoisie and his own aspirations, there stood still another power, that of the sated intellectuals of the Socialist Party, who held in their hands the whole apparatus of propaganda and organization—the cardinals and archbishops of a new creed, compared with whom he was only a humble village priest. The opportunity to get even with the old leaders, or at least to join their ranks, was to come soon.

LEADER

In 1911 Italy's long suppressed desire for imperialist expansion broke forth in the war with Turkey for the possession of Tripoli. A wave of annexationist fervor swept not only large sections of the population of the southern regions which expected immediate benefits from the conquest, but also all the bourgeois classes, including the intelligentsia. Italy had been the "proletarian" among the great powers who had swallowed up all the territory available for colonization. It was only fair, ran the patriotic argument, that she, too, should get her share, to provide for her surplus population; which, as was grimly stated by the defenders of the Italian claims, had so far served only as a sort of fertilizer for enriching the civilizations of the other lands.

The socialist and labor movement did not present a solid phalanx in opposition to that undisguised war for conquest.

A number of the most outstanding figures of the movement, representing the extreme right wing of the party came out openly in favor of the war. Their justification was expressed by their main spokesman in these words: "We need the courage, the discipline to die for a cause, today for the interests of other people, tomorrow for the ideal." Outside the party, the most prominent of the syndicalist intellectuals, such as Arturo Labriola and others, likewise engaged in a defense of the Tripoli expedition. They argued that a victory in a foreign war would raise the workers' self-esteem and thus enhance their militancy in the class struggle, and that the use of violence in a foreign war would encourage the returned soldiers likewise to resort to violence in their domestic conflicts.

Ingenious as these arguments sounded, they were only a blind. The unadorned truth was that the Right-Wing Socialists and the syndicalist intellectuals were afraid of the forthcoming class struggles, and that jointly with their own bourgeoisie, they were out to solve their country's internal problems by means of imperialism. Subjugation and exploitation of other countries, accompanied, as in Britain, by certain benefits for the working class, was to take the place of domestic conflict and to open the road for peaceful class collaboration. And it was exactly these syndicalist intellectuals who—with the exception of Labriola—less than ten years later were to supply some of the most active representatives of Fascism, with its perfectly frank "ideology" of conquest for the benefit of the Italian masters. Poor Georges Sorel, with his gospel of violence, meant originally as a proletarian revolt against capitalism, had to provide the ideological camouflage of "continuity" for their volte-face.

The moderate "center" of the party, and the extreme left as represented by Mussolini, whose provincial paper was coming more and more into national prominence, did not see it that way. Perhaps they did not believe that Italy was able

to get a "place in the sun" in a world already partitioned by
the stronger powers; perhaps they were afraid lest the wave
of war-enthusiasm, if unopposed, might weaken the labor
movement and leave them with diminished prestige and numbers—at any rate, they firmly opposed the expedition. Mussolini, in his provincial district, even took part in the organization of serious anti-war disturbances, such as tearing up
the rails in order to prevent the departure of trains carrying
soldiers. A prison sentence of five months was the result of
these activities. This happened in October, 1911. He had had
his troubles with the authorities before—but this was the
heaviest penalty he had ever incurred. He became a national figure. . . .

At the convention of the Socialist Party held in the following year, Benito Mussolini was the spokesman of the Left.
Two questions agitated the assembly; the imperialist deviation of the extreme Right in 1911, and their undignified attitude after an anarchist attempt on the king's life in 1912.
In the official jubilation at the king's escape, the leaders of
the extreme Right, who had endorsed the African expedition of the previous year, joined chorus with the monarchists. This had greatly scandalized all the more radical
elements in the party, with resulting benefit to the anarchist
and syndicalist competitors of official socialism.

It is here that Mussolini appears as the savior of the party
from a deviation to the Right which unwittingly was
strengthening the heterodox Left competition. His scathing
arraignment of the king's adulators, does not appear in his
official biography, otherwise not poor in details. "Why," he
asked, "should one be moved and weep about a king and only
about a king? Why this excessive and hysterical sensibility
when crowned heads are involved? Who is the king? He is
the citizen who by very definition is useless! There are peoples who have driven out their kings, when they were unwilling to protect themselves more effectually by sending them

to the guillotine, and these peoples are in the vanguard of civilized progress. For socialists, an attempt on the life of a king is a historical event or a news item, as may be. Socialists cannot associate themselves with monarchist mournings or festivities. . . . It is known that there is in existence a telegram, reading : 'I beg you to present my deep-felt salutations to His Majesty.' And this from Bissolati, who, twelve years ago, was shouting, 'Death to the king!' "

Mussolini got the scalps of his opponents, and four of the most prominent right-wingers, including Bissolati and Bonomi, were expelled from the party as a result of their war records and their betrayal of Republican principles. The excluded soon founded a party of their own, which though not as strong as the official party, had considerable representation in the parliament.

An interesting detail : the deputy Bonomi, one of the men whose expulsion was due to Mussolini's insistence, later became Minister of War in the cabinet of Giolitti in 1920-21, at the time of the Bolshevist scare. It was he who instructed the military authorities to supply the Fascist groups with all necessary ammunition, motor lorries, and other assistance, thus becoming mainly instrumental in Mussolini's later triumph. It was a truly Christian revenge. . . .

Having smashed the "right danger" and restored the radical reputation of the party, Mussolini, at the age of twentynine, was raised to one of the highest positions the party had to offer; he became editor-in-chief of the party's only daily paper, its central organ, *Avanti!* published in Milan.

With the central organ in his hands, he let himself go in a propaganda of ultra-radicalism which was quite out of tune with the actual policy of the party. Actually, the aspirations of the party were so moderate that four years before, in 1908, the bourgeois progressive *Secolo* of Milan could thus sneer at the Socialist Party decisions adopted at the convention at Florence: "But all this, that is *our* program. It took

the Socialists twenty years of struggle to get to this point.
Was it worth while?" On the other hand, Mussolini's wild
stuff was pleasant reading for the working masses, whom
the party politicians were out to rescue from the danger of
anarchist or syndicalist seduction, and he was permitted to
proceed. He touched upon one of the most ticklish questions
of the Italian socialist movement—the fact that all the candidates running for parliament were college-bred intellectuals; he attacked those party leaders who were Freemasons
—and most of them were—accusing them of a secret understanding with the Liberal bourgeoisie; he exhorted the workers to counter violence with violence—thus arousing the anger of the German Socialists, who considered such language
highly improper and Blanquist rather than Marxian.

LOSING HIS FAITH

It is possible that the violent language in which he was
indulging was only meant to drown the voice of his own
doubt of the cause he had embraced. His doubt, in this case,
affected not merely that ardent belief in the ideal of human
brotherhood and equality which a socialist intellectual usually loses before he gets out of his teens. It also touched his
belief in the more practical aspects of socialism, so to speak,
its ambition successfully to use the pressure of the masses
to curb private capitalist privilege, and finally to replace
it by the rule of the intelligentsia in the form of various
schemes of government ownership. The slow progress of the
cause, the disconcerting indifference or stupidity of the
masses, and the influence of his philosophical reading, particularly Nietzsche and other aristocratic despisers of the
lowly, all had their share in undermining the faith which he
was preaching—and kept on preaching even after he lost it.
For it is hard to start all over again, after one has reached
the age of thirty.

Two months before the outbreak of the War, Italy was on the brink of revolution. Clashes with the police which occurred in connection with a nation-wide antimilitarist campaign precipitated the general strike of June, 1914, and the struggles known as the "red week."

The great *élan* shown by the masses during that week may for a while have re-awakened Mussolini's waning faith. In the issue of *Avanti!* for June 12, 1914, immediately after the strike had been called off, he expressed his joy over the events of those "days of fire and blood" and his disgust with the trade-union leaders, whose decree ordering the cessation of the strike he described as "an act of treason."

Mussolini's bitterness against the moderate leaders of the General Confederation of Labor was no doubt genuine. He was not a hero himslf, but their cowardice disgusted him. The old rivalry between the *déclassé* intellectual, now hungry chiefly for power and ready to take a chance, and the self-complacent upstart ex-workers or other trade-union bureaucrats, who did not look beyond their safe jobs, sprang forth again in his diatribe. He might have had his doubts about the possibility of the ultimate aims of Socialism; but these doubts would not have stood in the way of his assuming power, or sharing in it with others, if as a result of that movement the governmental fabric had collapsed. Next to the Anarchist Malatesta, he was then the most popular figure among the revolutionary elements. Under his editorship the circulation of the daily had risen from 40,000 to 100,-000. . . . He knew his Marx well, and after assuming power, he could have explained to the impatient crowd that a transition period was necessary between capitalism and pure socialism; and that that transition period was a democratic republic, with or without a certain modicum of State Capitalism, controlled by the working class—that is, by the Socialist Party, headed by Mussolini. Before the masses had recovered from their joy at the overthrow of the monarchy, he would have consolidated the power in his hands and the whole crowd of hungry *déclassé* intellectuals, more numerous in Italy than in any other country, would finally have had their day—that is, their steady government jobs. . . .

To the attacks of the bourgeois press, which dwelt upon the excesses committed during that week by the underworld elements, he replied in his grand manner. Harking back to Marx, who "had justified all the measures taken by the Paris Commune of 1871," Mussolini wrote in the *Avanti!* of June 22, 1914; "We repeat it calmly, that as regards the latest general strike we accept what was good and what was bad; the proletariat and the underworld; legality and extra-legality; protest and insurrection."

Deep in his heart, however, one may assume, something else was going on simultaneously. The ease with which the moderate leaders had succeeded in extinguishing the flame of revolt and in getting the workers back to their factories made him include in his contempt not only the pusillanimous leaders but also the docile herd.

Some heretics, of whom there is always an unwelcome and uninfluential crop in every movement, thought at the time that the masses would not have let themselves be sent back to work so easily, if they had struck for higher wages and shorter hours as well. But such a simple thought did not occur to Mussolini; for a socialist intellectual, Marxian or no Marxian, always thinks of the "higher aspects" of the workers' struggles; and these higher aspects go beyond the mere slavish demand for fuller stomachs. They visualize, first of all, better political institutions with better politicians to head them and to take care of the bread-and-butter demands of the masses.

And thus, his ambition disappointed both by the masses and by his fellow leaders, Mussolini plunged into that limbo of cynicism, where honor, consistency, loyalty to one's friends and to one's party, are engulfed in the boundless egotism and unscrupulous self-seeking of the Renaissance man who is "beyond good and evil."

THE WAR

Two months later, the world was at war. Italy was not in it at first, and the Socialist Party advocated neutrality, as did in the beginning most of the other political parties and the grand old man of Italian politics, Giolitti. For about ten weeks Mussolini adhered strictly to the party line and was outspoken in his denunciation of the War. What he really thought of it all, while he was fulminating against the idea of Italian participation, is hard to make out. By the revolutionary reputation he had established for himself, he was bound to assume an intransigent attitude. Actually he had ceased to believe in anything and his mind was drifting. The signs were multiplying that eventually Italy would be dragged into the fray. Powerful interests were working in that direction. For a man in Mussolini's exposed situation to maintain his attitude, once Italy's participation had been officially decided, would mean to invite the fate of Jaurès, the French Socialist pacifist who was murdered on the eve of the declaration of war. To die for convictions which no longer meant anything? In private conversation Mussolini expressed himself in favor of intervention while openly he still opposed it in the paper he was editing. He was obviously preparing a gradual change of front. Right and left of him, old acquaintances, Socialists, Syndicalists, Anarchists, who like him had been preaching an ideal they no longer believed in —and who from all their past revolutionary convictions, had preserved only their appetites and the primeval faith in the efficacy of violence—were urging him to fall in with them. He still wavered. After all, his friends were only adventurers, who would never reach the summit of anything and were ready to serve one cause to-day and another to-morrow. He had a very promising career at stake. But his doubts ceased, once strong financial backing was assured him. When he no longer concealed his new alignment, he was forced out of the *Avanti!* and, five weeks later, began to publish the daily *Popolo d'Italia,* in which he immediately embarked upon preaching the very opposite of his own ideas of a short time before.

The opponents of Mussolini, whether radicals or liberals, have charged, ever since the War, that the financial backing necessary for the establishment and maintenance of *Popolo d'Italia* came from France. Names have been mentioned, notably that of the secretary of a French cabinet minister, who was said to have been in charge of transmitting to Mussolini the monthly subsidies from the French Government. The name of that French cabinet minister was Jules Guesde, the ultra-radical founder, and for more than a generation supreme leader, of French Marxism. At the outbreak of the War, he had discovered his patriotic heart and had joined the War Cabinet of the former Socialist Viviani. The accusation has been repeated time and again in Italy and abroad —a refutation has never been seriously attempted. Thus the chief exponent of revolutionary Marxism in Italy seems to have been brought or bought into the imperialist venture by the chief exponent of revolutionary Marxism in France. History offers few such grim pieces of humor.

The new paper called itself a "socialist journal" and carried two significant mottoes. One of them, "He who has steel has bread," was by Auguste Blanqui, the famous French Socialist and conspirator, who had spent half of his long life in prison for his various attempts to seize the government in order to establish a revolutionary dictatorship. By the middle of the eighties, only three or four years after his death, large numbers of his adherents had joined the movement of General Boulanger, reactionary aspirant to a military dictatorship and would-be emulator of Napoleon. The second motto had an even more illustrious author. It was by the great Corsican himself, and it read: "The revolution is an idea which has found bayonets." Was this selection of mottoes mere journalistic rodomontade—or was the journalist actually out for great adventure?

Soon afterwards Mussolini was expelled from the Socialist Party. A month later (January, 1915), referring to his "Groups for Revolutionary Action" which he organized in support of his propaganda for Italy's intervention in the War he wrote: "I think something great and new can emerge from these platoons of men who represent heresy and the courage to represent heresy. To-day it is War—it will be Revolution to-morrow. . . . Our intervention has a double scope, a national and an international one. . . . It means a contribution to the breakdown of the Austro-Hungarian empire; it means, perhaps, revolution in Germany, and, by an inevitable counterblow, revolution in Russia; it means, in short, a step forward for the cause of liberty and revolution. . . . The War is the crucible in which the new revolutionary aristocracy is being prepared. Our intervention is that of rebels, or anti-constitutionalists, and not the intervention of moderates, of nationalists, of imperialists."

The value of his protestations for "liberty and revolution" and against "nationalism and imperialism" may be measured by the fact that he was at the same time protesting against the participation of Greece in the war on the side of the Entente. The country of Venizelos would have interfered with Italy's ambitions in the eastern Mediterranean—"which is destined to be our field of expansion to-morrow." Thus, while the regular Socialists were courting the favor of the masses with the promise of their humanitarian ideal, and the Nationalists were tempting them with the prospect of a great empire, Mussolini tried to outstrip competition by promising both.

Italy entered the War, and Mussolini, who was conscripted, returned a scar-covered hero. These scars he owed to the explosion of a defective trench mortar, after a very short stay in the trenches proper. Long before the end of the War, though completely recovered from his wounds, he was permitted to return to his editorial occupation and to the fight for "liberty and revolution." . . .

The Socialists, whom, in his paper, he fought with the greatest violence, were in reality not "defeatists" like the Bolsheviks in Russia or the followers of Karl Liebknecht and Rosa Luxemburg in Germany. Their country had not been attacked, and as they had opposed its entrance into the war, they favored a speedy conclusion of peace. Following the great catastrophe at Caporetto and the invasion of Italy, they were as much for national defense as any other party.

THE AFTERMATH

The War was over but Mussolini's day had not yet come. The revolution which he had predicted while preaching intervention was in the air, but it was not to him that the masses directed their eyes for leadership. He was either disregarded or despised.

The "victory" had brought none of the things the masses had been led to expect as a prize for their sacrifices. The Socialists and other anti-war radicals, with their "I told you so," enjoyed greater popularity than ever, but for Mussolini there was no way back to the fold. The gulf of hatred between the party and its former favorite, who had passed into the camp of the war mongers, could not be bridged.

Mussolini now ceased calling himself a "Socialist" and dropped the word from the front page of his paper. It was to be from now on a paper defending the interests of the "fighters and producers"—this could mean everybody, but actually meant first of all, the ex-combatants. Having long lost all faith in socialism, he declared himself frankly an "individualist," giving an anarchist coloring to that term. In doing so, he was greatly influenced by Libero Tancredi, before the war a famous exponent of individualist anarchism, who had also contributed largely to Mussolini's conversion to interventionism in 1914. Under the name of Massimo Rocca, Tancredi was later to become one of the high dignitaries of the Fascist State—until he fell into disgrace for having ventured the impudent admonition that "the revolution was made by the Fascisti for Italy, but not for the Fascisti alone."

It is difficult to believe, but on April 16, 1920, only two and a half years before his assumption of power, Mussolini actually delivered a denunciation of the principle of organized government, equal to anything Bakunin or Kropotkin might have written on that subject, and certainly sufficient to bar him forever from landing on our shores. The occasion was the government's decision to introduce the daylight saving system which had called forth strong opposicion among the population. Mussolini joined the opposition and wrote in this connection the following passages taken at random from a long article: "Down with the State in all its forms and incarnations—the State of yesterday, of to-day and to-morrow, the bourgeois State and the socialist State! For us who are about to die for individualism, there remains nothing in the dark present or the cloudy to-morrow but the religion—absurd, it may be, yet always consoling— of Anarchy!"

In the light of his later policy as chief of the Fascist State, tending to denationalize certain public utilities and to turn them over to powerful private corporations, this classical sample of anarchist prose assumes a particularly ironic significance.

During the first two years after the conclusion of the War —roughly speaking, throughout 1919 and during 1920 until after the occupation of the factories in August-September—

his generally acclaimed rôle as "savior of Italy from the Bolshevist peril" is not so evident, for he himself, to all appearances, was part and parcel of that "peril."

Shunned by the other radicals, he founded a group of his own, which adopted and outdid the slogans of other radical currents in order to win over adherents from them all. The original members of his group were those deserters from the other revolutionary parties and organizations who in 1914-1915 had rallied around the banner of intervention. A pamphlet compiled by Giacomo Matteotti shortly before his assassination presents a remarkable collection of quotations from Mussolini's daily *Popolo d'Italia,* culled during the first two years after the War. There is no weapon in the arsenal, or demand in the programs, of socialism, syndicalism, anarchism, and communism that was not advocated in the columns of this paper: the class struggle; strikes for higher wages; strikes of public servants; direct action; the general strike; the 44-hour week (as against the 48-hour week demanded by the General Confederation of Labor which was under moderate Socialist control); separation of the Church from the State; confiscation of church property without indemnity; partial expropriation of capital to the extent of the public debt; abolition of the Senate; establishment of a republic; universal suffrage for both sexes; expropriation of the land with compensation for the former owners at the pre-war value; nationalization of industries, with workers' and government representatives on the Boards of Management; nationalization of banks; declaration of the First of May as a national holiday; abolition of the censorship and of all restrictions against the liberty of the press, of associations and of propaganda.

Mussolini advocated violence against the merchants who were responsible for the high prices and even suggested hanging them on lantern posts; he protested against the adoption by the municipalities of measures of economy involving the dismissal of workers; he attacked the authorities for denying to Anarchists the same right of assembly that was granted to the Socialists. . . . There was only one radical demand he would not subscribe to, and that was . . . Dictatorship. He was implacable in his opposition to this idea. For while he was ready to promise to the masses all the possible moons and to encourage them in any enterprise, he apparently wanted nothing for himself—except that dictatorship which he execrated. . . . Nor did he ever speak of the red flag, for he espoused the national tricolor and had always, since 1915, presented his ideas in a solution of flowery nationalist verbiage.

Nevertheless, the workers were in no hurry to desert the other radical organizations and to rally around Mussolini's eclectic revolutionarism. The efforts of the first year were almost entirely wasted, and Mussolini began to realize the hopelessness of his ambition to recover his old popularity among the working masses. The results of the elections of December 1919 were very disappointing. Out of 346,000 votes cast in the Milan district, his own group polled less than 5,000.

It was at this time, in expectation of the election results and without any strong backing either from the workers or from the bourgeois elements, that he turned down D'Annunzio's idea of a "March on Rome" for the overthrow of the government and the establishment of a republic. That "march" would have carried to the top his then dangerour rival, D'Annunzio, leaving Mussolini to play second fiddle. He had no taste for such a part. A political outcast, he was dreaming in the terms of Cesare Borgia's *"Aut Caesar, aut nihil."* Closer to the latter than to the former, he outdid himself in a flood of bombastic verbiage that was a mixture of aristocratic, individualist anarchism with complete philosophical nihilism. He hailed the return of Errico Malatesta, grand old man of romantic anarchism, and his very antipode in every respect; he sneered at "the bellowings of the herd that is getting tired waiting for a paradise that will never come, while we are supported by the security that the day of our full vengeance is not far." That full vengeance he was to have soon—and the Socialists did their best to help him get it.

THE TURN OF THE TIDE

In the summer of 1920 the Metal Workers' Union, embracing nearly half a million members, addressed to their employers a demand for higher wages. When the demand was rejected, the workers resorted to "obstructionism," or "striking on the job," as it is called here, whereupon the owners decided upon a lockout. In reply, the workers occupied the factories.

There was undoubtedly a strong element of syndicalism in this action—but it was approved not by Syndicalists alone. Not only the Syndicalists and Anarchists, as well as the extreme Socialists (who later formed the Communist Party) but also the right-wing Socialists and the moderate trade-unionists of the General Confederation of Labor endorsed the move. The "People's Party," a large Catholic organization active mainly among the rural workers and taking its inspiration from the Catholic clergy, came out in support of the workers, advocating coöperative management of the plants. Revolution was in the air, and nobody dared to oppose the workers. The government's attitude was altogether passive. No attempts were made to dislodge the workers from the plants. Mussolini and his adherents did not set out to defend the present capitalist system against the encroachments of the rapacious workers. In the September 12, 1920, issue of his paper, he declared that "trade-union management of the industries and of the public services is a Fascist postulate. . . . With regard to the present case, we are venturing the question as to the manner and the time. Can the trade unions at present take the place of private initiative and enterprise? It is necessary to proceed gradually. But that does not mean that one should never begin." A year and a half before that time, in March, 1919, when the workers in a provincial town occupied the large metal plant in which they were employed, Mussolini had been invited to address them. He did so, and his paper (March 20, 1919) printed his speech. "I am telling you," he said, "that you are on the right path because you have liberated yourselves from your protectors; your gesture is new and worthy of sympathy, on account of the motives which have inspired it. . . . I am with you for the sake of your rights, which are sacred."

Thus Mussolini's intervention to avert a threatened Bolshevik dictatorship, has been, to say the least, greatly exaggerated in the telling. . . .

The occupation of the factories fizzled out because the various radical parties and groups hesitated to bring matters to a head. The "Bolshevist Peril" proved a myth. Where the propertied classes had suspected a firm revolutionary determination to do away with privilege and inequality, they found preachers, politicians, job holders, but practically no revolutionists—though, as a matter of fact the Socialist Party was affiliated with the Communist International. Here was a helpless crowd, ready to revolt but unable to do so without leaders. The bourgeoisie decided to take revenge for their own late fear and humiliation and to deprive the workers of all those advantages which their strong organizations and the respect they had inspired in the employers had obtained for them during the War and immediately afterwards. The instrument for that revenge was at hand.

A new element had appeared on the scene since the demobilization. Countless numbers of the educated and semi-educated sons of the lower middle classes had come out of the trenches, eager to find some occupation and to start life

over again. After all the sufferings they had endured during
the War, they found that they were not wanted: their former jobs had been taken by women, and all the other soft
jobs were in the hands either of government officials or of
leaders and employees of the various working men's organizations. There was no chance for emigration, and even the
manual workers, whom they despised as an uneducated rabble, were better off than they were. The manual workers at
least had jobs and in many respects they were better off than
even the white-collar slaves, for these had no strong organization to back up their demands. The wages of the railway
switchmen, actually exceeding those of government-paid village physicians, were often quoted as a case in point. The
workers' organizations kept doing imprudent and heartless
things which deepened the bitterness of the intellectual and
semi-intellectual *déclassés* as well as of the other ex-soldiers.
War veterans and invalids were refused admission to labor
organizations—as if to punish them for their participation
in the War—and men wearing uniforms were insulted; useless compensatory gestures on the part of a working class
waiting for a revolution that was not coming. All this was
grist to Mussolini's mill.

From these dissatisfied elements Mussolini began to re-
cruit his following. They were a minority group, compared
with the great mass of manual workers, but they were desperate, and they had fighting experience—which the workers,
to a large extent, had not. The latter had stayed in their factories to supply the combatants, who were mainly peasants.
They were joined by a great number of ordinary adventurers of the underworld type, who expected impunity in an
organization including so many former army officers and
"highbrows." Thus the *fasci di combattimento,* "fighting
groups" were organized, and they tried their hand for the
first time in April, 1919, by attacking and burning the office
of *Avanti!* the special object of Mussolini's hate.

With their leader, these *déclassés* were biding their time. They swam with the revolutionary tide as long as the revolutionary outlook was favorable. When the outcome of the factory occupation proved that there was no actual strength behind all the revolutionary show of power, Mussolini understood that his time had finally come. Until that time he and his followers had been ready to win power and influence fighting side by side with the workers; now he was ready to get that power and influence by throwing in his lot with the other side.

Was he a traitor? Mussolini, who until that time had tried to outdo all other radicals, could have countered the socialist cry of treason with the counter-charge that they themselves had betrayed the workers by letting the revolution run to seed—and that he was going only one step further. He found it better policy to attack the Socialists from the opposite angle, as dangerous revolutionists who were ruining the country with continuous strikes. He made himself a rallying point for every element which for any reason had a grudge against one form or another of socialist activities. Aside from the capitalists, these included the small merchants, who complained of competition from the coöperative stores, and the rural landowners, big and small, who were suffering from the pressure of the trade union of agricultural laborers. These all gave their adherence to Mussolini's party, and their sons joined his armed bands. Many workers, either unemployed or on the lookout for permanent occupation, likewise joined him to obtain steady factory jobs as loyal employees, ready to spy on their radical fellow workers. His main support, however, he found in the big corporations, eager to put the workers in their place once for all, and in the government itself. The government wanted to break the political influence of the Socialist Party, which controlled about 3,000 municipalities and sent 150 deputies to Parliament—nearly one-third of all the members. The big corporations gave the necessary cash, and the government gave weapons, lorries, officers and . . . impunity.

In 1919 Mussolini had vowed the great revenge. He could have it now, and he took it. Punitive expeditions were organized, first in villages and provincial towns; the Socialist administrations of the municipalities were forcibly compelled to resign, the premises of the Chambers of Labor, the cooperatives and other radical institutions were raided and their records destroyed. If the workers offered resistance and drove out the raiders, and if Fascists were killed or wounded in the fight, large detachments would soon return, this time not merely to destroy but to kill. Often they were under the protection of armed forces which remained neutral as long as victory was assured for the Fascists. During that civil war, as Professor Salvemini points out, the militant Red groups never resorted to the Fascist tactics of raiding offices of other parties or forcing the resignation of municipal or government authorities.

The attacks of the Fascist squads did not have the effect that might have been expected—of consolidating the forces Mussolini had set out to destroy. The Communists offered resistance, fighting back with what arms they could get hold of, and so did the Anarchists; but these were minority groups within the laboring masses. The greater number followed the Socialist Party and the General Confederation of Labor, the powerful trade-union organization closely connected with it.

The Socialist Party was indeed still very powerful. It had 250,000 members in 1920-21, as against 83,000 in 1919. The trade unions, influenced by it, had 2,500,000 members. Thousands of coöperatives were controlled by the party. The main daily *Avanti!* had risen to a circulation of 400,000, and only technical difficulties in printing prevented a larger issue. The socialist magazine, *Critica Sociale,* edited by the leader of the party, Filippo Turati, was subsidized by the

Banca Commerciale, a large financial institution whose heads were wise enough to see in the party a force for social preservation. The party had in its hand between 2,500 and 3,000 municipal administrations, with plenty of jobs and about as much favoritism and similar graft as in any other administration. It still had with it very large sections of the lower middle classes, and particularly of the intellectuals, whose party it had been by tradition for decades. Not without cause had it attached the book as the symbol of the unity of workers, peasants and intellectuals, to the Soviet hammer and sickle, adopted as emblem after the Bolshevik Revolution. The party, in spite of its non-revolutionary, peaceful character, was affiliated with the Communist International— to satisfy the revolutionary temper of the masses. Professor Arturo Labriola, formerly syndicalist theorist (but sufficiently cooled in 1920 to become Minister of Labor under Giolitti) much later expressed the opinion that the Socialist Party could have seized power either in 1919, at the time of the high-cost-of-living disturbances, or in 1920, at the time of the factory occupation—but its leaders having achieved middle-class affluence, recoiled from the risk.

Early in 1921, following recriminations on the part of the Communist International, after the fizzling out of the factory occupation of September, 1920, a split took place in the party. The communist element had tried to have the Right-Wing leaders expelled. The center ("Maximalists"), in theory one-hundred-per-cent Communist but in practice as afraid of revolution as their more outspoken right-wing neighbors, sided with the latter, and the Communists bolted, forming their own party. The "Maximalists," who believed that "a revolution cannot be made by leaders but comes automatically," were afraid that an expulsion of the Right-Wing reformists would lead to a breaking up of the party and to the loss of the many jobs it still had at its disposal in spite of violent Fascist attacks. Their leader, Serrati,

thought Mussolini a "fool" and expected the Fascist craze
to peter out soon, when the safe business of revolutionary
talk and law-abiding practice would be resumed as usual. In
the meantime they were determined to go on talking socialism, class struggle, opposition to collaboration with bourgeois governments, and the rest of the socialist "centrist"
vocabulary.

The Right-Wingers, including the most experienced and
astute politicians of the socialist movement, saw clearly the
seriousness of the situation—but this did not mean that
they were ready to offer any serious resistance. They were
frantically trying to make peace with the Fascists. They
boasted of having prevented the revolution which had im-
pended during the period of factory occupation. They urged
the workers to forsake all use of violence, and they demanded severe punishment for the carrying of arms, though
it was obvious to everybody that such punishment would
be meted out only to the radical workers. For it was the
minister of war himself, their late comrade Bonomi—once
expelled at the behest of Mussolini as too moderate—who
was now arming the hosts of the former revolutionary firebrand.

Premier Giolitti, the "Jesuit in the garb of a plain clothes-
man," who, a year before, had refused to interfere with the
occupation of the factories, now, in 1921, refused to interfere with the violences committed by the Fascists. As he
put it, the "Fascist movement is too vast to permit police
interference." A year ago, the old Liberal Machiavellian
had, so to speak, entrusted the intellectuals and upstart ex-
workers from the Socialist Party and the trade unions with
the task of breaking the spirit of the revolutionary workers.
Now he permitted another set of intellectuals and ex-
workers, headed for the most part by former Socialists,
Syndicalists and Anarchists, to break up forcibly all radical
and labor organizations. It was a triumph of the Liberal

principle of *laissez-faire*—for, officially at least, there was no interference by the government.

Giolitti's collaboration with Mussolini was clearly visible in the latter's attitude with regard to the occupation of Fiume by D'Annunzio and his légionnaires. Though honor-bound to help in the romantic adventure of the imperialist poet, whose "Arditi" had formed the first nuclei for the Fascist black-shirt squads, Mussolini did not budge when Giolitti under instructions from the League of Nations took the necessary measures to expel D'Annunzio from the city he had occupied.

The Socialists' frantic efforts to keep their vested interests, their hard earned jobs in the various labor institutions, now menaced by the Fascist torches, were truly pathetic. In the second part of 1921 a pact of peace was concluded between the Socialists and the Fascists, which was to put a stop to the raids. One of the obligations assumed by the Socialists was not to exhibit the red flag and to use the official tricolor instead. With the national flag, the Socialists also adopted the gentle ideas of the Sermon on the Mount. One of their papers published the following decalogue, preaching a new kind of revolutionary heroism: "(1) Create a void around Fascism; (2) Do not provoke; suffer any provocation with serenity; (3) To win, be better than your adversary; (4) Do not use the weapons of your enemy, do not follow in his footsteps; (5) Remember that the blood of guerrilla warfare falls upon the one who sheds it; (6) Remember that in a struggle between brothers, those are the victors who have conquered themselves; (7) Be convinced that it is better to suffer the wrong than to commit it; (8) Don't be impatient. Impatience is extremely egoistical; it is instinct; it is the yielding to one's "ego" urge; (9) Do not forget that socialism wins the more when it suffers, because it is born in pain and it lives on its hopes; (10) Listen to the voice of the mind and of the heart, which advises you that the working people should be nearer to sacrifice than to vengeance."

Making peace with the Socialists almost cost Mussolini his leadership, for among his followers in the provinces there was general opposition to the establishment of normality. His party was growing by leaps and bounds. The incessant display of violence impressed many who had joined the Socialists as the coming power, destined to take over the government machine and dispense favors to its adherents. Now these expected rulers appeared as poltroons who dared not offer any serious resistance. The Fascists seemed about to win, and the sensible course was to get on their bandwagon. Besides, there was actual excitement and fun in mounting their lorries; money was abundant with the Fascists now; the Bolshevik scare and the Fascist readiness to fight it had succeeded in making "the bourgeois swine come across with their dough," as the black-shirts used to say among themselves. They could extend their activities, and they began to think seriously of taking over the political influence and jobs held hitherto by the Socialists. The Fascists began to build up their own political influence among the working population—even at the momentary expense of their paymasters or other bourgeois followers. The fall of the currency had brought about a rise in prices and great consequent distress among the poorer population. The Fascists therefore used force to compel the merchants and storekeepers to keep prices down. While this measure was not approved by all Fascists, the masses were often impressed and converted by it, particularly in the villages and small towns. Many of them began to join the trade unions which the Fascists themselves were re-organizing, having destroyed those managed by the Socialists. The Fascists also began to organize the unskilled workers, who had formerly been altogether unorganized, thus winning over an element which was to increase their political influence. Once started

on the road of eliminating socialist influence, the provincial
Fascists were loath to stop the civil strife, and they seriously and successfully challenged Mussolini's authority.

The March on Rome

The peace agreement, ineffectual as it was, was soon
officially broken by the Fascists. The large cities had so far
remained the domain of the radical organizations, the Fascist squads not daring to challenge the compact working
population of such cities as Rome, Milan or Turin. When in
November, 1921, they started a fray in Rome, they were
overwhelmed by the masses and forced to leave the city. It
is believed by many that an aggressive general strike, started
all over the country at that moment, would have checked the
progress of the Fascists and prevented Mussolini's triumph
a year later. But nothing happened. The Socialists still hoped
for peace.

Mussolini, having swelled his ranks in the provinces, particularly among the rural population, now began punitive
expeditions into the large cities as well. The moderates of
the General Confederation of Labor began finally to realize
that their doom was sealed. By the time they decided to
organize resistance and to call a general strike, what was
left of the fighting spirit of the masses was completely
broken. A threat on the part of Mussolini that his cohorts
would invade a city was sufficient to discourage any attempt
to continue the struggle.

Actually, Mussolini could now raise tens of thousands of
armed men at a moment's notice. He could not only destroy
labor organizations and terrorize socialist municipal administrations into resignation but he could also defy the government authorities openly, whenever the latter did not see eye
to eye with him.

He was now thoroughly conscious of the power which he

wielded. Here was a discouraged working class, thoroughly
demoralized by a leadership that was unwilling to engage
upon the course of revolution. Here was a frightened bourgeoisie and a wavering government helping him with money
and ammunition to cow the workers and to destroy their
organization. Did they think they could use him as their
latter-day condottiere, as a political gang-leader on a large
scale, whom they could drop as soon as they did not need
him any more? If they thought so they were mistaken. He
had succeeded in cowing the working class—couldn't he just
as well get hold of the government machine and show the
capitalists, who had hired him, who was the real master?
True, there was the army, which was loyal to the government, and his squads were no match for it. But the martial
exploits of the Fascist punitive expeditions had left their
mark upon the thought of the military commanders. If a
small group of armed men could terrorize the whole working
class, why could not the army assert its power against the
civilian government and set up its own rule? A conspiracy
for the establishment of a military dictatorship was soon
the result of conversations between Mussolini and a number
of army generals. The Duke of Aosta, uncle of the king,
who himself had designs upon the throne, was likewise in
the game. The assent, if not the collaboration, of the army
for a forthcoming coup by Mussolini was assured.

Strange and incomprehensible as it may appear, it was
another split in the Socialist Party which precipitated the
"March on Rome" and raised to power its former firebrand
leader. About four weeks before that "'March" took place,
the right wing of the party (which believed in collaboration
with the bourgeois parties and participation in the government) and the left wing (the former "Center," which believed in talking revolution but not making it) had finally
decided to part company. With a large section of Socialists
now becoming available for government majority combina-

tions, there loomed the possibility of a stable government by a more or less liberal-democratic bloc, including the Democrats, the "Popular Party" (Catholic Party) and the Right Wing Socialists, which might attempt to pacify the country by western democratic methods. This move would have put an end to Mussolini's ambition to head the government himself. To forestall it the "March" took place, on October 28, 1922; Mussolini waited in his Milan editorial office for a long-distance call from Rome. It came the next day. Parliament, cabinet, and king were helpless—for they had been warned that the army was with the "rebels." On the following day, Mussolini was the head of the government. Thus he saved the country not from the "Bolshevik peril," which in 1921 he had boastfully declared to be no longer in existence, but from the "danger" of a progressive combination *à la* Herriot, in France.

Mussolini's party was represented in the Chamber of Deputies only by a small group of thirty-five men, and the leader of the Fascists did not insist upon having a cabinet composed of his own adherents only. He took in representatives of every parliamentary party and even generously started negotiations with the moderate Socialists for their entrance into his government—an offer which they very eagerly accepted. It was their point of view that there were "only misunderstandings but not contradictions in principle" between the Fascists and the Socialists. Under the pressure of the ultra-conservative elements, however, Mussolini withdrew his offer later—a humiliation which still hurts the Socialists, and which they have tried to wipe out by denying that such negotiations ever took place. But Mussolini was cruel enough to publish the minutes of those negotiations. It was worse than forcible application of castor oil—one of the more civilized methods of persuasion used by the Fascists against the less prominent of their political enemies and dissenters.

POWER

Mussolini, now at the helm of his country, was free to carry out his program. But what was his program? Of the original radical demands put forward in 1919, there was not a single one on which he still insisted—either in the political or in the economic field. In September, 1920, when he had made up his mind to place himself altogether at the disposal of the capitalist interests, he had declared that "not being tied down to any fixed principles, they (the Fascists) proceed unceasingly towards one goal, the future well-being of the Italian people." Two years later, about a month before the "March on Rome," he had made plain in what the "future well-being of the Italian people" was to consist. "Our program is very simple," he said, "we want to rule Italy."

It sounded like a jest—but it was a program. "We" represented primarily that enormous number of intellectuals and semi-intellectuals, *déclassés* and adventurers, who were now on the point of assuming all the functions of government, from prime minister to policeman; functions which in themselves represent a vested interest affecting a considerable section of the population. The maintenance of their privilege, of their rule, became from now on the sole aim of the victorious party; all their seeming-contradictory measures were consistently adopted with that sole aim in view.

Though only three years before an adherent of the republican system, Mussolini soon found it expedient to recognize the monarchy, in order not to antagonize the army leaders and the conservative Nationalists, who were very valuable allies in obtaining and keeping power. Though at first an enemy of the Church, and eager to accept the help of the Freemasons during his struggles in 1921, he was later ready to throw them overboard—and even to exterminate them, when an alliance with the Church seemed to be more valuable. An advocate of all kinds of anti-capitalist measures in 1919, he became a stanch defender of private capitalism and practically abolished all inheritance taxes; yet that did not prevent him, from time to time, from favoring striking workers and forcing the manufacturers to grant concessions to their employees, whenever he found the favor of the workers necessary for maintaining his own power. In one respect only he did not change—his fierce nationalism and imperialism; though, from his original anti-German attitude, he switched over to a much fiercer anti-French antagonism.

The years following his assumption of power in October, 1922, have been marked by a continuous elimination of all vestiges of democratic parliamentary rule and the consolidation of the unchecked authority of Mussolini and his following. During the first year, by the application of the old guerrilla warfare of clubbing, he created such an atmosphere of fear among all the parties constituting the parliamentary majority, that he easily obtained their consent to a grotesque revision of the election law. This was the very opposite of his original program of 1919, but it was bound to secure him a full parliamentary majority. The law was adopted, since the legislators preferred undignified but painless political suicide to a violent physical death.

The elections held in 1924 turned out to be a landslide. With the methods used by Mussolini, Senator Heflin and the Dragons of the Invisible Empire could obtain landslides even in the Negro, Irish and Jewish constituencies of New York. An opposition, consisting of Democrats, Catholic Populars, Socialists and Communists, was nevertheless permitted to enter the Chamber in order to maintain an appearance of parliamentary government. It became truculent and occasionally quite embarrassing. Among the Socialists, Gia-

como Matteotti towered high above his comrades in courage
and strength of character. A large part of these—particularly the leaders of the trade unions—were ready to give up
the losing fight, to make peace, and even to ally themselves
with the victor. Matteotti was insistent upon holding out,
still hoping that a bourgeois-democratic coalition government might succeed the Fascist régime. A well-to-do country gentleman, one of the few incorruptibles who are in the
game neither for its financial rewards nor for a career but
out of a romantic sentiment of democratic duty, Matteotti
seemed a living reproach to Mussolini, who for the sake
of power had over and over again reneged every faith he
had ever professed.

THE MATTEOTTI MURDER AND AFTER

On the day after Matteotti had delivered his great speech
in the Chamber exposing the methods by which the "landslide" was obtained, Mussolini wrote an article in *Popolo
d'Italia* in which he said that Matteotti had made "a speech
of an outrageously provocative nature which should deserve
some more concrete reply." . . . Ten days later Matteotti
was dead.

The wave of indignation which followed the murder of a
member of parliament for a moment shook Mussolini out of
his self-assurance. He had to give orders for the prosecution
of the men who had acted under his orders. When the storm
subsided, the murderers got off with light sentences and
were released soon afterwards. The charge made was an
attempt to "kidnap" their victim, who had been "accident-
ally" killed as a result of "the practical joke of June, 1924,"
which had "degenerated into a horrible tragedy, independently of, or rather against the will of its authors"—to use
the words of Mussolini.

In reply to that "practical joke," the opposition withdrew

from parliament, leaving the Fascists to themselves. They were deprived of their seats—and a wave of "practical jokes" swept the whole country. The leaders of the radical groups (Communists, Anarchists, Maximalists) being in jail already, it was now the turn of the bourgeois opposition. Amendola, a leader of the moderate Liberals, was attacked and clubbed several times and died as a result of Fascist humor. The house of Nitti, an ex-premier and as "radical" as Mr. Lloyd George of to-day, was destroyed, though its owner succeeded in escaping. The same happened to the house of Count Sforza, formerly Minister of Foreign Affairs, and to that of the famous philosopher, Benedetto Croce. This was disciplined violence—not emotional or chaotic. It was the Duce's *mot d'ordre* that "life should be rendered difficult" or "impossible" to his opponents. Every Italian city and town was subjected to the unlimited authority of a local boss who enjoyed complete impunity. All local elective bodies were finally done away with, an appointed official taking their place. Criticism was suppressed entirely, and every paper had to become an organ of Fascist propaganda. Acts of violence committed by Fascists, when by some misunderstanding they came before the authorities, were declared to be part and parcel of the "revolution"—not subject to the ordinary moral standards. Amnesties followed each other in quick succession and were applied—with a few exceptions—only to crimes committed with a "national aim."

Occasionally the worm turned. People who in any other country would have been law-abiding pinks, Liberals, or moderate Conservatives, turned terrorists, and a few attempts were made on the life of the man who thirteen years before had glorified tyrannicide. An army general, Capello, the only military commander of high rank who had taken part in the March on Rome, outraged at the persecution of the Freemasons, began to support Mussolini's enemies and was accused of participation in a terrorist plot. Every such attempt called forth a new fury of bloody reprisals.

After a few years, every single organization, every single institution that remained was in the hands of the Fascists. Their success had attracted adherents from everywhere, from all parties and organizations. These all had to be placed. Members of the old bureaucracy were discharged by the thousand, to make place for younger talent drawn from the Fascist ranks. Tens of thousands of new government positions were created to take care of aspirants—draining the country's finances. The trade unions were now altogether under Fascist leadership—with a former Italian-American "Wobbly" who had edited the *Proletario,* an I. W. W. organ in New York, at their head. The moderate-socialist General Confederation of Labor was completely destroyed. All the jobs held formerly by socialist and other radical intellectuals and ex-workers were now in the hands of the Fascists, and the old, formerly so proud, leaders of the General Confederation of Labor had to beg the Fascists for modest jobs in an auxiliary or consultative capacity. It was a triumph all along the line.

The strong-arm men, sluggers, rowdies and ex-soldiers, formerly members of the punitive squads, unwilling to work, had likewise to be provided for—for a revolution, with or without quotation marks, is made and maintained not only by intellectuals, semi-intellectuals and self-taught ex-workers. A new praetorian guard was created for this purpose, the Fascist Militia, knowing no loyalty but to the party which had raised them from the depths of gangdom or the misery of manual work to the glories of a better-class policeman's job. The creation of this militia was the answer to all those who put their hope in the army as a potential means for overthrowing Fascist rule. With infinite foresight, Mussolini has gradually increased the militia to such an extent that numerically it now exceeds the army.

This was his way of keeping faith with the army generals who expected the establishment of military rule as a result of the March on Rome. But then, would they have kept faith with him?

Still, there were not enough jobs to satisfy all the aspirants who since the "March" had begun to crowd the organization. The stock of the "revolution" was watered, and the stockholders began to fight among themselves. Directors, preferred shareholders, common shareholders, they all had a hard life of it. Anti-Semitism, a scourge hitherto unknown in Italy, made its appearance within the Fascist ranks. There were too many Jews, they found, in all the more enviable branches of the nation's administration. More power, more jobs, were demanded for the uncircumcized Fascists . . . But it turned out that the Jews had infested the highest ranks of the Party itself. Signora Margherita Sarfatti, editor of the party's theoretical organ, closest friend and official biographer of the Duce, is a Venetian Jewess; and Signor Finzi, Under-Secretary of State, Mussolini's right hand man and one of the main organizers of Matteotti's murder, belongs also to this terrible breed, supposed to be able to create chiefly Freemasons, Bolsheviks and other non-conformists.

To reduce the number of aspirants for jobs, party cleanings were effected from time to time, involving sometimes the simultaneous expulsion of as many as a hundred thousand members of the new aristocracy. Even other, more radical, remedies had to be applied to restrict the ever increasing competition. The Fascist Party was closed to newcomers altogether. Only a privileged minority from among the members of the Fascist children's and youth organizations can expect to be admitted to the new order. A new class, or rather caste of rulers, to whom the rest of the population is subjected, has been created—the frankly avowed aim of the "Revolution."

CAESAR

To perpetuate his régime, Mussolini has borrowed from contemporary and past history all methods in any way suited to the purpose. Restrained by no prejudices, he has learned from his enemies, adopting alike the propaganda and organization methods of the Russian Communists and the educational methods of the Catholic Church. While ruling the present generation by the methods of a dictatorship, he is determined to make the next generation accept his system as a matter of conviction and voluntary consent. Growing youth is to be brought up entirely in the spirit of Fascist rule, and the interference by any other spiritual influence is being systematically eliminated. Hence his conflict with the Vatican, which having enjoyed this monopoly of education in a previous historical period, now sees its power and influence challenged by a new creed and a new lay clergy. The cult of the Duce and of the new régime is gradually to supplant any other cult. Though Mussolini reinstated the crucifix in all the schools immediately after his assumption of power, and though he always invokes the Lord in his speeches, the new articles of faith now taught to the youngsters do not dwell on the infallibility of the Pope but on the fact that "Mussolini is never mistaken." It is not so much "Suffer the children to come unto me," as "The Duce loves the children; the children love the Duce," which is hammered into the babies in teaching them the alphabet. In their primers are descriptions of pilgrimages to the village and the house in which He was born. . . .

When the babies grow up, and their religious devotion to the Duce and his régime needs some intellectual reinforcement, they are dosed with the various philosophers in whose works some justification for Fascist rule and its methods can be discovered. Machiavelli, with his glorification of

Cesare Borgia and all his treacheries and double-crossings; Sorel, with his justification of violence; William James, with his rationalization of practical results; Nietzsche, with his superman—obviously embodied in the Duce and his duce-lets; Vilfredo Pareto, with his theory of the *élites;* Babeuf and Blanqui, with their revolutionary dictatorships—all have had to supply an idealistic cloak for a movement whose first adherents were accomplished cynics with strong appetites.

But counter to these appetites go the appetites and the dissatisfaction of the great laboring masses, whose position has grown worse, wages having, by 1931, declined from twenty to forty per cent since the "revolution." During his early revolutionary career, Mussolini had found that faith in the socialist ideal was a good sedative for the impatient element; the benefits of a terrestrial paradise in the distant future were an even better compensation for the miseries of the present than those blessings of the Beyond which had lost their glamor. Now that the socialist ideal has in turn begun to fade, Mussolini and his crowd have created a new one which for some proletarians may be even more attractive than the dream of human equality. It is the creation of a New Roman Empire—the reëstablishment of the old glories of the period when Rome was the mistress of the civilized world and the *populus Romanus,* a self-glorified parasite, living upon the back of the rest of humanity. That even in those days Rome and the rest of Italy harbored millions of slaves, who had no share in the plunder, the Duce and his minions usually forget to mention. . . .

But his dreams of imperialist expansion have so far been doomed to futility. It is easier to destroy labor organizations and to club, shoot, or at least "castor oil" their leaders than to "smash up" the colonial empires and to annex the dependencies of France and Great Britain. . . .

Being unable to give his subjects an Empire to live on, he is now consistently preparing to give them at least an

Emperor—not only *de facto* but also *de jure*. All open political opposition to him was finally destroyed in 1926, when there were no longer any other parties and every single field of any public activity had been completely appropriated by the Fascists. "Parliament," since 1928, has ceased to be an elective body; all candidates permitted to run for "election" are appointed by the Fascist "Grand Council"—the only ruling body—and the population is permitted to vote "yes" or "no," with no secrecy of the ballot. In the hypothetical case of the majority voting "no," it is given the privilege of voting for another set of—Fascist candidates.

But supreme as Mussolini is, the highest authority still nominally rests with the king, whom he now never meets, though he elected to tolerate him as a concession to his aristocratic allies of the conservative Nationalist Party. These gentlemen were anxious to be spared the indignity of being the direct subjects of an upstart commoner. Mussolini was as willing to abide by this concession as by certain other agreements; and when a time-bomb nearly blew up the whole royal family, the Anarchists, who seldom disclaim their own performances even when they are failures, did not protest when radical and liberal public opinion almost unanimously pointed to the man who fifteen years before had been so merciless to the socialist detractors of regicide.

Be that as it may—all his activities of the last years tend to show that he is out not merely for a dictatorship surrounded by an aristocracy of merit. The man who in 1919, three years before his March on Rome, demanded the abolition of all titles of nobility, has now undertaken to protect the existing titles against all kinds of interlopers. He even includes in his protection the papal nobility, hitherto not recognized in Italy. Nobility of birth, cheapened by past Italian disunion and misrule, is to be restored to its ancient splendor and to become a closed corporation, like the Fascist nobility. For the upstart has always an admiration mixed with envy for the parasitic descendants of ancient free-booters and adventurers—a well-nigh atavistic sentiment of servility, shared alike by the Jacobin general who marries the Hapsburg princess, the proverbial American meat-packer who craves to be presented at the Court of St. James—and the son of a revolutionary blacksmith, who wears spats and brags about taking a bath every day—now.

Thus, to emphasize his eligibility as the legitimate successor of that aristocratic adventurer who was Caesar—he has his scholars ransack the archives to establish a connection between his own humble family and the lords of Bologna of the twelfth century. Signora Sarfatti, in her biography of the Duce, speaking of those medieval captains remarks with a certain hesitation that "we do not know whether Alessandro Mussolini (Benito's father) was their descendant." But since that time Mussolini himself has settled the question, for in his "Autobiography" he refers to his medieval namesakes with an obvious purpose and implication.

When, if ever, he will find the moment opportune for proclaiming himself Caesar, is hard to predict. The financial condition of his country is as bad as it can be, and the great waste entailed in keeping up an enormous machinery of oppression is not the least of the items contributing to this situation. The reduction of the salaries of all government employees, Mussolini's most faithful supporters, is an ominous sign. His own ranks are torn by dissensions, rivalries, internal squabbles. Large groups of non-Fascist intelligentsia are meanwhile embracing the republican-socialist gospel and conspiring for Mussolini's overthrow. The workers, long cowed and demoralized by the extermination or desertion of their most energetic elements, are now restive again and give vent to their dissatisfaction in strikes and demonstrations. For though the prospect that "by 1940 'white coal' will have entirely supplanted the imported black article, and that there will no longer be a market for foreign wheat in Italy," may be perfectly satisfactory to Mussolini's American apologists, such as Mr. Littlefield, it is not very encouraging to those who during that interval have to live on hope alone and to remain "industrious, silent, and disciplined," as Mussolini expects them to be.

Moreover, many things may happen before that messianic 1940. American finance and diplomacy are no longer as unanimous in their support as they were ten years ago, when Mussolini appeared to them as a savior from the Red Caliban threatening modern civilization. The Duce's hosts have proved to be not altogether selfless protectors of the fine flower of that civilization, as embodied in the capitalist interests. Their "protection" looks very much like blackmail or even outright expropriation. The Fascists made their "revolution" neither for "Italy" as the official story goes, nor for "capitalism" as the Socialist and Communist story goes and as Pierpont Morgan and the American Ambassador Richard Washburn Child believed. They have conquered Italy for the Fascists alone and are quite impudently interfering with all the most sacred laws of profit-making and hiring-and-firing, whenever they feel that an infringement upon these laws is necessary for the prevention of labor disturbances. However much capitalists may prefer the reactionary or futuristic verbiage of the Fascists to the class struggle terminology of the various brands of socialism, they cease seeing any difference, as soon as their property rights are seriously impugned. No wonder then that in many very conservative spheres, such as are represented by the publishers of the largest American periodical, Mussolini is now being attacked, although he received such lavish praise at the time of his first glory. More and more, Mussolini with his army of intellectuals, semi-intellectuals, ex-workers and praetorian guards, intent exclusively upon the preservation of his own power, begins to look to his capitalist critics suspiciously like a kind of freak Bolshevik, merely cleverer than his Moscow teachers; for *they* never concealed their open hostility to the capitalists, while the Fascists not only made the Italian "bourgeois swine come across with their dough"—but also induced the haughty Americans to do likewise.

There is yet another danger to Mussolini's rule—much more serious than the loss of American official sympathy. It is the possibility of a war which the Duce really fears— all his martial talk and appearance notwithstanding. For, like the Cossacks of the Tsar's time, his Fascist militia is formidable only against a disarmed population. Should a war come, and with it general conscription, the armed black-shirts who in peace time outnumber the regular army may be faced not only by a frontal attack of "barbarians"— so they refer to the foreigners—but also by a rear attack from their own armed population.

Mussolini has now begun to talk peace. He knows why. He also has announced a recession from the good aristocratic policy of seniority within the party, and, after having for years kept his party a closed corporation, he is again opening it up for membership from outside. It is undoubtedly a step towards democracy which may placate part of the malcontent elements. Barring his downfall, more reforms are certain to come. Will they be in the direction of more democracy, in order to placate the middle-class elements, or in the direction of more infringements upon the rights of private capital, in order to placate the dissatisfied workers?

JOSEPH PILSUDSKI

Liberator of Poland

To a detached observer the advent of Pilsudski, his coup d'état, his mock elections, his ruthless suppression of minorities, the horrors of his torture chambers, are likely to suggest a comparison with similar phenomena in southeastern Europe or Latin-America. Such a view would do a grave injustice to the picturesque man now at the helm of his country's government. For Pilsudski is not merely one of the many enterprising politicians or adventurous soldiers who were raised to power by an unforeseen *coup de main* in Balkanized Europe or America. He is in a class by himself—a character as romantic, as contradictory, and as grotesque as the history of his country.

Of the three sections into which Poland was partitioned over 130 years ago, Russian Poland was numerically, territorially, and economically the most important. It had a well-developed and steadily growing industry, while the Prussian and Austrian sections of the ancient kingdom were still predominantly agricultural. It had a rising middle class, engaged in trade and industry. It also had an ever growing group of lower-middle-class intellectuals who, under the rigid rule of the Russian oppressor, had little opportunity of coming into their own.

It was this dissatisfied group that at the close of the nineteenth century first began to disturb the apparent harmony between the Russian bear and the Polish lamb. Of Poland's educated classes it was the only one that had not given up the seemingly hopeless struggle against Tsarist rule. The vast Russian markets which were open to Polish industrial products proved a good anodyne for the wounded national pride of the Polish merchants and manufacturers, but they meant very little to the intelligentsia. What this class needed was not markets but—jobs; and these were not forthcoming as long as the country was under foreign rule—as long as Poland was not independent.

Alone, left to its own resources, this class was too weak to drive out the invader; hence it turned to socialism, the new gospel that was affecting all European countries. Here was the rising force that one day would change the world. Socialism raised the slogans of democracy and independence for oppressed nationalities. It had succeeded in enlisting the enthusiastic support of myriads of workers the world over. It had won their confidence by helping them in their early struggles for better conditions. It had given them a far-away ideal that had proved useful in encouraging them to fight against the very real relics of absolutism and feudalism.

The Polish intelligentsia did not fail to see the advantages of allying itself with this potent international factor. Were not the leaders of the new movement flesh of their own flesh: students, educated *déclassés,* journalists, lawyers, aspiring politicians? Were not the foremost spokesmen of European socialism at the same time the most ardent champions of Polish independence?

"Long live Poland!" was the concluding phrase of "A Letter to the Polish Socialists," written by Marx and Engels in 1880. That letter praised the Poles as "international champions in the struggle for proletarian emancipation" outside of their country, and was one of the most striking expressions of the interest shown by the pioneers of socialism in the cause of Polish independence. This interest was not a one-sided affair. By the first half of the nineteenth century some of the most brilliant of the Polish patriotic émigrés were known not only as knights errant of liberty in Western Europe but also as protagonists of socialist ideas. Lelewel, the famous Polish historian and patriot, participated at the convention that decided to issue the *Communist Manifesto* shortly before the Revolution of 1848. Count Stanislaw Worcell, another Polish patriot of note, developed ideas anticipating the patriotic socialism or socialist patriotism of Pilsudski's Polish Socialist Party (P. P. S.) of half a century later. Adam Mickiewicz, greatest of Polish poets and patriots of the same period, likewise combined his patriotism with socialist ideas.

Polish patriotic interest in Socialism, and early socialist interest in Poland converged on the issue of political democracy, which was paramount for all advanced elements at that time. Marx and his circle were, first of all, radical German and Western democrats. The worst enemy of democratic Europe was Tsarist Russia, the self-elected guardian of medieval reaction in the West. The establishment of a Polish democratic republic would create an effective barrier against intervention by this Asiatic policeman of Europe, who had choked off the Hungarian revolution of 1848-9. Socialism, as propagated by Marx and the other lower-middle-class intellectuals, was only the extreme expression of their demand for democracy. A stimulating promise, dangled as a bait to obtain the support of the workers, its educated protagonists saw it at best as a form of democratic State Capitalism, to be relegated to a distant future as soon as political democracy was attained. As conceived by the Polish patriots, socialism was to be the extreme democratic force which, once triumphant in the West with the support of the workers, would sooner or later clash with the colossus of the East and reëstablish Poland.

The Polish revolutionary movement of the eighties of the past century was greatly influenced by the political events going on in Russia proper. The activity of the Russian terrorists had dealt heavy blows to Tsarist rule, almost forcing it to capitulation. Even the serious setback which the movement had suffered shortly after the killing of the Tsar now seemed to be only temporary, and a large part of Poland's malcontent intelligentsia turned hopefully towards Russia. The struggle for a democratic, Europeanized Russia actually held out great hopes for Poland. It would not mean national independence at once, but eventually it would result in broad autonomy, with the consequent economic advantages.

A combination of Russian terrorism with western Marxism, the Polish socialist organization created at that time considered itself as part of the great revolutionary movement that was to emancipate the entire population of the Russian Empire. As a result, it did not stress the specifically Polish national issue at all. After a few years, however, that organization succumbed under the blows of Tsarist persecutions, along with the Russian terrorists in the heart of the Empire. In Russia proper, where industry was still in its infancy, the flame of revolution seemed to be extinguished for good; in Poland, economically more advanced, the labor movement, once started, did not halt. Continuous strikes kept the authorities busy and were not checked by either jails or executions.

This phenomenon was of paramount influence in molding the conceptions of the Polish revolutionary intelligentsia of the subsequent decade. Not expecting any help from Russia —for in their opinion the Russian revolution was dead for at least a generation to come—the intelligentsia abandoned the internationalism of the eighties, and reverted to the nationalism of the Polish democrats and socialists of the forties. The outcome of that change of front was the organization of the Polish Socialist Party (P. P. S.), founded in the early nineties of the past century, and to this day influential with a large section of the workers.

JOSEPH PILSUDSKI

The Tribune and the Hero

At its inception the Polish Socialist Party drew into its ranks the most brilliant minds of the country's youth, and these later became the leaders of the various political parties of present-day Poland. Its foremost figures were Joseph Pilsudski, its fearless man of action, and Ignatius Daszynski, the silver-tongued propagandist, who later became the Chairman of Poland's parliament until it was dissolved by his former comrade in arms.

There is a striking resemblance in the origin of the two men and in their early careers. Both are scions of the petty nobility and were born in 1867 on territory ethnically non-Polish; Daszynski in Eastern Galicia, where his ancestors lorded over the Ukrainian peasantry; Pilsudski in the Vilna region, a district now claimed by Lithuania. Like so many sons of the impoverished nobility whose only fortune was a glorious past, they inherited the romantic creed of the Polish exiles of the early nineteenth century, who dreamed of their country's independence and fought on the barricades of all the revolutions of Europe. Leaving the completion of college courses to their more sedate contemporaries, they entered the ranks of the *déclassé* intelligentsia, that turbulent brotherhood which, in all countries in need of a revolution, supplies rebels and renegades, idealists and adventurers, statesmen and job-hunters; and more often than not, that human, all-too-human specimen, which is a composite of all of these types.

Daszynski, gifted with a striking personality and with extraordinary oratorical powers, ranks in these respects with Jaurès and Trotsky, though lacking their wide culture. Ambitious, cunning, and "eclectic" in his principles, he was bound to become a leading politician, for his native Galicia, being a part of Austria, enjoyed a certain degree of political

democracy. At the age of thirty he was a member of the
Austrian parliament, to which he was elected by the workers
and peasants of the Krakow district with the active support
of a large section of the lower-middle-class intelligentsia.
Such was the wave of enthusiasm called forth by this great
orator that numbers of peasants, in their simplicity, actually
believed that their leader was going to Vienna to "learn the
trade from Emperor Franz Josef," in order to become king
of Poland after his apprenticeship was over.

But he was not to become king of Poland. This rôle,
mutatis mutandis, was reserved for his friend, whose name
had been practically unknown to the public until the outbreak of the World War. This man was Joseph Pilsudski—
the Orsini, the Garibaldi, and the Mussolini of Poland; the
conspirator and terrorist, the military leader and national
hero, and finally the Fascist dictator of the country he "liberated."

Pilsudski had none of those qualities of the successful
tribune and politician which had made Daszynski famous
among the parliamentarians of Central Europe. He did not
need them. Of what use would they have been to him under
Tsarist rule? He was, however, possessed of iron energy and
physical courage, as exceptional as Daszynski's oratory. He
wanted an independent Poland. An independent Poland was
as indispensable for the vast crowd of half-starved, impecunious intellectuals as jobs are for the unemployed. And
he was going to drive out the Tsarist invader, though millions of bayonets and thousands of gallows constantly
threatened him.

Curiously enough, Pilsudski got his revolutionary baptism
in connection with the events which led to the execution of
Lenin's brother Alexander. He became remotely and acci-
dentally implicated in the terrorist attempt on the Tsar's
life organized by Russian students in 1887, and had to spend
five years of exile in Siberia. There he evolved that combina-

tion of socialist and nationalist ideas which for more than a generation put its stamp upon the mental make-up of a large section of the malcontent Polish intelligentsia. Shortly after his release from Siberia he became one of the founders of the Polish Socialist Party (P. P. S.).

The first plank in the program of the P. P. S. called for the reëstablishment of Poland's national independence. Queer as it may seem, there actually was no other important organization that could seriously take up this slogan. The well-to-do strata of Polish society—the landed nobility and the capitalists—had long ago made their peace with the Tsar and were opposed to any dangerous venture of a nationalist character, on the ground that it might result in labor disturbances in industry and agriculture. The peasantry was largely illiterate and completely under the sway of the Catholic clergy. Thus, the only groups likely to respond actively to patriotic propaganda were the impecunious intelligentsia and the manual workers, who, in the liturgical words of Marx's *Communist Manifesto,* had literally "nothing to lose but their chains."

But "patriotism was not enough." A purely nationalist platform would have been strongly suggestive of the old Poland, ruled and ruined by the all-powerful nobility. To make the patriotic gospel more palatable to the workers, and also to secure the support of the radical parties of Western Europe, the new "proletarian" slogans were hitched to the old nationalist stage-coach. In other words, the reëstabment of Poland's independence, with its consequent new bureaucracy of Polish intellectuals, was proclaimed as a necessary prerequisite of socialist emancipation of the Polish working class. On occasion the Polish Socialists would give away the innermost secret of their "proletarian" yearnings. For instance, in discussing the prospects for democratic reforms in Russia and their possible consequences for Russian Poland, the London *Przedswit,* the chief organ of the

Polish Socialist Party, in one of its issues (No. 10) of 1894, questioned the advantages of a constitutional régime in Russia as far as Poland was concerned, on the ground that "the Poles would be excluded from all government positions." The naïve egotism of the remark shows that they considered this a matter of vital importance for the factory workers whose interests the party was championing.

The monopoly of the P. P. S. in the leadership of the Polish workers was not altogether uncontested. Ever since its foundation, the party had had to meet the competition of an internationalist group called "Social Democracy of Poland and Lithuania," which was headed by Rosa Luxemburg, later the associate of Karl Liebknecht during the German revolution. This group, however, wielded no great influence, and the international socialist conventions always sided with the numerically stronger P. P. S. against it.

THE GOOD FIGHT

In the eyes of Western socialists, the Polish Socialist Party was for many years surrounded with a halo of heroism like that of the Russian terrorists of the eighties. It organized strikes, not so much to obtain higher wages as to bring the Polish workers into conflict with the Tsarist authorities. It operated secret printing plants, in which underground papers were published, propagating a curious combination of Polish patriotism and Western socialism. It terrorized the Tsarist authorities by killing scores of stool-pigeons. policemen and higher government officials. It engaged in spectacular hold-ups ("expropriations") of government buildings, post offices, railway stations, and trains, in order to obtain funds for the conduct of all these activities. Joseph Pilsudski actively participated in and personally directed all these undertakings. It was he who was in charge of the secret printing plant in which the main organ of the party was published. Arrested and facing a life sentence, he simulated insanity and escaped from the St. Petersburg prison in 1901. It was he who in 1908 personally conducted the great attack on the Besdany Station, which helped to replenish the empty treasury chest of the party. He has a record of courage and adventure equaled in modern times only by that of the Russian terrorist and novelist, Boris Savinkov (Ropshin), of similar fame, though less fortunate destiny.

While calling himself a Socialist, Pilsudski had at heart a deep contempt for all theories—a quality in which he again closely resembles Savinkov. The story is current among Polish revolutionists that once Pilsudski saw a copy of the *Communist Manifesto* by Marx and Engels, which was published by his party abroad. He shrugged his shoulders, asking: "What for? Can a single Russian soldier be killed with that?"

During the Russo-Japanese War, in 1904, Pilsudski went to Japan in the hope of obtaining financial aid for the organization of an uprising in Poland. The Mikado's statesmen seem to have taken his socialism seriously and were afraid to enter into entangling alliances with the red specter.

The Russian Revolution of 1905 called forth a succession of strikes in Poland. Pilsudski's party used its influence to direct them exclusively against the Tsarist government, with the effect that the Polish Socialist Party earned the sympathy and the support of the Polish propertied classes, who were saved the inconvenience of paying higher wages. For the first time the Polish bourgeoisie began to realize that the socialist devils were not as red as they painted themselves.

In 1906 his party was rent apart. The less romantic set of Poland's revolutionary intelligentsia revolted against the purely nationalist policy of Pilsudski and his fellow social-patriots. Now that a revolutionary mass movement was on in Russia, they began to think about the possibility of broad constitutional and democratic reforms all over the Romanov empire. They shelved the far-away ideal of Polish independence, which at that time was as hazy a dream as an independent Czecho-Slovakia or a Soviet Republic, and advanced the demand for Polish autonomy within a democratic Russia. Pilsudski and his following found themselves in the minority at the 1906 Convention. They bolted and founded a new party "P. P. S.—Revolutionary Section," while the majority became henceforth known as "P. P. S.—Left." But in the public mind the name of P. P. S. remained always associated with Pilsudski and his patriotic brand of socialism. The other section rejected not only Polish independence as part of their platform, but terrorism as well. After the War they merged with Rosa Luxemburg's Polish followers to found the Polish Communist Party.

After the defeat of the Revolution of 1905, Pilsudski transferred his headquarters to Austrian Poland (Galicia), where, barring occasional terrorist and "expropriatory" excursions to Russian Poland, he stayed until the beginning of the World War. During this stay the obscure underground propagandist and terrorist pursued his strategical preparations for the "day" to which he had devoted his life. The "day" nearly came in 1909, when Austria-Hungary annexed Bosnia, that northwestern corner of the Balkans inhabited by Serbians, which nominally belonged to Turkey, and according to Russia, should have gone to Serbia. The ensuing Austro-Russian conflict, which well-nigh precipitated a war between the two countries, revived the hopes of the Polish Socialists. For, contemptuous of their less civilized eastern neighbors, they conceived the restoration of Poland not as a result of a revolution in Russia, in the success of which they had no faith, but as an outcome of an international conflict. For this reason, the world carnage, which was dreaded by the other parties of European socialism, was actually hailed by its Polish followers. Apparently, in the opinion of its leaders, twenty million dead and crippled was not too high a price for bestowing a new set of rulers on twenty million Poles. Was not Marx an ardent advocate of Polish independence in which he saw a bulwark of European democracy against the Tsarist menace? And did not the noblest figures among the old Russian revolutionists, such as Bakunin and Hertzen, openly sympathize with the Polish insurrection of 1863?

The actual conflict did not come until five years later. In the meantime Pilsudski had reached an understanding with the Austrian authorities. With their permission he began to organize his "sharpshooters" on Galician soil, from among the Polish refugees from Russia. They were to be the nucleus of the future Polish army which was to help Austria in a possible war against Russia. And after 1909 Pilsudski was in direct contact with the general staff of the Austro-Hungarian Army, which lent a willing ear to this peculiar Socialist's informative talks about Russian conditions.

COMMANDER OF THE POLISH LEGION

With the outbreak of the World War, the coöperation of the Polish Socialists with the Austrian general staff blossomed forth in the formation of the Polish legions. Once again Pilsudski entered Russian territory. This time, however, not as a disguised conspirator and terrorist, using his own automatic pistols and his own home-made bombs. The days when he was responsible only to the central committee of his party, i.e. to himself, were over. He was in full uniform now, and subject to the orders of the Austrian military authorities, which, however, never entrusted him with the full command of that Polish "national army" of a few thousand men. He was only a brigadier under the orders of a regular Austrian general of Polish descent.

Early in August, 1914, a manifesto was issued in Krakow (that is, on Austrian soil) to the effect that a "People's Government" had been established in Warsaw and that every Polish citizen ought to submit to its authority. It likewise declared that Pilsudski had been appointed leader of the military forces of Poland. That manifesto was a hoax, of course. Nobody had budged in Warsaw, but Pilsudski was perfectly serious about the contents of his own manifesto. From now on he saw himself as leader of the whole nation and not merely of one of its political parties.

His official connection with socialism became cumbersome, and he severed it, though continuing to call himself a Socialist until the end of 1915. Daszynski, while remaining leader of his own party, joined the Polish parliamentary group of the Vienna Reichsrat, which was controlled by the interests of the Polish landed nobility. Thus, while Pilsudski with his legions was fighting the Russians as comrade-in-arms of Austrian and German generals, Daszynski was heroically exerting himself to assure the Austrian emperor of the loyalty and devotion of the Polish people and of the Socialist Party. "Our program," he said in a speech made in October, 1916, "twines like an ivy on the Hapsburg throne," adding, however, that "this ivy has had its roots likewise in Polish soil." For this Polish soil he hoped to obtain independence by the grace of the Central Powers, which were to appoint one of their imperial princes to the royal throne of Poland. To meet possible objections on the part of more radical Socialists, Daszynski elaborated an interesting theory, according to which, not a democratic republic, but a constitutional monarchy offered the best safeguards for democracy and political liberty. This Polish constitutional monarchy was, by the way, to be a rather diminutive affair, consisting solely of Russian Poland, since not only the gov-

ernments, but even the German-speaking Socialists of the
two central empires refused to part with the Polish sections
incorporated in their respective countries. Such was socialist
internationalism in practice. . . .

Pilsudski's military activities in alliance with the Central
Powers came to an abrupt end in 1916, when the unfriendly,
anti-Polish attitude of the German and Austrian authorities
made a further collaboration impossible for him. He opposed
the attempts of the Central Powers to impress into their
armies the inhabitants of the occupied Russian-Polish territories and to make them swear an oath of allegiance to the
"future King of Poland" and to the supreme command appointed by the German and Austrian emperors. Before he
could carry out his plan to cross over to revolutionary Russia, then in its Kerensky stage, and to join the Polish military formations established under the new régime, he was
arrested and interned in a Prussian fortress. After sixteen
months he was freed by the German revolution of November, 1918.

CHIEF OF STATE

The Russian Revolution and the defeat of the Central
Powers actually resulted in the restoration of Polish independence, and Joseph Pilsudski, grand master of the knights
errant of national liberation, became the chief of the new
State. A government next had to be organized—a government which would steer safely between revolutionary Russia
and revolutionary Germany and at the same time avoid civil
war and any disturbance of the existing class relations.
Pilsudski understood that such a task could be carried out
only by a government composed of Socialists, of men enjoying the confidence of the underdog. For this task of
organization he selected the engineer Andrzej Moraczewski,
a Galician Socialist of old standing, who had served as captain in the Polish legion during the War. It is a standing

joke in Poland how upon the latter's refusal to undertake the task the national hero and not-yet-dictator commanded his subordinate officer to "stand at attention," how he ordered him to become prime minister, and finally how he enjoined him not to do anything that might disturb the existing social system.

Pilsudski's orders were carried out. The government was held by the Polish Socialist Party, in trust, so to speak, until after the elections to the Constituent Assembly. Having "their own government," the Polish workers, in spite of their revolutionary traditions, showed no ugly temper. They waited, and they assailed nobody's property. In the meantime Pilsudski organized his army around the remnants of the old Polish legion that had fought during the World War. The workers were not given arms. It would not have been safe. The Socialist Party received specific instructions from its former leader to avoid anything of the kind. It conscientiously obeyed him.

After the elections to the Constituent Assembly, a regular bourgeois government was formed. The Socialists, who based their influence upon the adherence of a large section of the industrial workers and intellectuals, constituted only a comparatively small fraction of the total number of deputies. These socialist deputies were very sagacious and indulged only in "constructive" criticism of the various administrations which kept following each other in quick succession. As a reward, they reaped all the advantages of a privileged group. Government printing offices were leased to the party newspapers at a nominal rental which practically amounted to a donation. Members of the party, all the former half-starved intellectuals and semi-intellectuals, as well as former manual workers who had won their distinction in the underground or open fight against the Tsar, were provided for in the various government departments, the army, the secret police—unless they preferred careers as party politicians, lecturers, editors, organizers of trade unions, educational and sporting societies, and so on.

The idol of a large part of the population—workers, intelligentsia, and poorer farmers—and first president of his reborn country, Pilsudski had no intention of resting on his laurels; particularly as he had rivals and enemies who refused to concede that he was the liberator of his country. They were disrespectful enough to call Poland's independence simply the incidental result of Germany's victory over Russia and of the Allied victory over Germany, which was as much as to say that Pilsudski was a *Chantecler,* who thought that his crowing made the sun rise. Pilsudski was resolved to silence these scoffers and to cover himself with immortal glory of his own making. Had not Poland once been a great empire, stretching from the Baltic to the Black Sea, embracing Lithuania, White-Russia, and the Ukraine? Could not history be repeated? A humanitarian formula, so necessary in the days of Wilsonism, was soon found for this noble undertaking. It was not to be an annexation, but a liberation of all these territories, which, with Poland, would form a great federation of free peoples under the hegemony of the nation that had freed them from the Russian yoke.

WAR WITH SOVIET RUSSIA AND AFTER

The moment came in 1920 when the civil war in Russia was over and the Red Army had crushed its enemies on all fronts. The Allies, to save Denikin and Kolchak, had urged the Poles to attack the Bolsheviks from the west in order to weaken their resistance against the White Armies. Pilsudski accepted their orders, as well as their ammunition, supplies, and money, but he sent word to the Red Army not to worry and to go about its business. Romantic and dreamer as he was, Pilsudski was not such a fool as to help in the

restoration to power of his old Tsarist enemies who would
have never recognized the independence of his country and
from whom he certainly could not hope to recover the "lost"
provinces. However, no sooner was that danger disposed
of, than he started the invasion of Soviet Russia, an enterprise which all but cost him his reputation and "his" country.
The strategic talents which had been so effective in organizing hold-ups of Tsarist currency depositories, failed him in
a real war against a real army, led by Trotsky and Budenny.
Driven back to the very gates of Warsaw, he was saved
only by the timely assistance of the able French general
Weygand.

Pilsudski's mad venture did not meet with unanimous
approval on the part of the whole nation. The wealthier
classes, manufacturers, and landed noblemen (except those
among them whose lands had been nationalized in Soviet
Ukraine and White-Russia) feared the aftermath of a possible defeat, with its concomitant revolution and expropriation. As little did they like the idea of a possible increase
of prestige for Pilsudski whose radical past they had not
yet forgotten. Quite different was the attitude of the less
prosperous elements, who saw a way out of their economic
difficulties in the conquest of the eastern territories. The
lower middle classes expected to find there more opportunities for economic independence; the intellectuals, new government jobs; and the peasant parties, "free land" to be
gained by driving out the Ukrainian and White-Russian
farmers, who would thus become "hewers of wood and
drawers of water" for the Polish conquerors. The industrial
workers were opposed to the war at first, but when the Russian Red Army repulsed the Polish invasion and began to
advance on Warsaw, special workers' battalions were
formed, by the Socialists, which fought, under the red flag,
against the hosts of Trotsky. The old hatred and fear of the
Russian proved stronger than proletarian solidarity.

Victory did not enhance Pilsudski's authority in the eyes of the reactionary parties—the National Democrats and the Christian Democrats—who represented the interests of the landed nobility, the manufacturers, and the very influential Catholic clergy. These groups had many grievances against the Marshal and his following. For all his imperialism, he was a progressive who stood for agrarian reform, which was to help the peasantry at the expense of the landed nobility; he was a representative of the educated middle classes, as against the obscurantism of an intolerant clergy; he was not particularly interested in Jew-baiting; he defended the adoption of laws like those of other civilized countries for the protection of industrial workers. Worst of all, strange as it may seem, he was not nationalist enough for them. After over a century of national nonexistence, they had all of a sudden obtained not only independence, but also the right to lord it over several millions of Germans, Ukrainians, White-Russians, Jews, and Lithuanians, making up in all about forty per cent of Poland's total population. Did not simple justice demand that these people should be forcibly Polonized, Catholicized, disfranchised, driven away from their soil and business? Pilsudski did not see it that way. Faced by the danger of a reactionary-clerical bloc, he preferred to win the support of these national minorities against the common enemy, and not to antagonize them more than was necessary for the maintenance of Polish supremacy. The reactionaries never forgave him this "betrayal" of the national cause, and immediately after the presidential elections of 1922, one of them killed Professor Narutowicz, progressive President-elect of the Republic, who had been indorsed by Pilsudski and returned to office by the bloc of progressives, socialists, peasants, and national minorities.

During the period between 1922 and 1926, the power gradually shifted from the hands of Pilsudski and his sup-

porters to those of the reactionaries. This was due chiefly
to the process of differentiation going on among the Polish
peasantry. The "Piast" party, representing the more prosperous peasants and headed by the former Premier Witos,
formed a bloc with the "Rights." As a result, Pilsudski had
to restrict his activities exclusively to the army, but even in
this field his political and personal enemies and rivals made
life unbearable for him. Resigning his command, he retired
resentfully to the country seat which his grateful countrymen had donated to him in recognition of his heroic record.
Before retiring, however, he shot a last Parthian arrow at
his adversaries. At a banquet arranged in his honor in July
1923, Pilsudski delivered himself of a speech which aroused
doubts as to his sanity. It was not so much the vehemence
of the attacks and insults directed against his enemies, as
the tone of self-glorification which astounded friend and foe
alike. "I am not going to attribute to myself greater merits
than those which the world concedes to me. They may say
that I was unable to manage the Polish nation, but no criticism, no audacity will dare to question my military laurels.
I have covered the Polish arms with glory. During the first
days of Poland's life I gave her victories so brilliant, so
unheard of, that only in the remote past can one find the
like of them. . . . I have conquered an enemy before whom
others were trembling. . . ."

His Military Coup

In 1926 Pilsudski decided to give up his sulking attitude
and to call his opponents into the open. The appointment of
his old enemy Witos to the post of premier was the spark
that started the conflagration. The causes lay, of course,
much deeper. Witos and the "Right" parties were making
preparations for a complete elimination of Pilsudski's influence. The old guard of his friends, the officers who had

fought with him in the Legion and built up the national army, were to be weeded out by retiring them from service, and his opponents were to be placed in all commanding positions. Within a generation, with the public education in the hand of his enemies, even his deeds and his name would be forgotten. Such things can be done. . . .

Pilsudski struck and won. His coup of May 12-15, 1926, was a purely military affair. He did not want it to be anything else, and during those three days he did not issue a single appeal to the population. The old national hero was not mistaken in his conviction that the bulk of the army, and particularly of the officers, were still with him. A large part of the population—the workers, the poorer peasantry, the lower middle classes, and particularly the intelligentsia—acclaimed his victory, but they took no part in the struggle. The Polish Socialist Party, which he had founded over thirty years earlier, was non-committal until the evening of the second day of the coup. The outcome was still uncertain and to stake everything on one card was permissible to an erratic old hero, but not to a respectable political party of job-holders, who had forgotten the old glorious days of starvation, prison, and martyrdom. The first political group to come out openly for Pilsudski during this struggle was, strangely enough, the Communist Party. This was indeed curious, since Pilsudski loathed the Communist Party as a gang of Russian agents; he alleged that their Soviet propaganda aimed at the reëstablishment of Russian rule over Poland in another form; he and his successors had been persecuting the Communists with all the rigor of the Tsarist code which had been retained for political dissenters. However, the Communists argued as follows: Pilsudski was the representative of the democratic strata of the population, engaged in a struggle against the reactionary bloc of capitalists, landed nobility and clergy; it was accordingly the duty of the Communists to come to his rescue. They there-

fore called for a general strike and for the arming of the
workers. The good intentions of the Communists failed to
improve their standing with Pilsudski. They only succeeded
in impairing their reputation in the Communist International. For while these democratic sentiments were perfectly
sound communist theory for out-of-the-way countries
where the petty bourgeoisie usually sympathizes with Russia, they were downright treason in the case of Poland.
There the lower middle classes, represented by Pilsudski,
were in favor of an aggressive policy against the Soviet
Republic, much more so than any other section of the
population.

In their ill-fated appeal in favor of Pilsudski, the Polish
Communists called for the organization of detachments
against the Fascists. There were, as a matter of fact, a
group at the Extreme Right, calling themselves Fascists, in
whose eyes even the clerical-reactionary régime was not
sufficiently reactionary, and who clamored for a stern dictatorship that would exterminate all radicals, whether underground Communists or perfectly respectable Socialists, and
would put the Jews and the other national minorities in
their place. The actual Fascist peril, however, was to come
from quite another direction. . . .

Following Pilsudski's victory on the streets of Warsaw
and the elimination of his two chief enemies, the President
Wojciechowski and the Premier Witos, the parliamentary
life of the country was permitted to proceed as if nothing
had happened. A new President had to be elected, of course,
and everybody expected the victor to accept again the supreme office which, under the title of "Chief of State," he
held during the first years of the Republic. Pilsudski declined the empty title; he passed it on to some innocent professor, whose name nobody ever had heard before, and retained for himself the modest post of Minister of War. This
symbolic gesture was to denote that from now on the repre-

sentatives of the people were to be only the parliamentary embellishment of a thinly disguised military rule.

The continued support which the majority of the electorate had been bestowing for so many years upon Pilsudski's political enemies had, no doubt, made him skeptical about the divine character of the *vox populi*. He had risked his life a hundred times, had created a national army, restored his country's independence—and all this seemed to make no difference to the ungrateful majority. His old sympathies for the civilian underdog went the way of the socialist dreams of his youth. Henceforth all his tender sentiments were to be reserved for "the most popular man in the country," as he was wont to call himself, and for his uniformed brothers in arms. They were the salt of the earth; their readiness to die for their country elevated them to the dignity of a true aristocracy, entitled to rule over a cowardly rabble that thought only in terms of material comforts. That rabble would have to obey. . . .

But the representatives of the civilian rabble did not always do as they were bid. Both the conservative and the progressive parties of the Sejm (Parliament) repeatedly balked. They seemed not to be particularly afraid of the Polish Napoleon. Not even the threat of a Fascist dictatorship could bring them to their senses. In October, 1926, this threat was expressed quite openly by Pilsudski's paper, *Glos Prawdy*. In an article directed against the reactionary National Democrats the paper stated indignantly that "the National Democrats had no right to call themselves Fascists. If an analogy with the fascist movement is to be looked for in Poland at all, we must declare frankly that it can only be found in the camp of Pilsudski's followers. Up to the present we have not transferred fascist methods to the Polish scene, solely for this reason—that we did not consider it necessary."

Cynical observers had some suspicions as to why "it was

not considered necessary." The economic situation of the country was most unfavorable, and in order to obtain foreign credits it was essential to preserve certain semblances of popular control such as is possible only under a parliamentary régime. There is little doubt that some unmistakable hints to that effect were given to Pilsudski by foreign creditors, who did not share his confidence in the stability of a régime to which the great majority, and especially the wealthier classes, were opposed. For, aside from his faithful officers and a part of the middle-class intellectuals, the national hero had few unconditional adherents. There was in Poland no terrifying red specter as in the Italy of Mussolini's coup, with which to secure unlimited contributions from the propertied classes and a lavish influx of foreign credits. Neither did Pilsudski have a well-organized party of his own to lean upon. He soon proceeded to organize one and called new elections, hoping against hope to carry the electorate. His main issue was the "graft" and "corruption" practiced by his opponents—as if this could be an issue in our sophisticated age! His disappointment was bitter, for the official government ticket polled only a small fraction of the total vote. With the aid of the government machinery in his possession, Pilsudski sought to win over various sections from all classes of the population. He made promises to the manufacturers and landowners, as well as to the poor peasants and industrial workers. He held out his hand to the myriads of ambitious intellectuals and semi-intellectuals who had failed to get seats on the overcrowded bandwagon of their liberated country. He carried the war into the Polish Socialist Party and induced the Warsaw section of the party, as well as the trade unions of the capital to come out unreservedly for his personal rule. A government job in the country's capital is a convincing argument and so is a subsidy granted from the chests of the State Treasury. The liberation of his country, for which in his younger days he was willing to sacrifice his life, had now given way to another ideal—the preservation of his power. A fitting anti-climax to an eventful life: The man who in 1908 held up a Tsarist train to get a few hundred thousand rubles for Poland's freedom, twenty years later held up his own country for a much bulkier sum, in order to build up his own party. It was the famous affair of the 560,000,000 zloty (about $62,000,000), spent without authorization on the part of Parliament, that precipitated the crisis of 1930 in which practically all parties united against Pilsudski's unconstitutional methods.

DICTATOR

Since 1929 there has no longer been any doubt that Pilsudski is openly heading towards the establishment of an unrestricted personal dictatorship and the elimination of all political life. The government has ceased to be a parliamentary, or even a civilian affair. It has passed into the hands of the "group of colonels," headed by Colonel Slawek, the Marshal's right-hand man. Since 1929 the Sejm has been called only for occasional one- or two-day performances, for the purpose of voting the budget—and for their pains the deputies have been addressed by Pilsudski as "prostitutes" and "scoundrels," not to mention other unprintable "military" terms. Needless to say, his popularity has not been particularly enhanced by such arguments. Meanwhile the economic situation of the country has been going from bad to worse, exemplified by a 20 to 40 per cent reduction of wages, while over 30 per cent of the revenues have been spent for military purposes.

No wonder that even his oldest friends and admirers in the Socialist Party, who stood by him during the first three years of his dictatorship, have been finally forced to break with him politically and personally. The last of them was the Chairman of the Sejm, Ignatius Daszynski. The brilliant

parliamentarian could not stand being reduced to the rôle of
a bellboy. Pilsudski's attempt to impress the budget commission by the presence of a few score of his picked officers,
caused the clash between the two former friends and brought
the Polish situation to the attention of the whole world.

Late in June, 1930, the representatives of the various opposition parties, in a convention called while the Sejm was
not in session (it practically never was), for the first time
openly voiced their protest against Pilsudski's dictatorship.
Two months later Daszynski, in a public speech, deplored
the fact that "any noncommissioned officer thinks he has
the right to bully the members of Parliament" and appealed
to "Pilduski's honor to renounce the present principle of
ruling the Poles as if they were a conquered nation." Pilsudski was not impressed. He simply ordered the arrest of
the opposition leaders or called them to the colors for military service, having first dissolved Parliament and called for
new elections to take place in November, 1930. But this time
he was taking no chances. "I cannot be defeated" he declared candidly in an interview given to the press a few
weeks before the elections, and he forthwith canceled as
many election tickets of the opposition as stood in the way of
a safe majority of the government bloc. The victims of this
cancellation policy were not his old reactionary foes of the
National Democratic Party; these were permitted nearly to
double their seats; the sufferers were his former friends of
the socialist and peasant parties, as well as the national minorities. The former editor of an underground Socialist
paper, the ex-champion of the underdog, had now the support of the landed nobility and of the banking and manufacturing interests.

Thus, after thirteen years of independent existence, Poland returned to the old traditions of the "Galician elections," which before the War were a byword in Central
European politics. Special favorites with the Vienna authori-

ties, the representatives of the Polish nobility of those days, got themselves elected—with military assistance—not only in the Polish rural sections but even in purely Ukrainian constituencies of Eastern Galicia where the big landed estates are owned by Polish noblemen.

Having adopted and surpassed the electoral principles of the Galician junkers, Pilsudski has been only too eager to emulate and to outdo them in his attitude towards the national minorities. After the War, Eastern Galicia, which is ethnically Ukrainian, remained a Polish possession, as it had been under the rule of the Hapsburgs, who had favored the Polish nobility at the expense of the Ukrainian peasantry. The internal struggle between Pilsudski and his opponents awakened the hopes of the militant Ukrainian nationalists and they opened a desperate campaign of arson and violence against the Polish landed nobility which in many respects was a perfect replica of the old struggle of the Irish Land League against the English landlords.

Pilsudski, whose policy towards the Ukrainians had hitherto been rather conciliatory as compared with that suggested by his more reactionary opponents from the Right, was thoroughly aroused by this showing of ingratitude, and he countered with a campaign of violence which made the exploits of the Black and Tans appear as mere horseplay. Ukrainian schools, educational societies, coöperative stores, and other institutions were closed or destroyed; hundreds of peasants were flogged or killed.

In justice to the old hero it must be admitted, however, that in his sadistic outbursts he displays no national prejudice or political partisanship. While the punitive expeditions were in full swing in Eastern Galicia, while, in the prison of Luck, Communists and other extremists were subjected to indignities and maltreatments customary only in Balkan countries—the fortress of Brest-Litovsk was converted into a torture chamber for the parliamentary leaders of the various moderate opposition parties. Socialists of the MacDonald type (among them a former Prosecutor at the Highest State Tribunal), Catholic clericals of the Christian Democratic Party, deputies of the Peasants' Party (among them a former prime minister), they all shared equally in the personal vengeance inflicted upon them by an embittered old man who chose to treat a whole nation worse than his ancestors had treated the serfs attached to their fief. In the course of December, 1930, those horrors were widely reported in the press the world over. Naturally enough, the demand for an investigation of the Brest-Litovsk occurrences was turned down by the Sejm. For now Pilsudski had a majority at last—no matter how obtained.

Late in 1930 the Warsaw *Robotnik*—in a passage suppressed by the censor—stated that "Poland is passing through a period which is even worse than that of Stolypin" —the most ruthless of Tsarist prime ministers. Thirty years before Pilsudski had lain in a Russian dungeon for publishing secretly the same *Robotnik*—then as now the organ of the Polish Socialist Party—in which he advocated socialism, democracy and national independence. . . .

*   *   *

The trial of the prisoners of Brest-Litovsk—the mildly socialist and bourgeois-progressive opponents of Pilsudski's personal régime which ended early in 1932, has confirmed old rumors current about him for several years. The former socialist terrorist and *guerrillero* is seriously contemplating the assumption of the Polish throne, vacant since 1795. Members of his party are frankly voicing this idea in Parliament. It is being supported by Prince Radziwill, of the oldest Polish aristocracy. The next step may be another effort to reëstablish and to excel the glory that once was Poland. It may be an attempt to realize Polish hegemony not only over all the Ukrainians, White-Russians, and Lithuanians who were once Polish subjects, but over the entire Slavic world, from the western mountains of Czecho-Slovakia to the Pacific coast of the Russian Far East. For Pilsudski is a dangerous and curious sort of romantic—a grotesque mixture of Napoleon and Caligula, with the latter's peculiar strain prevailing.

WILLIAM Z. FOSTER

Apostle in the Land of the Infidels

O LD Huxley once spoke of the tragedy that sooner or later confronts a scholar whose beloved hypothesis is killed by a merciless little fact. Apostles of otherwise successful gospels of celestial and terrestrial salvation are occasionally victims of similar heartbreaking defeats. Their firm belief that they alone are the dispensers of spiritual or material "uplift" for the whole human race is often rudely shaken by the recalcitrant attitude of whole countries or even continents. Most of Africa and Asia, for instance, simply will not take to the gospel of love, and the meek Gallilean died in vain, so far as that section of humanity is concerned. Modern socialism, in all its various ramifications, is in no better case in regard to America. Since the middle of the last century, generation after generation of unsuccessful apostles has gone down in bitter discouragement over the unresponsiveness of the American worker. For this ungrateful wretch, in his overwhelming numbers, still prefers the gospel of Billy Sunday to that of Gene Debs; he votes for Al Smith rather than for Norman Thomas; he organizes under Gompers and Brindell rather than under Haywood and Foster; he celebrates Labor Day instead of the First of May; and he will join the Ku Klux Klan or the Knights of Columbus rather than the Socialist or Communist International—in short, he is altogether under the mental sway of his capitalist masters.

The usual explanation is based chiefly on conditions in

the early part of the last century, when there was abundant free land on which any worker could settle as an independent farmer. Immigration from Europe on the tremendous scale of the second part of the nineteenth century had not yet begun, and labor was consequently scarce. The wage worker's status was a transitory one, a mere prelude to economic independence, as a farmer, an urban merchant, or other employer of labor.

With such opportunities an actual possibility before his eyes, the early American worker preferred the concrete fleshpots of the capitalist present to the abstract delicacies of the socialist future. Socialism, with its terrestrial "Beyond" for future generations, might have catered to his more spiritual needs as it does at present for some of the economically hopeless; but the American worker of that period was not economically hopeless, and he was contented to set his hopes on a celestial "Beyond" which promised him eternal bliss for himself—and not mere temporary happiness for his grandchildren.

Moreover, preachers of that terrestrial paradise were hardly to be heard in the early days. There was no rebellious, dissatisfied intelligentsia to stir up America, as it stirred up the England of the Chartist period, and the France and Germany of the forties—before the revolutions of 1848. No remnants of feudalism invited attack, no political disfranchisement excluded all but the very richest from participation in political life and public affairs. There was no hopeless, desperate crowd of impecunious lower-middle-class intellectuals dreaming of a revolutionary or post-revolutionary dictator of Robespierre's or Napoleon's type. American intellectuals did not have to help the workers in their wage struggles and to preach to them the socialist Beyond in order to induce them to snatch at an immediate democratic heaven for their educated liberators. The Napoleonic ideal of the "career open to talent" was an actual reality in the new continent. A job, and with it the prospect of unlimited advancement unhampered by any particular adverse discrimination on account of the lack of family connections, was open to every man of ability. The arduous way of democratic revolution, enlivened with socialist *Zukunftsmusik,* was as unnecessary to the career of the American intellectual as were martyrdom and self-sacrifice to that of a clergyman of the time of Constantine. *Thus no tradition of the worker-loving socialist intellectual was connected with the early struggles of American workers* and the absence of this tradition was one of the great obstacles to the spread of socialism in a later period.

True, even in those early years, there were individual adepts of socialist theories in America. Albert Brisbane, an ancestor of the versatile Hearst journalist, brought from France an enthusiasm for the socialist theory of Charles Fourier. A protest against the ravages of early industrialism, Fourierism did not preach revolt against the propertied classes. It rather tried to reconcile the conflicting interests of the various classes and to avoid the repetition of such bloody catastrophes as the Great French Revolution. Horace Greeley, Charles A. Dana, and some other intellectual notabilities of the period became converts to the new gospel. These pioneer liberals, however discontented they may have been with the privileges enjoyed by the money lenders and land grabbers, were, like their teacher, dreamers rather than fighters. Their favorite activity—the founding of socialist colonies or communities—was an attempt at escape from, rather than a struggle against, existing evils. There were also communities inspired by the teachings of Robert Owen and Etienne Cabet, hailing from England and France respectively. The communities invariably failed and the founders returned to the capitalist fleshpots. Socialist colonies with a religious tinge, inspired by other prophets and set up by various immigrant and native dreamers, had no better fortune. A town or village here and there still bearing the name of "Utopia," and occasional reminiscences of the Oneida free love community, the Shakers and other sectarians, are all that now testify to this early epoch of socialism in America.

When William Foster was born in 1881 these idyllic forms of social protest were already quaint antiquities. The American worker, however, could look back upon a long history of struggle conducted quite independently of outside support. The weapons of that long fight included strikes for higher wages and shorter hours, attempts at creating a strong trade-union organization, and individual and mass violence against employers and their tools. But, except in a few isolated cases, it had been fought without accompaniment of socialist ideas or the use of a socialist vocabulary. As yet there were no large numbers of impecunious, starving intellectuals to teach the workers that language.

Nevertheless, the American workers had not altogether dispensed with the diverting pastime of forming political parties of their own. That, they did with a vengeance—every successive decade after the late twenties of the nineteenth century saw a new outbreak of futile attempts at dislodging the old party machines. But these mushroom parties were not socialist in character, whether socialism be conceived as advocacy of equality of incomes, or simply as government ownership with unequal rewards, that is State Capitalism. The leaders of all of these parties, as a rule working men by origin, looked upon the worker as a potential independent farmer or small property holder, and their respective programs depended for support on proposals for free land, currency reform, and such-like panaceas, in which the workers could forget the real issues of the moment. The launching of one of these parties and its temporary success usually expressed the workers' reaction to some temporary reverse in the industrial field, whenever an economic depression strengthened the hand of the employers and weakened the trade unions.

Simultaneously with these native attempts to win American workers over to some erratic scheme—such as "Greenbackism," "free silver," single tax, and what not—the continuous influx of German immigrants prepared the soil for the formation of a Socialist movement in the European style. A large percentage of the newcomers consisted of seasoned propagandists, imbued with the ideas of Marx or Lassalle. These succeeded in founding numerous papers for, and organizations among, the German workers, who then made up the most important section of immigrant labor—aside from the Irish. Gradually, they began to win some influence among the English-speaking workers as well, and after a few unsuccessful attempts at the creation of socialist parties, the Socialist Labor Party was founded in 1876. Like all socialist parties of the Old World, it believed in electing State and Federal representatives to fight anti-labor laws, and at the same time it was in favor of the workers organizing in trade unions and obtaining better living conditions. It was a very moderate, law-abiding affair, and its leaders strongly objected to the practice, then current among the German immigrants, of organizing societies of riflemen, meant to oppose violence to the armed forces continually used against workers on strike.

The seventies, with their economic depression, saw the American workers involved in repeated and violent struggles. Individual terrorism, as practiced by the devoutly Catholic "Molly Maguires" in the Pennsylvania coal mines, as well as numerous strikes and uprisings in other sections of the country, characterized the period. The rise of the first permanent socialist organization was not the only change which marked the end of that decade and the beginning of the next. The same period saw the inception and development of other movements or schools which were to affect,

Courtesy of Workers Film Photo League

WILLIAM Z. FOSTER

either temporarily or permanently, the subsequent course of the American labor movement.

THE ANARCHISTS AND THE KNIGHTS OF LABOR

One of these was anarchism, then still in its extremely militant form. Anarchism as a philosophic theory had its native representatives, in the early period, in the persons of Josiah Warren, Stephen Pearl Andrews, and Henry David Thoreau: in the eighties and later, in Benjamin Tucker. But the individualist philosophies of these men had no connection whatever with the labor movement, or with any form of revolutionary activity. The anarchism that actually played a certain part in the struggle of the American masses was of German importation and centered chiefly around the person of Johann Most. It was the expression of the militant mood of a great number of German exiles who had left their country as a result of the anti-socialist persecutions begun by Bismarck in 1878. Most had his eyes and his mind chiefly directed towards Germany, and the terrorist tactics which he advocated were in reality meant for his native country only. His anarchism was not the pure millennial article, as propounded by Peter Kropotkin for the descendants of the great-grandchildren of the living generation. It was strongly influenced by such seemingly disparate thinkers as Karl Marx, Michael Bakunin, and Auguste Blanqui; the system it proposed looked like a decentralized socialist state, with that strict accounting of individual production and rewards which is anathema to the present-day orthodox communist-anarchism of Kropotkin and his followers. The American authorities did not object to the gospel of violence openly preached by Most in his unequaled and peculiarly picturesque language, so long as it was apparently for German consumption exclusively. Only after the heartbreaking disappointments of the movement in the United States and the triumphant progress of moderate socialism in Germany had destroyed his faith in the nearness of the revolution, did Most fall into line with the anarchists of other countries and accept the unearthly dream of Kropotkin's Arcadia.

In the eighties, however, the situation looked rather hopeful. In 1881 the left wing of the Socialist Labor Party seceded. It was disgusted with the party's dickerings with the "Greenbackers" (currency reformers) and it set up a separate "Revolutionary Socialist Party." These malcontents were mostly German workers, originally followers of Lassalle and sharers in his exuberant faith in the messianic virtues of the ballot box. It had taken the vote-stealing practices of democratic ·America finally to convert them to the gospel of physical force. In 1883 they organized the "International Working People's Association"— a revival of the defunct First International, or, more correctly, of the anarchist wing of that body. A mixture of ideas taken from Bakunin, Marx, and Lassalle, the program of the new organization attracted all the more rebellious elements in the labor movement, particularly among the Germans and the Czechs. In the early eighties, they were actually stronger than the official Socialist Labor Party.

While the Anarchists were fighting the Socialists for influence among the immigrant element, two other organizations were struggling for the souls of the native workers. These were the Noble Order of the Knights of Labor and the American Federation of Labor. The Knights of Labor, founded in 1869 but grown to their fullest power in the eighties, succeeded for a time in holding under their influence hundreds of thousands of skilled and unskilled workers, white collar men and even farmers. It was a federation of local bodies, organized along territorial rather than craft or occupational lines. Many of its members aspired to "independence" rather than to an improvement of their situation by fighting against their employers. Their leaders offered them all kinds of panaceas, such as free land, currency reform, nationalization of certain public utilities, and a general struggle of all the people against "money power" and the legislators. They spoke a language that was extremely humanitarian and in many respects influenced by current socialist ideas: they knew no color bar and their organization was open to unskilled and skilled workers alike. They had but one prejudice—they were against strikes, for these might prove an obstacle to their political ambitions. In their opinion, it was much simpler for the majority of the people to take over the industries and work them in the national interest; for then "it would not be necessary for coal miners to strike in order to secure living wages."

Arguments of that kind were not convincing to all workers. Large numbers of them—particularly the skilled mechanics—preferred to organize in trade unions and to get the immediate benefits of higher wages, modest as they were, rather than to wait for the "pie in the sky" which would be obtainable only after the great majority of the people had been won over to vote one ticket or another.

Trade unions for the purpose of improving the situation of the American workers had been in existence ever since the early part of the nineteenth century. The specific conditions of the country's development, which gave the most energetic and enterprising elements from the working class an opportunity to become prosperous farmers and business men, had delayed, however, the process of organizational consolidation. It remained for an immigrant Jewish cigarmaker to create that *rocher de bronze* of loyal American labor which was to withstand all the enticements of German anarchism and socialism, native and French syndicalism, and Russian communism. This outstanding man was Samuel Gompers—for nearly half a century the most prominent, though not always the most glorious, figure of the American labor movement.

These four groups within the American labor movement had the opportunity to show their colors during the eight-hour agitation that culminated in the Chicago Haymarket tragedy of 1886. The agitation had been initiated by the trade unions which in 1881 had formed the Federation of Organized Trades and Labor Unions—since 1886 called the American Federation of Labor. At a convention held in 1884, the organization fixed May 1, 1886, as the date for the beginning of the general strike that was to obtain the eight-hour day. The leaders of the Knights of Labor, all their protestations against "the thraldom and loss of wage slavery" and their thunders against the money interests notwithstanding, were ordinary politicians, anxious to create a political machine able to compete with the old politicians. They opposed all action that could bring them into active conflict with the powers that be, and the leaders issued a secret circular to their members, enjoining them to keep away from the eight-hour campaign. The official Socialists were likewise opposed to the agitation, and they declared openly that only through the ballot could the workers obtain their objective. The Anarchists alone threw themselves body and soul into the struggle and paid for it with the lives of their leaders and the destruction of their movement.

While Gompers was laying the foundation for a powerful organization of the American labor aristocracy, William Foster was growing up in a milieu that was almost as much below that of the skilled mechanic as the latter was below the great average of the middle classes. When at the age of eighteen he joined the socialist movement, he had gone through a school of life unknown to all but a few of the labor leaders of this country. Data published by *American Labor Who's Who* established the fact that most of the labor and socialist agitators and organizers in America come either from the lower middle classes or from the skilled workers—social groups in which most children can obtain

fairly good elementary or even secondary schooling. William
Foster had no such chance. Born in Massachusetts, in the
family of an unskilled Irish worker—and is there any more
unskilled work than that of a cab-washer?—his formal education actually included no more than three years of public
school. At the age of ten he had to go out to earn his living,
and from that time on he worked in more than a dozen different manual and semi-manual occupations, as unskilled,
semi-skilled and skilled worker, on land and sea, in industry
and farming, on railways and on steamships. The number
of occupations he has essayed is not exceeded even by the
number of social philosophies he has adopted and in turn discarded—and that number is large enough.

SAMUEL GOMPERS AND DANIEL DE LEON

At the time when Foster took that step which expressed
his protest against the system that had robbed him of his
childhood, the radical movement in the United States was in
a condition of distressing confusion. Anarchism had been
declining ever since the tragic events in Chicago during
1886-87. The bomb of the 4th of May, 1886, thrown in the
heat of the eight-hour agitation, had as its sequel the condemnation and execution of the most prominent Anarchist
propagandists of Chicago, the heart of the movement. Those
executions were judicial murder pure and simple, and were
established as such six years later, by Governor John P. Altgeld, who proclaimed the innocence of the hanged men and
pardoned those of their comrades still confined to prison.
Altgeld's political death following on that courageous act
has been an effective damper upon similar Quixotic attempts
to interfere with the accepted course of justice in Massachusetts, California, and elsewhere. Anarchism, which, however naïve in its ideology, represented in those years the
most violent expression of working-class protest against the

existing system, gradually shrank after this tragical setback to the insignificance of a vituperative sect, torn by personal jealousies and engaged in theological hair-splittings. During the subsequent periods as soon as new, less visionary and more matter-of-fact revolutionary currents appeared, its most vigorous and combative elements joined either the I. W. W. or the Communists.

The Knights of Labor had meanwhile disappeared. Abe Lincoln's opinion about the impossibility of fooling all the people all the time may have been exaggerated in its optimism; but in this case it proved true. The free-land and cheap-money panaceas soon lost their attraction; the working class elements, particularly the unskilled workers, began to drop out after a number of unsuccessful strikes, the more readily as the leaders of the organization were actually opposed to that weapon. It was not, however, until 1892, after the defeat of the Homestead steel strike, that they openly declared this stand. Soon afterwards Terence V. Powderly, Grand Master Worker of the Noble Order since 1879, having been dropped by his organization, gave up his attempts at playing the third-party game and accepted a well-paid political job from the Republican party. The noble Knight of Labor had become a lowly flunky of capital.

The field was now free for a straight fight for supremacy in the labor movement between socialist would-be politicians on the one side and trade-union leaders on the other. Both sides were headed by men of no mean intellectual power. After 1890 the socialists had a gifted leader in Daniel De Leon, in whom erudition was added to oratorical and literary talent to make one of those fortunate combinations rarely encountered in one man. But just as rare was his utopian blindness and his uncanny ability to hurt the cause he had gone out to help. Samuel Gompers, his chief opponent, could juggle with ideas and phrases just as skilfully as De Leon, and he had a far more acute perception of the

driving forces of social life. He remained victor all along
the line.

Daniel De Leon did not believe that the workers could
materially improve their situation under the capitalist system. Consequently, strikes played almost no part in his
scheme of the class struggle for abolishing capitalism. Nevertheless, he believed in trade unions, for he understood that
the process of winning the masses over to a political party is
necessarily a slow one. After a bitter and futile struggle
against Gompers he gave up the idea of gaining support
from the existing trade unions, which were entirely under
the sway of Gompers, and were, moreover, organizations of
the skilled workers only. He accordingly attempted to form
his own trade-union organization—the Socialist Trade and
Labor Alliance. Its purpose was to smash the American Federation of Labor by tearing away some of the unions affiliated with it and by forming new ones. The Socialist Trade
and Labor Alliance was to organize all workers, skilled and
unskilled alike. The struggle for immediate improvements
was not stressed in these organizations. In De Leon's opinion this was hopeless in any case, and after the lost Homestead strike (1892) the professors and journalists of the
Socialist Labor Party had expressed themselves in the same
vein as the upstart mountebanks and demagogues of the
Knights of Labor—to the effect that the time for strikes was
over. What, then, were these trade unions to do? Well, they
were to keep themselves ready to take over the management
of the industries as soon as a majority in Congress had given
the government into the hands of the "working class"—that
is, into the hands of De Leon and the other socialist politicians. In other words, those trade unions were to be voting
agencies for De Leon and his friends, and the union members were to be given, in the cosmic future, the right to elect
the managers and the administrators of the socialist commonwealth. De Leon never could understand why this bril-

liant program failed to win over any considerable body of
workers. He blamed its failure upon the incredible wickedness of Gompers and his associates, whom he never tired in
belaboring with the most extraordinary and ingenious insults, such as "slick political faker," "disreputable renegade
and inebriate," "cold-blooded crafty villain," "entrapped
swindler," and the like.

Gompers, who retaliated in kind, was at heart as much of
a politician as his rivals from the S. L. P., and equally
averse to any revolutionary action. But he was incomparably
more intelligent than they were, and he knew how to set a
realizable goal for his ambition. He was not a self-complacent ignoramus like the present-day type of trade-union
leader, who has only the haziest and most distorted conception of the various socialist theories. He had been himself
under the influence of the revolutionary gospel of the First
International; he had admired Marx for his championship
of the trade unions as a means of improving the workers'
situation. He had likewise caught some of the spirit of syndicalism, already current among the anarchist sections of the
International, though the name and the official French theory
had not as yet appeared. This was expressed in his idea that
"the trade unions, pure and simple, are the natural organization of the wage workers to secure their present material
and practical improvement and to achieve their final emancipation." He also, no doubt, remembered Marx's famous
warning to the followers of Bakunin against that exaggerated and exclusive worship of the "ideal" which might trans-
form their movement into a religious sect. Gompers knew
how to use that argument very skilfully against all kinds of
Socialists and other Radicals, whom he accused of "diverting
the attention of the workers from the present struggle to idle
dreams." He was undoubtedly a very wise man.

Yet Gompers's devotion to the underdog was limited in
range. It included only a minority of the working class—its

skilled section. Skilled workers were easy to organize, and since they could not easily be replaced, they had a chance to improve their position in a peaceful strike contest against the employers. Moreover, their organizations could be maintained even in case of defeat, since the members were able to pay dues high enough to establish and support all kinds of mutual aid and benefit services. These services, in turn, kept the members financially interested in their organizations —and also enabled them to pay fairly good salaries to their organizers. Such unions were a practically effective means for holding in line large crowds of dues-paying adherents, much more so than a political party would have been, united only by vague hopes of a distant future, or by the peculiar satisfaction a workingman derives from sending his favorite orator to Congress.

Gompers did not have the anarchist's or the syndicalist's aversion to political action as a matter of principle. Though he occasionally used anarchistically sounding arguments against social insurance and other government measures for the protection of the workers, these were prompted not by any doctrinaire anarchist protest against the "State" as such but simply by a fear lest the assumption of such social insurance functions by the State might weaken the grip of the trade unions on their membership.* He was a perfect cynic in politics, firmly convinced that the capitalist system would last and, on occasion, not averse to giving the support of his organization's voting strength to those members of the two big parties who assumed an attitude not altogether hostile to the interests of organized labor and particularly of its leadership. He consistently refused to be identified with socialist politics. This was safer and more practical than espousing the cause of a political party that had the stain of foreign importation. For the native worker, as a general

* The early Marxian socialists in Germany, when they first began to help in the formation of the trade unions, likewise insisted that sick benefits, old-age benefits, etc., were proper functions of the unions.

rule, though himself the son of an immigrant, cordially
hates all newcomers as job-competitors and wage-slashers,
and the gift of socialism, offered by them, appears to him
suspicious. Moreover, most of the immigrant skilled workers—except the former very active militants—begin after
a number of years gradually to "go native" under the influence of improved conditions and to become indifferent
to the political affiliations of the old country.

Gompers considered the labor movement a privileged hunt-
ing-ground for former workers like himself, upon which
intellectuals had no right to trespass. It was with particular
glee that he used to refer to a letter—not meant for publication—of the once prominent American socialist, A. M. Si-
mons, who (in 1909) stated that the Socialist Party had no
following among the workers and was composed, on the one
hand, of a "bunch of intellectuals" and on the other of a
veritable riff-raff of "never-works, demagogues, and would-
be intellectuals." In Gompers's opinion the Brindells, "Big
Tims," and similar underworld heroes of whose doings he
was aware, but whom he never dared to discipline, had a
greater moral title to labor leadership than the socialist intellectuals and would-be intellectuals; for they had worked
at the bench once upon a time and would not dispute his
chieftainship. Besides, they were financial successes. . . .

In the struggle for leadership, Daniel De Leon lost utterly
and ignominiously. Not only did he not succeed in undermining the strength of the American Federation of Labor, he
gradually lost all personal influence in his own party as well.
The gifted scholar of Curaçao, descendant of half a dozen
races, including those of Torquemada, Baruch Spinoza, and
Toussaint L'Ouverture, graduate of as many universities in
as many different countries, displayed highly dictatorial propensities. This, as well as his trade-union policy which alienated the organized workers, led to a revolt of the majority
of the party in 1899.

From the schism that took place a new party developed in 1901. This included the bulk of the Socialist Labor Party as well as another socialist organization which a few years before had been formed by Eugene Debs, Victor Berger, and a few other socialist dissenters. The most outstanding personality of the "Socialist Party"—this was the name of the new body—was Morris Hillquit, a young lawyer of great ability. His Russian-Jewish origin and his foreign accent had not prevented him from rising to the very first rank of successful American corporation lawyers, but he chose to devote a large part of his time to the building up of a strong socialist party on the German model. The continuous growth of the party up to the beginning of the World War —it polled nearly a million votes in 1912 and had 120,000 dues-paying members—seemed to bear out his wildest hopes. As anti-War candidate for the mayoralty of the City of New York in 1917, he polled more votes than any other socialist candidate before or since that time. A group of Irish liberals, the Irish Progressive League, came out in his support with the statement that "the Hillquit party is the only party which endorsed His Holiness the Pope's peace note." But the tide turned soon afterwards. Hillquit is now a disappointed, rich old man; and his recent attempt to go to the American courts on behalf of the expropriated Russian oil magnates, against the Soviet Government, has all but destroyed his good name even among what is left of the Socialist Party.

THE RISE OF AMERICAN SYNDICALISM

In the early years of the new century Foster was still merely one of the rank and file of the growing Socialist Party. During those years, however, a new movement was gradually taking shape, which was to determine all the later course of Foster's career.

This was the movement which in time became known as "syndicalism"—though its adherents referred to themselves officially as "industrial unionists" and impressed themselves upon the popular mind as "Wobblies," from the initials of their organization, Industrial Workers of the World (I. W. W.).

Curiously enough, syndicalism in America originated as a protest against conditions diametrically opposed to those which caused the rise of the movement in the country of its origin. In France—as was shown in the chapter about Briand—syndicalism was the trade-union protest against the growing moderation of the socialist politicians. In the United States it began as a protest of the politically inclined socialist workers and intellectuals against the more or less unpolitical official leaders of the trade unions. It was only later that it was to clash with the socialist parties as well.

The growth of the American Federation of Labor, with its well-paid skilled workers supporting a generously rewarded trade-union bureaucracy—Gompers's salary gradually grew to $12,000 annually—resulted in the consolidation of the latter as a highly privileged group. This group became anxious to placate the powers that be and to avoid any clashes that might disturb their own peace and their own digestion. In 1894 the Pullman shop workers' strike threatened to develop into a nation-wide conflict between the workers of all industries and the combined forces of the social *status quo*. Gompers, who in the beginning had endorsed the strike, did not want to be involved in such a gigantic struggle with all its attendant responsibilities. Repeating the procedure of the Knights of Labor during the movement of 1886, he sent out a circular enjoining all the members of the American Federation of Labor to return to work. Ever since, the more radical element among the American workers has looked upon the A. F. of L. leaders as the "labor lieutenants of capital," to use a famous epithet flung at them by

Daniel De Leon. Gompers himself, conscious of the revolutionary potentialities dormant in every major strike, increased from that time forward his efforts toward social peace. These efforts found their expression in his membership in, and vice-presidency of, the National Civic Federation—an organization in which conservative labor leaders of the Gompers type were to join in amicable discussion with the representatives of American business. The peculiar policy of this *bona fide* labor leadership towards workers not affiliated with, or not obeying the orders of, the A. F. of L., sometimes assumed remarkable aspects. Thus, during the momentous Passaic textile-workers strike in 1926, the organ of the "regular" textile-workers union and the main publication of the A. F. of L. (*The American Federationist*) both carried large advertisements of the mills on strike—advertisements which were of no strictly commercial value, and which usually are classified as . . . subsidies. Another aspect of that peculiar policy was to have, in many cases, the membership dues collected by the employers and delivered to the union bureaucracy, which in turn showed its appreciation by concluding agreements highly acceptable to the collectors. For, as if by a strange coincidence, the contracts concluded with the coal companies, for instance, always were made to expire on April 1—as propitious a time for miners to strike as January would be for ice-wagon drivers, to quote the comparison used by Joseph Ettor, one of the leaders of the opposition to this policy.

A twofold movement set in as a reaction against Gompers's policy. On the one hand, the more militant element of the rank and file and of the leadership within the A. F. of L., supported by an imposing number of malcontent immigrant and native intellectuals, advocated an independent use of the ballot for the purpose of carrying out various reforms restricting capitalist privilege. These made up the new Socialist Party, then just rising into prominence.

Protest of another aspect came from the Western sections of the United States. The peculiar conditions of the labor struggles in the mining districts, where nearly every strike developed into a bloody fight between the troops and the armed workers, gave rise to the idea of organizing all workers, skilled and unskilled alike. The founding of the Industrial Workers of the World, in 1905, was the outcome of a combination of widely differing factors. There was the militant spirit of the Western miners, steeled as they were by their tragical struggle against the unsophisticated savagery of a virginal capitalism. There was discontent among some of the unions which had found that the peculiar conditions of their industries made it imperative to organize both skilled and unskilled workers, and which, for one reason or another, were dissatisfied with the American Federation of Labor or with their old leaders. There was the general influence of socialist propaganda, with its acceptance of the socialist ideal and of the ballot as a means of arriving thereat. There was De Leon's dual trade-union organization, the Socialist Trade and Labor Alliance, which joined the new movement in the hope of bolstering up the declining fortunes of the Socialist Labor Party, of which in fact it was only a duplication. Last, but not least, there was the influence of syndicalist and anarchist ideology. The anarchist element gradually destroyed the influence of the socialist would-be-politicians and was helpful in infiltrating the ideas of French syndicalism, to the effect that the labor union was both the instrument of struggle and the basis of social reconstruction after the elimination of capitalism. The finally accepted theory of the new organization, however, was not pure French syndicalism. French labor unions ("syndicats") were still largely craft organizations, while the official point of view of the I. W. W., as formulated by William E. Trautmann— editor of the German organ of the United Brewery Workmen's Union and generally acknowledged theorist of the movement—laid its main emphasis upon the formation of industrial unions, embracing all employees, skilled and unskilled workers as well as office men.*

In William D. Haywood the "Industrialists" found an inspired leader. In the earliest years of I. W. W. activity he had to fight for his very life against a trumped-up murder charge—an accusation intended to destroy the militant Western Federation of Miners, of which Haywood was the soul. The pressure of progressive opinion throughout the country forced an acquittal. Haywood remained a storm center of revolutionary activities in the United States until 1920, when a twenty-year sentence imposed upon him during the anti-Bolshevik hysteria forced him to flee to Soviet Russia, where a few years later he died, a broken man. Though an advocate of all revolutionary methods, such as the general strike, direct action and sabotage, Haywood did not consider it inconsistent at the same time to remain a member of the National Executive Committee of the Socialist Party, from which he was recalled in 1913 after the party had adopted a resolution damning the militant tactics of the I. W. W.

William Foster joined the I. W. W. in 1909, and at about the same time he left the Socialist Party. That party was then on the road to becoming what the *New Republic* (December 2, 1916) called "little more than an organized appetite for office—a Socialist Tammany, exploiting the devotion of its members instead of the funds of corporations, for the benefit of a little circle of perfectly honest, but perfectly incompetent and selfish politicians, who persist in thinking themselves idealists." The Industrial Workers of the World were meanwhile becoming more definitely aligned against the Socialist Party. The latter kept on growing more and more respectable and persisted in trying to remain on good terms

* The origin of the I. W. W. has been presented admirably in Louis Levine's (Lewis L. Lorwin) *Development of Syndicalism in America,* New York, 1913.

with the American Federation of Labor. That organization
with its steadily increasing membership seemed to offer a
fertile soil for socialist propaganda. The I. W. W., in
spite of the publicity it was getting on account of its spectacular fights, was still a small group of militants rather
than the mass organization which it had set out to become.
The few larger industrial unions which it had originally included, such as the Brewery Workers and the Western Miners, had withdrawn—frightened at their own creation.
More and more the I. W. W. was becoming the organization
of the unskilled, migratory, "hobo" element of the working
class, though occasionally it conducted strikes of the semi-
skilled, such as the textile workers in the Eastern sections of
the country. Its advocacy of the interests of the migratory
and the unskilled, such as the railroad construction and the
lumber workers, often brought it into conflict with the authorities in districts and towns which refused to permit its
meetings. William Foster, then a young and enthusiastic
militant, actively participated and suffered arrest in more
than one of those epic "free-speech fights" carried on by the
Wobblies in San Diego, Spokane, and other places on the
Pacific Coast.

There was a tragic internal contradiction involved in the
whole theory and organization of the I. W. W. which
damned it to futility. Its founders had set out to build up an
organization which should include the whole working class
and particularly those sections of it which hitherto had never
been organized. To accomplish this feat, they understood
that they would have to resort not only to revolutionary propaganda but also to such revolutionary methods as sabotage,
direct action, general strike. At the same time they apparently expected the authorities to stand by in judicial detachment and to observe the provisions of a "Bill of Rights"
which had been originally intended to protect respectable
property holders, or at best skilled mechanics, but certainly

not the countless host of unskilled pariahs whose demands, if satisfied, would engulf all the profits of the present industrial system.

Apparently, bitter experience was needed to teach them that revolutionary methods and an open mass organization do not well go together, and that either the organization will be suppressed by the authorities or the revolutionary methods must be given up. Their alternative was either to remain revolutionists by becoming underground conspirators, like the malcontent Russian intellectuals under the Tsar or the rebellious British workers early in the nineteenth century, or to give up all revolutionary methods and to be tolerated as a law-abiding dual organization, trying to compete with the A. F. of L. They chose the latter. Organizing with them has now become an aim in itself, as when they insist upon organizing a special "industrial" union for the unemployed, each of the unemployed having his membership card. Which all goes to show that at bottom their leaders were not real revolutionists but only non-conformist labor organizers with a radical vocabulary. They have now foresworn sabotage and all the other violent methods and they have refused to join the labor-union international of either the Communists or the Syndicalists because of possible suspicion that they are in favor of illegal, violent methods.

Though not a spectacular personality, like other outstanding leaders of the movement—Haywood, Elizabeth Gurley Flynn, Ettor, Giovanitti—and figuring little in the reports of the heroic struggles of the organization, Foster soon found his abilities appreciated by his comrades. An international trade-union conference was held in 1911 in Budapest, and Foster was sent there as the representative of his organization. The American Federation of Labor likewise sent a representative. As it was the practice of such international conventions to recognize only one central body for each country, the trade-union delegates of the rest of the

world, or, more properly, of Europe, had to choose between
the gigantic A. F. of L. and the I. W. W. The latter was
supported only by the French unions, then still in the heyday
of their unreformed syndicalist glory. The delegates of all
the other countries, in spite of their adherence to socialism,
were more impressed by the numbers of the conservative
craft unionists than by the enthusiasm of the socialist and
revolutionary "Industrialists." Foster had to quit the conference, and being out of funds, he slept the following night
in a park. . . .

Foster stayed in Europe more than a year. During that
year he came in contact with the syndicalist movement in
France, Germany, and England. As a result of his observa-
tions, he came to the conclusion that dual unionism, such as
professed and practiced by the I. W. W., was an altogether
hopeless undertaking. No sooner was he back in the United
States than he began to entreat his comrades to change their
ways and to join the old unions. This he did in a since famous letter, which he sent to the *Industrial Worker* after he
was offered the position of editor of that paper. He pointed
to the total failure of the I. W. W., both in America and in
England, as well as of a similar organization in Germany, to
make any headway as compared with the labor unions already
in existence. He contrasted that failure with the success
achieved by the French syndicalist militants, who had "cap-
tured and revolutionized" the existing trade unions; he likewise emphasized the progress made by the "boring from
within" tactics of the British syndicalists, who, under, the
leadership of Tom Mann, were trying to win over the old
trade unions to more militant methods.

His efforts to convince his old comrades were of no avail.
Haywood answered, quite pertinently, that the unskilled
workers whom the I. W. W. were trying to organize, were
simply ineligible for the A. F. of L., owing to a "vicious
system of apprenticeship, exorbitant fees," and a number

of other causes. "Unskilled labor must become skilled before it can gain rights," as John P. Frey, an influential
leader of the A. F. of L. once said. Ettor, another prominent organizer of the I. W. W., declared, both pertinently
and impertinently, that "the most unscrupulous labor fakers
now betraying the workers, were once our 'industrialist,'
'anarchist' and 'socialist' comrades, who grew weary of the
slow progress we were making on the outside, went over,
and were not only lost, but became the greatest supporters of
the old and the most serious enemies of the new."

Curiously enough, both Foster and his opponents were
right. Dual unionism—i.e. the creation of parallel unions in
competition to those already existing—was opposed to the
very essence of syndicalism. Basically syndicalism postulated
a non-partisan organization, in which workers of all opinions would join and which would sooner or later become permeated with the revolutionary spirit of the syndicalist militants. A dual organization, once created, was bound to
attract only those elements which were already consciously
revolutionary. The great majority, those who were simply
wage-minded, would be inevitably attracted to the organization that had numbers, respectability and . . . safety. The
dual organization would thus become a political or revolutionary body and would cease to be a non-partisan labor union. Haywood was equally right in his contention that it was
useless to tell unskilled workers to join the A. F. of L.—
that organization definitely did not want them. Yet, there
was no assurance that the I. W. W. was able to absorb these
workers. Under ordinary conditions the unskilled are simply
unorganizable. They are ready to fight; but as they are easily
replaced, nothing short of a nation-wide upheaval (or a war
with its resulting scarcity of labor) can actually improve
their situation and induce them to remain in a labor union
for any length of time. The I. W. W., whose ambition was
to organize all the millions of the unskilled, in its whole

quarter century of existence was always outnumbered
by the American Federation of Labor twenty to one—a mere
"corporal's guard," to borrow the contemptuous expression
of Samuel Gompers. The whole tragedy of American syndicalism was reflected in the controversy between Foster's
orthodox syndicalism on the French model, and Haywood's
native "industrialism." The one wanted to infuse revolutionary methods into an organization composed of a privileged group of skilled workers, who by their very position
were moderate and law-abiding, occasional acts of violence
notwithstanding; the other wanted to organize an instinctively revolutionary mass, which by its very nature resisted
organization. A decade later the Communists, under Foster's leadership, were to set themselves both these tasks. . . .

Undaunted by the stubbornness of his former comrades of
the I. W. W., Foster proceeded to found his "Syndicalist
League," which was to propagate his ideas among the radical elements and to bring them into the path of his "boring
from within." At the same period he collaborated with another syndicalist in writing and publishing *Syndicalism,*
a pamphlet which contains a comprehensive presentation of
his ideas at that time. Seven years later, during the great
steel strike of 1919, this pamphlet was used by the Steel
Trust and the anti-labor press as a means of working up
anti-Bolshevik hysteria; its author was then in the public
eye as the leader of that strike, conducted under the auspices
of the A. F. of L.

"Boring from Within"

In the meantime Foster had become general organizer of
the Brotherhood of Railway Carmen, an organization affiliated with the American Federation of Labor. He collaborated with the progressive wing of the Chicago labor leaders, who fought the corrupt practices of the unspeakable
gang of freebooters controlling the unions of the building

trades. His history from this time forward becomes a tangle of Machiavellian policy, in which it is hard to distinguish between the triple process of deceiving his opponents, misleading his friends, and deluding himself. At heart he no doubt believed that he was still working in the spirit of his old revolutionary aspirations. So did, probably, his syndicalist teacher, Leon Jouhaux, head of the French General Confederation of Labor, when, after the beginning of the War, he became a "bitter-ender" and with practically his entire organization—it had begun to grow in numbers and respectability—switched over to moderate, patriotic trade unionism on the German socialist model. Growth in numbers is dangerous to the radicalism of a labor organization. With their improved material standing the leaders inevitably and unconsciously begin to think in terms of "responsibility" rather than of consistency, particularly if the latter may land them in prison and destroy their organizations.

Foster's language changed completely. In 1916 he had founded the International Trade Union Educational League, under whose auspices he published the pamphlet *Trade Unionism, the Road to Freedom*. It was a diluted syndicalism of a sort—a two-per-cent solution one might say—with all the revolutionary slogans omitted. It was written with the tongue in the cheek, so to speak, promising the workers full emancipation on the day when *all* of them would be organized.

"As they [the workers] organize," he wrote, "and job competition diminishes, they gain strength and the bargaining power passes gradually from the employers' hands into theirs. They force an ever-lessening degree of exploitation. And with the flight of time this process will go on until finally, when the workers are fully organized, job competition will have been abolished and the bargaining power shifted wholly into their hands. Then, on that happy day, in their irresistible might, they will refuse to be exploited at all, the thieving wage system will collapse: . . . a prosperous era will be instituted in which industrial justice shall prevail."

It was all so simple. . . .

It is very likely that this pipe dream of well-nigh Gandhist tenuity was considered by Foster as an indispensable strategical move for placating the distrust of Gompers and of the other leaders of respectable trade unionism. In his book on *The Great Steel Strike,* written in 1920, in defending the moderate tone of the pronouncements of official trade unionism, he says: "Like various other aggressive social movements [the trade unions] have more or less instinctively surrounded themselves with a sort of camouflage or protective coloring, designed to disguise the movement and thus to pacify and disarm the opposition." This was meant not only as an alibi for the A. F. of L.; it was likewise intended as an excuse for his own behavior since the time he had begun to "bore."

In fact, ever since his descent into practical activity along with the regular trade unions, he had done everything possible to alienate the more revolutionary elements of the labor movement. It may have been the subtle strategy of a man who seemingly breaks with his past only in order to strike all the harder when the proper time shall arrive. But some saw in it common cynicism of a man who, having lost his revolutionary faith, is trying to do his best for himself by cashing in on the knowledge and experience obtained in the labor movement; at any rate Foster was apparently proceeding along the path so bitterly described by his former comrade Ettor, in the passage previously quoted.

A glimpse of Foster's activities during this period of his life can be gained from the deposition made by Samuel Gompers during the Senate investigation of the Steel Strike of 1919. Asked about his relations to Foster, the grand old man recounted how in 1913 "about a year after that pamphlet [*Syndicalism*] had been printed" he [Gompers] had spoken at a meeting of the Chicago Federation of Labor. "One of the delegates arose after I had concluded," the deposition goes on, "and expressed himself that it would be wise for the men in the labor movement of Chicago and of the entire country, to follow the thought and philosophy, and so forth, which President Gompers had enunciated in his address. . . . Much to my amazement, after the meeting was over I was informed that the delegate was Foster. . . . I think I addressed a letter to him expressing my appreciation of his change of attitude, his change of mind, and pointing out to him that pursuing a constructive policy he could be of real service to the cause of labor. He was a man of ability, a man of good presence, gentle in expression, a commander of good English, and I encouraged him. I was willing to help build a golden bridge for mine enemy to pass over. I was willing to welcome an erring brother into the ranks of constructive labor."

It was in the same spirit of long-range strategy, or complete surrender, that William Foster, the "radical anti-patriot knowing no country" (so he had described himself in *Syndicalism*), whole-heartedly accepted Gompers's position during the War. He had been entrusted with the organization of the Chicago packing-house workers, a job which he did extremely well. Simultaneously, however, by his own admission, he "carried on a regular campaign in our organization in the stockyards"—for the sale of Liberty bonds. And this was while his former comrades of the I. W. W. were being lynched by vigilantes or facing indictments that brought them twenty-year terms. . . .

THE GREAT STEEL STRIKE

In the course of 1918, great restlessness prevailed among the steel workers. Ever since the early nineties, all attempts to obtain any better terms through strikes or to extend the union organization beyond the highly skilled upper crust of native American workers had proved dismal failures. Twelve hours work a day and seven days' work a week was practically the rule, with a supervising spy system unequaled in any other industry—or any other country, for that matter. The improved conditions won by so many other categories of workers during the War at last aroused the hopes of the steel operatives as well. The situation seemed to the I. W. W. a propitious opportunity for organizing large groups of unskilled workers—such an opportunity as had not offered itself since their foundation.

It was not, as already explained, the policy of the A. F. of L. to organize the unskilled. A wage movement of the unskilled, underpaid and desperate as they usually were, could easily take on the proportions of a revolutionary mass struggle—and this the trade unions, and particularly their well-paid leaders, were keenly anxious to avoid. Moreover, so long as the unskilled could be kept at low pay, employers were more amenable to higher wage demands from the well-behaved and respectable skilled workers. . . .

On the other hand, it was even more dangerous from the A. F. of L. point of view to let the unskilled be organized by a competing organization. These I. W. W. daredevils, who were still, so to speak, at the beginning of their career, with practically nothing to lose, might—at that particular juncture—by their militant tactics, achieve some success and thus undermine the influence, and lower the prestige, of the A. F. of L. That could never be permitted, and to forestall any such calamity the A. F. of L. decided to steal a march on the I. W. W. and to do the organizing itself. Once organized, the unskilled workers could more easily be controled, misguided and betrayed, and their discouragement would keep them, for a time at least, unresponsive to the siren songs of radical competition. It was a subtle move and it was later adopted as a general policy by the A. F. of L.

Whenever the I. W. W. seemed to have even the slightest chance of extending its organization among the unskilled workers, native or foreign, white or colored, the A. F. of L. would suddenly shed its old prejudices against the categories in question. Sustained by its prestige as a *bona fide* organization, it could easily crowd out its disreputable and well-nigh outlawed competitor.

Foster was hardly conscious of the part he was playing when the A. F. of L. placed him in charge of the unskilled. No sooner had he finished laying the foundation of the stockyard workers' organization than he proposed to begin organizing the steel workers. In April, 1918, he made that suggestion to the Chicago Federation of Labor, and soon the National Committee for Organizing the Iron and Steel Workers was formed. Samuel Gompers became president of the committee, and Foster its secretary-treasurer. Twenty-four unions, representing a total of two million workers, backed its activities.

The story of that organizing campaign, which lasted for over a year, and of the strike which broke out late in September, 1919, is given in Foster's book, *The Great Steel Strike,* published in 1920. The cold report—Foster was still an active organizer of the A. F. of L. and not yet associated with the Communists—shows all the tragedy which attends the unskilled worker in his struggle for a more adequate share in life. For one thing, the unions which constituted that National Committee for Organizing the Iron and Steel Workers, were only half-heartedly supporting the whole campaign. Their monetary contributions were exceedingly meager, and they placed a mere "corporal's guard" of organizers at the disposal of the Committee. They thus prevented that quick attack, which, if undertaken while the War was still on, would have forced the steel magnates to the wall. Foster called the delay a "blunder"—for he was not at liberty to call it by its right name. Then, too, there was the

Amalgamated Association of Iron, Steel and Tin Workers,
a union for the highly skilled, which was supposed to absorb
the hundreds of thousands of unskilled workers won by the
campaign. This union was frankly hostile to the whole movement, and it actually broke the backbone of the strike by
"discouraging the men and advising them to return to work,"
to use Foster's words. This "dyed-in-the-wool skilled workers' union," made up mainly of native Americans, issued
150,000 dues cards during the strike, cashing in at two dol-
lars per member. Of the $300,000 thus collected from the
striking "Hunkeys," the union generously paid out $11,881
to the National Committee, for the conduct of the strike,
retaining the rest in its treasury. It was a good haul, and
after the defeat of the strike the unskilled workers who had
paid their entrance fees were terrorized by the companies
into abandoning the union. . . .

If such was the attitude of "friends"—what could be expected from open enemies? Twenty-five thousand armed
men were in the service of the Steel Trust in the Pittsburgh
district alone. The constitutional right of assembly was simply abolished in most places, and to an extent never practiced
even in imperial Germany, against which a war for democracy had just been waged. Pickets and labor organizers were
brutally murdered, and the perpetrators of the crimes were
acquitted. In giving a moving account of the death of Mrs.
Fannie Sellins, an organizer of the United Mine Workers
who was helping in organizing the steel workers, Foster
dispassionately notes that "rightly or wrongly, the steel
workers, almost to a man, felt that this devoted woman was
a martyr to their cause." Rightly or wrongly! What superhuman "detachment" was required of an A. F. of L. organizer! William Foster himself barely escaped a similar
fate in Johnstown. He was arrested by a mob led by the secretary of the Y. M. C. A. and the president of the Chamber
of Commerce, guns were stuck against his ribs, and he was

forcibly put on board an eastbound train. Civil liberties were obviously not meant for times like these.

An attempt to break the strike before it was actually begun was made by President Woodrow Wilson, aided by Gompers. Ten days before the date set for the beginning of the struggle, both of them asked for a postponement—Gompers obviously afraid of the turn the strike might take. But it was then too late. I. W. W. agitators were already active among the steel workers, the workers themselves were at the highest pitch of dissatisfaction, and the fight would have begun even without the consent of the A. F. of L. leaders. The strike was called.

After the strike had begun, a committee of the Senate undertook to investigate its causes. The Senators, anxious to prejudice public opinion against the strikers, kept harping upon Foster's past affiliations and opinions, particularly as expressed in his *Syndicalism*. Under their cross-examination he spent what must have been some of the most unpleasant hours of his life. The interests of the struggle, as understood by the A. F. of L., required that he should not reaffirm his past heresies; his personal honor and his standing among all radical opponents of the present system required that he should not forswear them. Adroitly he tried to dodge the countless irrelevant questions from the inquisitorial senators; questions which certainly had nothing to do with the steel-strike situation. But his cross-examiners were relentless and forced him to say things which he can hardly remember with pride; for instance, that his views were "in the main" in harmony with those of Gompers.

Finally, in January, 1920, the steel strike was broken—to a large extent with the help of Negro labor, which thus took its tragic revenge for the contempt in which it had been held by the white workers, whether skilled or unskilled.

The failure of the steel strikers did not discourage other categories of workers. Miners and railway shop workers also came out with their demands, and both the authorities and the press continued to associate all these movements with the name of Foster. Even at the time when Foster was writing his book on the Steel Strike, and was entirely absorbed by his task, he was accused by Attorney General Palmer of being one of the leaders of the railway strike. *The Herald* of Donora, Pa., one of the less inhibited papers, went so far as to declare that "the best remedy for that bird would be one of those old-fashioned hangings."

THE ROAD TO DAMASCUS

The great steel strike had made William Foster a national figure. He had become a headliner and the best-hated man in the country. It placed him, too, at the parting of the ways. He could return to his work in the A. F. of L., where a soft and well-paid position was assured him on condition merely that he live down that Red reputation which the steel interests and a pliable press had deliberately made for him. With his intellectual equipment, he was certainly competent to step into the shoes of Samuel Gompers, should the latter choose to retire or to die. This, however, the powerful bureaucrats in charge of the Federation would never permit. They did not trust him. Soft and pink as he seemed to have become, they felt a lurking suspicion that this might be mere make-believe, and that at heart his repentance and conversion were not genuine. He was still openly monkeying with his old I. W. W. ideal of organizing the unskilled; he was not fraternizing with the representatives of big business; he was not a "regular fellow," but a studious bird, keen to find out anything that was to be known about the labor movement in every country of the world. No, decidedly, he was not their kind. Gompers likewise towered intellectually miles above them; but the old man was a thorough cynic, and as such, flesh of the flesh of these Tammanysouled and -minded trade-union officials. Irish though Foster was—as they were themselves for the most part—he seemed to be an Irishman of a different kind; one of those fine, dead, incorruptible pioneers of Ireland's and America's freedom, whom they celebrated in florid speeches but with whom they certainly would not have liked to work. In brief, Foster made them uncomfortable, for they could never feel sure that it was the pink Sancho Panza and not the red Don Quixote who was the real man. . . .

Foster himself could hardly have felt happy when, in 1920, he looked back upon the work he had accomplished since he had entered the American Federation of Labor. He had been entrusted with the organization of the stockyard workers, mostly unskilled and semi-skilled, and he had succeeded in enrolling about 200,000 of them. It was largely due to his efforts that they had obtained the eight-hour day, higher wages, and substantial improvements in their living conditions. But his work, accomplished with so much ardor, had been frustrated by the malicious intrigues of the Butchers' Workmen's Union, an organization of skilled workers; and the man who headed that organization had been backed and supported by Gompers himself. By 1920 Foster's packing-house workers' union was completely destroyed. His promising activity in behalf of the steel workers had likewise been brought to naught, and to a large extent by the same all-powerful element in the trade-union organization. . . .

The hope remained that a change in the spirit of the great mass of organized workers would force their leaders to a change of policy; or, if that was not possible, would bring new leaders to the fore. This hope came from Europe. The Russian Revolution was holding out against a world of enemies and had finally succeeded in crushing, or at least in repelling, both domestic enemies and foreign invaders; and the Spirit of Revolution moved upon the face of the Earth.

In 1920 Foster founded the Trade Union Educational League, which was to stimulate the amalgamation of craft unions and further the cause of industrial unionism.

Socialism, in its moderate as well as its radical manifestations, had heretofore been treated as a joke in America—as the "lunatic fringe of the labor movement," to use one of the historical sayings of President Roosevelt. After the November Revolution in Russia and its victorious stand against its enemies, that amused attitude yielded to hysterical fear and rage. Cynical bourgeois and tired, sceptical radicals alike began to entertain the possibility of a social revolution. Foster's old faith, dead or sleeping since his first enthusiasm, was again rekindled. No sooner was Clemenceau's *cordon sanitaire* broken than Foster went to Russia—to see with his own eyes. He saw the workings of a revolution that had swept away the capitalists and the landlords; he saw the seething turmoil that was presented by the rest of Europe; he returned to America a convinced admirer of the Bolshevik revolution and a believer in the application of its methods to other countries as well. This was a dangerous game to play, but the prize was worth the danger. For he could never have doubted that *he,* and no one else, would be called to head the forces of revolution and to go down in history as the American Lenin. . . .

At the time when Foster returned to America, the incipient communist movement was in a very bad plight. So was the Socialist Party, whose offshoot it was, in America as in all the other countries of the world. After their "palace revolution" against the dictatorship of Daniel De Leon, the American Socialists had for a time made continuous headway, not only among immigrant workers but also among native Americans. They had a number of native American intellectuals in their ranks. They even exerted an appreciable influence on the A. F. of L., assuming toward its policy an attitude which, unlike DeLeon's, was critical but not hostile.

The progress of the War and its later developments put a stop to the further growth of the party. A large number of the native intellectuals—among them some of the best-known names in the party—reverted to type and became frankly Anglo-American jingoes in their sympathies. A few of the leaders, such as the great native orator Debs, took an internationalist attitude. The greater number of the leadership, while not exactly "pro-German," were anti-Ally. The Jews and the other oppressed nationalities hailing from Russia wished above everything else for the defeat of the Russian armies, from which they quite logically expected the overthrow of the Tsarist régime. The Irish took a similar attitude with regard to England. As for the German and German-Austrian element, with the exception of their New York daily, they openly or covertly adopted the nationalist attitude of Scheidemann in Germany.

The anti-War attitude assumed by the majority of the party when America entered the fray resulted in the secession of Anglophile American intellectuals already mentioned. They have ever since remained detached from all radical activities. The rest of the party had a drastic grinding between undiscriminating persecution on the part of the Department of Justice and mutinous criticism from the younger set, which now began to talk seriously of overthrowing the existing system—with the conquest of the Socialist Party machinery as the first step.

The formation of a Left Wing within the Socialist Party; its expulsion as a precautionary measure, in order to protect the vested party interests of the job-holding old guard; the emergence of three mutually hostile communist parties (the Communist Party, the Communist Labor Party, and the Proletarian Party) from the former Socialist Left Wing; so events unfolded within the socialist movement during the years between America's entrance into the War in 1917 and the firm establishment of Soviet rule in Russia after the defeat of all its enemies in 1920-1921. True, the old Socialist Labor Party remained—a sect of personal worshippers at the shrine of Daniel DeLeon, who had died embittered and almost forgotten, in 1914. His party paper still appeared weekly and still religiously reprinted all the most insignificant editorials written by the great man ten or twenty years before; it called itself the only revolutionary Marxian party, and at the same time strenuously fought all "uncivilized" forms of struggle, taking a peculiar pride in the fact that it never had been prosecuted by the authorities. . . .

There was also the I. W. W., still bleeding from the thousand wounds it had suffered during the atrocious War-time persecutions. This organization was now torn between its enthusiasm for the Russian revolution and its dislike of the American Communists; for the latter were attracting ever-increasing numbers of once-loyal "Wobblies," now tired of dreaming of "One Big Union," while remaining a heroic "corporal's guard." In time their dislike of communist competition turned the I. W. W. against Soviet Russia as well.

Foster's conversion to communism was a godsend, for the movement was sorely in need of an outstanding personality with a nation-wide reputation. The Socialists had one: old Eugene Debs, the greatest American orator, a man known for his integrity. The Left Wing had in vain tried to win him over to the cause of Communism. He sympathized with them; he was an enthusiastic admirer of the Bolshevik revolution; but he was opposed to anything that smelled of violence or illegality. In his saintly naïveté, he apparently believed that the majority of the people could actually be won over to Socialism by sound arguments and good oratory. After the majority had adopted the cause of socialism, violence would be unnecessary in any case. . . . It was in this spirit that he always opposed *sabotage* and direct action, and that he dismissed as "ridiculous, arbitrary and autocratic" the policy of "armed insurrection" demanded by "Moscow."

THE WORKERS' PARTY

At that time the Communists were an outlawed "illegal" party. The persecutions of the authorities had driven them underground, and they were preaching civil war, armed insurrection and a proletarian dictatorship, the various groups into which they were split trying to outdo each other either in revolutionary ardor or in revolutionary realism. All of it bore no relation to the actual conditions of the country. The great mass of workers in America were interested in better wages and were ready to fight for these. The purely political revolutionism of these enthusiastic would-be dictators left them indifferent, if not amused. . . .

The Communists did not lose courage. They merged, split again, organized various bodies of a non-secret type which, to avoid persecution, did not openly call themselves communist; last, but not least, they wrote "theses" attacking each other and pointing to each other's ignorance, cowardice, and bourgeois prejudices. The whole proceeding was full of unconscious humor; a grotesque caricature of the tragic revolutionary struggles of Russia and Central Europe. Whether the leaders of the various mutually hostile "parties" or groups realized it or not, their theoretical differences were only a camouflage for their personal and group ambitions fighting for predominance within the movement.

By 1922-23 the anti-Bolshevik hysteria was abating. In the opinion of the Communists, illegal parties were no longer necessary in the countries where the existing laws permitted open organization. Capitalism, so ran official communist opinion the world over, had entered upon an era of temporary stabilization after the stormy post-war period, and another revolutionary wave could not be expected in the very near future. Heretical opinion among revolutionary malcontents in Europe had it, however, that the Russian

Communists (whose word prevailed in the Communist International, the central body shaping communist policies in all countries) having victoriously repulsed all enemies and begun to stabilize themselves in their peculiar form of State Capitalism, were no longer interested in world revolution. From now on, so these malcontents claimed—and Trotsky had likewise preferred these charges against his opponents—the chief task of the communist parties the world over was to secure the sympathy of the workers for the Soviet Republic and for its defense against possible agression.

A new era had begun for the American communist movement at the time when William Z. Foster decided to join the cause. The first step on the new road was the formation of a legally permitted "Workers' Party" and preparation for the winding up of the underground activities. A secret convention of the underground Communist Party, held in Michigan in August, 1922, ended in disaster. It was betrayed by a stool-pigeon, and Foster was arrested together with most of the other delegates. His "boring from within" activities would probably have been more successful if he had not been thus publicly identified with the Communists. On the other hand, Foster and his new comrades probably thought that his open affiliation with their cause would add prestige to the party whose leader he was to become.

The consequences of that arrest to Foster himself were not as calamitous as might have been expected. By the time he was tried, in the early part of 1923, the Bolshevik scare had subsided, and there was no longer that remarkable unanimity of feeling among American jurors, whether capitalists or organized workers, that had been so effective in securing heavy sentences for every radical. The jury disagreed.

During the same year the "Communist Party"—as the underground organization had been called—was finally scrapped. The Workers' Party (aside from a small Michigan group calling itself the "Proletarian Party") remained as the only communist organization in the country. Numerically it was not very strong, having a total membership of only fifteen or twenty thousand and an exceedingly small native following of no more than one or two thousand, but what adherents it had were enthusiasts. The party certainly monopolized the affections of the great majority of those foreign-born workers who were radically inclined, with the sole exception of the Jewish needle workers, who were about equally divided between the "Rights" and the "Lefts." Though not polling as many votes as the Socialists—this was due to the large percentage of the foreign element—it was organizationally much stronger than the latter.

Once the Communists had become an open party, they set out to fulfill their task of winning over the majority of the working class. This was to be the preliminary to the overthrow of the existing system—the nebulous aim of a dim future. The less distant and more real aim was to produce a "united front" of the working class. It was of course out of the question that this "united front" of radicals and moderates should aim at the overthrow of the capitalist system or at a substantial improvement of the situation of the working class by means of extensive wage struggles. The socialist and trade-union leaders were opposed to both of these objectives. The only direction in which the "united front" could proceed must therefore be the striving for moderate reforms, and before everything else, the defense of the Soviet Republic and the struggle for its recognition—all tasks to which any bourgeois Liberal could give his hearty support. There was also, of course, though unadmitted as a rule, the intention of getting into close contact with the masses now held in tow by other organizations, with the aim of winning them over to the communist cause.

In 1923 a number of progressive trade unions in Chicago and certain western and middle-western organizations of dissatisfied farmers called a convention for the purpose of forming a nation-wide Farmer-Labor Party. The Socialists, now a weak party with a membership of no more than 12,000, declined to participate in the effort, since a majority of the trade unions of the country had not been won over to the project. The Communists, who were likewise invited, accepted the call and succeeded in capturing the convention. Most of the non-communist elements withdrew, and the Federated Farmer-Labor Party, which the Communists organized as a result of their victory, became merely a duplication of the Workers' Party. It soon disappeared.

In the following year the various progressive and liberal elements of the country decided to get together, in view of the impending presidential election. A "Third Party" movement was to be set on foot, and the Socialist Party was ardently active in preparation for the so-called Conference for Progressive Political Action. Senator Robert LaFollette was to be the presidential banner-bearer of the new movement. The Socialists were hoping for an American Labor Party on the British model, in which they expected to play the part of the Independent Labor Party of England. The Communists likewise hailed the new movement. They again took part, as during the previous year, in preparations for the formation of a national Farmer-Labor Party, the initiative coming this time from the Minnesota State Farmer-Labor Party. At the same time they were declaring that "the Farmer-Labor Party must enter an electoral alliance with it [LaFollette's third party] against the old capitalist parties and the capitalist government." There were voices among the Communists and communist sympathizers to speak against this stand of their leadership, for—they said—it simply meant that the party of proletarian dictatorship was to become involved in a coalition with small capital against big business—a policy for pink-and-yellow Socialists rather than for red Communists. These dissenters pointed also to the danger involved in a policy dictated exclusively by the consideration of the needs of the Soviet Republic, for which LaFollette's election meant official recognition and possibly credits. They declared that such a stand meant the renunciation, for some time, of the class struggle. Otherwise the frightened small capitalists would be driven back to the fold of reactionary big business.

In the end no united front could be arranged for Foster and LaFollette. To explain and to justify that collaboration to the proletarian world at large, a leading American Communist wrote in an international communist press service: "The campaign will allow us to enter the third party wherever the opportunity presents itself, to form a left wing within it and split it away from the third party." The writer had forgotten that one's Machiavellian intentions are seldom served by their open revelation, and sure enough the Wisconsin Senator came out quite rudely against his would-be supporters. The Communists thereupon nominated William Foster as their own presidential candidate. Their ticket received hardly more than 33,000 votes. Four years later, in 1928, running again as the presidential candidate of his party, he obtained 75,000 votes.

From the violent debates and internal struggles which racked the party late in 1924, it appears that Foster was not particularly enthusiastic about the course its policy had taken. The responsibility for that course lay chiefly with a certain John Pepper, who for a number of years was official representative of the Communist International in this country. Pepper, now expelled from the Communist International and generally discredited in every respect, was the type of unprincipled adventurer—a modern political *condottiere*—that has sprung up and infested the labor movement particularly since the War. A moderate Socialist in pre-war Hungary, he had become a member of the democratic Karolyi government after the War. In this capacity he threatened the Communists around Bela Kun with "mass

terror." Two days later he was himself People's Commissar
for War of the Bela Kun government, only to be forced to
resign a month later, owing to an internal revolt of the
Communists themselves. It was he, who, as a delegate of
the Communist International in the United States, had conceived the idea that the election of LaFollette should be the
main task of the party in view of the great advantages
which the Soviet Republic would derive from it.

John Pepper had collected around himself most of the
intellectual, white-collar element of the party, and it was
this element that was so favorably inclined towards helping
in the formation of the Farmer-Labor Party and supporting
the Third Party campaign. Foster, in spite of his conversion
to communism, had still some of the old syndicalist aversion
to competition by intellectuals. He wanted, he announced,
"no substitute for the Workers' Party." He was undoubtedly
afraid that the organization of a broad Farmer-Labor Party
would give a preponderance to all kinds of white-collar politicians. Whatever theoretical reasons he propounded for it,
there was at the root of his opposition the old jealousy felt
by the leaders who, like himself, had risen from the ranks,
and who had had a long trade-union experience, against the
essentially politically-minded college-bred intellectuals and
semi-intellectuals, well enough versed in abstract political
theory and political wire-pulling, but without any actual contact with the hard-working masses of manual labor. Two
militants of the party, who belonged neither to the Foster
group nor to the opposing Ruthenberg group, and who were
seized by an impish ambition to spill the beans, declared that
a "great deal of the controversy in the party was of a
purely factional nature and not upon any issues of principle . . . Two groups in the party are brutally out for
power, and they subvert everything else to attain their ends."

The party referendum, as well as the party convention,
showed that Foster's influence was much stronger than that

of his opponents. But the Executive Committee of the Communist International in Moscow preferred to have the minority group of intellectuals at the helm. There was always danger—so some of the communist dissenters tried to explain the situation—that in a conflict between the policy of the Communist International and the specific requirements of the labor movement in America, the ex-workers grouped around Foster might balk and perhaps revert to a syndicalist policy.

As a result, both the referendum and the decision of the party convention, at which Foster had assembled forty votes against the twenty votes given for his opponents, were set aside by the International, and the direction of the party came into the hands of the minority. The losers were very bitter. Some of them asked themselves what was the use of conventions—of the clearly expressed will of the majority? But such was the organization of the Communist International, which, from its very inception, had been a large international party with nonautonomous national branches and with practically unlimited powers vested in the Executive Committee, seated in Moscow. It imposed an "iron discipline bordering on military discipline" * upon all affiliated communist parties, which these in turn, imposed upon their individual members.

Foster himself attempted to fight the decision and to appeal against it, but at once a large part of his following among the lesser leaders realized the hopelessness of such a course and swung over to the newly installed ruling group. The demoted leader soon saw himself surrounded by a mere minority of former trade-union militants.

* Point 12 of the 21 conditions of affiliation with the Communist International speaks of "iron discipline" which must prevail in every Communist Party. In a speech delivered at a session of the Executive Committee held on December 19, 1929, Stalin amplified the expression "iron discipline" by adding the words "bordering on military discipline." (*Daily Worker*, New York, January 30, 1929.)

It was a bitter pill. He had given up a brilliant and safe career in the *bona fide* labor movement for the honors of leadership in an outlaw band. The hopes that he had cherished for the new party had not materialized. It had remained a well-nigh hopeless sect, made up mainly of foreign-language groups. And now even the scant honor of that leadership was wrung from his hands. Some of his closest friends resigned from the party and retired from the movement. One of them was his son-in-law, a former structural iron worker, who returned to his old occupation, and, no longer used to the dangerous trade, fell off a scaffolding and was killed. Foster himself stuck it out and continued the work which he had ·begun at the close of the steel strike; building up the activities of the Trade Union Educational League, which by "boring from within" was to win over the big unions to the cause of communism.

CIVIL WAR

During the four years following Foster's demotion from leadership in 1925, the control of the party passed more and more definitely into the hands of the Ruthenberg group of intellectuals and semi-intellectuals. Ruthenberg died in 1927. His successor was Jay Lovestone, a brilliant and hard-working college graduate—a very young man for party leadership. James P. Cannon, a former worker and I. W. W. militant, and one of the founders of the party who at that time was in Foster's camp and later became the leader of the Trotskyist group, remarked of Lovestone and his general staff that from New York City College they "leaped directly into leadership of the Party without any intermediary steps in the turmoil of the class struggle." Indeed, a current overproduction of college graduates had been making it hard for young intellectuals to find any position leading into a hopeful career, and the more so if they were of Jewish descent. The labor movement accordingly, even in its most radical aspects, took on for them the character of a way of escape —though this was by no means a conscious mental process.

Lovestone and his following were stanch supporters of the Stalin-Bukharin group, then ruling both in the Communist Party of the Soviet Union and in the Communist International. Foster's group of former trade-union militants, as well as a large body of other militants of working-class origin, put up with Lovestone's dictatorship—but they hoped meanwhile for a comeback. Trotsky's struggle against the party machine, resumed in 1926 with renewed vigor as a result of the support given him by some of his former highly influential opponents, filled Foster and the other malcontents with hope. They were, indeed, not particularly interested in the theoretical aspects of the Russian party discussions, but a victory of the Trotsky opposition would mean a complete realignment of forces in the Communist International, and consequently a victory of the opposition in other countries as well as Russia. This was not to be. By 1928 it was obvious that Trotsky had lost and that his cause was entirely hopeless. Wm. Foster was no romantic, to stake his entire career on a lost cause, and indeed Trotsky, with his well-known attitude with regard to the trade unions, was theoretically the very antipode of everything Foster had ever stood for. Trotsky without the prospect of power had no further interest for the former apostle of syndicalism. Yet the latter was now faced with the prospect of complete party disgrace, or even expulsion, on account of his former sympathies with the great Russian Tribune; for the intra-party struggle, in Russia and elsewhere, had reached the stage of merciless eradication of all dissenters. The fight for power knows only one law—self-preservation. With hesitation or without, Foster therefore publicly denounced as Trotskyists a group (headed by J. P. Cannon) of his former fellow-sympathizers with the Russian Opposition. They were speedily expelled from the party.

After his expulsion Cannon founded his dissenting group, which now bears the name "Communist League (Opposition)," while its periodical conveys to the American public the regular messages of the Great Exile to a loyal Trotskyist host. Foster remained in the regular party, but his authority was greatly shattered even among those who opposed the Lovestone régime; and a split which occurred in his own group left him practically without a following. At the party convention called early in 1929, he was the sole "Fosterite" delegate, opposed to over ninety followers of Lovestone and half a dozen dissenters from his own former group.

Yet that convention brought his vindication and the utter ruin of his enemies. Not by a decision of the delegates, of course. Repeating the history of four years before, a telegram from the Executive Committee of the Communist International brought about the change. William Foster, lone delegate among a crowd of nearly a hundred opponents, was decreed head of the party. . . .

It turned out that Lovestone's understanding of the potentialities of America's economic development was entirely at variance with good communist theory. Lovestone believed that capitalism in America was still on the upgrade, not declining, as in the other countries. This was the so-called theory of "exceptionalism." Its practical conclusion was that the moment for large-scale revolutionary action in America had not as yet arrived. Lovestone's opponents branded this conception as a Right-Wing heresy and insisted that America's capitalism was just as much on the downgrade as that of the rest of the world.

This was all very interesting as theory, but it did not explain the real reasons for Lovestone's sudden fall from favor. The explanation of that sudden change lay in quite a different direction. After disposing of the Trotsky opposition in 1927-28, the victorious Stalin-Bukharin group came to grips within itself. The reasons of the clash between Stalin on the one hand and Bukharin, Rykov and Tomsky on the other, have already been explained in the chapter on Leon Trotsky. Bukharin, at that time at the head of the Communist International, was trying to use his connections for forming an anti-Stalinist bloc among the various parties affiliated with the International. Lovestone, like many Communists in other lands, believed that Bukharin would win, seconded as he was by such formidable allies as Rykov, the Premier, and Tomsky, the head of the Soviet trade unions. His guess was wrong. Before Bukharin could carry out his intrigue, he was outgeneraled by Stalin. By decree of the Executive Committee of the Communist International, Stalin had the right wing (that is, the more or less pro-Bukharinist element) in all the communist parties removed from leadership—or even expelled outright. In that process the communist parties of the various countries were greatly weakened.

When Lovestone and his following finally understood that the game was up, they hurriedly tried to prove their loyalty to the winner by knifing Bukharin and demanding that the latter be removed from the Communist International. They were too late. Lovestone's efforts to regain power in the party were of no avail. The Executive Committee of the Communist International was adamant; it obviously did not trust him. He finally found himself outside the party and a leader of that Right-Wing opposition which calls itself the "Majority Group." It is hardly necessary to say that, in the same manner as four years before, a large number of lesser Fosterite leaders had gone over to the winning Ruthenberg-Lovestone group, so, now, large numbers of Lovestone adherents fell immediately into line with the new Foster leadership. All the theoretical discussions had been only a cover for a "factional strife" that was "not based on any

serious differences on principles," to use the words of the
theses of the Communist International on the American
party situation.

The internecine struggle of the three factions—the official
party and the "Left" (Trotskyist) and "Right" (Lovestone-
ite) outlaw groups—now became extremely . bitter. Bur-
glaries of each other's offices in the search of compromising
documents; breaking up of heretic meetings by the enthusiastic followers of the official line; Trotskyist taunts at the
strict conformity of the "Stalinites" in view of "subsidies received from Moscow"; anti-Semitic gibes, in the
party's daily, against the Right-Wingers (such as the "Git-
low-Lovestone-Wolfe Hester Street concern") ; the renewal
of the long-since-withdrawn charges that Lovestone was a
stool-pigeon; accusations of charlatanism and low demagogy
against the official party, which was charged with having
urged fantastic relief measures on behalf of the unemployed,
for whom doles virtually amounting to double the average
wage were said to have been demanded. These were some
of the episodes of that struggle.

The non-conformists have been violently denounced by
the official party as counter-revolutionists, tools of American
imperialism, enemies of the Soviet Republic. The enthusiastic, but simple-minded, followers religiously believe those
charges. One of Lovestone's henchmen, who later recanted,
gave vent to his bitterness by declaring that "the leadership
of the Russian party is interested in the weakening of the
leadership of the Communist Party of the U. S. A., in order
that the Soviet Republic should get credits, diplomatic recognition and commercial advantages." Unpleasant reminiscences also began to crowd the press columns of the three
groups. The Right-Wingers recalled that one of the highest
leaders of the party, a former editor of the party's daily and
a deserter from Lovestone's camp, had declared that "fair-
ness is a conception imported from a hostile class; it be-

longs to the columns of the *Nation* and the *New Republic*."
Cannon's left-wing organ dug out the past of another editor
of the same daily, who, during the anti-Bolshevik hysteria,
had deserted to the red-baiters, and later on came back to
play a prominent part in the movement. Both "Rights" and
"Lefts" attacked Foster for his weak-kneed attitude during
the War. All this contributed to enliven the movement and
to hurt it far more than the hostility of the government and
of the official trade union leadership could do. The membership of the official party sank to 6,000, but it has since picked
up and by 1932 was reported to be about 10,000.

Foster's uneasy triumph was not of long duration. Was
it the ineradicable stigma of his syndicalist past? He apparently was not yet *persona grata* in the eyes of the Communist International, and he had been used only as a
stop-gap until another man could be chosen for leadership.
Significantly enough, several months after Foster's return to
power the theoretical magazine of the Russian Communist
Party printed a speech made by Stalin several months before, in connection with the internal struggles within the
American party. At that time Stalin had taken to task both
Lovestone and Foster and had expressed his indignation at
Foster's "indecent" attitude in trying to curry favor by
calling himself a "Stalinist." The reprinting of Stalin's un-
flattering remarks was taken by many as an indication that,
for some reason or other, Foster's leadership was not meeting with approval in the Communist International and that
he would soon be displaced. Not long afterwards, Earl
Browder, Foster's former associate in the struggle against
Lovestone, took his place at the helm of the party.

THE NEW TRADE-UNION POLICY

As in the previous years of Lovestone's domination, Foster was given charge of the party's trade-union activities.

His boring from within, begun several years before, had started out auspiciously. Particularly in the needle trades but also in the miners' union and in other organizations, the dissatisfied elements began to listen readily to preachers of a more militant strategy. The old trade-union officials of the Gompers tradition saw their means of livelihood threatened—and a pretty comfortable livelihood it was. In his *Misleaders of Labor,* a momentous collection of facts on American trade unionism, Foster presents a distressing picture. He shows the depths of Tammanyism and infra-Tammanyism to which nearly every union has been brought down by a leadership consisting not of commonplace officeholders with a lower-middle-class or middle-class standard of living, as in Europe, but, to a very large extent of high-powered racketeers, with the ethics of a Capone and the incomes of successful bootleggers. No wonder that such gentry refused to let themselves be displaced by those whom they saw only as envious competitors for their handsome capitalist incomes! A bitter campaign of expulsions, slugging, serious bodily harm, vote stealing, and all the other amenities of a struggle for power was instituted, rendering the work of the radicals extremely difficult and greatly weakening the unions; for the leaders in possession were willing to ruin "their" unions rather than give up their jobs without a fight.

The last few years have brought about a definite change in the trade-union policy of the Communists. In 1928 the Congress of the Red International of Labor Unions (the trade union counterpart of the Communist International) reversed its old policy of "boring from within," so urgently recommended by Lenin. Dual unionism, the formation of revolutionary trade unions in opposition to the old ones, became the new *mot d'ordre.* In France and Czechoslovakia the internal struggles within the trade unions had already led to splits and to the establishment of competing trade unions.

The new policy was now to be extended to all the other countries as well. The actual reason behind this sudden change was hard to determine. The official version was that capitalism had entered its "third period," that of decisive revolutionary struggles; that the old trade unions had become hopelessly reactionary; and that the workers' struggles for better living conditions could best be conducted under the leadership of factory councils and of shop delegates, who were to be stimulated in their development by the new revolutionary trade unions. Cynical comment from various anarchist "smart Alecks" implied that in the final analysis the conquest of the old unions, even if possible, did not offer any particular advantage to the communist cause at large; for, once in possession of the trade-union machinery, the new leaders were likely to succumb only too willingly to the mollifying influences of respectable trade-union leadership, and to forget their old affiliations.

The new trade-union policy was a hard shock to Foster. It was a reversal of all his judgments, ever since he had left and fought the I. W. W. on account of that very same policy of dual unionism. He tried to oppose it at first, but in the end he submitted; he is defending it now as vigorously as he ever attacked it. To use his own words, the activity of the revolutionary elements who are still in the old unions is to consist in "drawing the trade union workers under the ideological leadership of the Trade Union Unity League (the name of the dual organization of the Communists), and as speedily as practicable, into mass affiliation with it."

The new unions have been conducting a number of very courageous fights in the textile, mining and other industries. They have ventured into newly industrialized sections of the South, which no other labor pioneers have dared to penetrate. They have stirred up great numbers of workers hitherto unaffected by propaganda. From the point of view of figures, their valiant efforts have borne no fruit so far. The membership of their unions is not increasing in numbers, and it is hard to predict whether Foster will be more successful in this new task than was the I. W. W. in its quarter century of heroism and self-sacrifice. Many of Foster's former admirers doubt the sincerity of his latest conversion. They suspect that behind the war-mask of this orthodox Communist, directing the weight of his official condemnation against all dissenters from his latest creed—who are all "social-fascists," it appears—there is hidden a very sad and disappointed man. . . .

In the meantime the Communist Party, regardless of the human—all-too-human—squabbles and failings of its leaders, is drawing into its ranks all that is vigorous, combative and enthusiastic among the dissatisfied elements of the younger generation of workers and intellectuals. They may still be unconscious of the deeper implications of the movement they are engaged in, of the lurking contradiction between the interests of its working-class contingents and those of the intellectuals and former workers constituting its upper crust. Nevertheless, they are the great advance guard in the struggle against a bankrupt system of chaotic private capitalism. Already scores of far-seeing economists are pointing the way by recommending one form or another of State Capitalism, with the government as the sole business concern, whose "stockholders" are bureaucrats, technicians, and other intellectual workers—the new ruling class to come. The growth of the communist movement, with its menacing host of hoboes, unskilled "hunkeys," negro workers, and déclassé intellectuals may hasten the process of transition to that higher form of capitalism.

A new form of class domination, State Capitalism simplifies the class struggle to a contest between manual and mental workers and may thus foreshadow the twilight of all class domination. For the workers' healthy envy of all those who are better off than they are, will continue to spur them on to struggle—with all the weapons of the revolutionary arsenal—for more and always more, until they have equalized their incomes, and consequently also their educational opportunities, with those of their office-holding masters.

When that time arrives, the American people will remember William Foster in spite of all his failings, weaknesses and inconsistencies, along with all the other luckless pioneers of a rising laboring mass, such as the Molly Maguires, the Chicago martyrs, and, last but not least, Bill Haywood and the other valiant militants of the early I. W. W.

CONCLUSION

THE deeper aspects of a historical event or process are seldom fully realized by its contemporaries or by its main personages. The actual economic implications behind the religious and idealist verbiage surrounding the Crusades, the Reformation, the French Revolution, though hardly understood by contemporaries and participants, are now self-evident to even the most superficial student of history.

There is no doubt at present that the socialist movement of the nineteenth and twentieth centuries constitutes the beginning of a new historical epoch. Only a few of the momentous events in the evolution of humanity can be compared to it. Its foremost pioneers have not only succeeded in arousing the masses of the dissatisfied; they have also permeated their contemporaries with a more realistic conception and interpretation of historical events. Naturally enough, they have applied that method to their own movement as well and have proudly declared that theirs is the first movement on a world scale to be conscious of its own historical significance. It is a boast which, given the profound scholarship of its authors, sounds almost convincing.

The socialist critics of the existing system pierced through all the shams, and laid bare the real motives of the defenders of capitalist privilege, just as their liberal predecessors saw through those of the feudal apologists. They discerned the general interests which united their privileged enemies, as clearly as the various cross- and under-currents which created internal conflicts within their ranks. These critics likewise penetrated through the unconscious "rationalizing" mental processes which had accompanied both the struggles of the capitalist bourgeoisie for domination and their efforts to maintain it when won: processes which had permitted the capitalists to identify their own specific interests with the interests of all the other dissatisfied classes; to consider the wrongs from which *they* suffered as the wrongs of the "people" at large, and to see in their own access to power the liberation of the country.

According to the socialist scholars, such deception and self-deception as that caused by the predatory character of the ruling class of to-day is alien to the socialist movement —including in that term all the traditional currents of anti-capitalist protest. Aiming, as it does, at the defense not of any privilege, but of the common interests of the majority —the manual and mental workers—it is not predatory in character; it needs no "rationalizing" psychological processes, and it can afford to be fully conscious of its motives and aims.

The theory of the community of interests of all wage and salary-earning toilers of brawn and brain has long seemed simple and convincing. Yet, just as convincing seemed also that earlier theory of the community of interests of all members of the "third estate"—capitalists and peasants, workers and intellectuals—as opposed to the feudal lords; or Thomas Jefferson's theory of the community of interests of all "producers"—manufacturers, large landowners and the rest—as against the "speculators"; or Henry George's theory of the community of interests of all the people, as against the owners of land.

The theory of the "third estate" rallied the less favored classes of the population around the banner of the capitalist bourgeoisie. The theory of Jefferson could have served a similar purpose, with the money lender substituted as enemy for the non-existent feudal lord; and Henry George's "single tax" was, in the words of Karl Marx, "the last attempt to save the capitalist system." But in the mind of that great scholar—as in that of any other socialist thinker—there was no fallacy in the theory that the hired manager, engineer, professor, all the innumerable more-or-less privileged salaried intellectual workers, were, along with the manual laborers, at bottom, wage-earning, propertyless, proletarians, belonging to the same class as opposed to the property-owning capitalists. Nor did he see, or want to see, that this fallacy was to serve a specific class-purpose: to rally the manual workers around the banner of a new, rising bourgeois class—the intellectual workers.

The development of modern industrialism and of the modern State has made higher education accessible to wider groups of the population than in previous periods. Originally the educated elements belonged chiefly to the priesthood. There was also a restricted group of descendants of the privileged classes who, for one reason or another, were willing to take up politics, the arts and the sciences, usually as the privileged minions of some king or feudal lord. The upper sections of this feudal intelligentsia enjoyed the same privileges and comforts as their property-holding lords. Its lower strata, as represented by the poorer clergy, had often grounds for dissatisfaction. In many cases the more energetic and adventurous elements of this section revolted against their more fortunate superiors. Spiritually, these revolts expressed themselves in heresies drawn from the primitive communism of the Scriptures; materially, in the support of ever-recurring uprisings of the downtrodden urban and rural masses. Whatever the conscious ideal of these heretics, their real subconscious aim is now plainly evident: the theocratic rule of the victorious lesser clergy.

Where the exclusive mental sway of the clergy was either absent, as in classical Greece, or vanishing, as in the Europe of the seventeenth and eighteenth centuries, the dissatisfaction of the intellectuals expressed itself in philosophical or fictional dreams of the perfect State, as a protest of the owners of intellect and culture against the predominance of the owners of land, money, serfs and other material goods. Consciously or unconsciously, these utopian dreams were the compensatory "wish-fulfilments" of a social group which was still too weak to express its ambition for domination in any other way.

The political and industrial revolutions of the declining eighteenth century saw the intellectuals arrayed with the various groups of the rising middle classes in their struggles against the feudal past—and among themselves. With the emerging of capitalist rule, hampered as it still was by many encumbering feudal remainders, the independent strivings of the intellectuals began to come to the fore. A part of the educated scions of the property-holding classes were provided for as members of the State bureaucracy and of the liberal professions, not to speak of the clergy and of the officers' caste. These were entirely satisfied with the *status quo* and defended it against its critics and opponents. Industries were still largely managed by their owners, but a separate class of managers, engineers and technicians was gradually becoming more and more indispensable for the growing scope of economic development. The rewards of this last group were not very generous as yet, and many of them began to visualize the possibilities of a social order managed by themselves in a more efficient, more scientific, way than by the often ignorant capitalist upstarts, whose blind greed and ruthless exploitation of the workers was pregnant with calamitous possibilities. They remembered the miseries that had followed in the wake of the French revolution, and they wished to avoid their repetition. Their aspirations found expression in the ideas and proposals of various divergent currents, usually referred to as "utopian," "philanthropic," "conservative," or "Christian" socialism.

However widely the advocates of these currents differed in their vocabulary or their point of departure, most of them had actually much in common with the moderate Socialists of the present time. Middle-class or upper-middle-class intellectuals in social status or in sympathies, they feared the impending uprising of the submerged masses. Aside from a few visionary plans for human brotherhood to be realized as a result of the benevolence of the privileged classes, their proposals had in view practical improvements for immediate application, tending in the direction of government ownership. Their hierarchical state was to compensate the capitalists, lavishly to reward the higher abilities of the educated managers and organizers of the nation's economic and cultural life, and to perpetuate the social status of the performers of manual labor. Their postulate for a socialized or regulated form of exploitation—or economic inequality, which amounts to the same thing—can be found in undisguised form in the ideas of the followers of Saint-Simon or in the theories of the "conservative" Socialist, Rodbertus. Anxious to preserve existing privileges, advocates of these ideas were to be found among the staunchest supporters of the Cæsarism of Napoleon III and the monarchical principle of Hohenzollern Germany.

But in the first part of the nineteenth century the time had not yet come for the adoption of those proposals. Private capitalism was still at the beginning of its career, and the danger threatening from below could still be coped with by other methods than government ownership or similar schemes.

That danger from below was represented not only by the underpaid manual workers. It threatened likewise from a numerous group of lower-middle-class intellectuals—students without the prospect of comfortable positions after graduation, teachers without appointments, journalists without purchasers for their intellectual wares, and all the other varieties of unemployed or underpaid mental workers with hearty appetites and empty stomachs.

Early in the nineteenth century, Napoleon, with his promise of the "career open to talent," regardless of origin or wealth, had been for a long time the ideal of that educated but almost hopeless younger generation. "Napoleon was indeed the man sent by God to help the youth of France!" was the sigh of Stendhal's hero of that period, Julien Sorel, in *Le Rouge et le Noir.* "Who is to take his place? What will the poor wretches do without him, who have just the few crowns needed to procure them a good education, and then not enough money . . . to launch themselves in a career?"

But Napoleon was not to return, and the young men with an education had to fall back upon another hero of the Great Revolution in decline: Babeuf, the organizer of the "Conspiracy of the Equals"—the first attempt of a group of communist intellectuals to seize the government with the help of the workers. Babeuf's gospel was revived a few decades later and was known first as "Babouvism" and then called after Blanqui, its most outstanding apostle and martyr. During a whole generation impecunious intellectuals kept on organizing conspiracies and coups aiming at the establishment of a revolutionary dictatorship.

That economic depression of the early nineteenth century which inspired the more desperate section of the French intelligentsia with ideas rather like those of the Russian Communists of three generations later, had its revolutionary effects in England as well. A powerful radical movement, known as Chartism, was on foot on the other side of the Channel. Headed by lower-middle-class intellectuals, it enlisted the working masses in a struggle for more democracy, as expressed by universal suffrage. It was in many respects the prototype of the continental socialist parties, with their propaganda for universal franchise of about half a century later.

Greatly differing from each other in their external manifestations and in their vocabulary, the French and the English radicals of nearly a century ago had two important features in common. Headed by lower-middle-class intellectuals, both movements aimed at a change in the political form of the existing system—but not at the immediate seizure and nationalization of capital. Socialism, though generally professed by the French conspirators and partly current among the Chartists, was reserved for a more-or-less-distant future; but the seizure of power, or participation in the government with the help of a democratic suffrage, was put forward as an immediate objective. Power for the intellectuals and hope for the workers—that division of . . . spoils has remained to the present day.

Both Blanquism and Chartism disappeared under the impact of new conditions. The economic upswing that took place in England around the middle of the nineteenth century brought the trade unions to the fore, as an instrument for immediate improvement in the situation of labor. For many decades, trade unionism pure and simple reigned supreme over the minds of the English workers. An analogous process, though under other forms, took place in France, where a similar revulsion against purely political radicalism led to a development of various coöperative schemes. In both France and England, the parvenu manual worker who had acquired a smattering of education forced out his white-collar competitor for leadership.

A coördination of the political radicalism of the lower-middle-class intelligentsia with the trade-unionist aspirations of the upper stratum of the manual workers was effected by a group, originally German, centered around Karl Marx and Friedrich Engels. Their ideas served as inspiration for three generations of socialists of the various schools. "Regular" socialists of the German prototype, Communists of the Russian brand, Syndicalists of the

French and American (I. W. W.) varieties, even Anarchists, at least those of the Bakunin tradition—all were under the spell of the Marx-Engels class-struggle theory. That theory proclaimed an irreconcilable antagonism between the proletariat and the capitalist class, the final outcome of which was to be the expropriation of the propertied classes and the establishment of a collectivist form of production.

In the conception, currently accepted by all divisions of modern socialism, the word "proletariat" includes both manual workers and brain workers—all those who have to rely for their livelihood on wages or salaries. In his *Communist Manifesto*, Marx found ardent speech to present the miserable plight of the intellectual workers who had become paid wage slaves of the capitalist class. That plight was very real indeed during the early period of the nineteenth century, and Marx, himself one of them, could not help identifying their fortunes with those of the manual workers. Yet poor as they were, there was a substantial difference between their misery and that of the manual workers. Their middle-class or lower-middle-class families had spent a certain capital "to procure them a good education"—their mental, invisible means of production. That investment was bearing no dividends as yet. But a change in the politico-administrative structure—without essentially altering the status of the manual workers—could remedy their situation. Political democracy with its opportunities for underpaid or unemployed talent, meant not only "dividends" on their investment—it was also the starting point from which the malcontent intelligentsia could eventually obtain a controlling interest in the nation's business: dispossess the capitalists and take charge of the government and of the management of the nationalized industries. In Marxian language this was called "conquest of political power" by the—working class.

The second half of the nineteenth century saw the inauguration of political democracy or near-democracy in most western countries. In accomplishing this the radical intelligentsia secured the assistance of the manual workers by helping them, in turn, in their struggles for their bread-and-butter demands.

This was to be succeeded by the second stage : the revolutionary struggle proper, for the removal of capitalism and the establishment of socialism. The establishment of socialism meant, of course, one thing to the intellectuals and self-taught ex-workers, who headed the movement, and another thing to the manual workers, who made up their following. The latter saw in it the fulfilment of their dreams of economic equality; while in the conception of the former, "socialism" was only an euphemistic expression for State Capitalism— that is, government ownership of industries managed by a bureaucracy composed of intellectuals, self-taught ex-workers and former capitalists.

Even so, that second step has never been attempted, in democratic Western Europe, at least. The Paris Commune of 1871, in spite of all the red glamor associated with it, was a venture in radical democracy rather than in socialism. The advent of democracy, coupled with a great upswing in industrial development, had cooled the ardor of the former implacable enemies of the existing system. The starving intellectuals, who in the middle of the nineteenth century had been ready, side by side with the factory workers, to fight on the barricades for democracy or even for a dictatorship as the first step to socialism, were starving no longer. There were plenty of well-paid positions at their disposal, and as a group they had become perfectly respectable bourgeois. A certain section of the intelligentsia continued, however, to dabble in "labor" politics. These were ambitious men who saw in the socialist and labor movement a career that offered unlimited possibilities. There was, of course, a sprinkling of idealists, who joined the movement because the socialist ideal appealed to their outraged sense of justice; and also, to be sure, the common adventurers and "cranks" who infest every heterodox movement.

But these leaders were no revolutionists. That specific capital which they possessed, the privilege of a higher education, placed them above the working masses and enabled them to establish themselves as one of the many privileged groups of the bourgeois world. They were editors, politicians, organizers; preachers of the new gospel of a Proletarian Kingdom, apparently not of this world—or, at least, several generations away. The prospect did not dismay them, for they had time to wait. . . . A peaceful, unprecipitated transition to State Capitalism was the apex of their revolutionary longings. In the interval they were ready to defend the existing system against unwarranted interference with the normal course of affairs. In this they were supported by a section of the working class, the highly skilled workers, who, to a certain extent, were allowed to participate in the benefits of industrial expansion and colonial exploitation.

Nevertheless, theirs was no bed of roses. They were beset by many dangers. There were, first, the too-eager careerists, who were ever ready to jump out of the ranks and to play openly capitalist politics, thus affecting the *morale* of the followers. There were also some younger leaders who were afraid lest the moderation of the official party policy might eventually alienate the more impatient elements of their own party's working-class following; these often indulged in too much loose talk about revolution, with a view to taking over the leadership from the party "fossils." Friction and jealousy were continually occurring between the college-bred "highbrows," in charge of the political end of the movement, and the self-taught ex-workers, controlling the trade unions in coöperation with the party. Finally there were the anarchist and syndicalist heretics who also aspired to leadership of the laboring masses.

In time, however, the inexorable laws of life under democracy took care of the radical competitors, both within and without the party. The oppositionists within became very reasonable as soon as they were themselves admitted to the highest councils of the great organization. The anarchist intellectuals who often succeeded in attracting the most rebellious elements opposed to the existing system could represent no serious menace to the socialist politicians. With their far-away ideal and their rejection of the class struggle (or acceptance of it only for propagandist purposes) they were bound to become an insignificant sect of peaceful preachers, demolishing the existing order in spirit only. The syndicalists, their more realistic counterparts within the trade unions, were likewise bound to lose their revolutionary souls. Wherever they have succeeded in getting control of the trade unions, they have gradually succumbed to the allurements of regular trade-union leadership with its steady rewards. In France, the classical country of its origin, syndicalism has made peace with the existing order, indignant protests of uninfluential groups notwithstanding. Spanish syndicalism, with a long tradition of heroic struggles under the semi-absolutist Bourbon régime, entered shortly after the downfall of the latter upon a similar road of evolution towards respectability. Over and over again the democratic opportunities of the more advanced countries have enabled intellectuals, semi-intellectuals and self-taught ex-workers, as leaders of the various forms of the labor movement, to avail themselves of the revolutionary discontent of the masses in order to divert it into futile political campaigns, into peaceful trade unionism, or into some utopian cult.

But the democratic idyll did not last forever. There came a time when industrial expansion ceased to keep pace with increasing opportunity for higher education. Once more, there were not enough soft jobs to go around. Colonial possessions could provide for a part only of the educated surplus of the population—and not all countries had that outlet. Moreover, there were two great countries of the east which had not yet passed through the democratic stage—Russia and China. Economically and politically undeveloped, they had an enormous army of hungry intellectuals with no share in the national income.

Again, as in the early part of the nineteenth century, the civilized world was confronted by a host of desperate, impecunious, lower-middle-class intellectuals, whose only hope was in a violent overthrow of the existing system. The War and the unrest coming in its wake made an opportunity for this section of the intelligentsia to assert itself. While the official socialist parties, representing the more prosperous and sedate labor politicians and trade-union leaders, rallied to the defense of existing conditions and were accepted as full-fledged members of the various government coalitions— or at best adopted a weak-kneed, temporizing attitude—the more desperate elements openly challenged in one way or another the prevailing *status quo*. The communist reversion to the Blanquist tradition of revolutionary dictatorship and the Fascist reversion to a sort of military dictatorship in the Napoleonic tradition, represent the final outcome of these revolutionary developments of the War and post-War periods.

In Russia that section of the intelligentsia and semi-intelligentsia (including a large percentage of self-taught ex-workers) which is organized in the Communist Party, has succeeded in eliminating the capitalists and large landowners, and in imposing its rule over the rest of the population, including the other sections of the intelligentsia. It is tirelessly at work establishing a well-knit system of State Capitalism headed by an all-powerful bureaucracy. In the other countries communist leadership represents the younger and more adventurous set of socialist politicians. They are mainly concerned with taking over the inheritance of the decaying and discredited socialist parties. In exceptionally desperate situations, particularly in countries devoid of political liberties like Italy or Poland, some of them may attempt to emulate the Russian example. In the democratic countries, their policy resembles more or less that of the left wing of the socialist parties prior to the War—with more revolutionary talk than action; particularly as the Russian Communists upon whom they depend for inspiration, have shelved the idea of "world revolution"—being now more interested in industrializing their country and in avoiding international complications.

Those of the intellectuals who have joined the Fascist camp in Italy and Poland, are mainly deserters from the radicals—in quest of a short cut to power and influence. In Germany and elsewhere, they are mostly scions of the ruined "newly-poor" middle classes. Their terminology and their "principles" change from country to country, and . . . from one meeting to another; but their purpose is unmistakable: to gain as much power as possible, both by helping the capitalists to cow the workers, and occasionally also by forcing the capitalists to make concessions to other classes of the population. Their chief support is drawn from those sections of the educated middle and lower middle classes whose economic security and prospects have been destroyed by the post-War developments.

*   *   *

Simultaneously with the struggle of the various sections of the educated lower middle classes for power and influence, there seethes, deep below the surface, a potential revolt of those laboring masses, who, subconsciously of course, continue to think in other terms than their leaders. Whatever theories and panaceas they may be offered, they *feel*, so to speak, in terms of wages and employment, and from time to time their violent outbursts give expression to their inarticulate longings for their own emancipation. To be sure, every demand for higher wages implies a step in that direction, a step towards economic equality. Extended to the dimensions of a general strike of all manual workers, skilled and unskilled, the struggle for higher wages and work for the unemployed may culminate in the total absorption of profits and the reduction of the excessive incomes of the higher salaried men. Faced by demands they are unable to meet, the private capitalist corporations may be forced to yield their place to a higher form of industrial management, the system of government ownership, or State Capitalism, which Socialists sometimes call "State Socialism."

This higher form of industrial management has ceased to be the mere theoretical fancy that it was in the early part of the past century, when it was first proposed by various schools of socialism. To avoid its violent inauguration as an alternative to gradual economic disintegration otherwise conservative men have ceased to "view with alarm" the idea of state control of the nation's economic life. Remembering the services rendered by socialist parties and cabinet ministers to the cause of social peace during and after the War, a confused and frightened bourgeois world may entrust these former alleged enemies with the task of reorganization.

Whether the new system is ushered in as a result of sweeping peaceful reforms adopted under the continuous, threatening pressure of the dissatisfied masses, or as a result of a violent cataclysm; whether the new government machine is headed by moderate Socialists and neo-Liberals, or by extreme left radicals, inequality of income, perpetuated in the higher wages assigned for mental work, remains the outstanding characteristic of State Capitalism. On this point, at least, there is no difference of opinion between Communists and Socialists, between the more impecunious and violent enemies, and the more contented and patient critics, of private capitalist privilege. That principle of inequality has been propounded by their common teacher, Karl Marx, in his famous statement on the "first phase of communism"— his euphemistic term for State Capitalism under the management of the socialist intelligentsia. (*On the Gotha Program.*)

Both Socialists and Communists assume that the progress of economic development will automatically result in the later disappearance of these inequalities of the "first phase"; though, like their teacher, they relegate the "higher phase of communism" to a rather distant and nebulous future. Forgetful of their Marxian realism, they candidly attribute to the educated, privileged, beneficiaries of the "first phase" a truly—unworldly disinterestedness. Voluntarily they are to level their own incomes with those of the manual workers, thus creating equal educational opportunities for all, and wiping out their own intellectual monopoly and class predominance.

It is not very likely that such promises will keep the workers in their place. The continuous mass struggle for higher and higher wages will remain an accompaniment of State Capitalism (the "first phase of communism") as it is of private capitalism. Discontented groups of intellectuals will continue to embrace the cause of the manual workers and to assist them in their struggle, prompted either by an heroic urge to the good fight, or by their own ambition for leadership.

With the eventual equalization of wages for manual and mental workers, the apparent goal of such struggle, higher education becomes accessible to all alike. The rest is a new page in human history.

BIBLIOGRAPHY

ERRICO MALATESTA, OR THE ROMANCE OF ANARCHISM

BRUPBACHER, FRITZ, *Marx und Bakunin*, München, no date.
ELTZBACHER, PAUL, *Anarchism*, New York, 1908.
FABBRI, LUIGI, *Errico Malatesta*, Milano, 1921.
GRAVE, JEAN, *Le Mouvement Libertaire sous la 3° République*, Paris, 1930.
Il Processo agli Anarchici nell'Assise di Milano, Milano, 1922.
KROPOTKIN, PETER, *Memoirs of a Revolutionist*, Boston, 1899.
——, *The Conquest of Bread*, New York, 1927.
——, *Paroles d'un Revolté*, Paris, 1885.
——, *L'Anarchie, sa Philosophie, son Ideal*, Paris, 1896.
NANNI, TORQUATO, *La Gente di Mare e Giuseppe Giulietti*, Bologna, 1924.
NETTLAU, MAX, *Errico Malatesta, Das Leben eines Anarchisten*, Berlin, 1922.
——, *Der Vorfrühling der Anarchie*, Berlin, 1925.
——, *Der Anarchismus von Proudhon zu Kropotkin*, Berlin, 1927.
——, *Anarchisten und Sozialrevolutionäre*, Berlin, 1931.
Pensiero, Theoretical Anarchist Review, Rome, 1903-1911.
Pensiero e Volontà, Theoretical Anarchist Review, edited by Errico Malatesta, Rome, 1924-26.
SCARLATTI, GIUSEPPE, *L'Internazionale dei Lavoratori e l'Agitatore Carlo Cafiero*, Firenze, 1909.
TAGLIAFERRO, TRENTO, *Errico Malatesta, Armando Borghi e Compagni davanti ai Giurati di Milano*, Milano, 1921.

For the details concerning Errico Malatesta's life the author is particularly indebted to the valuable historical publications of Dr. Max Nettlau who has saved from oblivion very much of the early history of anarchism. The author likewise thanks Mr. Arnold Roller and Mr. Carlo Tresca for personally vouched-for data not available in any published source.

ARISTIDE BRIAND, CHAMPION OF THE GENERAL STRIKE

AUBERT, ALFRED, *Briand, Sa Vie Politique,* Paris, 1928.
DOMMANGET, MAURICE, *Babeuf et la Conjuration des Égaux,* Paris, 1922.
GEFFROY, GUSTAVE, *L'Enfermé* (Auguste Blanqui), Paris, 1897.
KRITSKY, *L'Evolution du Syndicalisme en France,* Paris, 1908.
LAGARDELLE, HUBERT, *Le Socialisme Ouvrier,* Paris, 1911.
——, *La Grève Générale et le Socialisme; Enquète Internationale,* Paris, 1905.
LEVINE, LOUIS (Lewis L. Lorwin), *Syndicalism in France,* New York, 1914.
LISSAGARAY, P. O., *History of the Commune of 1871,* New York, 1898.
LOUIS, PAUL, *Histoire du Mouvement Syndical en France 1789-1906,* Paris, 1907
Mouvement Socialiste, Theoretical Syndicalist Review, edited by Hubert Lagardelle, Paris, 1899-1914.
PELLOUTIER, FERNAND, *Histoire des Bourses du Travail,* Paris, 1921.
——, *Le Congrès Général du Parti Socialiste Français, 1899, précédé d'une Lettre aux Anarchistes,* Paris, 1900.
POSTGATE, R. W., *Out of the Past,* New York, 1926.
POUGET, EMILE, *Les Bases du Syndicalisme,* Paris, no date.
SEILHAC, LÉON DE, *Les Congrès Ouvriers en France de 1876 à 1897,* Paris, 1899.
——, *Les Congrès Ouvriers en France, Deuxième Serie (1898-1906),* Paris, no date.
SOREL, GEORGES, *Reflexions sur la Violence,* Paris, 1909.
Vie Ouvrière, Syndicalist Review, Edited by Pierre Monatte, Paris, 1909-1912.
WEILL, GEORGES, *Histoire du Mouvement Social en France, 1852-1910,* Paris, 1911.
ZÉVAÈS, A., *Le Syndicalisme Contemporain,* Paris, no date.
——, *Les Debuts Politiques de M. Aristide Briand* (in *Nouvelle Revue*), Paris, 1910.

J. RAMSAY MacDONALD, LAST RAMPART
OF EMPIRE

BAX, E. B., *Reflexions and Reminiscences of a Mid and Late Victorian,* London, 1918.

BEER, M., *A History of British Socialism,* London, 1919-20.

BERNSTEIN, EDUARD, *My Years of Exile,* London, 1921.

CRAIK, W. W., *A Short History of the Modern British Working Class Movement,* London, 1919.

CROOK, WILFRED H., *The General Strike,* Chapel Hill, 1931.

ENGELS, F., *Condition of the Working Classes in England in 1844,* London, 1892.

HAMILTON, MARY AGNES, *J. Ramsay MacDonald,* London, 1929.

HOGUE, R. W., *British Labour Speaks,* New York, 1924.

HYNDMAN, HENRY MAYERS, *The Evolution of Revolution,* New York, 1921.

MACDONALD, J. RAMSAY, *Socialism, Critical and Constructive,* Indianapolis, 1924.

——, *The Awakening of India,* London, 1910.

——, *Syndicalism, A Critical Explanation,* London, 1912.

——, *Parliament and Revolution,* London, 1919.

——, *Labor and the Empire,* London, 1907.

——, *A Policy for the Labor Party,* London, 1920.

NEARING, SCOTT, *The British General Strike,* New York, 1926.

POSTGATE, R. W., Out of the Past, New York, 1926.

PUMPIANSKY, L., *Zur Geschichte der Anfänge des Englischen Trade Unionismus,* Stuttgart, 1912.

SCHLÜTER, HERMANN, *Die Chartisten-Bewegung,* New York, 1916.

SHAW, GEORGE BERNARD, *The Intelligent Woman's Guide to Socialism and Capitalism,* New York, 1928.

TILTMAN, H. HESSELL, *J. Ramsay MacDonald, Labor's Man of Destiny,* New York, 1929.

TROTSKY, LEON, *Whither England,* New York, 1926.

TSIANG, TINGFU F., *Labor and Empire,* New York, 1923.

VARGA, EUGEN, *Die Sozialdemokratischen Parteien,* Hamburg, 1926.

WALLING, W. E., *Progressivism—and After,* New York, 1914.

WEBB, SIDNEY and BEATRICE, *The History of Trade Unionism,* New York, 1920.

PHILIPP SCHEIDEMANN, OR FROM MARX TO HINDENBURG

Bax, E. B., *Reflexions and Reminiscences of a Mid and Late Victorian*, London, 1918.

Bernstein, Eduard, *Von der Sekte zur Partei*, Jena, 1911.

——, *Die Deutsche Revolution*, Berlin, 1921.

——, *Die Voraussetzungen des Sozialismus und die Aufgaben der Sozialdemokratie*, Stuttgart, 1899.

——, *My Years of Exile*, London, 1921.

Die Neue Zeit, theoretical organ of the German Social-Democratic Party, edited by Karl Kautsky, 1890-1915.

Engels, Friedrich, *Introduction to Karl Marx's "Class Struggles in France,"* New York, 1893.

Frölich, P., *Zehn Jahre Krieg und Bürgerkrieg*, Berlin, 1924.

Grumbach, S., *Das Annexionistische Deutschland*, Lausanne, 1917.

Gumbel, E. J., *Vier Jahre Mord*, Berlin-Fichtenau, 1922.

——, *Verschwörer*, Berlin, 1924.

Junius (Rosa Luxemburg), *Die Krise der Sozialdemokratie* (1915), München, no date.

Kautsky, Karl, *Bernstein und das Sozialdemokratische Programm*, Stuttgart, 1899.

——, *The Class Struggle (Erfurt Program)*, Chicago, 1910.

——, *The Road to Power*, Chicago, 1909.

——, *Vergangenheit und Zukunft der Internationale*, Wien, 1920.

Lorwin, Lewis L., *Labor and Internationalism*, New York, 1929.

Luxemburg, Rosa, *Gesammelte Werke* (Vol. IV.), Berlin, 1923-28.

Mehring, Franz, *Geschichte der Deutschen Sozialdemokratie*, Stuttgart, 1897.

Michels, Robert, *Die Sozialdemokratie im Internationalen Verbande* (in *Archiv für Sozialwissenschaft und Sozialpolitik*, Vol. XXIV/1. 1907).

——, *Political Parties*, New York, 1915.

Nieuwenhuis, Domela F., *Le Socialisme en Danger*, Paris, 1897.

Proceedings of the Conventions of the German Social-Democratic Party, 1890-1931, Berlin.

ROCKER, RUDOLF, *Johann Most, das Leben eines Rebellen*, Berlin, 1924.

SCHEIDEMANN, PH., *The Making of New Germany; the Memoirs of Philipp Scheidemann*, 2 v., New York, 1929.

Spartakusbriefe, Berlin, 1920.

STRÖBEL, H., *The German Revolution and After*, London, 1923.

TROTZKI, L., *Der Krieg und die Internationale*, Zurich, 1914.

UNGER, EMIL, *Politische Köpfe des Sozialistischen Deutschlands*, Leipzig, 1920.

VAHLTEICH, J., *Ferdinand Lassalle und die Anfänge der deutschen Arbeiterbewegung*, München, 1904.

VARGA, EUGEN, *Die Sozialdemokratischen Parteien*, Hamburg, 1926.

WALLING, W. E., *The Socialists and the War*, New York, 1915.

WOLSKI, A. (Waclaw Machajski), *The Evolution of Social Democracy* (in Russian), Geneva, 1905.

LEON TROTSKY, OR GRANDEUR AND MISERY OF POWER

Avant Thermidor, Platforme de l'Opposition de Gauche dans le Parti Bolshevique (*Sapronov, Smirnov*, etc.), Lyon, 1927.

BALLOD, KARL, *Sowjet-Russland*, Berlin, 1920.

BAUER, OTTO, *Bolschewismus oder Sozialdemokratie*, Wien, 1920.

BERKMANN, A., *The Kronstadt Rebellion*, New York, 1922.

BUCHARIN, N., *Kautsky und Sowjet-Russland; eine Antwort*, Wien, 1925.

EASTMAN, MAX, *Since Lenin Died*, London, 1925.

HILLQUIT, MORRIS, *From Marx to Lenin*, New York, 1921.

KASSIOR, *Our Differences of Opinion—About the Rôle and the Tasks of the Trade Unions* (in Russian), Moscow, 1921.

KAUTSKY, KARL, *Terrorism and Communism*, London, 1920.

——, *Die Internationale und Sowjet-Russland*, Berlin, 1925.

——, *Bolshevism at a Deadlock*, New York, 1931.

KORNILOV, A., *Modern Russian History* (2 vols.), New York, 1916.

KULCZYCKI, LUDWIG, *Geschichte der Russischen Revolution* (3 vols.), Gotha, 1910.

LANDAU-ALDANOV, M. A., *Lenin*, New York, 1922.
LENIN, V. I., *What is to be Done?*, New York, 1931.
———, *The Proletarian Revolution and Kautsky, the Renegade*, London, 1920.
———, *The Crisis in the Party* (in Russian), Moscow, 1921.
———, *Wahlen zur Konstituierenden Versammlung und die Diktatur des Proletariats*, Moscow, 1920.
———, *Will the Bolsheviks Maintain Power?*, London, 1922.
———, *The Soviets at Work*, New York, 1918.
———, *The State and the Revolution*, London, 1917.
LENIN and ZINOVIEV, *Gegen den Strom* (Articles Written in 1914-1916), Hamburg, 1921.
LUXEMBURG, ROSA, *Die Russische Revolution* (posthumous), Berlin, 1922.
(MACHAJSKI, WACLAW), *The Bourgeois Revolution and the Workers' Cause* (in Russian), Geneva, 1906.
———, *The Workers' Conspiracy* (in Russian), n.p., Sept.-Oct., 1907.
———, *The Workers' Revolution* (in Russian), Moscow, June-July, 1918.
MARTOV, J., *World Bolshevism* (in Russian), Berlin, 1921.
MASARYK, THOMAS G., *The Spirit of Russia* (2 v.), London-New York, 1919.
NACHT, M., *Die Revolutionäre Bewegung in Russland*, Berlin, 1902.
Party and Opposition on the Eve of the 15th Party Convention, Discussion materials (in Russian), Moscow, 1928.
RADEK, KARL, *Wege der Russischen Revolution*, Hamburg, 1922.
Russia, Official Report of the British Trade Union Delegation to Russia, London, 1924.
SERGE, VICTOR, *L'An I de la Revolution Russe*, Paris, 1930.
STALIN, JOSEPH, *About the Opposition*, Moscow, 1928.
STEPNIAK, *Underground Russia*, New York, 1883.
TROTSKY, L., *My Life*, New York, 1930.
———, *The Permanent Revolution*, New York, 1931.
———, *The Real Situation in Russia*, New York, 1928.
———, *Lenin*, New York, 1925.
———, *The Lessons of October 1917*, London, 1925.
———, *Dictatorship versus Democracy*, New York, 1922.
WOLSKI, A. (Waclaw Machajski), *The Mental Worker* (in Russian), Geneva, 1905.

YAROSLAVSKY, E., *Against the Opposition* (in Russian), Moscow, 1928.

——, *Short Outline of the History of the Communist Party of the Soviet Union* (in Russian), Moscow, 1926.

YUDOVSKY, V. (editor), *Our Adversaries* (in Russian), Moscow, 1928.

BENITO MUSSOLINI, AN ADVENTURE IN CAESARISM

Almanacco Socialista, 1922, Milano, 1922.

ANGIOLINI, A., *50 Anni di Socialismo in Italia,* Firenze, 1908.

BALABANOVA, A., *Wesen und Werdegang des italienischen Fascismus,* Wien, 1931.

BORGHI, ARMANDO, *L'Italia tra Due Crispi,* Parigi, 1924.

——, *Mussolini in Camicia,* New York, 1927.

FABBRI, LUIGI, *La Contro-Rivoluzione Preventiva,* Bologna, 1922.

Fascismo, Inchiesta Socialista sulle Gesta dei Fascisti in Italia, Milano, 1922.

LANZILLO, A., *Le Mouvement Ouvrier en Italie,* Paris, no date.

MATTEOTTI, GIACOMO, *Il Fascismo della Prima Ora,* Roma, 1924.

MICHELS, ROBERT, *Sozialismus and Faszismus in Italien,* München, 1925.

——, *Der Sozialismus in Italien, Intellektuelle Strömungen,* München, 1925.

——, *Il Proletariato e la Borghesia nel Movimento Socialista Italiano,* Torino, 1908.

——, *Die exklusive Arbeiterpartei in Norditalien (1882-1892)* in *Archiv für die Geschichte des Sozialismus und der Arbeiterbewegung,* Leipzig, 1911.

MUSSOLINI, BENITO, *My Autobiography,* New York, 1928.

MUSSOLINI, TANCREDI, HERVÉ, *Dio e Patria nel Pensiero dei Rinnegati,* New York, no date.

POR, ODON, *Fascism,* New York, 1923.

POZZI, G. B., *La Prima Occupazione Operaia della Fabbrica in Italia,* Bergamo, 1921.

Protokoll des III. Kongresses der Kommunistischen Internationale, Hamburg, 1921.

Protokoll des IV. Kongresses der Kommunistischen Internationale, Hamburg, 1922.

ROMANUS, JUNIUS, *Mussolini und sein Gefolge,* Wien, 1928.

SALVEMINI, GAETANO, *The Fascist Dictatorship in Italy,* New York, 1927.

SARFATTI, MARGHERITA G., *Dux,* Milano, 1928.

SCHNEIDER, HERBERT W., *Making the Fascist State,* New York, 1928.

Università Proletaria, Parigi, 1928.

VARGA, EUGEN, *Die Sozialdemokratischen Parteien,* Hamburg, 1926.

WALLING, WILLIAM E., *The Socialists and the War,* 1915.

JOSEPH PILSUDSKI, LIBERATOR OF POLAND

By Order of Marshal Pilsudski, The Hell of Brest-Litovsk Before the Polish Sejm (in English, French, German and Polish), Zurich, 1931.

DASZYNSKI, IGNACY, *Memoirs,* (in Polish), 2 Vols. Krakow, 1925-26.

Die Polnische Sozialdemokratie, Documents Concerning the Attitude of the Polish Socialists During the War, in *Archiv für die Geschichte des Sozialismus und der Arbeiterbewegung,* Leipzig, 1916.

ETCHEGOYEN, OLIVIER, *The Comedy of Poland,* London, 1927.

LANDAU, ROM, *Pilsudski and Poland,* New York, 1929.

LIMANOWSKI, BOLESLAW, *Fighters for Freedom* (in Polish), Krakow, 1911.

——, *Stanislaw Worcell* (in Polish), Krakow, 1909.

MARX, KARL, ENGELS, F., and LAFARGUE, P., *Letter to the Polish Socialists, 1880,* in *Class Struggle,* New York, 1918.

MAZOWIECKI, M., *History of the Socialist Movement in Russian Poland* (in Polish), Krakow, 1903.

PILSUDSKI, JOSEPH, *The Memories of a Polish Revolutionary and Soldier,* London, 1931.

——, *The Revolutionary Struggle in Russian Poland* (in Polish), Krakow, 1903.

Political Strike in Poland (in Polish), Krakow, 1905.

Przedswit (Dawn), Theoretical Socialist Review, London, 1891-1905.

Przeglad Socialdemokratyczny (Social-Democratic Review), Theoretical Socialist Review, Krakow, 1907-11.

RJASANOFF, N., *Karl Marx und Friedrich Engels über die Polenfrage*, in *Archiv für die Geschichte des Sozialismus und der Arbeiterbewegung*, Leipzig, 1916.

VARGA, EUGEN, *Die Sozialdemokratischen Parteien*, Hamburg, 1926.

WOLSKI, A. (Waclaw Machajski), *Evolution of Social Democracy* (in Russian), Geneva, 1905.

WILLIAM Z. FOSTER, APOSTLE IN THE LAND OF THE INFIDELS

ADAMIC, LOUIS, *Dynamite, The Story of Class Violence in America*, New York, 1931.

BRISSENDEN, P. F., *The I. W. W. A Study of American Syndicalism*, New York, 1920.

COMMONS, JOHN R., and Associates, *History of Labour in the United States*, 2 Vols. New York, 1921.

Crisis in the Communist Party of the U. S. A., New York, 1930.

DE LEON, DANIEL, *The Burning Question of Trade Unionism*. New York, 1904.

——, *Two Pages from Roman History (Plebs Leaders and Labor Leaders)*, New York, 1903.

FINE, NATHAN, *Labor and Farmer Parties in the United States, 1828-1928*, New York, 1928.

FORD, EARL C., and WM. Z. FOSTER, *Syndicalism*, Chicago, no date.

FOSTER, WM. Z., *The Bankruptcy of the American Labor Movement*, Chicago, no date.

——, *Trade Unionism, the Road to Freedom*, Chicago, no date.

——, *The Great Steel Strike and its Lessons*, New York, 1920.

——, *Misleaders of Labor*, New York, 1927.

GOMPERS, SAMUEL, *Seventy Years of Life and Labor*, 2 Vols. New York, 1925.

HILLQUIT, MORRIS, *History of Socialism in the United States*, New York, 1903.

HILLQUIT, MORRIS, SAMUEL GOMPERS and MAX J. HAYES, *The Double Edge of Labor's Sword*, Chicago, 1914.

LEVINE, LOUIS (Lewis L. Lorwin), *The Development of Syndicalism in America* (in *Political Science Quarterly*), 1913.

LORWIN, LEWIS L., *Labor and Internationalism*, New York, 1929.
ONEAL, JAMES, *American Communism*, New York, 1927.
——, *The Workers in American History*, New York, 1921.
PERLMAN, SELIG, *A Theory of the Labor Movement*, New York, 1928.
ROCKER, RUDOLF, *Johann Most, das Leben eines Rebellen*, Berlin, 1924.
SCHLÜTER, HERMANN, *Die Anfänge der Deutschen Arbeiterbewegung in Amerika*, Stuttgart, 1907.
SORGE, F. A., *Die Arbeiterbewegung in den Vereinigten Staaten* (a series of articles published in the Marxist Review, *Die Neue Zeit* in Stuttgart, 1890-91).
VARGA, EUGEN, *Die Sozialdemokratischen Parteien*, Hamburg, 1826.

CONCLUSION

Archiv für die Geschichte des Sozialismus und der Arbeiterbewegung, Leipzig, 1911-31.
BALLOD, K., *Der Zukunftsstaat, Wirtschaftstechnisches Ideal und Volkswirtschaftliche Wirklichkeit*, Berlin, 1927.
BEER, M., *Allgemeine Geschichte des Sozialismus und der sozialen Kämpfe*, Berlin, 1929.
BERNSTEIN, EDUARD, *Der Sozialismus Einst und Jetzt*, Berlin, 1923.
——, *Wie eine Revolution zugrunde ging*, Stuttgart, 1921.
KAUTSKY, KARL, *The Social Revolution*, Chicago, 1912.
LENIN, V. I., *The State and the Revolution*, London, 1917.
LOZINSKY, EUGENE, *What is the Intelligentsia?* (in Russian), St. Petersburg, 1907.
MARX, KARL, *The Gotha Program*, New York, 1922.
MARX, KARL, and F. ENGELS, *The Communist Manifesto*, New York, 1930.
MENGER, ANTON, *The Right to the Whole Produce of Labor*, London, 1899.
Proceedings of the International Socialist Congresses (Paris-1889, Brussels-1891, Zurich-1893, London-1896, Paris-1900, Amsterdam-1904, Stuttgart-1907, Copenhagen-1910).
WOLSKI, A. (Waclaw Machajski), *The Bankruptcy of Nineteenth Century Socialism* (in Russian), Geneva, 1905.
——, (Waclaw Machajski), *The Mental Worker*, 3 v. (in Russian), Geneva, 1905.

INDEX

Engels, Friedrich, 10, 68, 83, 89, 95, 161, 312, 319, 398-399
Equalitarian socialism, 49, 258
Equality of incomes, 57, 157, 208, 239, 249, 341, 391, 406
Equalization of wages, 208, 239, 258, 391, 406
Erzberger, Matthias, 139
Ettor, Joseph, 355, 359, 361, 364
"Exceptionalism", 384
"Expropriations", 220, 318
Ex-workers, 86, 109, 172, 181, 264, 268, 278, 380-381, 383, 400, 402 (see also Trade Union Leaders)

F

Fabians, 156, 164-166, 189
Falsification of history, 94, 251
Farmer-Labor Party, 378, 380
Fasci di combattimento, 289
Fascism, 8, 27, 283-310, 403
Fascist Grand Council, 307; elections, 307; militia, 310; punitive expeditions, 42, 290
Fascists: German, 80, 143, 404; Italian, 36, 291-298, 302-304, 307, 309-310; Polish, 330-331, 404
Faure, Sebastien, 1, 66
Federated Farmer-Labor Party, 378
Federation of Organized Trades and Labor Unions, 346
Ferrer, Francisco, 74
Finzi, Aldo, 304
First International, 4, 9-11, 17, 86, 151, 350
"First Phase of Communism", 250, 406
Five-Year Plan, 257-258
Flynn, Elizabeth Gurley, 359
Food requisitions, 234
Foster, birth, 341; youth, 346-347; joins socialist movement, 346; member of Socialist Party,

353; joins I.W.W., 357; I.W.W. militant on Pacific Coast, 358; delegate to International Trade Union Convention, 359-360; becomes Syndicalist, French style, 360; tries to convert I.W.W. to French syndicalism, 360-361; founds Syndicalist League, 362; publishes pamphlet Syndicalism, 362; begins "boring from within", 362; organizer of Railway Carmen, 362; founds International Trade Union Educational League, 363; publishes pamphlet Trade Unionism, the Road to Freedom, 363; Gompers on Foster, 364-365; during the War, 365; organizes stock-yard workers, 365; organizes steel workers, 367; leader of Steel Strike, 367-370; stand before Senate committee, 369; efforts thwarted by A.F.L., 371; influence of Russian Revolution on, 371-372; founds Trade Union Educational League, 372; goes to Soviet Russia, 372; converted to communism, 374-376; arrested, 376; presidential candidate of Workers' Party, 379; participation in intra-party struggles, 380-381; loses party leadership, 381; favors and then combats Trotsky opposition, 383; reinstated as leader, 384; attacked by Stalin, 387; demoted from leadership, 387; in charge of communist trade-union activities, 387-390
Fourier, Charles, 340
Fourierism, 340
Frankfurter Zeitung, 127
Free land, 341
Freemasons, 277, 299, 302
"Free silver", 342

early nineties, 22; insurrectionary and underground activities,
22-24; in Ancona, 29; in the
United States, 30; in London
1900-13, 30; the Sidney Street
affair, 31-32; the Tripoli war,
32; during the "red week," 33,
278; on Revolution, 33; during
the War, 34-35; against "Pro-
Government Anarchists," 35;
returns to Italy, 1919, 36, 286;
arrested, 41; hunger strike, 42;
on trial, 43; on Russian Revolution, 45; on anarchist practical
program, 45; on Lenin's death,
46; in 1932, 3
Malato, Charles, 1, 22, 34
Mann, Tom, 158-159, 161, 169-170,
360
"March on Rome", 37, 286, 297
Martov, Julius, 204, 210
Marx, Eleanor, 154
Marx, Karl, 7-11, 17, 40, 51, 70,
83, 86, 89, 95, 99, 108, 147, 150-
151, 155, 161, 172, 231, 250, 268,
278-279, 312-313, 317, 319, 321,
342-344, 350, 393, 398, 399, 406
Marxism, 8, 19, 52-53, 81, 96,
158-159, 161, 187, 201-202, 204-
205, 210-211, 213, 271, 281, 313-
314
Marxists, 9, 59, 71, 86, 104, 176-
177, 209-210, 216, 351, 374, 398,
405 (see also Bolsheviks, Gues-
dists, Mensheviks)
Matteotti, Giacomo, 285, 301, 304
Max, Prince of Baden, 123-124,
126
Maximalists, Italian, 292
Maxton, James, 193
Mazzini, Giuseppe, 3, 5, 13
Mazzinians, 12
Mensheviks, 50, 210, 213-216, 218-
220, 222-223, 225-226, 234, 238,
254
Merlino, Saverio, 28-29

Mesopotamia, 191
Metal workers, Italian, 287
Mickiewicz, Adam, 313
Milan uprising, 1898, 29
Military communism, 233-234, 249
"Military-feudal exploitation of
the peasantry", 256
Miliukov, Paul, 222, 224
Millerand, Alexandre, 34, 61-62,
66-67, 71-73, 75-76, 80
Ministeriels, 68, 265
Minority Socialists (see Independ-
ent Socialists, German)
Misleaders of Labor, 388
Moderate Socialists (see Right-
Wing Socialists)
Molly Maguires, 342, 391
Molotov, Viacheslav. 245, 254
Monatte, Pierre, 39
Moraczewski, Andrzej, 323
Morgan, Pierpont, 309
Morris, William, 154
Morrison, James, 150
Most, Johann, 1, 89, 343-344
Müller, Hermann, 84
Mussolini, Benito, birth of, 263;
school teacher, 264; departure
for Switzerland, 266; revolutionary and atheist propaganda,
266-267; return to Italy, 269;
teacher again, 269; goes to
Trentino in Austria, 270; expelled from Austria, 270; editor of Lotta di Classe, 270;
intellectual influences affecting,
271; defends terrorist acts, 271;
opposes Tripoli war, 274-275;
fights Right-Wing Socialists,
276; editor of Avanti, 276; losing his faith, 277; "red week",
278-279; favors Italian intervention in War, 280-282; expelled
from party, 282; advocates imperialist socialism, 282; "groups
for revolutionary action", 282;
after the War, 283; individual-